*1989*

The EMERGENCE of MORALITY in

Young Children

# The EMERGENCE of MORALITY in
# Young Children

## Edited by Jerome Kagan and Sharon Lamb

THE UNIVERSITY OF CHICAGO PRESS · CHICAGO AND LONDON

JEROME KAGAN is professor of psychology at Harvard
University. He is the author of *Birth to Maturity, The
Nature of the Child, Infancy,* and *The Second Year.*

SHARON LAMB is an Ed.D. student in the Graduate School of
Education at Harvard University.

The University of Chicago Press, Chicago 60637
The University of Chicago Press, Ltd., London
© 1987 by The University of Chicago
All rights reserved. Published 1987
Printed in the United States of America

96 95 94 93 92 91 90 89 88 87     5 4 3 2 1

The University of Chicago Press gratefully acknowledges a
subvention from the John D. and Catherine T. MacArthur
Foundation in partial support of the costs of production of
this volume.

LIBRARY OF CONGRESS CATALOG-IN-PUBLICATION DATA

The Emergence of morality in young children.

Papers presented at a conference sponsored by the
MacArthur Foundation's Health Sciences Program held
at Harvard University in 1985.
    Bibliography
    Includes index.
    1. Moral development—Congresses. I. Kagan, Jerome.
II. Lamb, Sharon. III. John D. and Catherine T.
MacArthur Foundation. Health Sciences Program.
BF723.M54E48   1987      155.4'23      87–10952
ISBN 0–226–42231–3

This book is dedicated to the memory of Lawrence Kohlberg.

# Contents

# Introduction

*Jerome Kagan*

In the spring of 1982, as part of an extensive program devoted to research on mental health, the Board of Directors of the John D. and Catherine T. MacArthur Foundation voted to create a network of developmental scientists concerned with the psychological processes mediating the transition between infancy and childhood. With the exception of scholars studying the emergence of speech, most investigators had neglected the months between the first and third birthdays, despite the fact that empathy, self-awareness, and a concern with right and wrong appear for the first time during this era. As with most cases of scholarly neglect, the blame could be ascribed to weak theory and insensitive methods. Although groups of investigators within and across the five centers of the network were actively studying most of the competences of this period, the members of the New England group felt that insufficient attention was being given to the emergence of a moral sense in the second year. In response, they hosted a two day conference on 2–3 November 1984 devoted to the growth of moral standards. This volume contains the papers presented at that meeting, together with two commissioned essays.

## Perspectives

The papers and group discussions returned continually to three deep issues. The most controversial was whether young children are biologically prepared to display a moral sense as they approach their second birthday. Are a preoccupation with correct behavior, anxiety following the violation of adult prohibitions, and empathy with another's distress part of a universal hominid ontogeny, or are these phenomena no different from the child's learning to wave "bye-bye"?

In contrast to the nineteenth-century continental views of the acquisition of moral standards, most twentieth-century American scholars assumed that standards were learned through the proper application of reward and punishment. The prototypical explanation was that a child learned that hitting another or destroying property was wrong because adults punished such acts and praised their restraint. Hence, learning to inhibit striking or stealing from another was no different in principle from learning to remain quiet at the dinner table. However, recent empirical work, some of it summarized in this volume, suggests that by the second birthday children from many cultures show uncertainty with regard to broken or flawed objects, empathy with the distress of another, and anxiety over possible task failure. Because it is unlikely that parents across the world begin to socialize these acts at the same time, the temporal concordance implies a biologically based preparedness to judge acts as right or wrong, where preparedness is used with the same sense intended by linguists who claim that two-year-old children are prepared to speak their language. Because linguistic competence requires a prior maturation of relevant cognitive abilities, it is likely that a sensitivity to right and wrong can not appear until children are able to infer possible causes and feeling states in others and to anticipate the reactions of adults to their actions. It is probably not a coincidence that the first signs of a moral sense occur close to the time when most children begin to make inferences about symbolic meanings. One of the nicest examples is the two-year-old who treats an unfamiliar word as if it referred to an unfamiliar object.

Although inference is probably a necessary prerequisite, emotionality is the more obvious feature of the preparedness for accepting and imposing standards on behavior. The child's face, body, and voice change when he or she breaks a glass, dirties a dress, or makes another child cry. And many, including Marion Radke-Yarrow and Martin Hoffman, have noted that the capacity for empathy with another's feeling state is accompanied by special displays. The child also manifests emotional distress when he or she fails at a self-imposed task—like building a tower—or when a difficult challenge is imposed on the child by an adult. Most examiners of two-year-olds have seen the familiar tightening of the face and the whining request, "I want to go home now," after a child fails a difficult problem. These reactions imply that the recognition of a deviation between what one did, or was about to do, and the representation of a more perfect performance generates uncertainty. By the third birthday the child's reactions come close to matching the popular criteria for shame and guilt.

The sources of this family of emotions differ from those that generate affect in the first year in several ways. First, the incentive is not simply an external event—a stranger entering or the mother leaving the room—but a cognitive structure representing a possible event—perhaps someone is hurt or one anticipates failure at a task. The emotion a two-year-old shows upon hearing a younger sibling cry requires recognition of a relation between the crying and the idea that something or someone has caused the baby's distress. Because it appears that most children display these qualities by their second birthday, despite the dramatic differences in everyday experience across time and culture, it seems likely that the maturation of particular cognitive abilities has permitted these phenotypic characteristics. It is of interest that recent data on the ontogeny of the infant monkey's brain suggest that synaptic density in human limbic structures reaches a peak during the second year.

However, even if all children were biologically prepared to believe that some acts are classed as right and wrong, with the exception of restraint on harming others and meeting criteria for mastery, humans from varied societies do not agree on the actions that are treated as deeply felt obligations. The content of moral standards seems to be a product of history, culture, family values, and the individual's personal reconstruction of his or her past experience. However, the psychological processes that mediate the acquisition of a moral standard remain disguised. Investigators who promote a relatively strong environmental view—Carolyn Edwards provides one example—place most of the power in direct tutoring and instruction. Others, like Elliot Turiel, acknowledge the role of exhortation but want to give as much power to autochthonous cognitive syntheses as psycholinguists do in their explanation of the appearance of speech. Proponents of the nativist argument claim that adult moral standards are not always copies of parents' views but often dramatically opposed to family beliefs. The "generation gap" would not exist if the moral standards of youth were simply carbon copy incorporations of conversations heard at the dinner table. This suggestion does not deny the relevance of social transmission of some standards, but it reminds us that the child, like Francis Bacon's bees, transforms information in creating a morality.

A second somewhat less controversial theme dealt with the usefulness of the theoretical distinction between conventional and principled moral standards. Although this distinction has broad acceptance, there is far less agreement on the bases for the distinction, aside from the general intuition that the difference rests on the seriousness of violating a particular standard. Thus, if obeying authority is a conventional standard, perhaps because the person views conformity as expedient, disobedience will not generate much guilt or moral uncertainty. But if obedience is a principled standard because it is part of a deeply held philosophy of how one should relate to legitimate authority, then nonconformity will produce serious emotional consequences. A standard demanding nonconformity to authority could be the product of imitating a college roommate or the slowly crafted ideology of a later-born son who wanted to understand why his older brother unjustly commanded so much more privilege than he. If acquiescence to all of the requests of an employer generated less guilt in the former than in the latter individual, the standard would be regarded as conventional for the first agent and principled for the second.

Conceptualizing the distinction in this manner places the discussion of morality in a broader context. Violation of conventional standards like "Don't slurp while eating" or "Say 'excuse me' when you pass in front of someone" are usually learned in order to maintain a close emotional tie to another or to avoid adult disapproval. But some standards are established through identification with another or as a result of attempts, not always conscious, to understand one's role or to reduce the dissonance among a set of inconsistent beliefs. For example, a child who aspires to possess a parent's power and capacity for nurture and has identified with that parent will treat the parent's standards as obligations with special force. When a standard on tolerance is part of the support for the child's belief that he shares the power of the parent, violation is more serious than when the standard was shaped only through fear of punishment. When the adolescent with formal operational talent attempts to resolve inconsistencies in sets of related attitudes, the resulting standards that successfully resolve the dissonance have the capacity to provoke strong emotional sequelae because violation of these standards makes it necessary to question the premises that guide everyday decisions. If a fourteen-year-old girl justifies her loyalty to an alcoholic mother because of a standard that makes family devotion supersede all other considerations, it will be extremely difficult for her to disobey the family's insistence that she marry a member of her own ethnic or religious group. Each adolescent and adult arrives at a small number of deep moral assumptions that serve to keep the large corpus of conscious attitudes in some degree of logical coherence. If a person decided, as a result of reflection on experience, that the beliefs "Knowledge is basically good," "Marriage is a sacrament," or "Love is salvation" were false, he or she would probably feel anxiety, or at least unpleasant tension. The distinction between a class of moral, in contrast to conventional, standards seems to rest, therefore, on two important processes: mode of establishment and quality of conscious feelings after a violation. When a class of events in nature has both distinctive origins and consequences it deserves special epistemological status.

However, this brief for two types of standards is based on functional criteria rather than the inherent features of actions. However, most moral philosophers and psychologists who study morality—Turiel is a good example—believe that principled standards share specifiable objective features that differentiate them from conventional ones, as gases are distinguished from metals. Nonetheless, many useful scientific categories are based only on functional consequences. For example, epinephrine and norepinephrine, which are very similar structurally, are distinguished by their differential effects on target tissues. If the intensity of guilt, uncertainty, or shame generated by violating a standard is treated as a primary defining quality of a standard, one would argue not for a dichotomy, but for a continuum from conventional to principled on which any standard could be placed. Standards whose violation is followed by strong moral affect would be principled; those whose violation leads to minimal emotion would be conventional. This view would at least explain why the standard to treat all human beings as equal under the law is principled in contemporary America but not in fourth century Greece, or why adultery in some parts of contemporary American culture has, over the past century, moved from principled to conventional status.

Most philosophers, however, have wanted to make the power of rational argument rather than emotion the basis for the distinction between the two categories. Such a position fails when applied to young children, for whom the ideas of good and bad appear to originate in feelings linked to acts, or the contemplation of acts, that cause distress to another or provoke adult disapproval. Although the exact origins of these two feeling states are unclear, each is phenomenologically recognizable and usually unpleasant in tone, and, for the child, constitutes the core of the sense meaning of bad. Subsequently, events that become linked to the cognitive structures that represent bad acts and intentions, and their associated unpleasant feeling states, also become members of the category bad. It appears that, at least for children, David Hume was correct when he suggested that feelings, not reason, lie at the heart of morality.

But feelings are private, subjective phenomena, and empirical scientists require public referential meanings in order to discuss the domain of morality. The sense meaning of a standard is the idea that a particular class of acts is proper and good, but the referential meaning is contained in the empirical context that affirms that idea. The primary moral constructs in all moral theories combine sense and referential meanings. What is not always recognized, however, is that the theoretical meaning of a construct is vulnerable to change when the referent changes. This fact is a major reason for scholarly controversies on the nature of moral development, for investigators often choose different referents in their empirical explorations of moral stages.

Lawrence Kohlberg, for example, uses a person's answers to a set of orally presented dilemmas that oppose the morality inherent in preserving human life with the morality of respect for another's property. But Richard Shweder uses a person's answers to questions like "Is this act right or wrong?" for specific acts issued by particular agents in well-defined situations. A six-year-old who told Kohlberg that a husband should not steal a drug to save his dying wife because stealing is wrong might also tell Shweder it was wrong for the husband to let his wife die, implying that he should steal the drug necessary for her health. Shweder and Kohlberg come to different conclusions about the development of morality, in part because they use different sources of evidence. Judy Dunn, Carolyn Edwards and Robert Emde use changes in overt behavior and emotional display following violations of standards as evidence of morality rather than a child's verbal answers or explanations. Some three-year-olds will show obvious signs of emotion when someone takes a toy from another, even though they might not be able to answer the moral questions posed by Kohlberg or Shweder. And, if a hypothetical investigator measured a child's psychophysiological reactions to questions about the morality of stealing there is a strong possibility that the correlation between the physiological reactions and the answers to the Kohlberg and Shweder questions would be very low. Such a result would imply that the meaning of the phrase "seriousness of violation" or "moral stage" depends on the specific evidence quantified.

The third and final question that dominated discussion probed the relevance of empirical data on moral development for the concerns of philosophers. Put plainly, would it make any difference to a moral philosopher if a child were or were not biologically prepared to acquire the right-wrong distinction, or if strong emotion rather than rationality were the primary criterion for the difference between principled and conventional standards? This question is not easily answered. Greek philosophers intended their reflections to reveal truths about nature, but after the Enlightenment it became clear that some of the empirical sciences were doing better at discovering nature's truths than those who brooded deeply in their study. Hence, philosophers selected a different set of challenges to solve. Initially, and understandably, they chose to analyze human characteristics that seemed beyond empirical inquiry, especially the moral and intellective qualities of humans. But when psychologists, anthropologists, and sociologists entered this territory the philosophers moved to analyses of the logical coherence of the texts the scientists prepared. It is not a serious distortion to suggest that during this century most philosophers took as their assignment the analysis of the logical relations among sets of propositions about particular ideas. If the idea happened to pertain to morality, philosophers tried to invent an argument that was logically consistent and commanding, given a small number of intuitively attractive premises. With only a few exceptions, one popular premise was that moral decisions should rest on cognitive analyses. It is not surprising that so many Western philosophers chose to make morality a product of rationality, for it is easier to invent a logically coherent brief for personal honesty if humans make this moral decision on logical grounds than if telling the truth originates in emotions and the rational explanation is an afterthought required to make the behavior appear more reasonable.

It is only during the past decade that some philosophers have begun to accommodate to psychological data. In "Epistemology and Cognition" (1986), Alvin Goldman addresses epistemological issues by taking into account new laboratory data on cognitive functions. In a second example of this trend Stuart Hampshire rejects the traditional emphasis on rationality in moral reasoning and relies on empirical evidence to emphasize the significant role of emotion in moral decisions. Piaget also believed that conclusions about morality should be rooted in evidence; that is why he described developmental changes in the moral reasoning of children.

The truth value of statements about living cells is determined by empirical scientists; the logical coherence of a theory of meaning is evaluated by philosophers. But the basis for human morality is claimed by both social scientists and philosophers; hence, it is not clear whether moral philosophers must accommodate to the information gathered by child psychologists. Although Rawls's essay on justice won wide acclaim as a coherent argument for an egalitarian standard, it is totally indifferent to the empirical data on human cupidity.

## The Papers

Richard Shweder's thoughtful essay notes that cultures can be divided into those that conceive of humans as autonomous agents and
those that conceptualize the individual as part of a larger group. Freedom, rights, and justice will be principled moral standards and guilt
a major moral emotion in societies that celebrate the unconnected individual, for each agent must be free to act in whatever ways are necessary for self-actualization, as long as another's liberty remains un-
compromised. However, if the person's relation to the group is primary, respect for social roles and adherence to rules and rituals will
be principled moral standards, and anxiety over the disapproval of
others will be the primary moral emotion.

One reason freedom is a primary, principled standard in the
West is that our society has insisted for a very long time that each
person's fate depends on the making of correct decisions. However, if
one's future is determined by the events of a previous life, an agent's
actions are not totally in his hands and personal freedom is less
central. Justice is a salient moral standard in the West because we
believe that if the weak are not protected from the strong the former
will be exploited. But justice will be a less pressing moral standard in
societies that believe that being poor, sick, or disenfranchised is a
result of a prior life, a witch's curse, or a tainted heredity.

Shweder accepts the division between moral and conventional
standards, although he does not rely on emotions to make that
distinction. Shweder suggests that the West has fewer moral and
more conventional standards because the nature of our economy
demands free entrepreneurial agents who cannot be restrained by
categorical imperatives. In other cultures (India is Shweder's example), loyalty to and interdependence on the group always take precedence over an individual's will and personal liberty. Shweder argues
there is a relation between the conception of an agent as free and a
preference for conventional standards, because conventionality
awards to each individual the freedom to abrogate a consensually
based obligation for action.

There is one possible point of vulnerability in Shweder's conclusion that Americans prefer conventional standards and Indians
favor principled ones. Had Shweder asked his American informants
about behaviors related to love and affection he might have found
Americans as principled as Indians. Few Americans would say that it
was conventional for parents to tell their children they do not love
them. But this obligation is less binding in other cultures. Jean Briggs
notes that among the Eskimo of Hudson Bay, aunts tease four-year-

olds by saying, "You don't love your baby brother, why don't you tip him out of his parka and let him die."

Judy Dunn relies on young children's behaviors with their siblings as the major source of evidence for moral concerns. She finds that young children are sensitive to the emotional states of their brothers and sisters and apply the ideas of good and bad as adults do. But Dunn chooses to emphasize the importance of parental behavior and sibling interactions rather than the child's preparedness as the basis for the establishment of these moral ideas. Dunn also corrects the popular bias to look only at anxiety, shame, and guilt as signs of comprehension of a standard by noting that joking, teasing, and laughing are regular accompaniments to the witnessing of a mischievous act.

Carolyn Edwards also awards formative power to the role of indirect instruction, especially when the child decides on conventional rules. This decision followed an analysis of observations of adults and children in a village in Kenya and a school in the northeastern United States. After presenting a rich set of exemplars, Edwards suggests that the distinction between principled and conventional standards lies with the socializing adult, not with the child. "It is the culture, not the child, that decides what normative and regulatory rules and standards are most important and necessary for social life and obligation."

Elliot Turiel's essay provides an instructive critique of Shweder, Dunn, and Edwards, each of whom is taken to task for awarding too much power to the environment. The seminal idea in this chapter is the qualitative distinction between moral (that is, principled) and conventional standards. But in sharp contrast to Shweder's essay, Turiel and his colleagues argue that morality is qualitatively different from convention because of the agent's feeling of obligation to meet the standard in action. This obligation does not depend on anxiety over disapproval or a wish to gain favor. Morality, unlike convention, is defined by an awareness that one cannot help but act in accord with a principled standard, even if that action means becoming an "enemy of the people."

Turiel's distinction between morality and convention is intuitively appealing. Most American parents feel obliged to love their children and find it difficult to tell them that they are hateful, no matter what the parent may feel at the moment. But Turiel acknowledges that the deeper basis for this distinction is unclear. We have three choices. The simplest is to declare, in the spirit of parsimony, that certain domains of action are inherently moral universally. This was G. E. Moore's strategy. To refrain from harming another is the one standard most citizens and philosophers endorse as a member of the set. But consensus fails after that concession is made. Turiel, along with most post-Enlightenment scholars, adds individual freedom to the list of moral standards, asserting that curbing another's freedom violates a moral standard. However, the practice of slavery by otherwise morally upstanding citizens in ancient Athens and eighteenth-century Virginia suggests that many adults apparently do not feel the obligation that Turiel believes they should experience.

A second criterion for morality could be the presence of moral emotions, particularly guilt and shame. If violation of a standard engenders guilt or its anticipation, the person feels obliged to meet it. This view permits one to conceive of the difference between morality and convention as a continuum, depending on the intensity of the moral emotion, felt, or, with Turiel, to treat the two categories as qualitatively different, depending on whether the emotion is present or absent. This issue remains undecided. Finally, the criterion for morality could be a version of Kant's categorical imperative. Any act that an agent has decided is part of a rationally constructed philosophy of action is moral by definition. This is, of course, Kohlberg's choice.

However, each of these criteria permits an agent to decide that almost any act is moral, as Shweder's data show. An Indian widow feels a moral obligation to avoid eating meat; a Shiite terrorist feels a moral obligation to murder an Israeli child; a Mayan priest feels a moral obligation to remove the heart of an adult the community has selected for a sacrifice to the gods. There remains, therefore, no clear consensus on the bases for the division between moral and conventional standards, despite agreement on the usefulness of the distinction.

Robert Emde and his colleagues emphasize the contribution of early emotions to moral development in their review of contemporary attitudes of psychoanalysts. The central change has been the recognition that the superego begins its formation in the second year and does not have to wait for the oedipal conflict. Modern analysts see the cognitive representations of sanctioned behaviors—the yeses—as emerging before the later representation of the prohibitions, although some psychologists would contend that the affirmations and prohibitions emerge together, or with the temporal order reversed. This essay emphasizes the possible relation between attachment and the growth of standards in the second year and carefully cites the new evidence that either affirms traditional hypotheses or requires some changes in traditional Freudian explanations. The two most important changes are a replacement of libidinal drive theory with a view that awards power to coping systems and a recognition that signs of morality in the two-year-old do not require conflict but originate in the maturation of empathy. These new premises bring psychoanalysts closer to what is becoming the dominant view among developmental scholars.

Carol Gilligan and Grant Wiggins are interested in the content of the standard rather than the conventional-principled dimension. They suggest that although justice and care are moral imperatives for all children, males are likely to make the former the primary basis for a private ethic while females are likely to choose the latter. No evaluation of "better" is implied by this fact; it is just that males and females choose different moral itineraries.

It is not clear why this hypothesis seems to match experience. It could be, as feminists suggest, that it is the simple product of propaganda from family, school, and media. But the recent return to the attractiveness of traditional female roles by young American women in the midst of a feminist revolution that is moving the other way makes that explanation unlikely. On the other hand, simple genetic arguments are unsatisfying because they provide no details; they solve the problem with a heavy club. It is possible that the two itineraries are not psychological operants but commitments made during childhood following recognition that the quintessential elements of the maternal role are an attitude of care, acts of nurture, and, above all, restraint on hurting another. Therefore, it would be unwise for a young girl to fight destiny. This decision might be helped by the young girl's premature inference that because boys are physically stronger they will always be more powerful. How could the average five-year-old girl know that adult power is held with symbols, not muscles? But having decided that power would always have to be shared or, worse yet, never gained, it would not be unreasonable for the average girl to commit herself to the only other major agenda available when relating to people; namely, as friend, supporter, and lover. Gilligan's imaginative thesis describes this outcome.

The single philosopher at the meeting, Lawrence Blum, sided with those who award importance to emotional states. Blum posits a state he calls "responsiveness" or "connection," which is a sense of relatedness to others that emerges prior to the cognitive ability to infer that others share functions with the self. Blum argues that a "sense of connection" to another is a basic human characteristic actualized in early childhood and, like the ethologist's released responses, emitted automatically under specifiable conditions. Blum realizes that psychologists prefer to derive this sense of relation from prior cognitive competences or to argue that a prior separation of self from mother is a prerequisite. Blum's relatively novel position would make the appearance of empathy a bit easier to explain, for this feeling would follow from a sense of connection to others. As a consequence, attempts to explain the differentiation of self from others on the basis of parent-child interactions would be less important to theories of the first stage of moral development.

Blum's second novel point is reminiscent of William James's remark that one can detect both an abstract principle and a concrete context in each moral act. Blum notes correctly that most contemporary Western psychologists have emphasized the abstract moral principle, what Blum calls the impartial feature of morality. The principles of justice, honesty, and freedom are applied by agents across a wide variety of situations with both strangers and kin. Kohlberg, Rawls, and Gewirth, as well as Shweder and Turiel in this volume, are concerned with impartial moral principles. Blum reminds us that every moral situation also has a particular actor, target, and situation that should not be ignored. When a wife tries to change a conversation before her husband makes a fool of himself she is not applying an abstract moral principle that directs her to protect those who might be vulnerable to unpleasantness. Rather, the wife is responding to her husband on that particular occasion. She might even be surprised if someone told her that she was acting morally. It is refreshing to find a philosopher who argues more vehemently for the psychology of the moral agent than many social scientists.

Although Blum comes close to suggesting that freedom is an impartial principle and compassion a particularistic one, it does not seem necessary to confound the content of the standard with its degree of impartiality or concreteness. The golden rule, which stresses compassion for others, is an impartial universal imperative, while awarding one's fourteen-year-old son the freedom to stay out after midnight is particularistic.

The editors thank the John D. and Catherine T. MacArthur Foundation for the support of this conference, Robert Emde, who directs the Network, for his continued support of this effort, and William Damon for an incisive critique. We also thank Jeris Miller and Helen Snively for their help in preparing this manuscript and Steven Reznick for wise counsel and loyal effort during the planning and implementation of the conference.

# Culture and Moral Development

Richard A. Shweder, Manamohan Mahapatra, and
Joan G. Miller

This essay reports the results of a cross-cultural development study of
ideas about the moral (its form) and ideas about what is moral (its
content). The informants for the study are children, five to thirteen
years of age, and adults, male and female, from Brahman and "Untouchable" families in the orthodox Hindu temple town of Bhubaneswar, Orissa, India; and from Judeo-Christian families in the secular
university neighborhood of Hyde Park in Chicago, Illinois.

The research reported was supported by a grant from the Human Learning and Behavior
program of the National Institute of Child Health and Human Development (R01
HD17067). The research in India would not have been possible without the support,
encouragement and advice of S. K. Misra, S. K. Mahapatra and M. K. Rout. Our deep
gratitude to those scholars and to those who, over the years, have eased our way: P. K.
Badu, Ashoy Biswal, Rita Biswal, N. K. Das (Nabi Babaji), R. N. Das, Babaji Patnaik, K.
S. Ramachandran, M. T. Rath, Babla Senapati, and Nilamani Senapati. An earlier
version of the chapter was read by several colleagues, whose comments, both critical
and supportive, were appreciated. Our thanks to Augusto Blasi, Roy G. D'Andrade,
Donald W. Fiske, J. David Greenstone, Jerome Kagan, Larry Nucci, James Stigler, Elliot
Turiel, and Alan Young. Manamohan Mahapatra's mailing address is Punama Gate
Area, Bhubaneswar 751002, Orissa, India.
    A special thanks to those who directly assisted in the development, translation,
collection, coding and interpretation of research materials, especially Barbara By-
houwer, Kathleen Chattin, Sandy Dixon, Alan Fiske, Chita Mohanty, Swapna Pani,
Deborah Pool, Mary Ruth Quinn, and Candy Shweder.

1

One aim of the essay is to assess the strengths and limitations of two prominent and important theories about the origins and development of moral understandings: Kohlberg's "cognitive developmental" theory (Kohlberg 1969, 1981; Kohlberg, Levine, and Hewer 1983) and Turiel's "social interactional" theory (Turiel 1979, 1983; Nucci and Turiel 1978; Turiel and Smetana 1984). A second aim is to highlight the role of social communication processes in the ontogeny of moral understandings by outlining a "social communication" theory of moral development and using it to interpret the similarities and differences in the moral understandings of children and adults in the two cultures.

## Three Theories of Moral Development

The three theories to be discussed present different portraits and accounts of the ontogenetic origins of the idea of a moral obligation. Kohlberg's "cognitive developmental" theory hypothesizes that a genuine understanding of the idea of a moral obligation (stages five and six) has its origins in the idea of a conventional, or consensus-based, obligation (stages three and four). The theory proposes, as a developmental universal, that the idea that obligations are rooted in convention precedes the idea that obligations are rooted in natural law.

According to the "cognitive developmental" theory, the development of the idea of a moral obligation is related to the development of general skills of rational reasoning. Those skills include deductive logic and the ability to distance oneself from what is personal, egocentered or consensus-based. Movement through the stages is related to the cognitive ability to construct, and to transcend to, a detached, impartial vantage point from which one evaluates right and wrong objectively.

By contrast, Turiel's "social interactional" theory proposes that the idea of morality and the idea of convention are not connected in development. Furthermore, it is proposed that the idea of a moral obligation and the idea of a conventional obligation are both present universally and differentiated from each other in early childhood.

According to Turiel's theory, the development of the idea of a moral obligation is related to social experiences with a restricted class of events that have objective or intrinsic implications for justice, rights, harm, and the welfare of others. A paradigmatic moral experience is the child's personal observation of the consequences of hitting and hurting a helpless victim. On the other hand, the idea of a conventional obligation arises from social experiences with a class of socially regulated events that lack any objective or intrinsic implications for justice, rights, harm, or the welfare of others. For Turiel, a paradigmatic conventional experience is the extrinsic or externally imposed social demand to use clothing styles (for example, skirts) as a mark of gender differences.

The "social communication" theory, to be outlined in this essay, presents a third account of moral development, diverging in different ways from both Kohlberg and Turiel. In contrast to Kohlberg, the "social communication" theory proposes that the idea of a moral obligation is a universal of childhood and is not preceded by the idea that obligations derive their authority from consensus or convention. In that respect the "social communication" theory converges with Turiel's "social interactional" account.

In contrast to Turiel, however, the "social communication" theory questions the hypothesis that there are universal developmental processes leading the child to differentiate and contrast moral versus conventional obligations. The research suggests that it is not a universal idea that social practices are conventional formations, deriving their authority from a culture-bound consensus. According to the theory a culture's ideology and worldview have a significant bearing on the ontogenesis of moral understandings in the child, and not all cultures have a place in their view of the world for the idea that social practices are conventions.

A basic claim of the "social communication" theory is that children develop an idea of a conventional obligation in those cultures, like our own, where the social order has been separated ideologically from the natural moral order. One way that separation can occur is by reducing, as far as possible, what's moral to free contracts, promises, or consent among autonomous individuals. In the purest version of our free contract worldview, "markets" are absolutely neutral as to the particular social arrangements into which individuals choose to enter. The terms of a contract are decided by those who enter it; between "consenting adults" anything goes. The "social communication" theory proposes that the idea that social practices are conventional or consensus-based takes on significance only in those cultures where social arrangements are thought to be secondary formations, derived from a more fundamental, natural moral authority—the will of the individual, voluntarily expressed through consent, promise, or contract.

As we shall see, not all cultural worldviews are like our own. The Latin word "mores," from which the term "morals" is derived, meant "custom" (Gewirth 1984), and in many parts of the world, including orthodox Hindu India, customary practices (for example, menstrual seclusion, arranged marriage, food taboos, kin avoidance, naming practices) are viewed as part of the natural moral order. Society is not separated conceptually from nature. What is natural or moral has not been narrowed down to the idea of an individual, empowered and free to create relationships at will through contract. Forms of human association are thought to be found (natural law), not founded (conventionism). In those parts of the world, the idea that social practices are conventions plays a minimal role in the child's developing understanding of the source of obligations.

Social practices are the primary focus of our study. The Hindu temple town of Bhubaneswar is a place where marriages are arranged, not matters of "love" or free choice; where, at least among Brahman families, widows may not remarry or wear colored clothing or ornaments or jewelry; where Untouchables are not allowed in the temple; where menstruating women may not sleep in the same bed as their husbands or enter the kitchen or touch their children; where ancestral spirits are fed on a daily basis; where husbands and wives do not eat together and the communal family meals we find so important rarely occur; where women avoid their husbands' elder brothers and men avoid their wives' elder sisters; where, with the exception of holy men, corpses are cremated, never buried; and where the cow, the first "mother," is never carved up into sirloin, porterhouse or tenderloin cut.

The study focuses upon thirty-nine practices including kinship avoidance, forms of address between inferiors and superiors, sleeping arrangements, incest avoidance, dietary practices, forms of dress, marriage and remarriage, personal possessions and private property, begging, nepotism, monogamy, wife beating, physical punishment for children, the division of labor in the family, the inheritance of property, the protection of persons from physical and psychological harm, funeral rites, and various practices surrounding the birth of a child.

One aim of the study is to determine how the obligations associated with those practices are understood by Indian and American children and adults, with special reference to the distinction between morality and convention. A second aim of the study is to make explicit the premises and principles that are implicitly conveyed by social practices. What do Indian and American practices tell us about each culture's conception of persons, society, morality, and nature and about the relationships among those orders of things? Similarities and differences are identified in the form and content of moral codes across different cultural or subcultural traditions. A third aim of the study is to use our cross-cultural evidence on moral thought to appraise Kohlberg's and Turiel's contrastive theories of moral development. Thus, before turning to our study it is necessary to review and critique in detail those two theories.

## Kohlberg's Cognitive Developmental Theory: Overview and Evaluation

### Overview

Kohlberg (1969, 1971, 1981) has proposed a comprehensive scheme for developmental and comparative research on moral understandings. The scheme builds upon the work of Piaget ([1932] 1965) by identifying three major levels in the attainment of moral understandings and dividing each level into two stages.

In the lowest, "preconventional" level of understanding (stages one and two) young children define the meaning of "rightness" and "wrongness" in terms of the subjective feelings of the self. What is right is what avoids punishment or brings one rewards. If the self likes it, it is right; if the self doesn't like it, it is wrong. There are no "higher" obligations. Egoism reigns.

In the intermediate, "conventional" level of understanding (stages three and four), older children and adults continue to define the meaning of "rightness" and "wrongness" by reference to subjective feelings, but now it is the collective feelings of others that matter. What is correct and virtuous is whatever agrees with the will and dictates of authority figures (the commands of parents; the role expectations of society; the laws of legislatures). If one's reference group likes it, it is right. If one's reference group does not like it, it is wrong. The idea of obligation is equated with the rules and regulations of society or the state. Conformity and consensus reign.

In the third and highest "postconventional" level of understanding (stages five and six in Kohlberg's earlier formulations; stage five in more recent formulations; Kohlberg, Levine and Hewer, 1983) "rightness" and "wrongness" are defined by reference to objective principles detached from the subjective feelings and perspective of either the self or the group. What is correct and virtuous is defined in terms of universalizable standards, reflectively constructed by the individual, of justice, natural rights, and humanistic respect for all persons, regardless of sex, age, ethnicity, race, or religion. For the postconventional thinker, there are objective obligations that any rational person can come to discover and is bound to respect, that stand above the feelings of the self or the demands of others. In Kohlberg's theory, the source of the idea of being obliged to do something is related to the hypothetical act of entering into a contract to form a society. Postconventional thinkers recognize that among the terms of any voluntary and rationally based contract to form a society, justice, fairness, and natural rights must reign.

There are several noteworthy features of Kohlberg's three-level scheme. First, the scheme is organized around the contrast between subjectivity and objectivity. By "objectivity," Kohlberg means relative distance from the perspective of the self, or seeing things from a detached or "decentered" vantage point. In principle, perfect objectivity, a transcendental state, is seeing things from "nowhere in particular" (Nagel 1979). Thus, for Kohlberg, the first major move in moral development is away from solipsistic subjectivism, away from exclusive involvement with personal pleasure and pain and one's own individual needs (preconventional understanding) toward a recognition of external group consensus, a concern with the approval of significant others and conformity to social conventions and laws (conventional understanding). The second major move is toward transcendental objectivity, away from exclusive concern with conformity to custom, law, or group consensus (conventional understanding) and toward respect for rationally defensible objective standards for right conduct (postconventional understanding).

A second noteworthy feature of Kohlberg's three-level scheme is that the three levels correspond to three different conceptions in moral philosophy about the meaning of the expression "It's right to do that." According to one view, associated with so-called emotivist conceptions of moral discourse (Stevenson 1944; see MacIntyre 1981), obligations, like tastes, are merely expressions of personal preferences. The underlying meaning of the expression "It's right to do that" can be translated as an exhortation: "I like it; you like it as well." According to a second view, associated with so-called positive-law or legal positivist conceptions of moral discourse (see Hart 1961) obligations are nothing more than the promulgations of other human beings. The underlying meaning of the expression "It's right to do that" can be translated as an empirical report that "It is permitted by existing rules, laws, and other commands promulgated by your group, and there are no existing penalties for doing it." According to a third view, associated with so-called natural-law conceptions of moral discourse, there are such things as "objective" obligations which rational persons can discover. The expression "It's right to do that" can be translated as an implicit argument that "There are certain impersonal, objective standards to which social practices and institutions, man-made rules and laws, and personal desires must conform if those practices, institutions, rules, laws, and desires are to be valid."

Whether or not Kohlberg is fully aware of it (although see Kohlberg 1981, chap. 9), he has arranged these three conceptions of moral discourse in a single developmental sequence with emotivism at the bottom, positive-law conceptions in the middle, and natural-law conceptions at the top. Thus, there appear to be several alternative ways to label Kohlberg's three levels: preconventional, conventional, postconventional; egoistic, consensual, moral; emotivist, positive-law, natural-law (see figure 1.1).

A third noteworthy feature of Kohlberg's three-level scheme is that adequate moral understandings are portrayed as emerging out of prior conventional understandings. Kohlberg's image of the development of moral understandings is a sequential process of differentiation and replacement in which postconventional or natural-law conceptions of right versus wrong come to be distinguished from conventional or positive-law conceptions and supersede them (Kohlberg, Levine, and Hewer 1983, 17, 32). Likewise, conventional or positive-law conceptions emerge out of prior preconventional egoistic, or emotivist conceptions.

A fourth noteworthy feature of Kohlberg's three-level scheme is that adequate moral understanding is equated with the postconventional level of thinking. It is Kohlberg's view that the postconventional level of understanding is rationally preferable to the conventional level, which in its turn is rationally preferable to the preconventional level. He argues that with the development of processes of rational reasoning (for example, formal operational reasoning as described by Piaget) and exposure to proper education (for example, engagement in Socratic dialogue), the individual will recognize the conceptual inadequacies of the lower level of understanding and adopt a higher, more rationally defensible conceptual level. The underlying assumption is that in a creature endowed with the capacity for rational thought, as that capacity is cultivated, the development of moral understanding will tend in the direction of what is most rational.

A fifth noteworthy feature of Kohlberg's three-level scheme is that the various criteria for characterizing postconventional understanding are not all equally secure in the moral philosophy literature. Consistent with Kohlberg's claims, most recent analyses in moral philosophy suggest that adequate moral understandings have something to do with the idea of objective obligations that rational people can come to know, and that moral understanding cannot be reduced to the idea of positive law, social convention, or personal desire. It is a matter of dispute, however, whether a formal decision criterion involving the ideas of justice and harm can account for all cases where we judge a moral transgression to have occurred (for example, incest,

**Figure 1.1:** Schematic Representation of the Parallel Distinctions Running Through Kohlberg's Three-level Cognitive Developmental Theory of Moral Development

| | | | | | | |
|---|---|---|---|---|---|---|
| *Level 3* | postconventional | morality | natural law | principle | it's right | transcendent objectivity | formal operations |
| *Level 2* | conventional | convention | positive law | consensus | the group approves | collective subjectivity | concrete operations |
| *Level 1* | preconventional | personal preference | emotivism | self-ego | I like it | solipsistic subjectivity | preoperational |

using contraceptives, between consenting adult brother and sister) (Feinberg 1980; Perelman 1963). Furthermore, there is disagreement in the moral philosophy literature about whether there are such things as natural or objective rights as described in the Bill of Rights (MacIntyre 1981) and about whether reference in moral justification to the commandments of a superior or divine being set forth in "sacred text" is to be classified as an instance of positive law, level two, as Kohlberg classifies it (1981, chap. 9), or natural law, level three (Dworkin 1977). There is disagreement about whether the theory of free contract or the idea of consent can provide a comprehensive or even compelling account of the sources of obligation to those shared expectations that constitute a society. In other words, it is not a settled fact that all Kohlberg's proposed criteria are mandatory features of any rationally based moral understanding. Some of the proposed criteria may be discretionary or permit rational alternatives or substitutes. There may be other rationally based moral codes besides the one proposed. Kohlberg may not have sufficiently distinguished between mandatory versus discretionary features in his conception of postconventional understanding. There may be alternative postconventional moralities for which no place has been provided in his scheme.

## An Evaluation of Kohlberg's Cognitive Developmental Theory

### The Strength of the Theory

It is widely acknowledged in moral and legal philosophy that moral understandings are not the same as conventional understandings. The difference is exemplified, for Americans, by the difference in the way they understand their obligation, construed to be moral, to feed their children, versus their obligation, construed to be conventional, to send their son to school in pants instead of a skirt. One of the more defensible ways to distinguish the two types of understanding is by reference to the abstract idea of natural moral law basic to Kohlberg's scheme.

One way to think about the abstract idea of natural moral law is to imagine that there are certain standards to which social practices, man-made rules, and personal desires must conform if those practices, rules, and desires are to be valid. These standards are natural, in at least two senses. First, adherence to those standards is thought to lead factually to certain ultimate, important, or categorical ends of life like liberty, equality, safety, salvation, or the elimination of suffering. Secondly, the standards themselves are thought to be objective

or external, hence natural. Just as the shape of an object is said to in-
here in that object regardless of a human perceiver, so too, certain actions (starving a child to death) are thought to be wrong independent
of any human acknowledgement of it. The wrongness is there regardless of whether anyone recognizes it as such. Declaring that a round
object is square does not make it so. So too, an action that is wrong
by virtue of natural law cannot be made right by any declaration,
vote, or legislation.

To select a parochial example, in those places in the world
where the idea of natural law is associated with the idea of natural
"rights," there are certain freedoms (speech, travel) that are placed beyond the realm of the subject and out of the reach of majority vote,
above convention and consensus. Of course, a government, a state, or
a court may fail to realize its objective obligations and may fail to
grant its citizens any rights at all. But, according to those who believe
that civil liberty is part of the natural order of things, the obligation
is present nonetheless. Being objective it does not go away for having
been misperceived.

Kohlberg is probably on the side of the angels in his use of the
abstract idea of objective obligations to describe the nature of genuine
(or postconventional) moral understandings. It is the appeal to an objective ought, a natural law, that genuine moral understanding is
about, both in Kohlberg's scheme and in the schemes of most moral
philosophers. Nonetheless, Kohlberg's account of moral development
and his conceptual scheme have been the target of much legitimate
criticism. Before summarizing those legitimate criticisms, however,
it is necessary to digress for a moment to discuss Kohlberg's most recent reformulation of his theory.

## The Reformulation

Kohlberg's recent reformulation of his theory (Kohlberg, Levine, and
Hewer 1983) is a lucid but complex statement, packed with revisions,
qualifications, concessions, and several new distinctions. It is complex enough to dazzle even the most sympathetic critic. An unsym-
pathetic critic might view the reformulation as the beginning of the
epicycle stage of the theory. "Soft" stages are now distinguished from
"hard" stages. Two substages (A and B) are introduced within each of
Kohlberg's stages to accommodate the Piagetian distinction between
autonomy and heteronomy. And while a "soft" seventh stage is added
to the scheme, the previously proposed "hard" stage six is dropped because it is not an empirically identifiable form of moral reasoning
(1983, 60).

The domain of the theory is narrowed. What was once to be a theory of moral development is now described as a theory of justice reasoning. Kohlberg, Levine, and Hewer (1983, 19) write: "We admit, however, that this emphasis on the virtue of justice in Kohlberg's work does not fully reflect all that is recognized as being part of the moral domain."

The claims of the theory are weakened. Kohlberg, Levine, and Hewer (1983, 63) state that they agree with their critics that genuine postconventional moral understandings need not be tied to any particular normative ethical position. They accept the criticism by Carter (1980) that " 'what Kohlberg really achieves with clarity is nothing more than a sequential typology of development in moral thinking from egoism to universalism, and from situation-specific rules to universalizable and reversible judgments of principle.' " Carter probably overstates the case. For Kohlberg has not discovered that adults are typically principled or universalistic postconventional thinkers, and stage one egoism is not a frequent empirical occurrence, even among children (Snarey 1985). What Kohlberg has firmly established empirically is that, with his interview methodology and scheme of concepts, children are more likely than adults to justify action verbally by reference to the subjective feelings of the self, and that adults make more reference to social and political institutions— majority vote, the state, the law—in discussing their obligations. The only empirically established sequential typology emerging from the Kohlberg framework is the shift in verbal justifications from reference to self to reference to social institutions. Research concerned with how society and social institutions are represented by mature adults does not support the idea of a sequential end point on the side of abstract universal principles. Most adults in most societies stabilize at stage three with a conception of society built up out of the mutual reliances and interdependencies, and the specific agreements and obligations, associated with particular status or role relationships— husband to wife, parent to child, friend to friend, stranger to stranger (Edwards 1980, in press; Gilligan 1982).

It is ironic that with the publication of his "current formulation" there is somewhat less clarity about what it is that Kohlberg believes. Some of his most fundamental reformulations are difficult to reconcile with each other, and his thinking seems to be in the midst of a, perhaps productive, process of change. For example, Kohlberg, Levine, and Hewer state that "at this point, our stage findings do not allow us to claim evidence for certain normative ethical conclusions which nevertheless remain Kohlberg's own philosophical preference for defining the ontogenetic end point of a rationally reconstructed theory of justice reasoning. In particular we cannot claim either that there is a single principle which we have found used as the current empirically highest stage, nor that that principle is the principle of justice or respect for persons. There may be other principles" (1983, 63). They allude to alternative principles such as "responsible love," and they acknowledge the existence of a rationally appealing "morality of particularistic relationships" (see Gilligan 1982). This particularistic morality need not be based on such principles as "contract" or universal respect for persons but is founded instead on such ideas as loyalty, caring, and responsibility (1983, 20). Yet later in the text Kohlberg, Levine and Hewer (1983, 75) assert: "We claim that there is *a* universally valid form of rational moral thought process which all persons could articulate, assuming social and cultural conditions suitable to cognitive-moral stage development" (our emphasis).

One way to reconcile the two apparently contradictory assertions would be to postulate that Kohlberg's idea of a single, universally valid form of moral reasoning does not include, as a mandatory feature, the principle of justice or respect for persons but only some very general features like the abstract idea of an objective obligation. The problem with that attempted reconciliation is that Kohlberg quite clearly wants to deny that *any* moral principles are culturally variable "in a fundamental way" (1981, 73–74). He wants to assert that *all* divergences of moral belief can be reconciled by rational principles and methods (1982, 73–74). To eliminate the apparent contradictions in the text, one is tempted to ask: Are the principles of justice and respect for persons, then, not "fundamental" principles? Are discrepancies between normative ethics founded on justice versus those founded on particularistic relationships, loyalty, caring, and benevolent love, not to count as "divergences in moral beliefs"?

Kohlberg's theory has become a perplexing and shifting target, which, given its current complexities and flexible epicycles, is more difficult to represent in 1985 than it was in 1982. At present, the theory that is influential in the field is the one that preceded the current reformulation, and it is that theory that we have tried to represent. Nevertheless, the only criticisms of Kohlberg worth considering are those that still seem relevant after reflection on his latest reformulations. It is to those enduring criticisms that we now turn.

## The Limitations of the Theory

*Is cognitive development stagelike?* One criticism of Kohlberg's theory addresses his claim that the development of rational reasoning, specifically the attainment of the cognitive stage of formal operational thinking as described by Piaget, is a precondition for genuine moral understanding. Unfortunately, the moral development literature has not clarified what is purely logical, as distinct from what is purely moral, about moral concepts like commitment, harm, duty, trust, or rights. Empirical studies have been inconclusive on the relations between performance on Piagetian logical tasks and performance on Kohlberg's moral dilemma interview (Haan, Weiss and Johnson 1982).

Moreover, the Piagetian account of cognitive development has taken a beating in recent years (Shweder 1982c). It has come to be acknowledged that human cognitive growth is not very stagelike, and no single cognitive stage (preoperational, concrete operational, formal operational) is a characteristic property of an individual's cognitive functioning. The most recent comprehensive review of Piagetian concepts concludes that "the experimental evidence available today no longer supports the hypothesis of a major qualitative shift from pre-operational to concrete operational thought" (Gelman and Baillargeon 1983, 167).

One implication of that evidence is that how an individual functions in Kohlberg's scheme may depend on what he or she is thinking about. Varying the manner of presentation of a problem limits the generality of a conclusion about conservation of number or liquid quantity. Similarly, by changing the content of a moral dilemma it may be possible to alter the modal stage response of a subject. For example, a subject may be stage four when thinking about stealing, but stage three when thinking about extramarital sex (see Gilligan, et al. 1971).

Doubts about whether moral growth is very stagelike are reinforced by two facts. Approximately one-third of the responses of a typical subject come from stages other than the modal stage, and for any particular subject almost all responses come from only two stages, typically in a two to one ratio. As a theoretical structure Kohlberg's scheme has three levels, each divided into two stages. Hence, *in theory*, there are six stages. As an empirical phenomenon, however, stages one, two, five, and six occur rarely in pure form among adults, and stages one, four, five, and six occur rarely in pure form among children. The typical child mixes concepts and principles from stages two and three. The typical adult mixes concepts and principles from stages three and four. The main thing that distinguishes children from adults is that adults stop talking about personal likes and dislikes and start talking about social institutions and social systems. Both children and adults talk about social roles and status ob-

ligations (which, as we shall discuss later, may be a promising starting point for an alternative conception of a rationally based postconventional morality). In the study of moral development, it may be
time to set aside the theoretical machinery of Piaget's stage theory of
cognitive growth. The evidence suggests there are diverse concepts
and forms of reasoning available to children and adults. What we do
not yet understand is how the particular case one thinks about and
the way it is represented make it more or less difficult to engage in
one form of reasoning or another.

   *Is the test biased in favor of Westernized elites?* A second criticism builds on Kohlberg's observation that certain populations receive higher stage scores than others. While it is not true, as is sometimes claimed, that men score higher than women on Kohlberg's
moral development interviews (Walker 1984; Snarey 1985), social
class is a major correlate of stage level. On a worldwide scale, the
highest scores are achieved by Israelis of European origin, upper middle-class Americans and Western oriented members of the urban elite
in countries like Taiwan and India. Some critics see this as an indication of bias in Kohlberg's scheme (Simpson 1974). An alternative
interpretation, compatible with Kohlberg's theory, is that processes
of rational reasoning and opportunities to engage in Socratic dialogue
are unequally distributed across human populations. In other words,
upper middle-class Americans are more rational than lower class
Americans; Israelis of European origin are more rational than Israelis
of African or Middle Eastern origin; and urban elite populations in
Taiwan and India are more rational than traditional rural populations
in those countries.

   The thesis that there is an unequal distribution of rationality
across populations has both supporters (Hallpike 1979) and critics
(Cole and Scribner 1974; Shweder 1982a, 1982b, 1982c). It is important, however, to distinguish this thesis from a less controversial one
with which it is sometimes confused, namely the thesis about the
distribution of self-consciousness or deliberate meta-analysis. It is
widely acknowledged among cognitive anthropologists and cross-cultural psychologists that individuals and populations do differ in the
extent to which they reflect on what they know and explicitly for-
mulate it. Few researchers would deny that those who are schooled
are better at self-reflection and more likely to think about or even
write down the rules for moral or logical thinking (see Scribner and
Cole 1981). Self-consciousness about thinking probably is a useful
cross-cultural and developmental variable. Not everyone has good
verbal access to their own processes of rational reasoning.

Notice, however, that the thesis about meta-analysis has nothing to say about the types of rational processes available to a person or people. There is an important difference between implicit versus explicit understanding of principles. The fact that some cultures are more ratio-nal*ized* (self-reflective or "meta") than others does not mean that they are more rational. What is controversial is the question of the distribu-tion of rational reasoning processes, as distinct from the mental skills of self-reflection, verbal access, and meta-analysis.

*Why is postconventional thinking so rare?* A third criticism comes closer to the concerns of this chapter. Perhaps the most strik-ing research finding using Kohlberg's scheme is that very few people are postconventional thinkers. On a worldwide scale, only 1 or 2 per-cent of all responses are pure postconventional, and mixed conven-tional/postconventional responses (so-called stage four/five) account for only about 6 percent of responses (Snarey 1985). Even pure pre-conventional responses are infrequent. The vast majority of responses fall within the loose boundaries of the conventional level of under-standing (stages three and four). If one accepts Kohlberg's moral di-lemma interview methodology and the underlying interpretive logic of his scheme, then one must conclude that almost all adults in all cultures conceive of virtue as conformity with the subjective prefer-ences of the group, and most never attain the idea that there are ob-jective obligations that take precedence over the preferences and will of the group. That conclusion is not consistent with several more eth-nographically based research findings on moral codes (Read 1955; Ladd 1957; Malinowski [1926] 1976; Firth 1951; Fortes, 1959). Firth's remarks on the Tikopia are typical of ethnographers' accounts of moral codes: "The spirits, just as men, respond to a norm of conduct of an external character. The moral law exists in the absolute, inde-pendent of the Gods" (quoted in Nadel 1957; 270–71). Moreover, if the idea of objective obligation does not occur to most people in most societies, it would suggest that most members of our species adhere to a rationally inadequate conception of morality. Not surprisingly, that conclusion has led some moral development researchers to raise doubts about Kohlberg's interview methodology, the logic of his con-ceptual scheme, or both.

## The Methodological Critique: Why Is Postconventional Thinking Rare?

Kohlberg's theory of moral development is about the development of moral understandings, yet his moral dilemma interview methodology is a verbal production task that places a high premium on the ability to generate arguments, verbally represent complex concepts, and talk like a moral philosopher. It is hazardous to rely on such a procedure when studying moral understandings because one of the most important findings of recent developmental research is that knowledge of concepts often precedes their self-reflective representation in speech. Young children know a great deal more about the concept of number, causation, or grammaticality than they can state. As Nisbett and Wilson (1977) have put it, people "know more than they can tell." A distinction is needed between implicit, tacit, or intuitive knowledge of a concept and the ability to state explicitly the knowledge one has.

To clarify the distinction between implicit and explicit knowledge of principles, consider research on adult understandings of natural language grammar. Most people do not have good verbal access to their own available concepts or intellectual processes. The ability to describe grammatical principles is a rather poor index of an individual's knowledge of the grammar of his language or of his ability to discriminate between grammatical and ungrammatical utterances. Most competent speakers of a language can make use of grammatical decision rules without being able to state what those rules are. Researchers would not confuse a theory about the development of grammatical competence with a theory about the development of the skills of a grammarian.

That, curiously, seems to be what has happened in the study of moral understandings. Those who study moral understandings with Kohlberg's moral dilemma interview have reduced the study of moral concepts to the study of verbal justification of moral ideas. The study of moral understanding has been narrowed, by methodological fiat, to the study of what people can propositionalize. That is dangerous because what people can state is but a small part of what they know.

Kohlberg's interview methodology requires subjects to access verbally their moral concepts, produce moral arguments, and talk like a moral philosopher. Several researchers (Turiel 1979, 1980; Nucci and Turiel 1978; Nucci 1981, 1982; Nucci and Nucci 1982; Smetana 1981a, 1981b, 1982, 1983; also see Shweder, Turiel, and Much 1981; Shweder 1982a) have relaxed the demand characteristics of the moral dilemma interview situation, requiring only that subjects be consistent in their responses to direct probes about the objective versus consensual status of moral versus conventional obligations. For example, children are asked whether an obligation is merely relative to the child's group or universally binding. "Suppose there is another country where parents and schools allow children to [pull each other's hair; wear no clothes at school]. Is that all right?" Others (e.g., Much and Shweder 1978) use a somewhat different technique and look at distinctions drawn between moral and nonmoral obligations, as revealed in the way children use language in "situations of accountability" to justify or excuse apparent violations of normative standards.

The findings from that research, where subjects are permitted to display their understandings by means of responses to simple, direct probes (or through naturally occurring language use), suggest a different portrait of the emergence of moral understandings, at least among children who are exposed to the family and school practices of Western liberal democracies. Probing their subjects about the impersonality, alterability, and relativity of obligations, Turiel, Nucci, and Smetana discover that even young children (ages three to five years) have an implicit understanding of the idea of an objective obligation. Young children distinguish moral rules (the prohibition on destroying the property of others without their permission) from conventional rules (it is wrong to eat horses but not wrong to eat cows; it is wrong for a boy to wear a dress to school every day). They recognize that, unlike conventional obligations, moral obligations cannot be altered by majority vote or the preferences of this or that group.

The Turiel, Nucci, and Smetana research suggests that young children understand the idea of an objective obligation. It also suggests that what children know is not necessarily revealed during a Kohlbergian interview. More directed probes may be needed to get at their implicit understandings. For example, children sometimes say such things as "it is wrong to steal because you'll be caught and sent to prison" (an apparent egoistic, preconventional response). However, when probed directly—"what if you would not be caught, you would get away with it?"—many of those same children maintain that stealing would still be wrong, and it would be wrong even if your father told you to do it, and even if most people voted to make it right. When children say "it is wrong to steal because you will be punished" they often mean "wrong things get punished, and stealing is punished because it is wrong." They do not usually mean "it's the punishment that makes something wrong." What children know and intend to communicate is not equivalent to the literal and surface interpretation of their often feeble attempts to identify and state in words the abstract principles underlying their judgments.

The Conceptual Critique: Why Is Postconventional
Thinking Rare?

A second reaction to Kohlberg's finding that so few people around the
world exhibit genuine moral understandings is to question the underlying interpretive logic of his scheme (Shweder 1982a, 1982b; Shweder and Miller 1985). One reason so few people are postconventional may be that most people reject the particular conceptual reference
points from which Kohlberg constructs his notion of a rationally appealing objective morality. It is important to recognize that for a person to reject Kohlberg's postconventional level of moral understanding is not the same as defining morality as positive law or subjective
preference; there may be alternative conceptual starting points from
which rationally to construct an objective morality. That type of critique of Kohlberg's interpretive logic is associated with the position
that there are "divergent rationalities" in the moral domain (Shweder
1986).

The idea of "divergent rationalities" in the moral domain can be
analyzed into the following claims. (1) There exists more than one
rationally defensible moral code. (2) In any moral code with rational
appeal, some concepts are "mandatory"; without those mandatory
concepts the code loses its rational appeal. Other concepts are "discretionary"; they permit replacement by alternative concepts whose
substitution into the code would not diminish its rational appeal.
(3) Every moral code that is rationally defensible is built up out of
both mandatory and discretionary concepts. The rational appeal of
a moral code would be diminished, it would become empty, if
it were divested of all discretionary concepts. (4) Kohlberg's particular conception of postconventional morality is not advocated by
most rational thinkers around the world because they reject one or
more of the particular discretionary concepts incorporated into his
scheme.

What are the mandatory and discretionary features built into
Kohlberg's conception of postconventional morality? As far as we can
judge, there are at least three mandatory features. Those features have
broad appeal among moral philosophers and are candidates for moral
universals. There are also at least six discretionary features. Not all
rational thinkers will find those particular features rationally appealing; they may elect to construct a moral code with substitute concepts or principles.

The three mandatory features are the idea of natural law, the
principle of harm, and the principle of justice. The six discretionary
features are a conception of natural law premised on natural "rights";

a conception of natural law premised on "voluntarism," "individualism," and a "prior to society" perspective; a particular idea of what or who is a "person"; a particular conception of where to draw the boundaries around the "territories of the self"; a conception of justice in which likenesses are emphasized and differences overlooked; and, finally, a rejection of the idea of divine authority. We consider briefly each of these features.

*Mandatory feature 1: The abstract idea of natural law.* The idea of natural law has already been described at some length. The idea is implicated whenever we speak of a discrepancy between what is and what ought to be. The idea of natural law implies that there are certain practices and actions that are inherently wrong regardless of how much personal pleasure they might give us and despite the existence of rules or positive laws that might permit their occurrence. It is the idea of an objective obligation.

*Mandatory feature 2: The abstract principle of harm.* The principle of harm states that a legitimate ground for limiting someone's liberty to do as they want is a determination that harm is being done to someone. Life in society is made up of the direct and indirect effects of people's actions and inactions. Every rationally appealing moral code defines what consequences are permissible and justifies the regulation of certain actions by reference to their harmful effects, however those are conceived.

*Mandatory feature 3: The abstract principle of justice.* The principle of justice states that like cases must be treated alike and different cases differently (Hart 1961). Alternatively, what is wrong for one person is wrong for any similar person in similar circumstances (Singer 1963). The principle of justice is the normative or prescriptive side of the abstract idea of categorization. In effect, the principle of justice forces us to group people into those we treat one way (in like fashion) and those we treat another way (in like fashion). Any social categorization (kin versus nonkin, teacher versus student) implements the principle of justice by defining the kinds of people there are to have similar or different kinds of relationships with.

*Discretionary feature 1: A rights-based conception of natural law.* One discretionary feature of Kohlberg's moral code is a rights-based conception of natural law. The feature is discretionary because not every rationally defensible moral code must be founded on a conception of natural "rights." A moral code may be founded on a conception of natural "duties" or natural "goals" and remain rationally defensible. Dworkin (1977) has important things to say about the difference between rights-, goal-, and duty-based moral codes. He points out that while all moral codes may have some place for social goals, individual rights, and individual duties, rational moral codes differ significantly in the scales over which goals, rights, and duties range, and in the priority given to goals over rights, duties over goals. In a goal-based code, a good like "improving the general welfare" or "national security" is taken as fundamental and given priority. In a rights-based code, a right like "the right of all men to the greatest possible overall liberty" is taken as fundamental and given priority. In a duty-based code, a duty like "the duty to obey God's will as set forth in the Ten Commandments" is taken as fundamental and given priority.

It is crucial for Dworkin's conceptualization that rights, duties, and goals are not merely three idioms for saying the same thing. If they were merely idioms, then every right could, in principle, be translated without loss of meaning into a parallel duty or goal, every duty into a goal or right, every goal into a duty or right. There are two reasons why perfect intertranslation cannot be achieved.

For one thing, there are duties and goals without correlative rights. In India, for example, it appears that the duty of a householder to feed a guest is owed to some third party or force like God or Hindu dharma, without any implication that the guest has a right to be fed, and in our own historical tradition parents had duties towards their children long before children could make rights claims against their parents.

Secondly, as Dworkin notes, rights and duties are not perfectly intertranslatable because even in those cases where duties and rights correlate "one is derivative from the other and it makes a difference which is derivative from which." He points out that the idea that "you have a duty not to lie to me because I have a right not to be lied to" is quite different in meaning from the idea that "I have a right that you not lie to me because you have a duty not to tell lies." They are different in meaning because "in the first place I justify a duty by calling attention to a right; if I intend further justification it is the right I must justify, and I cannot do it by calling attention to the duty. In the second case it is the other way around."

Duty-based codes have several distinctive features. In a duty-based code attention is focused on the moral quality of individual acts per se, on the degree of conformity of each act to a code for proper conduct. It is the code that takes precedence and it is the code that is the object of interpretation and elaboration, while the individual per se and his various "interior" states, preferences, appetites, intentions, or motives are of little interest or concern. The purity of the motive is less important than the quality of the act.

When moral codes are duty-based, the individual is supposed to match his or her actions to the code "or be punished or corrupted if he does not." The individual is not at liberty to deviate from the rule, or to call on others to do so. Within a duty-based code there is no such thing as a natural right (e.g., free speech) to encourage others to engage in wrong actions. In a duty-based code it would be incoherent to proclaim: "Do not impose your private morality on other people." Indeed, in duty-based moral codes, individual rights and the domain of what is private are typically subordinated to duties, and it is the duties associated with particular role relationships, of a wife to her husband, a host to his guest, that receive the most elaborate treatment in the code. It is the performance of duty, not the defense of liberty or personal conscience, that stimulates feelings of righteousness. To the extent that Kohlberg's scheme presupposes the existence of natural "rights" and gives them priority, the scheme will seem alien to any rational thinker who constructs a moral code on the basis of natural duties or natural goals.

*Discretionary feature 2: Natural individualism in the abstract.* A second discretionary feature of Kohlberg's moral code is the priority given to individualism. Societies are built out of roles and statuses (mother-child, doctor-patient, teacher-student, etc.), for which there are performance obligations, and out of individuals, who have differential talents, abilities, powers, intelligences, resources, and beauty. Both are necessary for social action. A discretionary feature in any moral code concerns what is taken as more fundamental, real, natural, or of value: "roles and statuses" (the parts to be played) or "individuals" (the people who play the parts).

The most fundamental entity in Kohlberg's moral code is the "abstract individual." Kohlberg's individual is "abstract" in two senses. First, the individual is abstracted from society. Conceived to exist as an autonomous entity prior to or outside of the social arrangements in which he or she is found, hypothetically stripped of any distinguishing social identity, each individual is assumed to have an intrinsic, and equal, moral value quite apart from that which attaches to him or her as an occupant of a particular status. Second, the individual is abstracted out of his or her personality and divested of all distinguishing marks of character, such as differential power, intelligence, beauty, charisma; the abstract individual, by definition, has no individuality.

The abstract individual is the fundamental entity in Kohlberg's scheme because society is viewed as a logically derivative product, formed when abstract individuals enter into a social contract. Kohlberg's commitment to an abstract individual is most apparent in his attempt, following Rawls (1971), to derive a just society from the idea of a social contract forged under an aptly labeled "veil of ignorance." Rawls and Kohlberg argue that a just society is the one to which any individual (free of duress and concerned only with self-interest) would voluntarily bind himself if he had to form a society ignorant of who the comembers of the society were going to be, that is, ignorant of his relative intelligence, talent, power. The most basic unit in Kohlberg's moral code is a theoretically idealized individual abstracted from society and abstracted from his own psychological qualities.

An alternative approach to the rationalization of a moral code is to start with the assumption that social arrangements are primary or fundamental and to attribute moral significance to the universal fact of role differentiation (for example, within the family) and the unequal distribution of health, wealth, status, beauty, and intelligence across individuals. That view argues that a differentiated social morphology is part of the natural order of things, that the moral value of a person is dependent on the position occupied within a system of particularistic interpersonal relationships (see Read 1955) and that the moral value of a person can be measured by reference to the skills, talents, and psychological qualities that are his or her just desert. It judges as fair whatever actions ensure that the proportions between differentiated social functions and social roles are adapted to the society as a whole (see Dumont 1970). This idea that social arrangments are part of nature, and that social forms are more permanent and fundamental than the individuals who happen to pass through them, has had its appeal to many rational thinkers.

*Discretionary feature 3: Who is a person?* A third discretionary feature in Kohlberg's moral code is his substantive conception of what or who is a "person" or "moral agent." Every moral code has some kind of more or less inclusive definition of who must abide by the standards of natural law and is entitled to just treatment and protection from harm. What is discretionary, however, are the category boundaries of the "person" or "moral agent." The rational defensibility of a moral code is probably unaffected by such decisions as, for example, whether illegal aliens have the same rights as citizens of the state or whether such entities as corporations, fetuses, cows, or dogs should receive protection from harm.

Kohlberg adopts a relatively inclusive definition of moral agent and treats as moral equivalents prisoners and free men, men and women, citizens and aliens, children and adults, heathens and non-heathens. His definition of a moral agent does not include fetuses, cows, fish, insects, plants, or other nonhuman living things. His definition is probably too inclusive for some rational thinkers who might argue that, just as the claims of one's children ought to take precedence over the claim of a stranger, so too the claims of a fellow "tribesman" ought to take precedence over the claims of an outsider. His definition of a person may not be inclusive enough for other moral thinkers who might argue that life is continuous and that even animals have a soul and should not be bred and raised in order to be killed and eaten.

*Discretionary feature 4: Which territories of the self?* A fourth discretionary feature in Kohlberg's moral code is his substantive conception of where to draw the boundaries around the "territories of the self." Within any moral code "moral agents" or "persons" are entitled to protection from harm; yet, even after it is decided who is a "moral agent," another discretionary decision must be made: how expansively to define the realm worthy of protection that surrounds the "person."

In other words which invasions of which territories of the self are to be considered harmful attacks? Are the protected territories to include only our bodies and physical possessions, or are they to include also our feelings, reputation, and honor? Not all rational thinkers would care to defend the proposition that "sticks and stones can break your bones, but words can never harm you," or that honor is always less important than life, so suffer the insult.

*Discretionary feature 5: Justice as equality.* A fifth discretionary feature is a substantive conception of justice in which likenesses are emphasized and differences overlooked. Kohlberg argues that justice requires every person's claims to be treated as equal, regardless of the person (1981, 144). What is moral vis-à-vis an American is moral vis-à-vis a Vietnamese; what is moral vis-à-vis a father is moral vis-à-vis a son (1981, 135). Kohlberg believes that in employing the utilitarian rule for maximizing general welfare the only just thing to do is count each individual as equal to one unit; no weighting is allowed. Thus, saving more lives is better than saving fewer lives, regardless of who it is that is saved, the old or the young, the good or the wicked. That conception of justice is not implied by the abstract idea of justice, which merely states "treat like cases alike

and different cases differently." The abstract idea of justice does not
state which likenesses or differences should count, whether or how
they should be weighted, or how, in particular, like cases should be
treated, other than being treated in the same way. When relevant
differences can be cited it is not unjust to treat different cases differently. That is the reason why some rational thinkers argue that
it can be a moral act to prohibit the son but not the father from
casting a vote, and by analogy that no one should be allowed to vote
who is uninformed about the issues or candidates or unable to exercise mature rational judgment. Within a population, rationality is
not equally distributed, and some individuals may have greater vulnerabilities than others and require greater protection from themselves.

*Discretionary feature 6: Secularism.* A final discretionary feature of Kohlberg's code is a secularism that rejects divine authority
(1981, 312–18). That rejection is revealed when Kohlberg (1981, 315)
argues that the statement "X ought to be done because it is a command of God (or is in the Bible, or is one of the Ten Commandments)"
is equivalent to the statement "X is right because it is approved of by
a majority of the Gallup Poll." In other words, the knowledge possessed by a superior or divine being set forth in sacred text has no
greater epistemological status than majority votes or other expressions of the subjective preferences of a group of human beings. That
idea commits Kohlberg to a particular, and in our view peculiar, definition of natural law, in which the only things that count as natural laws are things that human beings can discover *for themselves*
(1981, 313), without the assistance of revealed or handed-down
truths about right and wrong.

It is reasonable to presume that Kohlberg does not believe in superior beings who have privileged access to truths about natural laws.
He seems to reject the idea that there might exist natural laws that
human beings are unable to discover on their own, or that there might
exist natural laws whose underlying rationale is difficult for mere human beings to understand, even after the natural law is revealed. Yet
the idea of a superior or divine being (whose privileged access to truth
is revealed in sacred texts) is neither incoherent nor irrational. Unless
Kohlberg is prepared to argue that all rational thinkers must be atheists or that it is irrational to accept an account of the truth from beings thought to have superior powers of understanding, his attempt to
equate divine commands with convention or group consensus must
be seen as a discretionary act of a secular humanist that need not have
universal appeal to all rational thinkers.

We have examined in some detail several discretionary features in Kohlberg's conception of postconventional moral understanding. Most of those features are variations on the idea that society has a rational foundation in a hypothetical social contract, and the related claim that the idea of an abstract, rational individual standing outside of, or prior to, society can be used as the fundamental and common measure of moral conduct. The underlying logic of Kohlberg's scheme is premised on voluntarism, secularism, and individualism, premises that not every rational thinker must adopt. There is the possibility that there is more than one form of postconventional thinking and that individualism is not the only premise out of which to construct a rationally appealing objective ethics.

We suspect that so few people around the world meet Kohlberg's criteria for postconventional thinking because they reject his particular rationalization of morality. Subjects classified as conventional thinkers (stages three and four) may be expressing an alternative form of postconventional thinking that cannot be easily classified within the terms of Kohlberg's scheme. We believe that is the case with our Hindu informants, as we shall see later. It may be true of Kohlberg's American informants as well.

## Turiel's Social Interactional Theory: Overview and Evaluation

### Overview

Turiel, Nucci, and Smetana examine the young child's implicit understanding of abstract moral principles like natural law or universalizability. The research, however, does more than just provide a methodological critique of Kohlberg's verbal production interview task; it suggests an alternative theory of moral development. One way to conceptualize their theory is to imagine that Turiel, Nucci, and Smetana have turned Kohlberg's three-level scheme on its side. Instead of three levels of understanding (egoistic, conventional, and moral) they posit three domains of understanding (personal, conventional, and moral) which are distinguished from each other by young children, and which undergo separate courses of elaboration, and increased sophistication (see figure 1.2). Moral understandings do not emerge out of conventional understandings but rather coexist with them during early childhood. The differentiation of what is moral from what is conventional is explained not by reference to the development of rational reasoning and exposure to Socratic dialogue but by reference to the distinguishing qualities of social interactional events. "Qualita-

**Figure 1.2:** Turiel's Social Interactional Domain Theory of Moral
Development Turns Kohlberg's Scheme (figure 1.1) on Its Side

|                        | Domain A                                              | Domain B                                                          | Domain C                                              |
|------------------------|-------------------------------------------------------|-------------------------------------------------------------------|-------------------------------------------------------|
|                        | Moral                                                 | Conventional                                                      | Personal                                              |
| *Material* *Conditions* | Justice, harm, rights, welfare, allocation of resources | Social uniformities and regularities, food, clothes, forms of address, sex-roles | Psychological states, personal tastes and preferences |
| *Formal* *Conditions*   | Rational Universal Unalterable Objective Self-constructed More serious | Arbitrary Relative Alterable Consensus-based Socialized Less serious |                                                       |

tively distinct types of social interactions with different classes of
events or actions lead to the construction of different types of social
knowledge" (Smetana 1983, 134).

Turiel, Nucci, and Smetana accept Kohlberg's proposed criteria
for distinguishing moral understandings from conventional ones,
although they believe the distinction exists in early childhood. Morality refers to objective obligations concerning justice, harm,
rights, and human welfare, and it is instantiated by actions (e.g., hitting and hurting; stealing personal property) that have an objective
effect upon the well-being and rights of others. The idea of convention, in contrast, refers to certain actions that are right (or wrong) by
virtue only of social consensus (e.g., men wearing pants instead of
dresses; the idea that all work should stop on Saturdays for a day of
rest).

A convention is the idea of an obligation for which there is no
natural law. It is the idea that the rightness or wrongness of an action
(shaking hands when greeting another) is arbitrarily designated and
historically limited to a social consensus that happens to have
formed. It is arbitrarily designated in that, from an objective or rational point of view, what happens to be right or wrong (eating beef but
not pork) could have been designated otherwise. Turiel, Nucci, and
Smetana hypothesize that socially demanded behavioral uniformities
(traffic regulations, dress codes) are functionally advantageous for coordinating social interaction among members of a social system. That
functional advantage, they argue, is the major reason that any social
consensus develops at all around such issues as what to wear, what to

eat, how to eat, how to address others (first name or title) (see Lewis 1969).

Turiel, Nucci, and Smetana believe there are intrinsically moral events. They argue that, through social interaction, children quickly come to distinguish those events that inherently possess a moral quality (connecting them to issues of harm, justice, and welfare) from those events whose rightness or wrongness is merely an extrinsic matter of social consensus. Young children are said to develop the idea of a moral event and the idea of a conventional event and to distinguish them from each other because they have had direct experience with both types of events and have learned that they are not the same.

The Turiel, Nucci, and Smetana theory does not postulate that every event must be purely moral or purely conventional. The theory acknowledges fuzzy boundaries and various blending of types (Smetana 1983; Turiel and Smetana 1984; Turiel and Davidson, in press). The theory does postulate the existence of enough pure moral events and pure conventional events to stimulate in the mind of the child a distinction between morality and convention.

For Turiel, Nucci, and Smetana, morality refers to objective obligations concerning harm, justice, rights, and the welfare of others. They argue that actions or events possess that moral quality if those actions or events involve physical or psychological harm, personal or private property, promises or commitments, or the allocation of scarce resources. Conventional events do not possess a moral quality, since their rightness or wrongness is acquired solely by virtue of social consensus, should such a social consensus develop. Those conventional events include food "customs," clothing "styles," sex-role definitions, forms of address, and sexual practices. According to the theory, ridiculing a cripple will be universally viewed by children as a moral event, while the norms prohibiting male business executives from wearing a dress to work will be viewed as conventional.

Turiel, Nucci, and Smetana credit young children with inferential ability to recognize the moral quality inhering in some events. These skills include means-ends analysis, the recognition of cause and effect connections, and simple forms of hypothetical and counterfactual reasoning (for example, "if everyone were to do that, then . . . "). Those cognitive skills make it possible to recognize the objective connection between pulling someone's hair and inflicting harm and the desirability of the presumption that such behavior is wrong, unless overridden by other moral considerations.

Young children are also credited with the ability to detect regularities in their social environment. They recognize that some actions are, for no apparent objective or rational reason, consistently considered wrong by members of the group. Turiel, Nucci, and Smetana argue this leads children to infer that conventionally based wrongness is arbitrary, relative to one's group, alterable by consensus, and less serious in the breach. According to the theory, conventional wrongs, but not moral wrongs, can only be learned through exposure to group consensus via social transmission processes—commands, sanctions, instructions. Moral wrongs are learned primarily through direct observation of the harm or injustice caused by a transgression. Finally, Turiel, Nucci, and Smetana argue that children taken an interest in regulating, sanctioning, and intervening in other children's actions when those actions violate moral standards but remain relatively indifferent when children violate conventional norms for right conduct. Social conventions, they imply, are the concern of adults, not children.

In sum, Turiel, Nucci, and Smetana introduce an alternative methodology into the study of moral understandings, broad enough to include both implicit and explicit knowledge of moral concepts. They propose a theory of moral development in which moral understandings do not develop out of conventional understandings, but rather coexist with them from an early age. The central claims of the theory concern (a) the determinate content of moral versus conventional events (e.g., pulling hair vs. wearing brightly colored clothes to a funeral); and (b) the parallel series of oppositions (universal vs. relative; unalterable vs. alterable; serious vs. not serious; objective vs. subjective; inherent vs. extrinsic; rational vs. arbitrary; directly observed vs. socialized) that distinguish both moral events and the idea of morality from conventional events and the idea of convention.

## An Evaluation of Turiel's Social Interactional Theory

### The Strength of the Theory

The Turiel, Nucci, and Smetana research suggests that the mandatory principles of a rationally appealing moral code—the abstract or formal ideas of natural law, harm, and justice—are available between the ages of three and five years and can be elicited utilizing direct probes about the relativity, alterability, and importance of obligations. From the point of view of the young child, obligations are not overwhelmingly viewed as conventional, and, for at least a subclass of material events, the young child grasps the difference between objective, natural-law, reason-driven obligations and consensus-based, collective-preference, conformity-driven obligations. Happily, the research directs our attention to "social interaction" and to the child's intellectual and emotional appraisal of the consequences of his or her own actions (e.g., pulling someone's hair and making him or her cry), although the research gives relatively little weight to the way interactional events and their consequences are socially construed, or to the way children are assisted by others in appraising an event.

## The Limitations of the Theory

*Are events free of social meaning?* One potential difficulty with the Turiel, Nucci, and Smetana theory is that it underplays the way ritual observances and customary practices involving food, sex, dress, the exchange of greetings, and terms of address may be linked through social meanings to mandatory moral principles like harm, justice, and natural law. The theory underestimates the potential importance and moral significance of events classified by the theory as conventional.

That tendency to overlook the role of social meaning in the development of moral understanding may be a by-product of Turiel, Nucci, and Smetana's definition of morality. Morality is defined not only by reference to the idea of natural law and objective obligation (a mandatory feature of any rationally appealing moral code), but by reference to natural "rights" (a discretionary feature). And morality is defined not only by reference to the abstract idea of harm (a mandatory feature) but by reference to only certain kinds of harms (direct and intended physical and pyschological attacks) on certain types of "persons," namely sentient beings (a discretionary feature). Given that definition of morality, Turiel, Nucci, and Smetana have no difficulty identifying arbitrary assault (hitting and hurting), biased arbitration, and theft as prototypical examples of moral infractions. Yet with that definition of morality, how are we to classify the failure to perform funeral rites for deceased parents, or kissing and sexual foreplay between consenting adult brother and sister?

The theory is faced with a difficulty. On the one hand, the principle of harm could be broadened to include the distress or emotional upset that is caused when someone witnesses in others what they believe to be a violation of obligations. The concept of a "person" could be broadened to include such entities as the souls of deceased ancestors, God, nature, or anything else that is believed to be vulnerable to harm, insult, or abuse. Yet if the discretionary features which define a moral code are broadened in that way, it is no longer obvious why a domain of conventional events must be separated out from a domain of moral events; nudity or the violation of a dress code might be emotionally upsetting to someone, hence a moral event. On the other hand, if morality is equated with such discretionary features as natural "rights" and direct physical or psychological assaults on a sentient being, then we must classify as conventional events the obligation to perform funeral rites for your parents, and the taboo on incest between cautious, consenting adult siblings. That would be a misclassification from the point of view of most peoples of the world.

Such examples cannot be readily explained away as domain mixtures or second-order phenomena. It is not the case that our obligations concerning incest avoidance and a proper burial for the dead are understood as primarily conventional with secondary moral implications. On the contrary, at least for some peoples, the expectations associated with the incest taboo and funeral rites are the prototypes of a moral obligation.

An indirect, but fascinating, source of evidence on the issue of whether Turiel, Nucci, and Smetana's hypothesized domain of conventional events *must* be separated in development from the moral domain comes from Murdock's (1980) cross-cultural survey of theories about the causes of illness in 139 societies. Among the theories of illness surveyed by Murdock is the theory of "mystical retribution," in which acts in violation of some taboo or moral injunction cause illness directly (rather than through the mediation of some offended or punitive supernatural being) (1980, 18). Murdock lists six major types of rules, injunctions, and taboos in order of the frequency with which their violation is associated with subsequent illness.

It seems reasonable to assume that a rule whose violation is thought to make you sick is perceived as important. Thus, it is noteworthy that many of the actions that are thought, on a worldwide scale, to cause illness are from the class of actions Turiel, Nucci, and Smetana classify as "conventional." Violations of food taboos (e.g., a Muslim eating pork) are at the top of Murdock's list. Violations of sex taboos (e.g., adultery and incest) come next. Next come violations of "etiquette" taboos, especially "breaches of appropriate behavior towards kinsmen, strangers or social superiors," and violations of "ritual" taboos, defined as "breaches of appropriate behavior toward the supernatural." Fifth on the list are violations of "property taboos" (theft, trespass), a class of actions that Turiel, Nucci, and Smetana classify as "moral." The final class of transgressions frequently associated with illness are violations of "verbal taboos" (e.g., "blasphemy or the use of forbidden words"). In Murdock's data on theories of illness through mystical retribution, actions classified by Turiel, Nucci, and Smetana as conventional (e.g., forms of address to social superiors) are not necessarily treated as different from actions classified as moral (e.g., theft).

Turiel, Killen, and Helwig (155–244) have noted that children and adolescents sometimes make distinctions between moral and conventional (nonmoral) events by weighing the seriousness of the transgression; the more serious breaches are considered moral. If seriousness of breach is an indication of the moral (versus nonmoral) quality of an event, and if the belief that a breach will cause illness is an indication of perceived seriousness, then the cross-cultural evidence surveyed by Murdock does not support the proposition that food customs, sexual practices, modes of dress and address, and ritual practices will be excluded from the moral domain. One possible conclusion consistent with Murdock's result is that if food customs, ritual observances, sexual practices, and modes of dress are inherently nonmoral, then perceived seriousness of breach is not a measure of what is moral (versus nonmoral). A second, more appealing conclusion is that there are no inherently nonmoral events. Nothing in the first-order interactional experience of events per se demands a distinction between morality and convention.

In a discussion of 'domain mixtures," Smetana (1983, 134–41) stops just short of drawing that latter conclusion. Noting that events classified in her theory as conventional are not always viewed as conventional by her child informants, Smetana describes ways in which what she views as conventional events can be reinterpreted as moral. For example, a child addressing a teacher in front of the whole class by her first name or a child answering a question without raising his hand can be viewed as morally wrong by interpreting those events as psychological insults, unfair to the rights of others, causing injury, or hurting someone's feelings. While it is our view that there are other ways to moralize an event, for example, by reference to violations of natural duties, or by direct reference to a scriptural code of natural law, Smetana's observations on "domain mixtures" are sufficient to raise an important doubt for us about the *inevitability* of the development of domain distinctions between morality and convention in moral development. We are skeptical about the proposition that a class of nonmoral events must universally be distinguished from, and set in contrast to, a class of moral events in the minds of children and adults. We are skeptical because we do not believe there exists a universal class of inherently nonmoral events. Nor do we believe that every culture draws a distinction between what is moral and what is conventional, although some cultures do.

*Is thinking free of social communication?* A second potential difficulty with the Turiel, Nucci, and Smetana theory is that it underplays the importance of tacit and explicit social communication in the interpretation of an event as moral. It is conceivable that there are certain actions (e.g., poking someone in the eye with a stick) whose wrongness young children might, in principle, be able to figure out for themselves by observing the consequence and empathizing with the victim, or by working out the counterfactual, "what if that had happened to me?" That is the type of self-construction process, through direct interaction, that Turiel, Nucci, and Smetana associate with the acquisition of primary moral understandings; processes of social communication, they argue, are decisive only in the acquisition of conventional obligations.

While it is possible to conceive of self-construction processes in the development of certain primary moral obligations, it seems to us an open empirical question whether the wrongness of moral actions is learned that way in practice. It is also an open empirical question whether wrongs that are learned through social communication will be viewed as conventional and consensus-based, deriving their authority exclusively from the commands of the parent or group. Whether an event is interpreted as moral or conventional—indeed, whether a distinction is drawn between morality and convention— may be related to how events are talked about and represented.

The relevance of social communication to moral development is highlighted by Edwards' work (1985) on naturally occuring transgressions among Luo children in the South Nyanza district of Kenya. Edwards analyzed a corpus of 105 transgression events, observed in connection with a study by Carol R. Ember. The recorded events, which include verbatim transcripts of verbal accusations, commands, threats, excuses, and accounts between child caretakers (ages seven-and-a-half to sixteen) and their young charges, consist of violations that Turiel, Nucci, and Smetana classify as moral (e.g., aggression toward peers, aggression toward animals) and violations they classify as conventional (e.g., terms of address, displays of deference, appropriate greetings, etc.) Edwards draws several pertinent and provocative conclusions from the analysis of her corpus.

First, with regard to events that Turiel, Nucci, and Smetana classify as moral (e.g., aggression toward small children or animals), "the victim's response is not the main, and certainly not the only, source of information for Oyugis children. Luo culture contains strong prohibitions against the striking of infants and toddlers by older children. Adults clearly communicate to children, first, that infants and toddlers are too little to be beaten no matter what, and second, that hurting and striking small children is a punishable offense." Furthermore, observations suggest that children are not left to construct moral rules concerning cruelty to animals on their own, by simply observing the victim's response. Rather, aggressive children are assisted in inhibiting action by intervening adults and children, "who rely a great deal on the use of commands, threats and sanction statements to stop aggressive behavior." Edwards points out that prohibitions against hitting and hurting and other forms of aggression require "enforcing by sanctioning agents to convince children that these matters are serious and not to be forgotten."

Second, with regard to events that Turiel, Nucci, and Smetana classify as conventional, Edwards points out that the Luo "put a great deal of stress on proper social forms"—the correct use of titles, kinship, age and status terms, appropriate greetings, avoidance, and joking to communicate interpersonal difference in rank, status, and power. On the basis of the recorded episodes it appears that the Luo consider those events to be just as important as those events that we would view as harmful or unjust. Younger children are called by older children to account for violations of so-called conventional events, just as they are for violations of moral events. Indeed, Edwards argues that "justice, harm and welfare rules, on the one hand, and conventional rules, on the other, are not necessarily learned in different kinds of social encounters."

Third, with regard to the command, threat, and sanction statements that frequently accompany transgressions in both the moral and "conventional" domain, Edwards suggests that they do not lead the Luo child to conclude that rules are arbitrary or consensus-based, or that rules derive their force simply from punishment. She argues that in the Luo cultural context, commands and sanction statements convey information about the basic importance and unconditionality of rules. Luo children interpret a command or threat to mean, "These rules are not to be taken lightly. Obey them whether I am there or not."

Fourth, with regard to the finding that American children view conventional rules (dress styles, forms of address, food customs, manners, and etiquette) as less important and more negotiable than moral rules, Edwards suggests that such a differentiation of convention versus morality may not be a developmental universal. At least for the Luo, relationships of status, power, age and kinship, and the proper forms of address, greeting, avoidance, and deferential display are understood as part of the moral-natural order of things and do not stand in contrast to morality. One is tempted to suggest that for the Luo, and for many other people as well, forms of address are as important as the status relationships they are meant to signal or express.

Turiel, Nucci, and Smetana may be able to accommodate the Luo evidence within their theory. They might argue, for example,

that, for the Luo, certain conventional events have moral implications that are lacking in our society. Two decisive questions would
still remain. First, at what point do conventional events with moral
implications become moral events with moral implications? Second,
why is it not possible for all conventional events to become moral
events with moral implications? If it is possible, then a domain distinction between morality and convention may not be a cross-cultural or developmental universal.

## From Review to Preview

Kohlberg and Turiel have made important contributions to our understanding of moral development. But as indicated in our review, the
cognitive-developmental and social interactional theories of moral
development have raised as many conceptual and empirical issues as
they have resolved. Several of those problematic issues are addressed
in the cross-cultural developmental research from India and the United States reported below.

The research assesses Kohlberg's central claim that conventional understandings precede moral understandings, and the Kohlbergian finding that children and most adults do not possess an idea
of natural law or objective obligations. The research assesses Turiel,
Nucci, and Smetana's central claim that the distinction between conventional obligations and moral obligations is a universal of childhood and adulthood, and that some events are inherently moral and
other events inherently nonmoral.

We have discovered through our research that moral events cannot be distinguished from conventional events on substantive
grounds. For example, among orthodox Brahmans and Untouchables
in India, eating, clothing and naming practices, and various ritual
events are viewed in moral, rather than conventional, terms, and several practices (wife beating, sleeping in the same bed with a menstruating woman) that one culture views as harmful are not seen as harmful by the other culture.

Second, while we have discovered that some principles and practices (e.g., keeping promises, protecting the vulnerable, avoiding incest, justice, unprejudiced judgment, reciprocity, respect for personal
property) are strong candidates for universal features in any moral
code, we are far less confident that there exists a universal class of
inherently nonmoral events. Those "deep" moral principles that are
shared across cultures do not characteristically lead to similar judgments about what is right or wrong in particular cases. Any event can be
made moral by appropriately linking it to a deep moral principle.

Third, we have discovered (pace Kohlberg and Turiel) that, on a worldwide scale, the idea of convention plays a relatively minor role in everyday understandings of obligations. Postconventional moral conceptions of obligation represent the dominant mode of rule understanding held by all informants, Indian and American, child and adult, male and female. The postconventional emphasis in America is on the natural "right" to free contract, personal choice, and individual liberty. The postconventional emphasis in India is on the natural "duty" to respect the "truths" of Hindu dharma, which concern the justice of received differences and inequalities, the moral implications of asymmetrical interdependencies in nature (for example, parent-child), and the vulnerabilities and differential rationality of social actors.

The idea of convention, the idea that obligations are consensus-based, relative, and alterable, is not absent from the interviews, but it occurs almost exclusively in the thinking of American adults and older American children. American children and adults express the democratic ideology that any collection of like-minded individuals is free to construct for themselves their own design for living, as long as other differently minded individuals are free to "exit" and form their own society. When a practice (serving horse meat but not dog meat for dinner) is viewed as conventional, typically it is by an American adult or eleven-to-thirteen-year-old. Orthodox Hindu informants make little use of the idea of convention. They view their practices as direct expressions of natural law. Among American children under age ten, there is not a single practice in our study that is viewed predominantly in conventional terms, although as American children get older certain practices and events do evoke the idea of convention.

Fourth, we have discovered that the communication and the socialization of a moral code proceed rapidly over ontogeny and seem to influence the direction of developmental change in social cognition. The culture-specific aspects of a moral code seem to be acquired as early in childhood as the more universal aspects, although socialization pressures and communication channels seem to be far more intense and/or effective in Hyde Park than in Bhubaneswar. There is relatively little evidence for a spontaneous universal childhood morality unrelated to adult attitudes and doctrines. For the most part, the moral thinking of Indian and American children is much like the thinking of adults in their respective cultures and distinct from the thinking of the children in the other culture.

Moreover, the directionality of change in moral thinking seems to be culture-specific. As Americans grow older they rely more on the idea of convention and become more pluralistic or relativistic in their judgments. As Indians grow older they show a greater and greater tendency to view their practices as universally binding and unalterable.

While it is possible to argue from the data for a culture-specific domain distinction between morality and convention among American adults and older American children, the research suggests that the idea of a conventional practice does not necessarily stand in contrast to the idea of morality. Rather the idea of a convention may be a second-order moral concept, distinctive of a democratic world view with an ideology of free contract. In democratic societies with a preponderant free-market mentality, one ideally grants to people the natural right to freely choose the way they want to live, and the natural right to enter voluntarily into a covenant to "convene" a society with other free, like-minded individuals. The emerging consensus about how to organize a society becomes a natural source of obligations, and respect for the conventions set forth in the covenant becomes a moral obligation.

Finally, the research suggests that the abstract idea of natural law or objective obligation may be universal to childhood and adulthood while several discretionary features of moral codes, which help constitute the rationality of any particular code, need not be universal. There may be more than one type of postconventional moral understanding. Having previewed the major findings of the study we turn to the study itself.

## The Development of Moral Understanding in Bhubaneswar and Hyde Park

### Method

*Informants.* The American sample includes thirty male and thirty female children from each of the age ranges five to seven, eight to ten, and eleven to thirteen, as well as thirty male and thirty female adults, a total of 180 children and sixty adults. The informants, predominately white, and of middle-class or upper middle-class background, are descendants of the reformed to secularized branches of the Christian or Jewish traditions. Most of the informants would describe themselves as Protestant, Catholic, or Jewish. Some of the adults would describe themselves as secular humanists or atheists. Few would describe themselves as orthodox. Children were recruited from schools in Hyde Park, the residential community surrounding the University of Chicago. The adults in the sample were, for the most part, parents of children attending these schools, although only children and adults from different families were re-cruited in the sample. While the majority of the adults sampled are Hyde Park parents, there are some informants who are not parents of school-age children.

The Indian sample consists of two subsamples, Brahmans and "Untouchables." The Brahman subsample includes thirty male and thirty female informants from each of the age ranges five to seven, eight to ten, and eleven to thirteen, as well as thirty male and thirty female adults, a total of 180 children and sixty adults. The informants are orthodox Hindus residing in the old temple town of Bhubaneswar, Orissa, a residential community surrounding the eleventh-twelfth century Hindu temple of Lingaraj.

The Lingaraj temple is a pilgrimage site for Hindus from all over India. Most of the informants in the Brahman sample come from families in which at least one male member performs hereditary du-ties in the cycle of ritual activities in this functioning Hindu tem-ple. The deity residing in the temple is Lingaraj, a form of the Hindu god Siva, represented through a stone lingam. Each day in the tem-ple the deity is awakened, bathed, and dressed. Food is cooked for him and he is fed. He takes a nap. He holds audience. Functionaries from the resident Brahman castes assist him in these activities. They also serve as guides for pilgrims, possessing as they do heredi-tary privileges to escort pilgrims from designated districts throughout India. In addition to the scores of functions performed every day in the temple, there are astrologically determined dates during the an-nual cycle of the temple when the deity is brought out of the temple to, for example, visit his married sister, beg forgiveness for his sins at the nearby temple of the god of death (Yama), take a vacation to the temple of a maternal aunt, or go on an outing with his wife, the god-dess Parvati.

Temple duty is not a full-time occupation for most of the adult male informants in the sample. Most are employed or engaged in other activities or occupations, as shopkeepers, tailors, civil servants, teachers, or property owners and landlords. Nevertheless, the status of the Brahman families in the sample is defined by their role in the ritual activities of the temple. The orthodoxy of the social and family practices of the Brahman community in the old town is not unrelated to their desire to maintain the sanctity of the temple and preserve the pilgrimage trade. All of the adult Brahman women in the sample have maintained traditional female roles in a Brahman household or joint family, as wife, mother-in-law, or widowed matriarch. Brahman chil-dren in the sample were recruited from schools in the old town com-munity and from families familiar to the authors. The adults in the sample were recruited by word of mouth through friendship networks from Brahman families resident in neighborhoods surrounding the Lingaraj temple.

The "Untouchable" sample includes thirty male and thirty female informants in the age range eight to ten years, as well as thirty male and thirty female adults. The informants are members of those castes referred to as "scheduled" castes by the government of India (scheduled for affirmative action programs), as Harijans or "children of God" by Gandhi, and as "unclean" castes by the local Brahmans. They come primarily from the local Bauri, Hadi, and Pana communities. The traditional occupations of these informants include agricultural labor, latrine cleaning, and basket making. The men and women in the sample regularly seek employment as physical laborers in road and house construction, stone quarrying, and harvesting. Informants from these "scheduled" castes reside either in the old temple town of Bhubaneswar or in neighboring villages. A few of the children were recruited through local schools. Many were recruited with the assistance of local members of the respective communities. Adult informants were recruited through friendship networks. According to local doctrine, members of "Untouchable" castes do not maintain their own sanctity and thus are not permitted to enter or come in contact with any holy ground. And in India there are many holy grounds, including the physical body of a Brahman, the house of a high-caste family, the purificatory waters of sacred rivers, ponds and wells, and all temples. Untouchables are not permitted entry to the Lingaraj temple.

*The thirty-nine cases.* The core of the study is an examination of American and Indian childhood and adult interpretations and understandings of thirty-nine behavioral cases. The thirty-nine cases, representing a range of family life and social practices, were developed over a period of several months on the basis of ethnographic knowledge of community life in Bhubaneswar and Hyde Park. Mahapatra is an anthropologist and a native resident of the old temple town. At the time the study began (October 1982) Shweder had previously conducted eighteen months of field research in Bhubaneswar.

The examination of informant interpretations was undertaken by means of a standard set of interview questions designed to assess an informant's understanding of obligations as subjective versus objective or conventional versus moral. The interview questions are described below. Informants were also presented with a ranking task to assess the perceived seriousness of the potential transgression event in each of the thirty-nine cases. The thirty-nine cases were developed with several objectives in mind.

One aim was to determine the extent to which the social order is perceived as moral or conventional by children and adults in India and America. Thus, cases were selected to sample a set of existential issues that must be addressed by any social system. The existential issues of concern in this study are personal boundaries (what's me/what's not me?), sexual identity (what's male/what's female?), maturity (what's grown-up or responsible/what's childish or irresponsible?), autonomy (am I autonomous and self-reliant/am I interdependent and mutually reliant?), ethnicity (what's our way/what's not our way?), hierarchy and status (who's up/who's down; how should life's burdens and benefits be distributed?), identification-empathy-solidarity (whose interests do I take into account/whose interests do I not take into account?), personal protection (avoiding a power order or "the war of all against all") and the "state" (what I want to do versus what the group wants me to do) (see Shweder 1982a). Cases were developed that related to one or more of those issues.

A second aim was to test Turiel, Nucci, and Smetana's hypothesis that a distinction between moral and conventional obligations can be drawn on substantive grounds. Thus, certain cases were selected to exemplify practices that Turiel, Nucci, and Smetana would classify as primarily conventional (e.g., regulations and restrictions concerning dress, food, terms of address, ritual practices, sex role definitions). Other events were selected to exemplify practices that their theory would classify as primarily moral (e.g., regulations concerning property, promises, and physical and psychological attacks on another person).

A third aim was to identify principles and concepts that might be candidates for moral universals. The moral philosophy literature from Hobbes to Kohlberg suggests several candidate concepts: justice, harm, reciprocity, protection of the vulnerable, altruism, honesty, loyalty, the honoring of commitments, and various prohibitions related to theft, ingratitude, biased arbitration, arbitrary assault, and the use of irrelevant classifications. Cases were selected to represent those candidate principles.

The fourth and final aim in selecting a corpus of behavioral cases was to further the development of an ethnography of family life. Thus, culture-specific practices were included in the study, in addition to practices that might have a more universal distribution. Cases were developed having to do with sanctity (pollution), chastity and respect for status (central themes for Indians), personal liberty, privacy, and equality (central themes for Americans). The thirty-nine behavioral cases are listed in table 1.1. They are listed in order of the

**Table 1.1:** Thirty-nine Cases in order of Perceived "Seriousness of Breach" as Judged by Hindu Brahman Eight- to Ten-year-olds

1. The day after his father's death, the eldest son had a haircut and ate chicken.
2. One of your family members eats beef regularly.
3. One of your family members eats a dog regularly for dinner.
4. A widow in your community eats fish two or three times a week.
5. Six months after the death of her husband the widow wore jewelry and bright-colored clothes. (the widow)
6. A woman cooked rice and wanted to eat with her husband and his elder brother. Then she ate with them. (the woman)
7. A woman cooks food for her family members and sleeps in the same bed with her husband during her menstrual period. (the woman)
8. After defecation (making a bowel movement) a woman did not change her clothes before cooking.
9. A man had a wife who was sterile. He wanted to have two wives. He asked his first wife and she said she did not mind. So he married a second woman and the three of them lived happily in the same house. (the man)
10. Once a doctor's daughter met a garbage man, fell in love with him and decided to marry him. The father of the girl opposed the marriage and tried to stop it because the boy was a garbage man. In spite of the opposition from the father, the girl married the garbage man. (the daughter)
11. A widow and an unmarried man loved each other. The widow asked him to marry her. (the widow)
12. A beggar was begging from house to house with his wife and sick child. A homeowner drove him away without giving him anything. (the homeowner)
13. In a family, a twenty-five-year-old son addresses his father by his first name. (the son)
14. It was the king's order, if the villagers do not torture an innocent boy to death, twelve hundred people will be killed. The people killed the innocent boy. So the king spared the life of the twelve hundred people. (the people)
15. A poor man went to the hospital after being seriously hurt in an accident. At the hospital they refused to treat him because he could not afford to pay. (the hospital)
16. A brother and sister decide to get married and have children.
17. The day after the birth of his first child, a man entered his temple (church) and prayed to God.
18. A woman is playing cards at home with her friends. Her husband is cooking rice for them. (the husband)
19. A father told his son to steal flowers from his neighbor's garden. The boy did it. (the boy)
20. While walking, a man saw a dog sleeping on the road. He walked up to it and kicked it. (the man)
21. Two people applied for a job. One of them was a relative of the interviewer. Because they were relatives, he was given the job although the other man did better on the exam.
22. Immediately after marriage, a son was asked by his parents to live in the same house with them. The son said he wanted to live alone with his wife and that he and his wife had decided to live in another town and search for work there. (the son)
23. A man says to his brother, "Your daughter's skin is dark. No one will say she is beautiful. No one will wish to marry her." (the man)

**Table 1.1:** *(continued)*

24. A father said to his son, "If you do well on the exam, I will buy you a pen." The son did well on the exam, but his father did not give him anything, spending the money on a carton of cigarettes. (the father)
25. Two brothers ate at home together. After they ate, the wife of the younger brother washed the dishes. (the wife)
26. A man had a married son and a married daughter. After his death his son claimed most of the property. His daughter got a little. (the son)
27. At night a wife asked her husband to massage her legs. (the wife)
28. A wife is waiting for her husband at the railway station. The train arrives. When the husband gets off, the wife goes and kisses him. (the wife)
29. There was a rule in a hotel: Invalids and disfigured persons are not allowed in the dining hall.
30. You went to a movie. There was a long line in front of the ticket window. You broke into line and stood at the front.
31. You meet a foreigner. He is wearing a watch. You ask him how much it cost and whether he will give it to you.
32. In school a girl drew a picture. One of her classmates came, took it, and tore it up.
33. A father, his eldest son and youngest daughter traveled in a boat. They had one life jacket. It could carry one person. The boat sank in the river. The father had to decide who should be saved. He decided to save his youngest daughter. The father and the eldest son drowned. (the father)
34. A letter arrived addressed to a fourteen-year-old son. Before the boy returned home, his father opened the letter and read it.

35. A young married woman went alone to see a movie without informing her husband. When she returned home her husband said, "If you do it again, I will beat you black and blue." She did it again; he beat her black and blue. (the husband)*
36. In a family, the first-born son slept with his mother or grandmother till he was ten years old. During these ten years he never slept in a separate bed. (the practice)*
37. A boy played hookey from school. The teacher told the boy's father and the father warned the boy not to do it again. But the boy did it again and the father beat him with a cane. (the father)*
38. A man does not like to use a fork. Instead he always eats rice with his bare hand. He washes it before and after eating. He does this when he eats alone or with others.*
39. Two men hold hands with each other while they wait for a bus.*

*Not considered a breach

perceived seriousness of the transgression involved, as judged by eight to ten-year-old Brahman children in the old town of Bhubaneswar.

The descriptions of the thirty-nine cases and the interview questions (to be described below) were developed first in English, then translated into Oriya (the state language of Orissa) for use with Indian informants, and then back-translated into English for use with American informants.

*The interview.* Questions were developed to assess features of an informant's understanding of the nature of obligations. Some questions probed the extent and seriousness of the obligation. Other questions indexed the perceived impersonality or objectivity of the obligation, with special reference to the features of relativity and alterability. Responses to the questions made it possible to classify informant understanding along several axes and into several categories, including the distinction between conventional and moral obligations.

The thirty-nine cases were divided into three thirteen-case subsets for use with the standard series of questions. Each subset of cases was administered to one-third of the males and one-third of the females in each age-community subgroup. Having informants answer the questions concerning thirteen rather than thirty-nine cases was a strategy designed to avoid possible fatigue or boredom effects that might have resulted from a more lengthy interview. A list of the question probes appears in table 1.2.

The questions can be viewed as criteria for distinguishing moral or objective obligations from conventional or consensus-based obligations while identifying those areas of conduct where it is perceived that one has the moral right to do whatever one wants. The first three

**Table 1.2:** The Standard Questions

1. Is [*the behavior under consideration*] wrong?
2. How serious is the violation?
   (*a*) not a violation
   (*b*) a minor offense
   (*c*) a somewhat serious offense
   (*d*) a very serious violation
3. Is it a sin?
4. What if no one knew this had been done. It was done in private or secretly. Would it be wrong then?
5. Would it be best if everyone in the world followed [*the rule endorsed by the informant*]?
6. In [*name of a relevant society*] people do [*the opposite of the practice endorsed by the informant*] all the time. Would [*name of relevant society*] be a better place if they stopped doing that?
7. What if most people in [*name of informant's society*] wanted to [*change the practice*]. Would it be okay to change it?
8. Do you think a person who does [*the practice under consideration*] should be stopped from doing that or punished in some way?

questions assess the existence or nonexistence of an obligation and the perceived importance of the obligation, should one exist. Question 4, concerning self-regulation in the absence of external observers, indexes one aspect of the difference between moral and conventional obligations. Questions 5 through 7 tap the perceived universality (versus relativity) and unalterability (versus alterability) of obligations.

Obligations that are thought to be relative to particular groups and alterable by consensus or majority will are readily classified as conventional obligations. Obligations that are perceived as universally binding and unalterable are readily classified as moral obligations.

The perceived relativity of an obligation is a necessary but not sufficient criterion of conventional understandings, because obligations need not be perceived as universally binding to be perceived as objective or moral. It is not incoherent or self-contradictory for an informant to believe that a moral or objective obligation may be tailored to the special requirements of a population, its temperament, its climate, its local context. We return in a moment to the issue of how to classify obligations that are thought to be unalterable, but only binding on some particular groups and not other groups. Finally, question 8, concerning sanctions, and the perceived legitimacy or illegitimacy of outside regulation, makes it possible to identify cases where informants believe there is a moral right to freedom of choice to do what one wants.

Our use of the questions in assessing an informant's understanding of obligations is illustrated in the following responses given by a hypothetical Brahman adult and American adult to case 4 (table 1.1), concerning a widow in your community who eats fish two or three times a week. First, the Brahman interview:

1. Is the widow's behavior wrong? (Yes. Widows should not eat fish, meat, onions or garlic, or any "hot" foods. They must restrict their diet to "cool" foods, rice, dhal, ghee, vegetables.)
2. How serious is the violation? (A very serious violation. She will suffer greatly if she eats fish.)
3. Is it a sin? (Yes. It's a "great" sin.)
4. What if no one knew this had been done? It was done in private or secretly. Would it be wrong then? (What difference does it make if it is done while alone? It is wrong. A widow should spend her time seeking salvation—seeking to be reunited with the soul of her husband. Hot foods will distract her. They will stimulate her sexual appetite. She will lose her sanctity. She will want sex and behave like a whore.)

5. Would it be best if everyone in the world followed the rule that widows should not eat fish? (That would be best. A widow's devotion is to her deceased husband—who should be treated like a god. She will offend his spirit if she eats fish.)

6. In the United States, widows eat fish all the time. Would the United States be a better place if widows stopped eating fish? (Definitely, it would be a better place. Perhaps American widows would stop having sex and marrying other men.)

7. What if most people in India wanted to change the rule so that it would be considered all right for widows to eat fish. Would it be okay to change the rule? (No. It is wrong for a widow to eat fish. Hindu dharma—truth—forbids it.)

8. Do you think a widow who eats fish should be stopped from doing that or punished in some way? (She should be stopped. But the sin will live with her and she will suffer for it.)

Next consider the American interview.

1. Is the widow's behavior wrong? (No. She can eat fish if she wants to.)
2. How serious is the violation? (It's not a violation.)
3. Is it a sin? (No.)
4. What if no one knew this had been done. It was done in private or secretly. Would it be wrong then? (It is not wrong, in private or public.)
5. Would it be best if everyone in the world followed the rule that it is all right for a widow to eat fish if she wants to? (Yes. People should be free to eat fish if they want to. Everyone has that right.)
6. In India, it is considered wrong for a widow to eat fish. Would India be a better place if it was considered all right for a widow to eat fish if she wants to? (Yes. That may be their custom but she should be free to decide if she wants to follow it. Why shouldn't she eat fish if she wants to?)
7. What if most people in the United States wanted to change the rule so that it would be considered wrong for a widow to eat fish? Would it be okay to change it? (No. You can't order people not to eat fish. They have a right to eat it if they want.)
8. Do you think a widow who eats fish should be stopped from doing that or punished in some way? (No!)

It should be noted that questions 5 through 7 are asked regarding the rule or obligation that is endorsed by the informant and perceived by the informant as relevant to the case. In some cases, as in the Brahman example, this rule or obligation may concern the regulation or proscription of a particular practice. In some cases, as in the American example, the rule or obligation may concern the protection of an

**Table 1.3:** Categorizing Obligations into Types

|  | Questions 5 and 6 | | |
| --- | --- | :---: | --- |
|  | Universal Obligation | : | Relative Obligation |
| Unalterable obligation | Univeral moral obligation | : | Context-dependent moral obligation |
| Question 7 | - - - - - - - - - - - - - - | : - - | - - - - - - - - - - - - - - |
| Alterable obligation | Incoherent | : | Conventional obligation |

agent's freedom of choice or autonomous decision making, in which case the interview assesses whether personal freedom in such matters is moral or conventional.

In the two sample interviews presented above neither informant viewed the dietary practices of widows in conventional terms. Although they disagreed about the morally right thing to do, both the Indian Brahman and the American viewed the issue as a moral issue. Both viewed the obligations involved as universally binding (questions 5 and 6) and unalterable (question 7). For the Brahman the relevant obligation was a status obligation associated with widowhood and the continued mutual reliance of husband and wife. For the American the relevant obligation was the obligation to protect the personal liberties and zones of discretionary choice of autonomous individuals. For the American whether you eat fish or not is your own personal business. The right to personal liberty and discretionary choice concerning what you eat is a moral issue. The obligation to protect that liberty is an objective obligation. Neither informant argued that the obligations involved were relative to this or that group or alterable by consensus or majority vote.

Crossing the relativity versus universality criteria (questions 5 and 6) with the alterability versus unalterability criteria (question 7) produces four categories for classifying informants' understandings of obligations. See table 1.3.

*Classifying responses as conventional versus moral.* Much of our discussion of conventional and moral obligations will focus on informant responses to question 5 and 6, concerning the relativity of obligations, and question 7, concerning the alterability of obligations. For the sake of that discussion it is useful to distinguish the idea of a universal moral obligation from the idea of a context-dependent or culture-specific moral obligation. It is also useful to distinguish further both those types of moral obligations from conventional ones that are perceived not only as context-dependent or culture-specific but also as alterable. Treating relativity (versus universality) and alterability (versus unalterability) as independent dichotomous variables in a 2 × 2 factorial design, we generate four possible types of understandings of obligations: universal moral obligations (universal and unalterable), context-dependent moral obligations (relative and unalterable), conventional obligations (relative and alterable), and a logically incoherent fourth category in which it is held that obligations are universally binding but can be altered by consensus in a particular society.

The understanding of obligations as univeral moral obligations is exemplified by a Brahman informant who argues that it is wrong to let young children sleep alone in a separate room and bed because children awaken during the night and are afraid, and that all parents have an obligation to protect their children from fear and distress. The understanding of an obligation as a context-dependent moral obligation is exemplified by a Brahman informant who argues that an Indian parent has an objective moral obligation to physically punish his errant child, but that the obligation does not universalize to American parents because the temperamental qualities of American children make them less responsive to physical punishment and more responsive to warnings or reasoning. The understanding of an obligation as a conventional obligation is exemplified by an American informant who argues that it is all right for people in other cultures to eat dogs, just as it is all right for us to eat sheep, cows, or rabbits, and that the prohibition on Kentucky Fried Canine for dinner would cease to have force if most Americans wanted it to. After all, we raise turkeys for slaughter. Why not raise dogs for slaughter?

*Ranking task: Seriousness of violation.* A ranking task was administered to a subset of informants from the main sample. This subset included ten male and ten female children in each age-community subsample, ten male and ten female American adults, ten male and ten female "Untouchable" adults and twelve male and twelve female Brahman adults.

The thirty-nine cases, written on separate index cards, and also read aloud to most Indian children and some adults, were presented to informants for ranking. Informants were asked first to identify the cases in which they felt the practice under consideration was wrong. They were then asked to rank order those cases in response to the question, "How serious is each violation? Which is the most serious, the next most serious, and so forth"? To ease the cognitive demands of the ranking task, the ranking was undertaken in steps. Informants first divided the wrong behaviors into three or four gradations (e.g., minor offense, somewhat serious offense, very serious offense) and then rank-ordered the behavioral incidents within each subcategory. Ties were not permitted, except for the cases considered nonviolations.

Subsequent analysis of the data focused on the ranks accorded each of the thirty-nine cases, with the most serious breach numbered 1, and the least serious, 39. In that correlational analysis, cases considered nonviolations were considered ties and assigned the mean value of the nonoccupied rank positions. For example, in a case in which an informant judged four cases to be nonviolations, each of those incidents would be assigned the rank value of 37.5 (that is, the mean of the nonoccupied rank positions of 36, 37, 38, 39).

## Results

The results section is organized around a series of questions posed below.

*Question 1: Are there, in fact, cultural differences in judgments about what is right and what is wrong?* Anthropologists have long noted the existence of major culturally based variations in judgments about what is right and wrong. Some anthropologists have even set as their task the understanding and explication of the unstated premises, metaphors, and lines of reasoning that lend ethical force and justification to those startling judgments of right and wrong ("It's a sin to comb your hair during a thunderstorm") that to an outsider seem opaque or bizarre.

Murdock (1980) describes the category of sin among the Semang people of Malaysia. For the Semang, the category of sin includes combing one's hair during a thunderstorm or during the mourning period, teasing or mocking a helpless or tame animal, watching dogs mate, killing a sacred black wasp, sexual intercourse in the daytime, drawing water in a vessel blackened by fire, and casual informal behavior with one's mother-in-law.

As far as we know, there is little reason to doubt anthropological accounts of cross-cultural differences in judgments of right and wrong. Some scholars, however, have raised doubts about whether those native judgments are moral judgments, while still others are skeptical that there is any moral justification for such errant judgments of right and wrong. Even Murdock (1980, 89) expresses the view that for the Semang the category of sin is "arbitrary and devoid of ethical justification," and that to the extent the Semang conform at all to their prohibitions, it is merely out of fear of external sanctions by a superhuman, omniscient god.

Question 1 of the results section addresses the noncontroversial proposition that there are major cross-cultural differences in judgments of right and wrong. Question 2 addresses the more challenging issue whether those judgments of right and wrong are, from the point of view of the native, moral judgments, or merely judgments about obligations perceived to be conventional or conformity-based. Later, in a discussion of the conceptual foundations of the Hindu code in everyday reasoning in Orissa, we will explicate some of the premises, principles, goals, metaphors, and lines of reasoning that give ethical justification, and thus "internal" force, to apparently alien judgments about what's right and what's wrong.

With regard to the thirty-nine practices and cases examined in this study (see table 1.1) the judgments about what is right and wrong elicited from Americans and Oriyas are virtually independent. In contrast, there are high levels of agreement between Oriya Brahmans and Oriya Untouchables, with the notable exception of normative judgments about practices concerning widows (widows' diet and widow remarriage), practices over which there is considerable dissensus within the Untouchable community. Henceforth in this essay "dissensus" of judgment refers to judgments of right (or wrong) shared by less than 75 percent of informants within an age-community subsample. Conversely "consensus" of judgments refers to agreement about what's right (or wrong) among at least 75 percent of informants within an age-community subsample. Since sex differences are not an important factor in the findings, the responses of males and females have been pooled within each age-community subsample.

Table 1.4 presents the intercorrelations $(r)$ among the mean ranks of the thirty-nine practices in terms of perceived seriousness of breach, as judged by each age-community subgroup. Within the American community there are very high levels of mean agreement between each age group on the ranking task. On the average, American five-year-olds and American adults make very similar judgments about what is right and what is wrong $(r = .86)$. Levels of agreement are also high within and across the Brahman and Untouchable samples (the average within India, between age group correlation = .59). In contrast there are weak negative intercorrelations between the mean rankings of American children and adults versus the mean rankings of Brahman and Untouchable children and adults (mean cross-cultural correlation = −.21). At an unaggregated level of analysis, individual rankings of American adults intercorrelate with each other in the .60 range, Brahman adult rankings intercorrelate with each other in the .50 range, while American-Brahman rankings inter-

**Table 1.4:** Intercorrelations (*r*) of Mean Rankings of Thirty-nine Cases in terms of Seriousness of Breach

| | | Americans | | | | Brahmans | | | | Untouchables | |
|---|---|---|---|---|---|---|---|---|---|---|---|
| | | Ad | 11 | 8 | 5 | Ad | 11 | 8 | 5 | Ad | 8 |
| Americans | Adults | | .94 | .92 | .85 | −.16 | −.21 | −.34 | −.19 | −.29 | −.03 |
| | 11–13 | | | .93 | .90 | −.26 | −.27 | −.39 | −.25 | −.33 | −.13 |
| | 8–10 | | | | .92 | −.17 | −.25 | −.27 | −.11 | −.29 | −.03 |
| | 5–7 | | | | | −.22 | −.27 | −.32 | −.12 | −.24 | .01 |
| Brahmans | Adults | | | | | | .67 | .74 | .62 | .70 | .61 |
| | 11–13 | | | | | | | .54 | .38 | .60 | .44 |
| | 8–10 | | | | | | | | .68 | .56 | .52 |
| | 5–7 | | | | | | | | | .49 | .63 |
| Untouchables | Adults | | | | | | | | | | .72 |
| | 8–10 | | | | | | | | | | |

correlate with each other in a range that varies around .00, in a slightly negative direction.

Table 1.1 lists the full ranking of the thirty-nine cases in terms of seriousness of breach as perceived, on average, by Brahman eight-to-ten-year-olds. To appreciate fully the magnitude of the cross-cultural differences in judgments about right and wrong, the reader should compare his own judgments of seriousness of breach with those shown in table 1.1. With regard to the practices that are the focus of the study we seem to have found a relatively high consensus code, at least within each of the communities that are the focus of the study. There may, of course, be other issues over which there is more dispute within each community, and there may be other communities within each nation (e.g., the urban elite in India) who would display different patterns of judgment.

Over the entire set of cases, the judgments of our Oriya and American informants about right and wrong are virtually unrelated. The judgments are not uniformly opposed, nor are they typically in agreement. A display of the points of agreement and disagreement in normative judgments can be found in table 1.5. Inspection of table 1.5 reveals that, of the thirty-nine practices or cases, Brahman and American adults display similar jugments of right versus wrong concerning ten practices and opposed judgments concerning sixteen practices. For eleven other practices there is disagreement about what's right or wrong within one community or the other, although never in both.

What is not shown in table 1.5, and is important to note, is that several of the culture-specific wrongs are viewed by Brahman infor-

**Table 1.5:** Patterns of Disagreement and Agreement among American and Brahman Adults

| Case No. | Type of Practice |
|---|---|
| *Disagreement: Brahmans think it is right / Americans think it is wrong* | |
| 26 | Unequal inheritance, male vs. females |
| 35 | Beating disobedient wife |
| 37 | Caning an errant child |
| *Disagreement: Brahmans think it is wrong / Americans think it is right* | |
| 6 | Eating with husband's elder brother |
| 2 | Eating beef |
| 27 | Wife requests massage |
| 13 | Addressing father by first name |
| 1 | Cutting hair and eating chicken after father's death |
| 8 | Cooking in clothes worn to defecate |
| 5 | Widow wears bright clothes |
| 17 | Entering temple after birth |
| 18 | Husband cooks |
| 10 | Love marriage out of status |
| 11 | Widow remarriage |
| 4 | Widow eats fish |
| 7 | Menstruating woman cooks, etc. |
| 25 | Washing plates of husband's elder brother |
| *Agreement: Brahmans and Americans think it is wrong* | |
| 15 | Ignoring accident victim |
| 24 | Breaking promise |
| 30 | Cutting in line |
| 32 | Destroying another's picture |
| 20 | Kicking a harmless animal |
| 16 | Incest—brother/sister |
| 21 | Nepotism |
| 19 | Stealing flowers |
| 29 | Discrimination against invalids |
| 31 | Asking foreigner for his watch |

*Practices with dissensus in one or the other culture, with indication of consensual views of the other culture (B = Brahmans; A = Americans)*

| *Brahman Dissensus* | *American Dissensus* |
|---|---|
| 34 Father opens son's letter (A = wrong) | 36 Ten-year-old sleeps with mother (B = not wrong) |
| 33 Father saves daughter over son (A = not wrong) | 9 Polygyny (B = not wrong) |
| 28 Kissing in public (A = not wrong) | 12 Helping beggar (B = not wrong) |
| 22 Neo-local residence (A = not wrong) | 38 Eating with hands (B = not wrong) |
| 14 Sacrificing innocent child (A = wrong) | 23 "No one will marry your daughter" (B = wrong) |

mants as more serious transgressions than many of the events viewed as wrong in both cultures (see table 1.1). In the Oriya Brahman community it is considered a serious wrong for a doctor at a hospital to refuse to treat an accident victim because he is too poor to pay (table 1.1, no. 15), but that transgression is not quite as serious as a widow eating fish (table 1.1, no. 4). a relative eating beef (table 1.1, no. 2), or the firstborn son cutting his hair the day after his father's death (table 1.1, no. 1).

Tables 1.1, 1.4, and 1.5 illustrate what anthropologists have long known: different cultures display many differences in social and family practices and in ideas about what is right and what is wrong, and it is not always apparent at first blush, or to an outsider, why a particular event (like a widow eating fish or a man entering the temple the day after the birth of his child) is considered wrong at all.

It is, of course, important to recognize that the level of cross-cultural normative agreement and disagreement discovered in our study, or any study, is relative to the particular cases selected for investigation. With sufficient cunning it might have been possible to preselect cases to demonstrate higher levels of agreement or disagreement. What we would claim for our own findings is that the thirty-nine cases sample a broad range of practices of importance in India or America and represent key issues in the moral philosophy literature. With reference to those practices and issues one discovers what anthropologists experience when doing fieldwork: many things viewed as wrong on one side of the Atlantic are not viewed as wrong on the other side.

A far more controversial question is whether a culture's distinctive, and in many cases opaque, practices are invested with moral force. As noted above, Murdock described Semang sins as arbitrary cultural taboos without ethical justification. To what extent does the native agree with the anthropologist that culture-specific practices are conformity- or consensus-based matters of convention or "culture" rather than expressions of natural moral law or objective obligations? Later in the essay we will address the further question: Why is it that certain "innocent" events (e.g., cooking while menstruating) are viewed with disgust, outrage, or horror? What does the native know about such "innocent" events that we do not know? What does the native "see" in the event that we do not see? What premises, analogies, and lines of reasoning does the native use to comprehend the significance of the event and to render a judgment that it is morally wrong? Is there a rational ethical justification for such judgments?

*Question 2: "Culture" from the native point of view: a moral or a conventional order?* Our evidence suggests a strong tendency for informants to invest their practices with moral force and to view even their distinctive "cultural" practices from a naturalistic moral perspective. The dominant view among all informants, adult and child, male and female, American, Brahman, and Untouchable, is that society is a moral order, although the idea of a conventional obligation does play some part in the thinking of older American children and especially in the thinking of American adults. It is almost a nonexistent form of thought in our India data.

Table 1.6 examines sixteen culture-specific practices (see table 1.5), practices about which there is clear-cut disagreement between Brahman and American adults about what is right and what is wrong. Table 1.6 indicates whether informants perceive the obligation associated with each practice as a universal moral obligation (unalterable and universally binding), a context-dependent moral obligation (unalterable but relative) or a conventional obligation (alterable and relative). (See table 1.3 for a clarification of those distinctions.)

As indicated in table 1.6, the primary form of understanding among all informants is that the obligations associated with social practices are universal moral obligations. Understanding by reference to conventions occurs much less frequently than moral understanding. Notably, and in contrast to Kohlberg's theoretical formulations, American adults engage in reasoning by reference to convention more frequently than American five- to seven-year-olds. Conversely, American five- to seven-year-olds are more likely than American adults to engage in moral (versus conventional) judgment and to view their own obligations and rights (e.g., individual freedom of choice in matters of food, clothing, marriage) as universally binding, unalterable obligations. That developmental increase in the use of the idea of convention and "relativism" seems to be a culture-specific conceptual change, about which more will be said later.

The basic finding with reference to question 2 is that social practices and institutions are not typically, and certainly not universally, understood as conventional forms, and are usually perceived as part of the natural-moral order of things by most natives. One secondary finding with reference to question 2 is that the idea of objective moral obligation may be more, not less, widely distributed than the idea of convention, and the idea of morality may be ontogenetically prior to the idea of convention.

*Question 3: Can the distinction between moral and conventional events be predicted on substantive grounds? Is there some-*

**Table 1.6:** Sixteen Culture-specific Practices (see table 1.5) and Percentage of Responses of Each Type (see table 1.3)

| Practice (Case no. per table 1.1) | Brahmans Children (5–7) UM | CDM | Conv | Brahmans Adults UM | CDM | Conv | Americans Children (5–7) UM | CDM | Conv | Americans Adults UM | CDM | Conv |
|---|---|---|---|---|---|---|---|---|---|---|---|---|
| Love marriage out of status (10) | 56 | 31 | 00 | 100 | 00 | 00 | 85 | 05 | 10 | 85 | 15 | 00 |
| Menstruating woman cooks, etc. (7) | 66 | 11 | 16 | 94 | 00 | 00 | 85 | 00 | 15 | 60 | 30 | 05 |
| Cooking in same clothes used to defecate (8) | 62 | 18 | 12 | 94 | 05 | 00 | 70 | 00 | 25 | 55 | 15 | 30 |
| Addressing father by first name (13) | 75 | 12 | 06 | 87 | 06 | 00 | 85 | 05 | 10 | 20 | 50 | 30 |
| Husband cooks (18) | 83 | 16 | 00 | 75 | 20 | 05 | 75 | 15 | 10 | 70 | 20 | 10 |
| Widow eats fish (4) | 75 | 15 | 00 | 79 | 21 | 00 | 85 | 15 | 00 | 75 | 25 | 00 |
| Beating disobedient wife (35) | 75 | 12 | 00 | 100 | 00 | 00 | 100 | 00 | 00 | 95 | 05 | 00 |
| Caning errant child (37) | 100 | 00 | 00 | 60 | 33 | 07 | 90 | 00 | 10 | 85 | 10 | 05 |
| Widow wears bright clothes (5) | 60 | 33 | 06 | 71 | 14 | 00 | 95 | 00 | 05 | 35 | 45 | 20 |
| Eating beef (2) | 77 | 22 | 00 | 82 | 17 | 00 | 90 | 05 | 05 | 44 | 40 | 20 |
| Entering temple after birth (17) | 66 | 33 | 00 | 93 | 06 | 00 | 95 | 00 | 05 | 55 | 40 | 05 |
| Eating with husband's elder brother (6) | 75 | 00 | 00 | 56 | 18 | 18 | 85 | 00 | 10 | 55 | 35 | 10 |
| Wife requests massage (27) | 40 | 09 | 20 | 79 | 15 | 00 | 90 | 10 | 00 | 60 | 25 | 15 |
| Widow remarries (11) | 53 | 38 | 07 | 77 | 11 | 05 | 85 | 00 | 15 | 90 | 05 | 05 |
| Cutting hair and eating chicken after father's death (1) | 50 | 21 | 21 | 84 | 10 | 05 | 80 | 05 | 15 | 20 | 45 | 35 |
| Washing plates of husband's elder brother (25) | 62 | 25 | 00 | 94 | 00 | 05 | 100 | 00 | 00 | 60 | 20 | 20 |
| Average | 67 | 18 | 05 | 83 | 14 | 03 | 87 | 04 | 08 | 60 | 27 | 13 |

*Note:* UM = Universal Moral (unalterable and universal); CDM = Context-Dependent Moral (unalterable but relative); Conv = Conventional (alterable and relative).

*thing about certain events, for example, food, clothing, forms of greeting, that makes them resistant to moralization?* In our review of theories of moral development we asked whether the abstract idea of the moral and the abstract idea of the conventional have an objectively determinate content. That is to say, is there something about an event per se that determines whether the obligation associated with the event will be understood as moral or conventional? According to Turiel, Nucci, and Smetana's "social interactional" theory, certain types of events (food, clothing, terms of greeting and forms of address, the sexual division of labor) have no inherent consequences vis-à-vis justice, harm, and the welfare of others. Those events are, according to the theory, inherently nonmoral, or at least resistant to moralization, and the obligations associated with such events are more likely to be understood as conventional or consensus-based. Other types of events (physical and psychological attacks, allocation of resources, etc.) do have inherent consequences concerning justice, harm and the welfare of others, and it is highly likely that the obligations associated with those events will be understood as moral.

Table 1.7 presents data on informants' understanding of the moral verus conventional status of twenty-two practices. Eleven of those practices involve the type of material events (food, clothes, forms of address) theoretically defined as conventional by Turiel, Nucci, and Smetana. Those practices include the prohibition on eating beef, the restrictions on the color of clothes worn by widows, and the taboo against an adult son addressing his father by personal name. The other eleven practices involve the type of material events that would be theoretically defined as moral by Turiel, Nucci, and Smetana. Those practices include, for example, a husband physically beating a wife, a father breaking a promise to his son, and a child destroying a picture drawn by a schoolmate. For a full list of the twenty-two practices, see table 1.7.

In discussing the results presented in table 1.7 the first eleven events will be referred to as "morality-resistant" events. The second eleven events will be referred to as "morality-prone" events. The major claim we make for that division is that, within the framework of Turiel, Nucci, and Smetana's theory, the eleven "morality-resistant" events ought to elicit relatively higher levels of reference to conventions than the "morality-prone" events, all of which are relatively pure moral events.

A noteworthy feature of table 1.7 is that both types of events are viewed predominantly in moral terms. The obligations associated with such events as food (the prohibition on eating beef), clothing (the prescription that widows must wear white clothes for the rest of their lives), or forms of address (the prohibition against addressing your father by first name) are not typically viewed as alterable and relative. The hypothesized "morality-resistant" events are readily moralized. Over all age groups and cultural communities the "morality-resistant" events evoke the idea of conventionality only 7 percent of the time. Even among American adults, who are most likely to view obligations as conventional, the "morality-resistant" events are viewed as conventional only 20 percent of the time.

A second noteworthy feature of table 1.7 is that for three subpopulations, all American, the "morality-resistant" events elicit higher levels of reference to convention than the "morality-prone" events. Differences in levels of reference to convention between the

**Table 1.7:** Mean Percentage of Universal Moral, Context-Dependent Moral, and Conventional Reasoning for Each Age-Community Subgroup for Eleven "Morality-Resistant" Events[a] and Eleven "Morality-Prone" Events[b]

| | Reasoning vis-à-vis | | | | | |
| | Eleven Turiel-like "Morality-Resistant" Events | | | Eleven Turiel-like "Morality-Prone" Events | | |
| | *UM* | *CDM* | *CONV* | *UM* | *CDM* | *CONV* |
|---|---|---|---|---|---|---|
| | *Americans* | | | | | |
| Adult | 46 | 28 | 20 | 79 | 13 | 05 |
| Child: | | | | | | |
| 11–13 | 61 | 21 | 17 | 89 | 06 | 03 |
| 8–10 | 69 | 11 | 12 | 89 | 05 | 03 |
| 5–7 | 86 | 05 | 06 | 95 | 01 | 02 |
| | *Brahmins* | | | | | |
| Adult | 76 | 15 | 04 | 88 | 04 | 00 |
| Child: | | | | | | |
| 11–13 | 68 | 21 | 01 | 79 | 11 | 06 |
| 8–10 | 69 | 29 | 02 | 81 | 14 | 00 |
| 5–7 | 66 | 18 | 05 | 78 | 09 | 06 |
| | *Untouchables* | | | | | |
| Adult | 62 | 27 | 03 | 80 | 09 | 03 |
| Child: | | | | | | |
| 8–10 | 65 | 27 | 04 | 71 | 20 | 04 |
| *Average* | 66 | 20 | 07 | 82 | 09 | 03 |
| *Total Average of* | | | | | | |
| *UM and CDM* | | 86 | | | 91 | |

[a]"Morality-Resistant" Events = Table 1.1 Cases 1, 2, 3, 4, 5, 6, 13, 18, 25, 27, 38
[b]"Morality-Prone" Events = Table 1.1 Cases 15, 19, 20, 21, 24, 26, 29, 30, 32, 35, 37

types of events are statistically significant ($t$-test, $p = <.05$) for the American children ages eight to ten and eleven to thirteen, and for American adults. The differences in levels of reference to conventions between the two types of events are not statistically significant for any of the Brahman or Untouchable subsamples, or for the American five- to seven-year-olds.

The idea that obligations are conventional seems to be most prevalent among American adults. Over all samples and all thirty-nine cases there are six instances where an event is more likely to be classified as conventional rather than moral. All those instances come from the response of American adults or American eleven- to thirteen-year-olds. Importantly, those six events are much like the type of events Turiel, Nucci, and Smetana have often used to exemplify their theoretical domain of inherently nonmoral or conventional events. The six events are those referring to food and eating practices (nos. 3, 38, 1), forms of address (no. 13), and social organization (nos. 9, 36). For the Brahman and Untouchable samples, and for the American five- to seven-year-olds, there is no difference in frequency of reasoning by reference to convention between the two types of events and little support for the idea of a universal domain distinction in the mind of children or adults between conventional and moral practices.

The evidence in table 1.7 is not inconsistent with Turiel, Nucci, and Smetana's claim of a domain distinction between morality and convention in the reasoning of American subjects. For American subjects there are events that elicit relatively high levels of reasoning by reference to conventions, and those events are like the ones described by Turiel, Nucci, and Smetana. It is noteworthy, however, that even in our American sample, the idea of conventional obligations seems less pervasive, and begins to be evoked at a later age, than we had anticipated from the findings of earlier studies.

Methodological factors may explain the divergence between our findings and those of Turiel, Nucci, and Smetana. We find that reasoning by appeal to conventional obligations occurs relatively late among Americans and is a high-frequency mode of reasoning for only a restricted set of events. They find that such modes of reasoning by reference to convention occur early in childhood and are fairly common among Americans. A methodological factor that may explain that discrepancy concerns the specific questions used to assess the perceived relativity of obligations. Our interview questions concerning the "relativity" of obligations (table 1.2, questions 5 and 6) required that informants judge whether another society would be a "better place" if it stopped engaging in practices (for example, eating dogs) that the informant disapproved of in his or her own society. It is possible that the probes used in previous research were not as stringent tests of the perceived relativity of obligations.

In previous research on the perceived relativity of obligations, subjects have typically been asked whether it is "all right" for another society to permit practices that are prohibited in ones own society. Unfortunately, the question is ambiguous and potentially misleading, especially for subjects who are hesitant to meddle in the internal affairs of other nations. It has been our experience that when a subject says it is "all right" for another society to do things differently, all they may mean is "what right do I have to tell another society how to live." Such subjects may say "its all right" even when they believe the practices of the other society are morally wrong. Thus, in our research an informant who stated (perhaps moved by a liberal impulse to respect cultural differences) that it is all right for people in Nagaland to eat dogs would not be scored relativistic unless he or she also agreed, under cross-examination, that Nagaland would not be a better place if they stopped eating dogs (table 1.2, question 6).

The appeal to the idea of a convention is a rare occurrence among the Oriya Brahmans and Untouchables and the American five- to seven-year-olds. The young American children, like their American elders, believe that it is not wrong for a twenty-five-year-old son to address his father by his first name. But, unlike the American adults, the American five-year-olds do not think it is acceptable for Indians to prohibit first name use. Nor do these children believe, as do the American adults, that it would be legitimate to prohibit the practice if a majority of Americans decided it was wrong to be so informal with one's elders. Indeed, the idea of a natural right to personal liberty is highly developed in the American five- to seven-year-olds, and they are less willing than American adults to delimit that right or to relativize it. For the young American children (who believe one may address the father by his first name) and for the Oriya children and adults (who believe it is wrong to address the father by his first name), the issue is a moral issue, not a conventional one.

There is, however, one noteworthy difference between the "morality-resistant" events and the "morality-prone" events. Depending on the type of event, there seems to be a difference in the likelihood that informants will contextualize their moral obligations. Thus, while none of the events can be said to be truly "morality-resistant," and while the predominant view among all informants is that the obligations associated with social practices are universally binding and unalterable, there is a statistically significant tendency ($t$-tests) for the "morality-resistant" events to elicit higher levels of context-de-

pendent moral reasoning (unalterable but relative, see table 1.3) from
the adults in all three communities (Untouchable, Brahman, and
American) and from eleven- to thirteen-year-old Americans. The differences in levels of context-dependent moral reasoning between the
two types of events are not statistically significant for any of the five-
to seven- or eight- to ten-year-old samples or for the eleven- to thirteen-year-old Brahman sample.

That finding is supportive of Turiel, Nucci, and Smetana's notion that not all obligations are of the same kind. On a worldwide
scale, however, the crucial distinction is not between objective moral
obligations and consensus-based, conventional obligations. Rather
the distinction seems to be between context-dependent moral obligations and universally binding moral obligations. The obligations associated with food, clothes, terms of address, and sex roles are not
typically perceived as conventional. However, in comparison with
the obligations concerning physical assault, theft, and promises, the
obligations associated with food and clothes are less likely to be uni-
versalized.

It is important to emphasize that when context-dependent
moral thinking does occur, which is not often (20 percent with the
so-called morality-resistant events; 9 percent with the so-called morality-prone events, see table 1.7), it is not because the practices in
question are understood as arbitrary. On the contrary, a moral obligation is contextualized because the practice in question is viewed as
distinctively expressive of, or adaptive to, the special conditions,
temperament, or moral qualities of a population. One variant of
that view is verbalized in the minority position among Brahmans
that it is immoral for Brahmans to eat beef because (a) the human
body is a temple in which a holy spirit dwells (what we call the "self"
or the "witness" or the "observing ego" they view as a spirit or soul
or deity); (b) beef is a "hot" food; (c) "hot" foods stimulate the body
as a biological organism; (d) to stimulate the body as a biological organism is to violate the sanctity of the body as a temple in which a
holy spirit dwells. But it is permissible for Americans to eat beef because the colder American climate will counteract the effects of the
"hot" food.

As noted, that is a minority argument. Most Oriyas accept all
the premises of that argument. But, additionally, most Oriya Brahmans also believe that the cow is an incarnation of the "first mother,"
about whom there is much lore. They argue that we nurture our children using one of her holy gifts, her milk, and that even Americans
should not eat their mother! For most Oriya Brahmans the taboo on
eating beef is universally binding and its violation is a "great sin."

A second variant of context-dependent moral thinking is contained in the minority position among Brahmans that it is immoral for a Brahman widow to wear brightly colored clothes and jewelry because (a) she will appear attractive; (b) if she appears attractive she will invite sexual advances; (c) if she gets involved with sex she will disregard her meditative obligations to the soul of her deceased husband and behave disloyally. But it is acceptable for American widows to wear bright clothes and jewelry because (a) it is the destiny of America, *at this stage in its development as a civilization,* to be a world conqueror and the ingenious inventor of technology; (b) the off-spring of illicit sexual unions are more likely to be clever, dominating, and adventurous; (c) widow remarriage and other American practices, adolescent dating, and "love marriage," encourage illicit sexual unions, thereby producing those qualities of character appropriate to the stage level of American civilization.

A more abstract formulation of that context-dependent moral argument goes something as follows. America is a young civilization. India is an ancient civilization. It takes a long time for a civilization to figure out and evolve good or proper practices and institutions, those that are in equilibrium with the requirements of nature. You should not expect the young to possess the wisdom of the old. America is doing what is fitting or normal for its early stage of development. Its practices are not arbitrary.

In sum, there is little support for the hypothesis that a distinction between moral and conventional obligations is a universal of early childhood, encoding in thought the substantive differences between "morality-resistant" events and "morality-prone" events. For all samples, the obligations associated with practices in the proposed "morality-resistant" domain are understood primarily in moral terms.

The evidence is not inconsistent with the hypothesis of a culture-specific distinction between morality and convention in the American sample. American adults and older children do seem to show significantly higher levels (although not high levels) of reasoning by reference to conventions for the proposed "morality-resistant" events (food, clothes, forms of address, etc.) over the proposed "morality-prone" events (physical and psychological harms, etc.). For a small subset of events (tabooed foods, polygyny, titles versus personal names, eating with your hands) the idea of conventional obligations predominates in the reasoning of American adults or older children.

In both cultures the proposed "morality-resistant" events seem to elicit higher levels (although, again, not high levels) of context-dependent moral thinking, whereby informants appeal to an unalterable objective obligation that is tailored or specifically adapted to the distinctive nature or environment of a particular group. Nevertheless, for all groups, the predominant understanding of the proposed "morality-resistant" practices is not that they are arbitrary, alterable, and relative, but rather they involve universally binding objective obligations that cannot be altered by consensus or majority vote.

Question 4: Is there universal agreement among young children about what is morally right and wrong? Do young children "spontaneously" develop their own moral code? By age five, the young children in our study are well on their way to expressing distinctive culturally appropriate judgments about what is morally right and wrong; the Oriya children sound very Oriya, and the American children sound very American. That, of course, is not to say that the capacity to feel "lowered" or "elevated," "cleansed" or "stained," "pure" or "sinful," or to experience empathy, outrage, dread, shame, disgust, terror, guilt, pride, virtue, or any other moral sentiment is culturally acquired. It is to suggest, however, that what one feels "lowered" by, empathy towards, disgust at, pride in, or outrage about (that is to say, how moral sentiments are directed) is related to a judgment, not necessarily conscious or even verbally accessible, that bears many of the markings of received understandings by five years of age. The implication is that if children do subscribe to a universal moral code spontaneously generated independently of participation in social practices and socialization experiences, then researchers must search for it within the first four years of life. By age five, children around the world do not typically agree with each other about what is morally right or wrong.

As indicated in table 1.4, the rankings of the thirty-nine practices in terms of seriousness of breach by five- to seven-year-old Brahman and American children are virtually independent of one another $(r = -.12)$, while the rankings display marked similarities to the rankings of adults in the respective cultures $(r = .62$ between Brahman five-year-olds and adults; $r = .85$ between American five-year-olds and adults).

Whatever divergence in moral beliefs exists at age five becomes greater with age. The process of reproducing, in the next generation, the premises, principles, metaphors, and intuitions that make it possible to participate in social practices and generate culturally appropriate moral judgments seems to be a continuous one that goes on well into adolescence and probably adulthood. That can be seen by comparing table 1.8 with table 1.5. Table 1.8 shows the areas of agreement and disagreement about what is right (or wrong) between Brahman and American five- to seven-year-olds.

One noteworthy feature of table 1.8 is that there are fourteen practices about which the young children in both the cultures have strong convictions (75 percent agreement within a subsample) about what is right (or wrong). Across the two cultures, those convictions

**Table 1.8:** Patterns of Disagreement and Agreement among Brahman and American Five- to Seven-year-olds

| Case No. | Type of Practice |
|---|---|
| | *Disagreement:* |
| | *Brahman children think it is right / American children think it is wrong* |
| 37 | caning an errant child |
| 38 | eating with hands |
| 34 | father opens son's letter |
| | *Disagreement:* |
| | *Brahman children think it is wrong / American children think it is right* |
| 13 | addressing father by first name |
| 2 | eating beef |
| 8 | cooking in clothes worn to defecate |
| 1 | cutting hair and eating chicken after father's death |
| | *Agreement: Brahman children and American children think it is wrong* |
| 12 | ignoring beggar |
| 24 | broken promise |
| 32 | destroying another's picture |
| 20 | kicking harmless animal |
| 19 | stealing flowers |
| 7 | menstruating woman cooks* |
| | *Agreement: Brahman children and American children think it is right* |
| 39 | men holding hands |

For the remaining twenty-five practices there was dissensus within one or the other community.

*The Oriya term for menstrual pollution is *mara*. The general term for pollution, which can also be specified and applied to menstrual pollution is *chuuan*. Oriya children know those terms and associate with them certain menstrual practices (seclusion, no cooking by mother, etc.). They are not, however, aware of the fact of bleeding. There is no adequate translation in English of *mara* or *chuuan* for use in interviews with American children. The term "unclean," which was used, it obviously inadequate. With regard to case 7 the translation problem is theoretically fascinating yet may be practically insurmountable. Thus, the results on case 7 for American children, and the apparent agreement between American and Brahman youth, must be discounted.

are virtually independent of one another. Brahman and American five- to seven-year-olds agree about the moral status of seven practices and disagree about the moral status of seven other practices.

A second noteworthy feature of table 1.8 is that, at ages five to seven, there are still many practices about which children in one or the other culture have not yet formed a consensus. In adulthood the moral judgments of the two populations will still remain virtually orthogonal, but there will be many more practices (twenty-eight practices instead of fourteen) around which a consensus of moral understanding has emerged within each culture (see table 1.5).

A final noteworthy feature of table 1.8 is that, with the exception of driving away a beggar (no. 12), the wrongs about which Brahman and American five- to seven-year-olds universally agree are a subset of the set of wrongs about which there is universal agreement between Brahman and American adults. In other words, in areas of convergence in the moral judgments of young children, the children's views do not run contrary to adult views and may well have a common source in direct or indirect experience with routine social practices.

Table 1.9 compares the judgments of Brahman five- to seven-year-olds with those of Brahman adults. One feature to be noted in table 1.9 is that, of the sixteen practices for which there is a clear consensus within the child and adult samples, there is no case in which the children's and adult's view of right and wrong deviate from each other. In no case do the children think "X" is wrong while the adults think "X" is right, or vice versa. Either the adults have acquired their judgments from the children or the children have acquired their judgments from the adults, or both the children and the adults have acquired their judgments through participation in the same social practices, or some combination of those possibilities.

A second finding illustrated in table 1.9 is that there are twenty-three practices for which there is dissensus within either the adult sample or the child sample. That dissensus is typically among the children and not the adults. The one major exception is the practice of fathers opening and reading the mail addressed to their adolescent sons. The five- to seven-year-old Brahman children overwhelmingly think that practice is permissible while the Brahman adults are divided on the issue. In general, however, while the young children have many consensually shared views, the adults have convictions about many more issues. Not all practices are directly known or available to children, and it takes time to induce or comprehend the messages implicit in those practices that are directly experienced.

**Table 1.9:** Patterns of Disagreement and Agreement among Brahman Five-to Seven-year-olds and Brahman Adults

*Disagreement: Brahman children think it is right / Brahman adults think it is wrong*
NO CASES

*Disagreement: Brahman children think it is wrong / Brahman adults think it is right*
NO CASES

*Agreement: Brahman children think it is wrong / Brahman adults think it is wrong*

| Case No. | Type of Practice |
|---|---|
| 1 | cutting hair and eating chicken after father's death |
| 8 | cooking in clothes worn to defecate |
| 2 | eating beef |
| 12 | ignoring beggar |
| 24 | breaking promise |
| 32 | destroying another's picture |
| 20 | kicking innocent animal |
| 16 | incest—brother/sister |
| 19 | stealing flowers |
| 7 | menstruating woman cooks, etc. |
| 10 | love marriage out of status |

*Agreement: Brahman children think it is right / Brahman adults think it is right*

| Case No. | Type of Practice |
|---|---|
| 36 | ten-year-old sleeps with mother |
| 38 | eating with hands |
| 37 | caning an errant child |
| 39 | men holding hands |

*Practice with less than 75% consensus within Brahman adults or Brahman children between five and seven years of age*

| Practice | Is there consensus among children? | adults? |
|---|---|---|
| Eating with husband's older brother (6) | No | Yes |
| "No one will marry your daughter" (23) | No | Yes |
| Unequal inheritance, males vs. females (26) | No | Yes |
| Cutting in line (30) | No | Yes |
| Wife requests massage (27) | No | Yes |
| Ignoring accident victim (15) | No | Yes |
| Polygyny (9) | No | Yes |
| Eating a dog (3) | No | Yes |
| Beating disobedient wife (35) | No | Yes |
| Widow wears bright clothes (5) | No | Yes |
| Entering temple after birth (17) | No | Yes |
| Husband cooks (18) | No | Yes |
| Discriminating against invalids (29) | No | Yes |
| Widow remarriage (11) | No | Yes |
| Nepotism (21) | No | Yes |
| Washing plates of husband's elder brother (25) | No | Yes |
| Widow eats fish (4) | No | Yes |
| Asking foreigner for watch (31) | No | Yes |
| Father opens son's letter (34) | Yes | No |
| Father saves daughter over son (33) | No | No |
| Neo-local residence (22) | No | No |
| Kissing in public (28) | No | No |
| Sacrificing innocent child (14) | No | No |

A third feature of table 1.9 is that the culture-specific and universal aspects of the adult code seem to be acquired or constructed in the same way, or by the same process. Stated more cautiously, culture-specific moral beliefs and universal moral beliefs are constructed at the same rate. There are nine practices that seem to be strong candidates for universal moral prohibitions across adults in all three populations, American, Oriya Brahmans, and Oriya Untouchable. Those nine moral universals are listed in table 1.10. There are fourteen moral prohibitions that are specific to Brahman adults (nos. 1, 2, 4, 5, 6, 7, 8, 10, 11, 13, 17, 18, 25, 27) and five prohibitions that are specific to American adults (nos. 14, 26, 34, 35, 37). By age five to seven years, Brahman children have developed consensual moral convictions concerning four (44 percent) of those nine universal adult moral prohibitions (breaking promises, arbitrary assault, destruction of private property and incest). American five- to seven-year-olds have developed consensual convictions concerning seven (77 percent) of the nine prohibitions (all except incest and reciprocity-gratitude, asking for the watch; see table 1.10).

The same rate of acquisition seems to hold for the culture-specific moral practices and beliefs. Brahman five- to seven-year-olds hold consensual convictions concerning five (35 percent) of the fourteen culture-specific Brahman adult moral prohibitions (see table 1.9), while American children of the same age hold consensual convictions about all five (100 percent) of the culture-specific American adult moral prohibitions. Thus, while it remains to be explained why the moral judgments of their respective cultures are being acquired more rapidly by American than by Brahman children, in both cultures young children seem to be constructing the universal aspects of their moral code at about the same rate as they are constructing the

Table 1.10: Nine Candidates for Moral Universals across Adult
Populations—High Consensus Virtues and Vices for Brahman,
Untouchable, and American Adults

| Case No. | Type of Practice |
| --- | --- |
| 24 | keeping promises (a virtue) |
| 32 | respect for property (a virtue) |
| 30 | fair allocation (a virtue) |
| 15 | protecting the vulnerable (a virtue) |
| 31 | reciprocity—gratitude (a virtue) |
| 16 | taboo on incest (a virtue) |
| 20 | arbitrary assault (a vice) |
| 21 | nepotism (a vice) |
| 29 | arbitrary ("biased") classification (a vice) |

culture-specific aspects of the code (44 percent versus 35 percent for Brahman children; 77 percent versus 100 percent for American children).

It seems reasonable to hypothesize that the same process, whatever that might be, is responsible for the construction of the universal and culture-specific aspects of the code. Little support is to be found in this evidence for the hypothesis that the universal aspects of the code are constructed one way (e.g., self-constructed through the personal observation of objective consequences) while the culture-specific aspects are constructed in a different way (e.g., through acceptance of adult doctrines).

Whatever process explains the early similarity in the moral judgments of children (five years and older) and adults within a culture, it influences not only the content of judgments about right and wrong but also the more formal or structural aspects of those judgments. In the present context, what we mean by the formal or structural aspect of thinking is the idea of an obligation as a universal moral obligation (unalterable and universally binding) versus the idea of an obligation as a context-dependent moral obligation (unalterable and relative) versus the idea of an obligation as a consensus-based conventional obligation (alterable and relative).

There is a culture-specific directionality of change for some of the more formal or structural features of moral thinking. Thus, as Americans get older they are more likely to engage in reasoning by reference to convention and by reference to context-dependent moral reasoning, and less likely to engage in universal moral reasoning. Conversely, as Brahmans and Untouchables get older they are more likely to engage in universal moral reasoning, and less likely to engage in context-dependent moral reasoning or reasoning by reference to convention. Those culture-specific developmental trends are diagrammed in figures 1.3–1.5, where the average percentage of each type of response (universal moral, context-dependent moral, conventional) over all thirty-nine cases is indicated for all subjects interviewed in each age-community subgroup.

Examining the three types of thinking for each of the thirty-nine cases, the most general of all trends across the thirty-nine cases is the developmental waning of universalistic moral thinking in the American sample. While we cannot give a definitive interpretation to the trends displayed in figures 1.3–1.5 the five- to seven-year-old American children seem to believe there exists a universal natural right to eat beef if you want to, to choose your wife for yourself if you want to, to kiss your wife in public if you want to, to wear brightly colored clothes and jewelry even if you are a widow, if you want to. The

*Figure 1.3:* Universalistic moral thinking in children and adults in India and America. Universal moral—unalterable and not relative (see table 1.4).

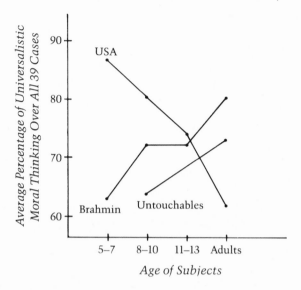

*Age of Subjects*

*Figure 1.4:* Context-dependent moral thinking in children and adults in India and America. Context-dependent moral—unalterable but relative (see table 1.4).

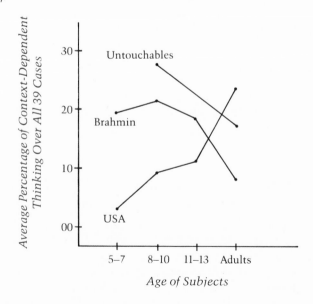

*Age of Subjects*

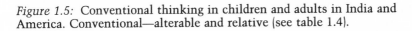

*Figure 1.5:* Conventional thinking in children and adults in India and America. Conventional—alterable and relative (see table 1.4).

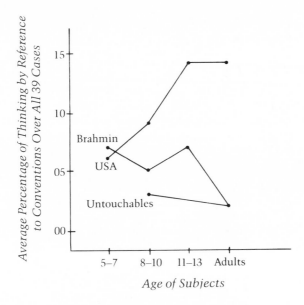

young American children are less willing than older American children and American adults to grant that rights to liberty in such matters are conventional or to accept that other societies can legitimately choose to do things differently. The developmental increase of universal moral thinking in the Indian sample is also relatively general across cases, while the higher average level of reference to conventions among American adults over young American children seems to be carried by a subset of cases, especially cases 1, 2, 3, 5, 13, 23, 25, 26, 27, 28, 34, 38 (see table 1.1).

There are several implications to the pattern of findings in figures 1.3–1.5. First, figure 1.5 raises the possibility that a distinction between moral and conventional practices may not be a universal of childhood or adulthood. The level of reference to conventional obligations in the Indian sample seems too insignificant to support the hypothesis of a universal domain distinction. Second, figure 1.3 suggests that obligations are not typically viewed as conventional or consensus-based by either children or adults. The idea of universal moral or objective obligations seems to be more widely distributed across ages and cultures than the idea of conventional obligations, and developmentally the idea of morality seems to take precedence over the idea of convention, even at an early age. Finally, taken together, figures 1.3–1.5 raise the possibility that the emergence of reasoning by reference to conventional or consensus-based obligations is a culture-specific development; however, the reason for the emergence of the idea of convention, in some cultures, like our own, but not in other cultures, like orthodox Hindu society, remains to be explained.

Far more research on these issues is needed, utilizing alternative methodologies. Directly probing about the relativity and alterability of family life and social practices, as we did in our study, is but one way to search for a domain distinction between conventional and moral obligations. Murdock's (1980) work on illness as a perceived consequence of transgression and Edwards' (1985) work on caretaker response to transgression suggest two other ways to study the degree of differentiation of domains. If a culture does distinguish conventional from moral obligations, that separation of domain might reveal itself in anything from differential patterns of emotional response to transgression to different types of sanctions or punishments. Reviewing our own research in light of Murdock's cross-cultural survey on illness and Edward's study of caretaker response in Kenya raises for us the strong possibility that the distinction between conventional and moral obligations is not a developmental universal.

*Question 5: What are the universal and culture-specific aspects of a moral code?* This essay is concerned with identifying the universal and culture-specific, mandatory and discretionary, features of rationally based moral codes. Given that aim, it is perhaps worth noting that to identify genuine differences in moral codes is to presuppose some common criteria for identifying moral issues. Meaningful differences presuppose a general likeness. However, contrary to Kohlberg's view that there are no fundamental differences from culture to culture in the ideal form of a rationally based moral code (1981, 71–74), it is our view that all rationally based moral codes are alike in some ways (the mandatory features) and in some ways different (the discretionary features). And, because the ways that moral codes differ are rationally discretionary, those differences (for example, in the assertion or denial of divine authority) are likely to persist even in the face of cognitive development and Socratic dialogue.

For the moment we shall put aside the issue of universal moral emotions (see Kagan 1984, especially chap. 4, on that issue). We believe there are such universal emotions—empathy, shame, guilt, outrage, pride, repugnance, disgust—and we believe the emotional reactions of others, their anger, disappointment, or hurt feelings, can play an important cuing function in the acquisition of a moral code. Recent experimental research on "social referencing" in infants and young children (Feinman 1982; Feinman and Lewis 1983; Campos and Stenberg 1981; Bretherton 1984) suggests that internalization of the evaluations of significant or powerful others is a prepotent onto-genetic process that does not wait patiently for an oedipus complex to develop. By ten months of age, infants make use of the mother's or experimenter's verbally or nonverbally conveyed affective interpretations of events (for example, distress or pleasure at the entrance of a stranger) and modulate their own emotional and behavioral reactions accordingly.

We even believe that some emotional responses are retained in the presence of conscious reflection and deliberate judgment, and that feelings (for example, righteous indignation) can form part of a rational response to a perceived transgression. Within the terms of a rationally based moral code, actions that are wrong, sinful or polluting may make you feel guilty, angry, afraid, or disgusted, and they may, in some cases, even carry with them an obligation to feel that way.

To acknowledge the universality and functional importance of moral emotions is not, however, the same as saying that actions become wrong, sinful, or polluting *because* they make you feel guilty, angry, afraid, or disgusted; or that you believe that actions are wrong, sinful, or polluting because they were learned in association with feelings of guilt, anger, fear, or disgust. We would reject, as do our informants, a pure emotivist view of the meaning of moral discourse. You may feel guilty because you have transgressed, but the transgression is not defined by the guilt, and, in many cases, a transgression is a transgression whether you feel guilty or not. To understand why a transgression has become defined as a transgression is to look outward, away from the emotions, in the direction of the moral code as a rational organization of concepts and principles. That is what our research is about. Thus, in considering moral universals, we put moral emotions to the side, for the moment, and focus on the form and content of the code itself.

Table 1.10 lists those nine moral prohibitions that are shared by American adults, Brahman adults, and Untouchable adults. One noteworthy feature of table 1.10 is that the nine universal prohibitions listed are *moral* prohibitions. They are viewed by all informants as objective, unalterable, and universally binding prohibitions. That suggests that the idea of an objective obligation, the idea of morality as natural law, is a universal. As we have seen (see table 1.6), the abstract idea of natural law is displayed relatively early in life, certainly by age five.

A second noteworthy feature of table 1.10 is that it is difficult to decide on a proper level of abstraction for describing moral universals. Some would argue that universality arguments are merely arguments about the generality of coding categories: the less specific the content written into the coding category the more universal the category. While there is much merit in that argument (see Shweder and Bourne 1982 on the "higher-order generality rule") it overlooks the fact that the peoples of the world sometimes do agree about relatively particularistic issues (e.g., that such-and-such a color chip is the reddest red, or that the offspring of an incestuous union are more likely to be deformed or in some way grotesque; see Berlin and Kay 1969; Burton 1973), and they frequently disagree about more general issues (e.g., whether people have transmigratory souls or whether or not justice means "to each according to his needs"). It is possible to discover pan-cultural universals without having to bleach one's coding categories of all interesting substance.

The research reported examines informants' judgments about particular cases (kicking a sleeping dog, cutting into a line at a cinema). As it turns out, it is possible to discover moral universals at the "case" level of description; Brahmans, Untouchables, and Americans all agree, for example, that "it is wrong when meeting a foreigner for the first time to ask him how much his watch costs and whether he will give it to you" (no. 31, table 1.1), and that "it is wrong for a hotel to make a rule that invalids and disfigured persons are not allowed in the dining hall" (case no. 29, table 1.1). It is possible for a concrete case to elicit a universal reaction of moral repugnance.

There is, however, an understandable temptation to identify the more general or abstract principle underlying a judgment about a particular case. In table 1.10 we have given in to that temptation. Thus, case 31 (asking the foreigner for his watch) is described as "reciprocity" and case 29 (no invalids in the dining hall) is described as arbitrary (biased) classification. There is also a temptation to reduce the list of principles in table 1.10 to a smaller set of highly abstract ideas. Thus, for example, the taboo on incest could perhaps be reduced to the idea of protection of the vulnerable (protecting children from sexual exploitation), and perhaps the idea of justice and the presumption that harm is wrong could "cover" most of the "middle-level" principles listed in table 1.10. Under some description, at some level of abstraction, justice, harm, and protection of the vulnerable might qualify as "deep" universals of all moral codes.

The rub is that if one focuses only upon the abstract principles underlying a judgment about a particular case, the abstracted principles do not make it possible to predict informants' judgments about particular cases. Thus, for example, while Oriya Brahman adults disapprove of kicking a dog that is sleeping on a street (no. 20), they do not disapprove of beating "black and blue" a wife who goes to the movies without the husband's permission (no. 35). And, while they disapprove of unfair treatment (nepotism, no. 21, cutting in line, no. 30, the hotel rule excluding invalids, no. 29), they believe it is permissible for a married son to inherit far more than a married daughter (no. 26). Indeed 60 percent of the female adult members of the Brahman community believe there is a positive moral obligation to save the life of the firstborn son over the life of the lastborn daughter if only one life can be saved (no. 33).

Needless to say, Oriya Brahmans do not view beating an errant wife as an instance of arbitrary assault, and they do not believe it is unfair to choose the son over the daughter in matters of life or inheritance. What Americans view as similar cases (kicking the dog, beating the wife) Oriyas view as quite different cases, and what Americans view as quite different cases (for example, addressing the father by first name, no. 13, and the wife requesting a massage, no. 27) Oriyas view as similar. The appeal to some small set of common abstract principles (justice, harm, protecting the vulnerable) does not help us understand or predict which cases will be seen as alike or different.

If we are to understand our informants' moral judgments about particular cases we are going to have to understand the culture-specific aspects of their moral codes and the way those culture-specific aspects interact with the more universal aspects to produce a moral judgment. Oriya Brahmans, for example, believe that beating a wife who goes to the movies without permission is roughly equivalent to corporal punishment for a private in the army who leaves the military base without permission. For Oriyas there are rationally appealing analogical mappings between the family as a unit and military units (differentiated roles and status obligations in the service of the whole, hierarchical control, drafting and induction, etc.). One thing the family is not, for Oriyas, is a voluntary association among coequal individuals.

## Discussion

### Implications for Kohlberg's Cognitive Developmental Theory

Our research in India and America suggests a portrait of the development of the understanding of obligations that differs from Kohlberg's. If one relaxes the demand characteristics of the interview task, utilizing direct probes about universality and alterability of obligations, it appears that major structural features of postconventional moral understanding are universals of early childhood and adulthood. Those features include the idea of objective obligations and natural moral law. And, if one relaxes the demand characteristics of the interview task, it appears that the idea of obligations as conventional or consensus-based is not the predominant form of understanding among either children or adults. Our research suggests that the idea of moral obligation does not develop out of the idea of conventional obligation. On the contrary, the idea of a conventional obligation is a special development related to certain discretionary features of a moral code, such as the ideas of individualism, individual rights, and "freedom of contract."

## Implications for Turiel's Social Interactional Theory

Turiel's theory hypothesizes an early, universal differentiation of a domain of moral obligations from a domain of conventional obligations. The theory hypothesizes that certain obligations are "morality-prone" while other obligations are "morality-resistant" because the events they regulate do not involve issues of justice, harm, or the welfare or rights of others. Our research suggests that the differentiation of moral events from conventional events is not necessarily a developmental universal and that the distinction between morality and convention, useful as it is within certain cultural worldviews, may well be culture-specific.

While it is not possible to prove definitely that *any* event can be moralized (i.e., treated as an objective obligation related to harm and justice), within the framework of our research, a moral and a conventional domain could not be distinguished on substantive grounds. For orthodox Hindus in the old town of Bhubaneswar, food, clothing, terms of address, sex roles, and ritual observances are conceived of as part of the moral order. The received orthodox Hindu conception of objective obligations or natural moral law leaves little room for the idea that culture or society is conventional, consensus-based, and arbitrary rather than an expression of natural law. Within a culture like our own where the morality versus convention distinction does play a part, there are undoubtedly events that fall on the boundaries or partake of both domains, and it is relevant and important to ask the question proposed by Turiel, Nucci, and Smetana, "Which are the pure moral or conventional events and which are the mixed events?" Within orthodox Hindu culture, however, the relevant question may well be, "Are any events purely conventional?"

Implications for Future Research

*Social communication.* What has not been emphasized sufficiently in past research on moral development is that children discern the moral order as it is dramatized and made salient in everyday practices. Children are assisted in constructing their notions of right and wrong. The inferences they draw about the moral (its form) and what's moral (its content), are, in substantial measure, personal reconstructions created within a framework of tradition-based modes of apperception and evaluation. The moral concepts of a people and their ideas about self, society, and nature are powerful ways of seeing the world that have been worked on, and applied to experience, over many generations. Every child is the beneficiary of a conceptual inheritance, received through communication with others.

Our "social communication" theory of moral development emphasizes the ways a culture's ideology and worldview have a bearing on the ontogenesis of moral understandings in the child. That highlighting is done by relating the ontogenesis of ideas about obligations to the representation of received permises and ideological tenets through routine social practices.

In our conception of "social communication," morally relevant interpretations of events by local guardians of the moral order (e.g. parents) are typically presented and conveyed to young children in the context of routine family life and social practices. Those moral premises are carried by the messages and meanings implicit in the emotional reactions of others (anger or disappointment or "hurt feelings" over a transgression). They are carried by the verbal exchanges—commands, threats, sanction statements, accusations, explanations, justifications, excuses—necessary to maintain routine social practices. Indeed, moral premises may be expressed through, and hence are discernible in, institutionalized behaviors; and those premises may be validated by the child, and hence reinforced for the child, because they help make sense of the experience of routine practices. Finally, it is an assumption of our theory that the emerging moral intuitions or unconscious moral inferences of the child are not only the product of social practices but are also the grounding for the child's later attempts to reflectively reconstruct its own moral code.

As an illustration of the social communication process we have in mind, consider the following case concerning one aspect of the socialization of moral understandings in the domain of pollution-purity-sanctity, with obvious implications for matters of interpersonal affiliation (see Shweder 1985, from which the following illustration is drawn and partly excerpted; see also Shweder and Much, in press).

"*Mara heici. Chhu na! Chhu na!*" is what a menstruating Oriya mother exclaims when her young child approaches her lap. It means, "I am polluted. Don't touch me! Don't touch me!" If the child continues to approach, the woman will stand up and walk away from her child. Of course, young Oriya children have no concept of menstruation or menstrual blood; the first menstruation arrives as a total surprise to adolescent girls. Mothers typically "explain" their own monthly "pollution" to their children by telling them that they stepped in dog excrement or touched garbage, or they evade the issue. Nevertheless, Oriya children quickly learn that there is something called "*Mara*" (the term "*chhuan*" is also used) and when "*Mara*" is there, as it regularly is, their mother avoids them, sleeps alone on a mat on the floor, is prohibited from entering the kitchen ("*Handi bahari heici*"—"I'm out of the kitchen"—is a local euphemism for talking about menses), eats alone, does not groom herself and is, for several days, kept at a distance from anything of value. Children notice that everything their mother touches is washed. In interviews, most six-year-olds think it is wrong for a "polluted" ("*mara*") woman to cook food or sleep in the same bed with her husband; most nine-year-olds think that "*mara*" is an objective force of nature and that all women in the world have a moral obligation not to touch other people or cook food while they are "*mara.*"

Oriya children learn that "touching" can be dangerous. They learn that "purity," "cleanliness," and status go together. Just as the pure must be protected from the impure, the higher status and the lower status must be kept apart or at a distance. These ideas are effectively conveyed in several ways. "Don't touch me" is heard on many occasions in many contexts. There's not only the menstruating mother (whose status in the family is roughly that of an untouchable for three days, and who is sometimes discussed as possessed by an evil spirit while bleeding). There's the father who tells his children not to touch him in the interim between bathing (a purification rite) and worshipping the family deity. There's the grandmother who does not want her grandchildren to touch her or climb into bed with her until the child has removed all his "outside" clothes, which have become polluted ("*chhuan*") as the child mixed with lower castes at school. Those attitudes and sentiments towards "*mara*" or "*chhuan*" also get coded and expressed in a children's game on the theme, "pollution tag." Several children stand apart from a lone isolated child and all together chant and tease: "You ate in the house of a Hadi (the lowest Untouchable caste). Don't touch me! Don't touch me!" The children scurry off, pursued by the hand of the "polluted" child.

The culture is providing the child with a practical moral commentary in which one of the many messages is ultimately that menstrual blood, feces, and lower status go together. For the sake of physical and spiritual well-being, they must be kept at a distance from what is clean, pure, and of higher status. Daily bathing and acts of purification and cleanliness become associated with status elevation and feelings of personal well-being. Ultimately, one's body becomes conceptualized as a "temple" with a spirit, the self, dwelling in it. Keeping the temple pure becomes a major goal of daily life, in eating, in bathing, in avoiding contact with pollutants and anyone of lower status.

The socialization process just described is affect-laden. The child wants to get in bed with his or her grandmother and is rejected. The child wants to approach the mother and is put off. The distress aroused in grandmother or mother can be palpable. Furthermore, the socialization process is carried by discourse that indexes a great deal of implicit knowledge. Since a great deal of what we call moral socialization is done through talking with others, the study of moral development calls for the identification of propositions about the way the world is and ought to be that are carried by discourse and other forms of symbolic action (see Much and Shweder 1978; Much 1983; Ochs and Schieffelin 1984; Shweder and Much, in press).

Finally, it is also interesting to note that the concepts that are inherited—pollution, impurity, separation, loss of status, purification, cleanliness—succeed at making sense of experience, from "the native point of view." Children reason, but not all the concepts they reason with are of their own making. Children observe the consequences of action, but those consequences include the encultured emotional reactions of others, and even those encultured emotional reactions are interpreted for the child by others, using concepts from tradition-based doctrines about psychological and social functioning. The child of moral development, it turns out, is not a lonely subject and is rarely left alone.

*Alternative postconventional moralities.* Our analysis of the mandatory and discretionary features in Kohlberg's conception of postconventional morality raised the theoretical possibility of alternative rationally based moral codes, based on a conception of natural law, justice, and harm (mandatory features), yet not founded on individualism, voluntarism, natural "rights," secularism, or the idea of a social contract (discretionary features). In the light of our experience in India and knowledge of the anthropological literature on moral codes, we think that it is more than just a theoretical possibility. We hypothesize that most adults around the world do not talk on Kohlberg's tasks like postconventional thinkers because they reject the discretionary features built into Kohlberg's definition of genuine moral understandings, not because they confuse objective obligations with consensus, convention, or positive law. There may be alternative rationally based moral codes that Kohlberg's scheme, founded on abstract individualism, voluntarism, and secularism, does not illuminate.

Our hypothesis implies that there is more than one way to rationalize a moral code and that the cluster of ideas associated with individualism, consent, voluntarism, promise, and free contract are discretionary rather than mandatory features of a rationally based moral code. The hypothesis raises the possibility that the ubiquitous stage three–four reasoning discovered by Kohlbergian researchers could be defended as a rationally based form of postconventional thinking, especially if interpreted in the light of a different set of discretionary moral concepts (see Gilligan 1982; Shweder and Much, in press).

One of the attractions of India for moral development researchers is the possibility that the orthodox Hindu moral code is an example of an alternative postconventional moral understanding. This is not the occasion to attempt a rational reconstruction of the moral judgments of our Hindu informants (see Shweder and Much, in press). Such a rational reconstruction would distill the numerous arguments, analogies, and premises used by our informants in defense of their practices (e.g., arranged marriage, the prohibition against widow remarriage, etc.) and form them into an "ideal" argument structure. By an "ideal" argument structure we mean a reasoned defense of family life and social practice that is not vulnerable to the criticism that its empirical claims are false or that its reasoning is viciously contradictory.

Our interviews with Hindu adult informants are rich in arguments. A distilled argument, for example, might go as follows: "A marriage is something that affects so many people, relatives, ancestors, neighbors, and friends, in serious ways. How can you possibly leave it up to one young person, driven by lust and passion, to make a sound decision?" Informants often reason by reference to similes and analogies. One argument asserts, "The husband is a moving god and should be treated with comparable respect." Another argument holds, "The body is a temple with a spirit dwelling in it. Therefore the sanctity of the temple must be preserved. Therefore impure things must be kept out of and away from the body." Factual claims are asserted, such as "Life on earth is organized around the division of things into male and female, and there is a natural assymetrical interdependency between them"; or, "The family is a natural institution." Fundamental assumptions and premises are implicitly or explicitly announced: "Nature is just. Virtue is rewarded and vice punished"; "Souls reincarnate"; "Received inequalities (male over female, elder over younger, Brahman over Untouchable) are a form of just desert"; "The family is the ideal prototype for all social relationships."

What one finds in the reasoning of our Hindu informants is a preference for paternalism and asymmetrical interdependency, the idea that most people need to be protected against their own vulnerabilities, and a rejection of the idea of autonomous functioning and self-sufficient voluntarism. There is an inclination to view the family, not the marketplace, as the prototype of moral relationships. There is a corollary tendency to represent the moral order as a natural order built up out of status or role obligations (wife to husband, stranger to stranger) rather than out of promises or commitments between abstract individuals living in the marketplace of a free-contract regime.

It is our hunch that the arguments of our Hindu informants are informed by an alternative postconventional morality (Shweder and Much, in press). A recent series of essays by the economist Schelling (1984), on the need to protect oneself against oneself, hints at one way for us rationally to reconstruct the Hindu code. States Schelling (1984, 100): "Actually, there is no a priori basis for confidence that enforceable contract is a generally good thing. People might just get themselves tied up with all kinds of regrettable contracts, and the custodians of legal wisdom might have decided that enforceable contract is a mischief. Suppose promises to second parties tended usually to get people into trouble, so that a wise legal tradition would readily excuse people from promises incurred in haste, or in passion or in disgust. Duress is recognized; if impetuosity were a problem, legally binding contracts might require something like a second or third reading before acquiring status. It is an empirical question whether the freedom to enter into contract, the freedom to make enforceable promises, or the freedom to emancipate oneself from a nicotine habit would prove generally to be a good thing."

What Schelling's remarks suggest is that, as a matter of fact, the human beings of a society may be highly vulnerable to exploitation or self-destruction and may not assume the idealized, and somewhat utopian, state of "voluntariness" presupposed by a free-contract regime. When people in the real world agree to the terms of a contract, they may do so impetuously, or under duress, while angry or depressed, or without foresight, willpower, or knowledge of relevant information, or lacking the skill to calculate consequences properly. An unwed mother in postpartum depression signs a contract permitting a childless married couple to adopt her infant in exchange for a sum of money. Later, no longer depressed, and willing to return the money, she wants her child back. Does she have an obligation to honor her contract? The legal system of a free-contract regime tries to adjust for the discrepancy between the idealized presumption of a "voluntary" agent and the fact of "involuntary" choice by specifying conditions (fraud, duress) for disqualifying contracts, by mandating certain terms that must be included in any contract, and by withholding freedom to contract from certain classes of agents (minors, the insane). (See Kennedy 1982, for a discussion of those issues and the role of paternalistic motives in a free-contract regime.)

It is instructive to construct hypothetically an alternative postconventional moral code, starting with the assumption that agents are naturally vulnerable. Since agents frequently display features of "involuntariness"—weakness of will, impetuosity, emotionality, ignorance, addiction, etc.—freedom to contract would not be deemed a general good. It either promotes exploitation, if the freedom is genuine and general, or promotes costly monitoring, regulations and correction by external authorities (judges and bureaucrats), if exploitation of the vulnerable is to be controlled.

Such an alternative postconventional conception of moral obligations might be self-consciously paternalistic, modeled after the family as a moral institution. It is noteworthy that in the Western legal-moral tradition, family obligations and law stand as a major exception to the general theory of free contract among autonomous, rational, voluntary agents (see Kennedy 1982). In contrast, it appears that in orthodox Hindu thought the family is not the exception to the basic principles of the moral order but rather the prototype of the moral order. It is credible to argue that the family exists as an institution because of the natural vulnerabilities and interdependencies of its members. Through a complex of relationships based on mutual reliance (e.g., husband and wife), asymmetrical interdependency (e.g., parent to child) and the obligations and agreements associated with kinship status (father, son, mother, daughter) the family seems to be able to function without the necessity of either a contract or outside regulation. In nonabusive families, of which there are many, a combination of loyalty, deference, empathy, altruism, love, and hierarchy protects the vulnerable from exploitation, while rewarding the powerful for caring for the weak. And all that is done without bureaucracies, legislatures, or the costly devices of centralized control.

Any rational reconstruction of a postconventional Hindu moral code is likely to be a rational defense of paternalism, sympathetic to the sentiment expressed in Tolkien's famous trilogy about the Middle Earth in its latter days: " 'Few now remember them,' Tom murmured, 'yet still some go wandering, sons of forgotten kings walking in loneliness, guarding from evil things folk that are heedless.' " In family relationships, we may come as close as we dare to restoring that lost sense of noble, or at least paternal-maternal, obligation.

# References

Berlin, B., and P. Kay, 1969. *Basic Color Terms: Their Universality and Evolution.* Berkeley: University of California Press.

Bretherton, I. 1984. Social Referencing and the Interfacing of Minds: A Commentary on the Views of Feinman and Campos. *Merrill-Palmer Quarterly* 30:419–27.

Burton, R. V. 1973. Folk Theory and the Incest Taboo. *Ethos* 1:504–16.

Campos, J. J., and C. R. Stenberg, 1981. Perception, Appraisal and Emotion: The Onset of Social Referencing. In M. E. Lamb and L. R. Sherrod, eds, *Infant Social Cognition.* Hillsdale, N.J.: Erlbaum.

Carter, R. E. 1980. What Is Lawrence Kohlberg Doing? *Journal of Moral Education* 2:9.

Cole, M., and S. Scribner, 1974. *Culture and Thought: A Psychological Introduction.* New York: John Wiley.

Dumont, L. 1970. *Homo Hierarchicus.* Chicago: University of Chicago Press.

Dworkin, R. 1977. *Taking Rights Seriously.* Cambridge, Mass.: Harvard University Press.

Edwards, C. P. 1980. The Development of Moral Reasoning in Cross-cultural Perspective. In R. H. Monroe, R. Munroe, and B. B. Whiting , eds., *Handbook of Cross-Cultural Human Development.* New York: Garland Press.

―――. 1985. Another Style of Competence: The Caregiving Child. In A. D. Fogel and G. F. Melson, eds., *Origins of Nurturance.* New York: Erlbaum.

―――. In press. Cross-cultural Research on Kohlberg's Stages: The Basis for Consensus. In S. Modgil and C. Modgil, eds., *Lawrence Kohlberg: Consensus and Controversy.* London: Falmer Press Limited.

Feinberg, J. 1980. *Rights, Justice and the Bounds of Liberty.* Princeton: Princeton University Press.

Feinman, S. 1982. Social Referencing in Infancy. *Merrill-Palmer Quarterly* 28:445–70.

Feinman, S., and M. Lewis, 1983. Social Referencing at Ten Months: A Second-order Effect on Infants' Responses to Strangers. *Child Development* 54:878–87.

Firth, R. 1951. Moral Standards and Social Organization. In *Elements of Social Organization*. London: Watts and Co.

Fortes, M. 1959. *Oedipus and Job in West African Religion*. Cambridge: Cambridge University Press.

Gelman, R., and R. Baillargeon, 1983. A Review of some Piagetian Concepts. In J. H. Flavell and E. M. Markman, eds., *Manual of Child Psychology*. Vol. 3, *Cognitive Development*. New York: John Wiley.

Gewirth, A. 1984. Ethics. *Encyclopedia Britannica*. 15th ed. Vol. 6.

Gilligan, C. 1982. *In a Different Voice: Psychological Theory and Women's Development*. Cambridge, Mass.: Harvard University Press.

Gilligan, C., L. Kohlberg, J. Lerner, and M. Belenky, 1971. Moral Reasoning about Sexual Dilemmas: The Development of an Interview and Scoring System. In *Technical Report of the U.S. Committee on Pornogrpahy and Obscenity*. Vol. 1.

Haan, N., R. Weiss, and V. Johnson, 1981. The Role of Logic in Moral Reasoning and Development. *Developmental Psychology* 18:245–56.

Hallpike, C. R. 1979. *The Foundations of Primitive Thought*. Oxford: Clarendon Press.

Hart, H. L. A. 1961. *The Concept of Law*. London: Oxford University Press.

Kagan, J. 1984. *The Nature of the Child*. New York: Basic Books.

Kennedy, D. 1982. Distributive and Paternalist Motives in Contract and Tort Law, with Special Reference to Compulsory Terms and Unequal Bargaining Power. *Maryland Law Review* 41:563–658.

Kohlberg, L. 1969. Stage and Sequence: The Cognitive-Developmental Approach to Socialization. In D. A. Goslin, ed., *Handbook of Socialization Theory and Research*. New York: Rand McNally.

———. 1971. From Is to Ought: How to Commit the Naturalistic Fallacy and Get Away with It in the Study of Moral Development. In T. Mischel, ed., *Cognitive Development and Epistemology*. New York: Academic Press.

———. 1981. *The Philosophy of Moral Development: Moral Stages and the Idea of Justice*. Vol. 1 of *Essays on Moral Development*. San Francisco: Harper and Row.

Kohlberg, L., C. Levine, and A. Hewer, 1983. *Moral Stages: A Current Formulation and a Response to Critics*. In J. A. Meacham, ed., *Contributions to Human Development*. Vol. 10, New York: Karger.

Ladd, J. 1957. *The Structure of a Moral Code: A Philosophical Analysis of Ethical Discourse Applied to the Ethics of the Navaho Indians*. Cambridge, Mass.: Harvard University Press.

Lewis, D. K. 1966. *Convention: A Philosophical Study.* Cambridge, Mass.: Harvard University Press.

MacIntyre, A. 1981. *After Virtue.* South Bend, Ind.: University of Notre Dame Press.

Malinowski, B. [1926] 1976. *Crime and Custom in Savage Society.* Totowa, N.J.: Littlefield, Adams and Co.

Much, N. 1983. The Microanalysis of Cognitive Socialization. Ph.D. diss., University of Chicago.

Much, N., and R. A. Shweder, 1978. Speaking of Rules: The Analysis of Culture in Breach. In W. Damon, ed., *New Directions in Child Development.* Vol. 2, *Moral Development.* San Francisco: Jossey-Bass.

Murdock, G. P. 1980. *Theories of Illness: A World Survey.* Pittsburgh: University of Pittsburgh Press.

Nadel, S. F. 1957. *The Theory of Social Structure.* Glencoe, Ill.: The Free Press.

Nagel, T. 1979. *Mortal Questions.* Cambridge: Cambridge University Press.

Nisbett, R. E., and T. D. Wilson, 1977. Telling More than We Can Know: Verbal Reports on Mental Processes. *Psychological Review* 84:231–59.

Nucci, L. P. 1981. The Development of Personal Concepts: A Domain Distinct from Moral or Societal Concepts. *Child Development* 52:114–21.

————. 1982. Conceptual Development in the Moral and Conventional Domains: Implications for Values Education. *Review of Educational Research* 52:93–122.

Nucci, L., and M. Nucci, 1981. Children's Social Interactions in the Context of Moral and Conventional Transgressions. *Child Development* 53:403–12.

Nucci, L. P., and E. Turiel, 1978. Social Interactions and the Development of Social Concepts in Preschool Children. *Child Development* 49:400–407.

Ochs, E., and B. B. Schieffelin, 1984. Language Acquisition and Socialization: Three Developmental Stories and their Implications. In R. A. Shweder and R. A. LeVine, eds., *Culture Theory: Essays on Mind, Self and Emotion.* New York: Cambridge University Press.

Perelman, C. 1963. *The Idea of Justice and the Problem of Argument.* New York: Humanities Press.

Piaget, J. [1932] 1965. *The Moral Judgment of the Child.* New York: Free Press.

Rawls, J. 1971. *A Theory of Justice.* Cambridge, Mass.: Harvard University Press.

Read, K. E. 1955. Morality and the Concept of the Person among the Gahuku-Gama. *Oceania* 25:233–82.

Schelling, T. C. 1984. *Choice and Consequence.* Cambridge, Mass.: Harvard University Press.

Scribner, S., and M. Cole, 1981. *The Psychology of Literacy.* Cambridge, Mass.: Harvard University Press.

Shweder, R. A. 1982a. Beyond Self-constructed Knowledge: The Study of Culture and Morality. *Merrill-Palmer Quarterly* 28:41–69.

———. 1982b. Liberalism as Destiny. Review of *The Philosophy of Moral Development*: Moral Stages and the Idea of Justice. Vol. 1 of *Essays on Moral Development*, by Lawrence Kohlberg. *Contemporary Psychology* 27:421–24.

———. 1982c. On Savages and Other Children. *American Anthropologist* 84:354–66.

———. 1985. Menstrual Pollution, Soul Loss, and the Comparative Study of Emotions. In A. Kleinman and B. Good, eds., *Culture and Depression.* Berkeley: University of California Press.

———. 1986. Divergent Rationalities. In D. W. Fiske and R. A. Shweder, eds., *Metatheory in Social Science.* Chicago: University of Chicago Press.

Shweder, R. A. and E. Bourne, 1982. Does the Concept of the Person Vary Cross-culturally? In A. J. Marsella and C. White, eds., *Cultural Conceptions of Mental Health and Therapy.* Boston: Reidel. Reprinted in R. A. Shweder and R. A. LeVine, eds., *Culture Theory: Essays on Mind, Self and Emotion.* New York: Cambridge University Press.

Shweder, R. A. , and J. G. Miller, 1985. The Social Construction of the Person: How Is It Possible? In K. Gergen and K. Davis, eds., *The Social Construction of the Person.* New York: Springer Verlag.

Shweder, R. A., and N. C. Much. In press. Determinations of Meaning: Discourse and Moral Socialization. In W. Kurtines and J. Gewirtz, eds., *Moral Development through Social Interaction.* New York: John Wiley.

Shweder, R. A., E. Turiel, and N. C. Much, 1981. The Moral Intuitions of the Child. In J. H. Flavell and L. Ross, eds., *Social Cognitive Development: Frontiers and Possible Futures.* New York: Cambridge University Press.

Simpson, E. L. 1974. Moral Development Research: A Case Study of Scientific Cultural Bias. *Human Development* 17:81–106.

Singer, M. 1963. *Generalization in Ethics.* London: Eyre and Spottiswoode.

Smetana, J. G. 1981a. Reasoning in the Personal and Moral Domains: Adolescent and Young Adult Women's Decision-making Regarding Abortion. *Journal of Applied Developmental Psychology* 2:211–26.

———. 1981b. Social-Cognitive Development: Domain Distinctions and Coordinations. Paper presented at meeting of The Society for Research on Child Development, Boston.

———. 1982. Children's Reasoning about Mixed Domains (Moral and Social). Paper presented at the annual meeting of the American Educational Research Association, New York.

———. 1983. Social Cognitive Development: Domain Distinctions and Coordinations. *Developmental Review* 3, no. 2, 131–47.

Snarey, J. R. 1985. Cross-cultural Universality of Social-Moral Development: A Critical Review of Kohlbergian Research. *Psychological Bulletin* 97, no. 2, 202–32.

Stevenson, C. L. 1944. *Ethics and Language.* New Haven, Conn., Yale University Press.

Turiel, E. 1979. Distinct Conceptual and Developmental Domains: Social-convention and Morality. In C. B. Keasy, ed., *Nebraska Symposium on Motivation, 1977.* Vol. 25. Lincoln: University of Nebraska Press.

_____. 1980. Domains and Categories in Social Cognition. In W. Overton, ed., *The Relationship Between Social and Cognitive Development.* Hillsdale, N.J.: Lawrence Erlbaum.

_____. 1983. *The Development of Social Knowledge: Morality and Convention.* New York: Cambridge University Press.

Turiel, E., and P. Davidson, 1985. Heterogeneity, Inconsistency and Asynchrony in the Development of Cognitive Structures. In I. Levin, ed., *Stage and Structure.* Norwood, N.J.: Ablex.

Turiel, E., and J. G. Smetana, 1984. Social Knowledge and Action: The Coordination of Domains. In W. M. Kurtines and J. L. Gewirtz, ed., *Morality and Moral Development.* New York: John Wiley.

Walker, L. J. 1984. Sex Differences in the Development of Moral Reasoning: A Critical Review. *Child Development* 55:677–91.

# Comment
## The Psychological Definitions of Morality
*Augusto Blasi*

The paper by Richard Shweder is a part of a larger and very ambitious project. His intention is not only to criticize Kohlberg's and Turiel's accounts of moral development but also to offer a constructive alternative description and explanation of moral development. Although Shweder qualifies his conclusions as preliminary, he suggests that his findings support the following claims: (1) Kohlberg is incorrect in postulating a universal sequence, in which the understanding of conventionality always precedes the understanding of morality; (2) Turiel is incorrect in postulating that the differentiation between conventionality and morality is universally present from a very early age; (3) the understanding of morality is universally present in children and adults, but the understanding of conventionality is a specialization of the former and only occurs in certain cultures; (4) moral understanding is not contructed by each individual but is "tacitly communicated" to the members of each culture through their participation in certain cultural practices.

These claims are more radical than they may appear initially. By rejecting the assumption of constructivism, Shweder places himself outside the currently popular cognitive-developmental understanding of moral development and seems to subscribe to a form of cultural determinism. In particular, his notion of cultural influence through "tacit communication," although ill-defined, is intriguing and worthy of reflection.

It is impossible to deal with each of Shweder's claims in such a short paper. Instead, I will limit myself to a central issue, namely, the ways in which morality, moral understanding, and moral behavior have been defined by psychologists. The relevance for Shweder's conclusions is obvious. If what Shweder means by morality is not what Kohlberg or Turiel mean by the same term, then his data may not be relevant to their accounts. But the issue of meanings goes beyond Shweder's, Kohlberg's, and Turiel's work and deserves to be considered in broad terms.

To simplify (and perhaps oversimplify) the history of psychological research in this field, one can say that morality was first defined as a list of specific behaviors, ranging from helping others to resisting the temptation to cheat. These behaviors were not understood by psychologists and social scientists in general as sharing any intrinsic characteristics; instead, their moral relevance was thought to exclusively depend on culturally relative classifications and labels.

The important shift occurred when it was acknowledged that morality does not consist of any specific behaviors but of a special perspective of the agent, a certain kind of understanding that the agent has of actions and situations. The "assumption of phenomenalism," as Kohlberg (Kohlberg, Levine, and Hewer 1983) calls it, was the starting point of cognitive developmentalism and remains one of its central characteristics. The reason why this definition is important and in my opinion should not be abandoned is that it made psychological research on morality (and not simply on moral reasoning) congruent with the meanings embedded in ordinary language. In fact, the level of ordinary language, or common understanding, not only creates shared social meanings, but allows interactions among people to be genuinely social.

Despite Kohlberg's contribution, two important questions still remain to be answered: first, which perspective is characteristic of morality and defines it; and second, which level of abstraction is most appropriate in studying people's moral understanding? The cognitive-developmental approach, particularly under Kohlberg's influence, relies for answers on philosophical theory or, at least, on the most common philosophical views. It takes justice to be the central characteristic of morality and one's understanding of justice as defining the moral perspective. Concerning the second question, the solution was to follow a formalistic approach to morality. Moral understanding would then consist of the most basic conceptual structure that determines the criteria used to justify one's moral actions.

It is useful to emphasize that these solutions are choices among several possible alternatives. These choices, moreover, do not necesarily depend on the meanings of ordinary language. In other words, it is possible to settle on a more concrete, more content-oriented, level of moral understanding. Moreover, one could have emphasized, together with or as alternatives to justice, other moral issues, such as kindness or obligations to oneself.

Another important observation concerns the influence of philosophy on psychology. As I noted elsewhere (Blasi 1986), even though this influence has been positive, there may be negative side effects when psychologists choose for their study of morality definitions that derive from specific philosophical theories. The reason is that philosophy is concerned with establishing a coherent and rational foundation for morality; namely, with determining what morality should be. Psychology, instead, is (or should be) interested in describing what morality in fact is, the way it is actually experienced by people, and in providing an account in terms of psychological processes, both rational and nonrational.

As a result of these different perspectives, philosophical theory may disregard, or eliminate as irrelevant to morality, behaviors and feelings that are relevant to the psychologist's questions. For instance, some philosophers (e.g., Habermas 1971; Hamm and Daniels 1979), starting from a theoretical conception of what morality should be, distinguish between moral issues and "good life" issues. In contrast with morality, good life issues would be relativistic, nonobligatory and mostly personal rather than interpersonal in content. They would include not only the pursuit of one's interests and the fulfillment of one's personality, but also loyalty to cultural customs and traditions and religious obligations.

If a psychologist were to follow the same guideline, he or she might disregard large samples of practices that in fact are viewed by many people as falling in the same category as moral obligations. The psychological theory of morality that would be based on this unnecessarily restricted sample of behaviors would consequently be much too narrow.

While it may generally be problematic to rely on philosophy to define what is to be studied as morality, the risks are even more serious in cross-cultural research. The reason is that those moral institutions on which the researcher relies, as well as Western moral philosophy that builds on them, may be inadequate to represent morality as it is understood in other cultures. One cannot rely on the similarities and differences among the practices, because morality cannot be defined without taking into account those subjective perspectives by which these practices are understood. And, in attempting to take these subjective perspectives into account, one cannot rely either on the simple use of terms such as "should," "right," "good," and "obligation," because it is precisely the meanings of these terms that are in question.

A possible approach to cross-cultural moral research would be to select a large number of culturally meaningful "practices" (in Shweder's sense of the term) and, for each, to gather rich networks of meanings (attitudes, reasons). This can be done at the level of the culture as a whole (e.g., through fairy tales, popular books, and newspaper accounts) as well as with groups of individuals of various ages and social backgrounds. Even then a working definition will be needed to differentiate moral from non-moral perspectives. The starting definition should be descriptive (i.e., involving a low level of theoretical reconstruction), emphasize psychological processes, and rely on as few philosophical assumptions as possible beyond the level of common understanding.

Elsewhere (Blasi 1986) I suggested a set of three criteria for morality. For the purpose of psychological research, a behavior or a practice is considered moral if it is intentional, a response to some sense of obligation, and if the obligation is a response to an ideal, even if vaguely understood. This definition may very well offer an adequate starting point, a middle ground between a behavioristic approach to practices and language on the one hand and a prematurely narrow philosophical view on the other. One may be able to determine, from the beginning, which practices are understood to be moral in different cultures. By relying on the network of meanings that are attached to each practice, one may be able to construct different categories of moral understanding and to establish, eventually, theoretical relations among these categories.

We can now return to Shweder's study and consider his claims in the light of these very general considerations. Shweder began his project with the decision to use as concrete material large samples of practices, not two or three dilemmas as Kohlberg and his associates used. These practices form a very heterogeneous group; while some seem to be good candidates for eliciting a universal moral response, others seem to be important only within certain cultures, and others, at least from the perspective of Western intuition and philosophy, seem to be irrelevant to morality. This last group includes hygienic and eating practices and prescriptions concerning dependence or independence, sex roles, and ethnic identity.

Shweder's selection of practices runs counter to the definition of morality as justice commonly accepted within cognitive developmentalism. But Shweder was probably correct in following his anthropological intuition rather than philosophical definitions. As I suggested earlier, his strategy seems to offer the only possible starting point, if one wants to find out to what extent moral understanding is universal, or whether justice is indeed the universal structural core of moral knowledge.

Unfortunately, this investigation, at least as presented in this paper, cannot keep its promise. In fact, Shweder relies on people's use of simple terms, such as "wrong," "best," and "okay," to indicate the presence of a moral judgment and does not seem to inquire how these and other terms are specifically understood by children and adults of different cultures.

He has asked eight questions concerning the necessity and the violation of each practice; each question contained key terms, whose meaning is ambiguous and open to different interpretations. Some of these are: "violation," "offense," "sin," "wrong," "serious," "best," and "okay." Childrens' and adults' answers were of two types. The first consisted in the choice of one of four alternatives concerning the degree of "seriousness" of violating a practice. On this basis, Shweder could find out how the practices are ranked by each subject in terms of their importance. He could then compare the rankings and determine the degree of similarity among children and adults of the same culture, as well as among the children and adults of different cultures.

The answers to the other seven questions consisted essentially of yes or no. Three of these questions are particularly important for Shweder: (1) Would it be best if everyone in the world followed practice *X*?; (2) In country *Z* people do practice *X* all the time. Would country *Z* be a better place if they stopped doing that?; and (3) What if most people in country *Z* wanted to change practice *X*? Would it be okay to change it? Shweder constructed the three most central categories of his analysis on the basis of the answers to these three questions. According to his classification, a practice is understood as establishing a universal moral obligation if one answers yes to the first question and not to the other two. The obligation is understood to be moral but context-dependent if one answers no to all three questions. Finally, the obligation is understood to be nonmoral but simply based on convention and consensus if one answers no to the first two questions and yes to the last. Shweder believes that these three categories represent "the more formal and structural aspects of normative judgments" (p. 35), and they allow him to address Kohlberg's and Turiel's views concerning the relations between conventionality and morality.

I believe, instead, that Shweder's findings are largely irrelevant to, and leave untouched, Kohlberg's and Turiel's claims. I will focus my discussion on Kohlberg's case. There are two reasons for my judgment. One is that Shweder tends to misinterpret Kohlberg's claims in important ways and ends up criticizing his own construction rather than the claims themselves. The second reason is that Kohlberg and Shweder define morality so differently in their respective empirical operations that it is impossible to see how their data can be relevant to each other.

Concerning the first point, Shweder misinterprets three central ideas of Kohlberg's scheme. First, he confuses the type of objectivity and universality characteristic of Kohlberg's postconventional level with his own concept of natural law. In Shweder's vocabulary, the idea of natural law seems to refer to a recognition that morality is based on the objective nature of things and actions. According to Kohlberg (Kohlberg, Levine, and Hewer 1983), instead, the postconventional understanding of universality seems to be based on the recognition that only a certain kind of ideal consensus establishes the ultimate moral rationality. Because of this confusion, Shweder interprets children's objectivistic approach to morality as indicating an understanding of natural law and concludes, then, that children are postconventional in Kohlberg's sense.

Second, Shweder appears to think that the conventionality of Kohlberg's level two (stages three and four) includes both the idea of conformity to rules and authority and the idea that the value of social rules is based on consensus. However, in Kohlberg's description, this level is social and authoritarian in perspective, but neither relativistic nor consensual, as Shweder seems to think. From Kohlberg's viewpoint, the moral value of consensus is understood much better at the postconventional than at the conventional level.

Finally, Shweder interprets Kohlberg's theory as claiming that genuine morality develops from the understanding of conventionality, namely, from a nonmoral position. But, again, Kohlberg's view is quite different. For him, moral development is always a matter of progressively clarifying those criteria that are specifically moral and differentiating them from those that are not. Thus, he believes that during level two there is a global understanding in which conventional and moral criteria are fused together and in which conventional criteria are given moral value. Level three, based on the understanding that moral criteria cannot be reduced to conventional criteria, would develop out of a genuinely moral, though partially undifferentiated, understanding.

However, even if Shweder had correctly represented Kohlberg's ideas, his data would not be adequate to test or criticize them. To use the currently accepted terminology, Shweder's data concern the *content* of people's thinking, whereas Kohlberg tries to capture the basic *structures* of moral understanding. More precisely, Kohlberg's stages are based on the reasons that people give to justify certain practices. Starting from these reasons, more basic criteria are isolated and the logic from which these criteria are derived is finally reconstructed. This information is missing in, and irretrievable from, Shweder's data, even from those categories that, in his view, reflect more formal aspects. For example, when a person says that a certain practice should be followed by everybody, in every culture, regardless of people's consensus, we still don't know why she or he thinks that this should be the case.

Faced with Shweder's finding that children's answers are more similar to the answers given by the adults of the same culture, Kohlberg would reply that similarity in content may hide more fundamental differences, while differences in content are compatible with similarity in structural criteria. In fact, Kohlberg (1969) has already pointed out that from an early age, children are familiar with and accept those attitudes and concrete judgments that are typical of their culture, but he has taken this fact to indicate the inadequacy of content responses to reveal structural moral development.

Of course, these considerations do not invalidate Shweder's findings. When they are considered alone and not in relation to Kohlberg's or Turiel's theories, Shweder's data are interesting and raise questions about the actual meaning and the limits of moral universals at the level of structural analysis. Shweder may say that the type of structural account that Kohlberg and others offer is only partial and ultimately not very useful to an understanding of how and why people do what they actually do. He may have a point, even if it does not seem useful to argue about the relative usefulness of approaches as different as Kohlberg's, Turiel's, and Shweder's. The real issue is one of integration; namely, of understanding how concrete moral judgments and abstract moral structures go together both at the level of individual consciousness and in functionally affecting behavior. This question of integration, it is fair to say, has not been solved; indeed, it is rarely asked.

However—and this brings us back to the main theme of my commentary—this work of integration presupposes that concrete judgments, as well as abstract criteria, are genuinely moral; that is, that they are understood to be moral by the individual who formulates them. Most of my doubts with regard to Shweder's research concern this point. It is of secondary importance that he did not intend to gather structurally relevant material. However, one frequently wonders whether the responses that Shweder accepts as having moral meaning are indeed understood as moral by his informants. When a person (American or Indian, child or adult) agrees that it would be best if everyone in the world followed a certain practice and that the world would not be a better place if other societies stopped the same practice, can Shweder be sure that this person understands and uses "best" and "better" in a moral sense?

In the methodological tradition that characterizes cognitive developmentalism, it is acknowledged that people's response only ambiguously reflect their conceptual competence. Therefore, an effort is made to facilitate the interpretive analysis and to clarify the subjects' real understanding by resorting to probes, alternative hypothetical situations, and countersuggestions. However, Shweder avoided this methodology and did so consciously. In his view and in the opinions of many others, this strategy unnecessarily relies on linguistic skills that many people do not possess and leads investigators to underestimate the actual level of conceptual competence. One may sympathize with Shweder's concern; however, the problem of inferring real meanings from the use of simple words still remains.

This inference is, of course, more problematic in the cases of children. And yet, it is this type of evidence that Shweder uses to conclude that even young children commonly approach cultural practices with the belief that they establish universal moral obligations and, thus, with a genuine moral understanding. My doubts are not simply based on the ambiguity of "better" and "best." We know from Piaget's (1932) studies that very young children do indeed attach some kind of strict necessity to social rules and generalize this necessity to everybody. However, Piaget had also pointed out that, in this case, necessity is not equivalent to moral obligation but reflects a confusion between physical laws and social rules, while generalization is not equivalent to moral universality but indicates children's basic inability to differentiate other people's perspectives from their own. Unless this type of ambiguity is resolved, it is very difficult to determine the precise way in which Shweder's findings are relevant to a theory of moral development.

# References

Blasi, A. 1986 Psychologische oder philosophische Definition der Moral. Schädliche Einflüsse der Philosophie auf die Moralpsychologie (How should psychologists define morality? Or, the negative side-effects of philosophy's influence on psychology). In W. Edelstein and G. Nunner-Winkler, eds., *Zur Bestimmung der Moral*. Frankfurt am Main: Suhrkamp.

Habermas, J. 1971. *Knowledge and Human Interests*. Boston: Beacon Press.

Hamm, C. M., and L. B. Daniels, 1979. Moral Education in Relation to Values Education. In D. B. Cochrane, C. M. Hamm, and A. C. Kazepides, eds., *The Domain of Moral Education*. New York: Paulist Press.

Kohlberg, L. 1969. Stage and Sequence: The Cognitive-Development Approach to Socialization. In D. A. Goslin, ed., *Handbook of Socialization Theory and Research*. Chicago: Rand McNally.

Kohlberg, L., C. Levine, and A. Hewer, 1983. *Moral Stages: A Current Formulation and a Response to Critics*. Basel: Karger.

Piaget, J. 1932. *The Moral Judgment of the Child*. New York: Free Press.

# The Beginnings of Moral Understanding: Development in the Second Year

*Judy Dunn*

In this chapter I am concerned with the earliest stages of children's understanding of the "standards" of their social world and the feelings of those who share that world. These two features of social cognition are crucial to the development of moral *understanding*, regardless of which theoretical approach to moral *judgment* is favored. In order to trace the beginnings of moral understanding, we must describe the child's growing grasp of social rules and of the consequences of his or her actions for other people's feelings or needs. My focus is on the second year of life—a period in which children make astonishingly rapid advances in this understanding.

Our studies of children observed at home show that adult standards become highly salient during the second year. They become a source of curiosity, distress, delight, and shared humor. Changes in children's emotional behavior and in the behavior of others in the children's world parallel the changes in children's understanding of rules and feelings, and I will argue that any attempt to understand the development of moral understanding must take serious account of both these changes. It is also important to examine the changes in children's behavior in the context of family relationships, taking full account of the emotional nature of those relationships. It is in the context of these social relationships that the dramatic advances in social understanding are made.

91

Evidence for changes in children's understanding will be drawn from observations of three social contexts—incidents of conflict within the family, pretend play between siblings, and discussion of feelings and rules between mothers and children. The interactions in these social situations suggest that affective experience may play an important part in these earliest stages of moral understanding. They also illuminate the relative influences of peers and adults, and of didactic, disciplinary, or role-taking experiences on the development of children's grasp of social norms.

## Understanding Standards and Emotions

What do we know about the earliest stages of children's interest in and understanding of family social rules and relationships? It could be argued on commonsense grounds that just as it is adaptive for children to be able to understand the emotions and intentions of family members, so too the ability to recognize features of the relationships between family members and of the social rules of the family is of major importance. The recent work on the abilities of nonhuman primates to recognize aspects of the relationships between other members of their social group supports this idea. Nonhuman primates behave differently toward others within their group not only on the basis of kinship and dominance but also on the previous history of alliances and prior support (Cheyney and Seyfarth 1982; Cheyney, Seyfarth and Smuts 1986). For very young children, however, our information on these issues remains sketchy. We know from mothers' reports in the studies of Zahn-Waxler and her colleagues (Zahn-Waxler, Radke-Yarrow, and King 1979) that during the second year most children become sensitive to the distress and anger of other family members. But other information on children's behavior within the family is lacking. Studies by Emde, Campos, and their colleagues (Campos and Stenberg 1981; Klinnert et al. 1983) show that by the end of the first year children monitor their mothers' emotional expressions in a situation of uncertainty and modify their behavior accordingly. But while such studies have provided illuminating demonstrations of children's capabilities, we remain ignorant of when and how children use such capabilities in their family lives.

Kagan's (1981) studies of the second year highlight a different feature of the developmental changes in children's understanding. The children in his studies showed an increasing interest in objects that were broken, flawed, or dirty and thus failed to conform to expected standards. Toward the end of the second year they also showed a distress at their own failure to achieve the goals set by adults in an experimental setting. Kagan argued convincingly that the common thread linking both classes of developmental change is an increasing understanding of and concern with the standards of adults.

Studies of children in group settings show that by three and four years old, children respond differently to different kinds of rule breaking or transgression (Much and Shweder 1978; Nucci and Nucci 1982; Nucci and Turiel 1978; Turiel 1983). Although the data do not show unambiguously a clear distinction between transgressions of social convention and of moral standards, they demonstrate that three-year-olds are sensitive to different kinds of cultural breach. It should be noted that the context of this research—the school setting—is one in which a rather special set of "social convention" rules is dominant. While three- and four-year-old children may be sensitive to the particular nature of "institutional" rules, we do not know how sensitive they may be to different kinds of family transgressions and rules.

How sensitive are children to moral breaches in the family? And when does their interest in family rules develop? Because it is within the family that an understanding of cultural rules first develops, studies of moral understanding should include observations of behavior within this family context. Disputes between family members over breaches of rules and conflicts of interest provide a context in which children's understanding is illuminated, and—it seems highly probable—also formed.

## Family Conflict

The focus of our two studies was on the interaction of secondborn children with their older siblings and mothers. Unstructured naturalistic observations were carried out in the home repeatedly during the second year. The methodology and results of the studies are described in detail elsewhere (Dunn and Munn 1985). The methodology was designed to include details of the conflict incidents, the verbal communication between family members concerning the incident, and the affective behavior of the participants. Family conversations during the observations were recorded on a portable tape recorder and transcribed by the observer following the observation. The observational record included not only precoded categories for the behavior of child, sibling, and mother during conflict but also narrative details of the incidents and a record of the expression of intense negative or positive affect by the participants.

Incidents of dispute and confrontation were frequent in these families as table 2.1 shows.

**Table 2.1:** Totals and Mean Frequencies of Conflict Incidents per Family

| Conflict Incidents | Mean Frequency at Various Ages (Months) | | | | |
|---|---|---|---|---|---|
| | 14 | 16 | 18 | 21 | 24 |
| Sibling conflict: | | | | | |
| Study 1 (N = 328) | 10.3 | 8.2 | 11.7 | 11.5 | 11.2 |
| Study 2 (N = 656) | — | — | 8.0 | — | 7.6 |
| Child-mother conflict: | | | | | |
| Study 1 (N = 298) | 5.8 | 8.2 | 9.2 | 12.0 | 12.5 |
| Mother-sibling conflict: | | | | | |
| Study 2 (N = 297) | — | — | 3.0 | — | 4.7 |

While there was not a significant increase in the frequency of such incidents over the course of the second year, there were striking developments in the children's behavior during the incidents and in the behavior of other family members toward the children. Three aspects of these changes stand out as particularly interesting in relation to the development of moral understanding. These are, first, changes in children's behavior related to the anticipation and understanding of others' feelings and intentions; second, changes related to understanding of and communication about social rules; third, changes in children's emotional behavior.

Let us consider first how behavior in sibling conflicts changed. The children's anticipation of others' feelings was revealed in two developments during the second year. The first was the development of teasing behavior. The children showed, with increasing frequency and with increasingly elaborate behavior, a pragmatic understanding of how to provoke and annoy the sibling during confrontation. At fourteen, sixteen, and eighteen months, most instances of such teasing involved the child removing the older sibling's comfort object or favorite possession, or attempting to destroy the sibling's valued possession or game. Some instances involved teasing the older sibling with a frightening object. The following incident occurred during an observation of an eighteen-month-old:

(Example 1—Family H)
**Mother to observer:** "Anny [sibling] is really frightened of spiders. In fact there's a particular toy spider we've got that she just hates."
Child runs to next room, searches in toy box, finds toy spider, runs back to front room, pushes it at sibling—sibling cries.

Such instances became significantly more frequent during the second year; by eighteen months they were observed in seventeen of forty children. The form of the teasing also changed; by twenty-four months verbal teasing was common and sometimes apparently reflected a surprisingly sophisticated grasp of what would irritate or upset the other child. One twenty-four-month-old, whose sister had three imaginary friends named Lily, Allelujah, and Peepee, would announce to her sister in situations of conflict that *she* was Allelujah— an act that infuriated her sister.

A second development during the second year was a change in the children's appeals to the mother for help during conflict with the sibling. By sixteen to eighteen months there was a striking difference in the likelihood that a child would appeal to the mother for help following an act of physical aggression or teasing by the sibling, as opposed to following the child's own act of physical aggression or teasing. In one study, for instance, the children appealed to their mothers after only four of 125 aggressive or teasing acts they initiated themselves. In contrast they appealed to their mothers after sixty-five of ninety-nine such actions *the sibling* initiated. It appears that the children showed some anticipation that help from the mother would not be forthcoming when they themselves had acted in a physically aggressive or teasing way.

Communication over sibling conflict changed in several ways during the second year. First, children began to refer explicitly to the responsibility of the sibling in the conflict incident:

*(Example 2—Family N)*
**Child, twenty-one months:** *(Looks at mother, points at sibling),*
  Anny got my book.

*(Example 3—Family N)*
**Child, twenty-four months:** *Child crying after sibling conflict, goes*
  *to mother.*
**Mother:** What happened?
**Child:** Anny bumped me.

There were also significant increases in the frequency with which both siblings and mothers, in addressing the children, referred to social rules and the feelings of others in the course of conflict incidents. These references suggest that the expectations of both siblings and mothers concerning the children's understanding of such rules and feelings were changing. In addition, there were interesting links between the mothers' comments to the *siblings* concerning rules and feelings and the children's behavior both at the time and six months later. For instance, in those families in which the mother referred frequently to social rules and feelings in talking to the sibling, the child was more likely to appeal to the mother during sibling conflict six months later. This finding suggests children may attend to and reflect on conversations about transgressions addressed to others, especially when such comments are made in the highly emotive context of disputes between family members.

Parallel to the developments in teasing and communicative behavior, there were striking changes in emotional behavior. During the second year children became more aggressive. When the younger sibling was fourteen months old, hitting and physical violence were most likely to be shown by the older sibling. But by eighteen months the secondborns were equally likely to be the first to escalate a dispute from verbal to physical aggression. Around eighteen months, they became increasingly agitated, angry, or distressed by conflict interactions. Self-abuse, tantrums, redirected aggression to the mother, and destruction of toys were increasingly common.

The same developmental changes also stand out when the children's behaviors in conflicts with their mothers are examined. There was an increased frequency of teasing the mother, of looking at the mother and laughing while carrying out a previously forbidden act, and of drawing the mother's attention to a forbidden act by pointing to the results of the act and vocalizing. These events highlight the child's developing capacity to anticipate the feelings or reactions of others. Deliberate evasion was also observed. One child went behind the sofa to pick her nose after being forbidden to do so, another hid when she wanted to pull the stitches in a cut on her forehead, and a third who had taken a pot of brandy butter out of the refrigerator carried it behind the sofa to eat it.

After sixteen months "conversations" between mother and child over transgressions were recorded in every family studied. The mothers' comments were often in question form, as if they expected and provided space for an answer. As early as sixteen months, children took part in such conversations about rules by shaking their heads, nodding, or giving verbal answers. A striking feature of these conversations was that the children explicitly commented on their own responsibility for transgressions.

*(Example 4—Family Ch)*
**Child, twenty-one months:** *Child spills drink on floor, looks at mother.*
**Mother:** Oh dear, oh dear!
**Child:** Look.
**Mother:** Look! Yes!
**Child:** *Rubbing at spilt drink with hand.* Rub it in. Rub it in. *(Looks at observer.)* I done it. I done it.

*(Example 5—Family Ho)*
**Ella, twenty-one months:** *At table, throws toy to floor (previously forbidden). Looks at mother.*
**Mother:** No! What's Ella?
**Child:** Bad bad baba.
**Mother:** A bad bad baba.

Children also joined in conversations between mother and sibling to comment on the transgressions of others.

*(Example 6—Family H)*
**Child, twenty-four months:** *Sibling shows mother that she has drawn on a piece of jigsaw puzzle.*
**Sibling,** *to mother:* Look.
**Mother,** *to sibling:* You're not supposed to draw on them, Caroline. You should know better. You only draw on pieces of paper. You don't draw on puzzles.
**Child,** *to mother:* Why?
**Mother,** *to child:* Because they aren't pieces of paper.
**Child:** Naughty.
**Mother:** Yes that is a naughty thing to do.

The teasing nature of the children's behavior in many of these exchanges was clear.

*(Example 7—Family C)*
**Child,** *eighteen months: Child pulls mother's hair hard.*
**Mother:** Don't you pull my hair! Madam! Don't pull hair. No it's not nice to pull hair is it?
**Child:** Hair.
**Mother:** Hair yes, but you mustn't pull it must you?
**Child:** Yes! (smiles)
**Mother:** No! No!
**Child:** No!
**Mother:** No. No. It's not kind to pull hair is it?
**Child:** Nice!
**Mother:** No it isn't.
**Child:** Nice!

Changes in the children's emotional behavior was particularly clear during the incidents of dispute with the mother. Physical aggression to the mother, destruction of objects, self-injury, and full-blown tantrums all increased significantly during the second year (see Goodenough 1931, for similar findings).

The data indicate that during the second year children begin to understand how to upset and tease other family members and show an increasing interest in what is permitted or prohibited behavior. These developments in understanding were apparent in conflicts and transgressions in which the children themselves were not initially involved. Disputes and arguments between mother and older sibling were rarely ignored by the secondborn children; however, their response to such disputes varied. Sometimes the eighteen- or twenty-four-month-olds responded to the conflict by imitating the forbidden act; sometimes they joined by prohibiting the sibling; sometimes they acted in a supportive way to mother or sibling, carrying out an action that *helped* either one or the other. "Collusion and conspiracy have begun" was the comment of one mother, describing the way that her two children now joined forces against her.

These incidents offer us the opportunity to examine whether differences in the children's behavior depend on the nature of the dispute—that is, whether the secondborns were responding to the emotion expressed by the participants and whether the topic of the conflict affected their behavior. The emotion expressed by mother or sibling was indeed linked to the nature of the children's response (see table 2.2).

If the mother or sibling expressed intense anger or distress during a dispute, the secondborns were most likely to watch or support

**Table 2.2** Children's Responses to Three Affect Categories of Sibling-Mother Conflict

| | Affect Categories | | | | | |
|---|---|---|---|---|---|---|
| | Sibling or Mother Intense Negative | | Sibling Laughs | | Neutral Affect | |
| Children's Response | *Mean Proportion* | *SD* | *Mean Proportion* | *SD* | *Mean Proportion* | *SD* |
| Imitates sibling | .14 | .29 | .34 | .39 | .25 | .31 |
| Supports sibling | .18 | .34 | .02 | .07 | .05 | .17 |
| Supports mother | .03 | .90 | .05 | .22 | .05 | .10 |
| Punishes/prohibits sibling | .01 | .04 | .00 | .00 | .02 | .06 |
| Laughs at mother/sibling (without other response) | .03[a] | .10 | .33[a,c] | .43 | .04[c] | .09 |
| Watches | .50 | .37 | .18 | .37 | .30 | .33 |
| Ignores | .12[b] | .25 | .08[c] | .16 | .30[b,c] | .30 |

[a]Difference between category 1 (intense negative) and category 2 (sibling laughs) significant at $p < .05$
[b]Difference between category 1 (intense negative) and category 3 (neutral affect) significant at $p < .05$
[c]Difference between category 2 (sibling laughs) and category 3 (neutral affect) significant at $p < .05$.

the sibling, and the participants were rarely laughed at. By contrast, if the sibling laughed during a dispute with the mother, the secondborn child usually responded to the incident by laughter or imitation. Incidents in which neither mother nor sibling expressed emotion were most frequently ignored, watched, or imitated.

It seems, then, that the children were sensitive to the emotions expressed by sibling or mother, and that their responses not only differed with the emotions that were expressed but were "appropriate." Children showed support to distressed or angry siblings but very rarely to laughing siblings. It is possible of course that the children were responding to some other feature of the conflict which was itself associated with the display of emotion. One possibility we examined was that the *topic* of the conflict was systematically related to differences in the children's response. We distinguished three categories of topic, those focused on "rules," those concerned with "power," and those focused on "aggression."

The investigation showed that children laughed at "rules" incidents more than at "power" incidents; they laughed at and imitated the sibling more in "rules" incidents than in "aggression" incidents; and they prohibited the sibling more in "aggression" incidents than in the "rules" or "power" incidents (see table 2.3). However, these topic categories were not independent of the emotion expressed by the participants. Intense negative emotion was more likely to be expressed in "aggression" incidents, while laughter by the sibling was more common in "rules" incidents than in "aggression" or "power" disputes.

**Table 2.3:** Children's Response to Three Topic Categories of Sibling-Mother Conflict

| | Topic Categories | | | | | |
|---|---|---|---|---|---|---|
| | Aggression | | Power | | Rules | |
| Children's Response | *Mean Proportion* | *SD* | *Mean Proportion* | *SD* | *Mean Proportion* | *SD* |
| Imitates sibling | .03[b] | .90 | .21 | .36 | .27[b] | .29 |
| Supports sibling | .19 | .37 | .04 | .13 | .05 | .11 |
| Supports mother | .00 | .00 | .07 | .16 | .05 | .11 |
| Punishes/prohibits sibling | .31[a,b] | .46 | .02[a] | .09 | .01[b] | .03 |
| Laughs at mother/sibling (without other response) | .00[b] | .00 | .04[c] | .19 | .09[b,c] | .14 |
| Watches | .31 | .46 | .25 | .34 | .36 | .28 |
| Ignores | .16 | .35 | .37[c] | .40 | .17[c] | .20 |

[a]Difference between category 1 (aggression) and category 2 (power) significant at $p < .05$
[b]Difference between category 1 (aggression) and category 3 (rules) significant at $p < .05$
[c]Difference between category 2 (power) and category 3 (rules) significant at $p < .05$

Clearly we cannot assume either that the children were responding solely to the topic of conflict or solely to the emotion expressed by the participants. It is of course important to note that the topic and the emotion expressed were closely related. But to examine the children's sensitivity to the topic of the conflict per se we need to consider their response to those incidents in which neither mother nor sibling expressed either positive or negative emotion. The results of this analysis showed that even when no extreme emotions were expressed, children did respond differently according to the topic of the conflict. They ignored more of the conflicts focused on "power" disputes than on "rules." Transgressions of the rules of the family, which involved breaches of rules of possession, rudeness, or wild boisterous behavior, were more salient to the children than "power" disputes between mother and sibling. In their verbal comments on the conflicts between mother and sibling, the children showed some awareness of their sibling's transgression. And in their supportive and comforting actions they demonstrated a practical understanding of the emotional state of the other and of how to alleviate this distress.

What inferences can we make from these observations about the child's understanding of social rules within the family? The children's behavior in conflict, or when others are carrying out transgressions, their attention-getting and evasive behavior, and their explicit comments all indicate that the children are developing some conception that rules are shared by family members. They show indisputable interest in what is expected and permitted, and what is forbidden.

### The Role of Others

What role do family members play in the development of social and moral understanding? The close meshing of adult reference to acceptable standards with the increasing interest of their children in such matters was evident not only in conflict situations (with reference to the rules) but also in another context—the discussion of broken or flawed objects. Kagan (1981) drew attention to children's concern with objects that were flawed, first observed at nineteen months in an experimental setting. In our home observations we found a steadily increasing interest in such objects that was, however, already evident at fourteen months (see figure 2.1). Note that the mothers drew their children's attention to such objects from the beginning of the second year and their communications about these flawed objects increased in frequency, as did those of the children. It is a strong possibility that

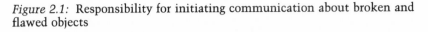

*Figure 2.1:* Responsibility for initiating communication about broken and flawed objects

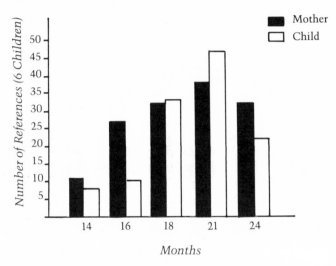

*Months*

such communications by the mother and the family conversations about rules and transgressions do play a part in the development of the children's understanding. Our analyses of the individual differences in children's behavior in conflict support such a view (Dunn and Munn 1986a). Children who were showing relatively mature behavior in conflict at two years—conciliatory acts, teasing, reference to rules, justification for prohibition—came from families in which the mother, in her interventions in sibling conflict, frequently referred to social rules and to the feelings of the siblings.

## The Significance of Emotions

Emotional behavior shown during transgressions changed markedly during the second year. The parallel between the increase in the violence of emotions expressed and the developments in social understanding was striking. Tantrums, self-abuse, destruction of objects, and physical aggression increased over the same period in which the social understanding reflected in the development of teasing, evasion, and collusion grew so dramatically. Others have argued that the increasing frustration and anger expressed by children during the second year is closely linked to the child's developing sense of self (Kagan 1981). In particular, Kagan (1984) has stressed the significance of emotional experiences in the development of moral understanding in these early years. He argues that emotions form the basis for the acquisition of standards—for a "principled morality." He emphasizes children's increasing worry and concern at failure to achieve adult-approved standards, their empathy with others' distress, and their distress at their own inability to master tasks. This emphasis on affect and on the close link between self-awareness and appreciation of standards is illuminating and important. But the results of our studies suggest two caveats.

The salience of the issue of adult standards and transgressions is unquestionable; the curiosity and interest children demonstrate is vividly clear. But in highlighting the links between emotion and the acquisition of standards we should not fail to recognize the "intellectual" and frequently rather *unemotional* interest children show in, for instance, broken, dirty, or flawed objects. At least some of the discussion of social rules is unemotional, explorative, and characterized by reflection rather than emotional drama.

Previous discussions of emotion and moral development have focused on the distress, anxiety, shame, or fear aroused by transgression or the failure to achieve adult-approved standards. These are seen as crucial for the development of social understanding; indeed, a functional argument is put forward in which these "negative" emotions are central in preventing the child from being a destructive force (Kagan 1984). But this stress on "negative" emotions should not obscure the other emotions children express in relation to standards and to their violation—namely their amusement and pleasure. Children show delight in sharing understanding that standards have been violated. They make *jokes* about rule violations and share them with others. Some of the looks and smiles given in such incidents may be generated by uncertainty or worry about the adult's reaction, but hardly all. If we are in the game of offering functional interpretations, there is an equally plausible argument that an important function of emotions, both positive and negative, is to heighten the child's awareness of others, of the feelings, the relationships, the rules and roles of the family world.

What is so important about focusing on the role of emotion in the acquisition of standards is that it forces us to think about a more general issue—the relation between emotion and cognitive changes. The conventional way to think about this relation is to see changes in emotional behavior as a reflection of changes in cognitive ability. But it is surely a more complex relation. The emotional experiences may well play some part in the growth of the children's understanding. It could be, for instance, that the emotion generated in relation to transgression of adult standards *heightens* the child's cognitive awareness—for instance, *because* he is so upset about *X* he thinks harder about it.

As Maccoby and Martin (1983) have pointed out, the work on state-dependent memory (Bower 1980) suggests that experiences are tagged with affective labels and that these labels have a great deal to do with the way in which past experience is brought to bear on current functioning. A good example of this is the finding of Zahn-Waxler and her colleagues. The importance of maternal communication about *not hurting others* lay not in the explanations that mothers gave for the others' distress or the consequences but in the affective intensity that accompanied it. The amount of sympathetic arousal and helpful action over others' distress that children showed at a later time was correlated with the emotional intensity of the mothers' communication. It seems particularly likely that affective experiences are significant in the development of moral understanding and particularly important that researchers be sensitive to this possibility.

## Pretend Play

Conflict is not the *only* context—or even necessarily the most important context—in which children begin to grasp the rules of the culture in which they grow up. Two other aspects of children's social life stand out as potentially interesting. The first of these is the context of joint pretend play. The significance of pretend play as a context in which children explore and exploit social rules and roles has been beautifully demonstrated in work with three- and four-year-olds by Garvey (1977) and by Martlew and her colleagues (Martlew, Connolly, and McCleod 1978). However, the beginnings of this ability to take part in social role play, which involves sharing a pretend framework with another person and taking on a role other than the self, have been little studied. We have examined the development of children's social role play in two studies (Dunn and Dale 1984), focusing on naturally occurring sequences of children's play at home, with mother, sibling, and alone.

During the second year, about a third of the children in each of these studies began to engage in joint role play with their siblings, play in which social rules and social roles were discussed, varied, and enacted. The play was a source of pleasure and amusement in which both children shared an understanding of their social world. Four features of this play deserve note.

The joint play between sibling and two-year-old took place predominantly in those families in which the relationship between the siblings was a warm and affectionate one. It was uncommon in those families in which the siblings did not get along well. A second point is that although the general framework for this social pretend play was almost always set by the older sibling, the younger children did make innovative contributions to the play. They did not simply follow the directions of their siblings but offered suggestions, negotiated rules and roles, and contributed to the shared world of play. This is strikingly sophisticated behavior for such young children. Until now such capabilities have been thought to be well beyond the powers of twenty-four-month-olds. The play shows one way in which an affectionate relationship with a sibling can provide experiences which may be of real developmental significance. The third point is that as early as eighteen months children who had an affectionate and supportive sibling were initiated into such play and began to demonstrate some powers of understanding that social roles and practices can be a source of play and humor and can be varied and even distorted. Finally, the studies showed that children of this age only engaged in such play with a sibling, never with their mothers. Mothers engaged in pretend play as spectators rather than as partners with their two-year-olds.

The general point of importance concerns the processes leading to the development of moral understanding. It appears that different relationships within a family have *different* potential for the growth of understanding of the standards, roles, and rules of the social world in which the children grow up. To put it another way, different aspects of children's developing understanding of social rules are likely to be fostered in different relationships—a point to which I will return.

## Conversations about Inner States and Feelings

Children learn about the rules of their culture not only in conflict interactions and pretend play but also in communication between family members about feelings and inner states. It has been argued that the experience of empathic feelings is important in the development of moral understanding (Hoffman 1976). It has also been shown, as we noted earlier, that parental explanations to children of the cause of other people's distress, especially explanations with a strong affective component, are particularly effective in promoting altruistic behavior. A plausible case can be made for the potential influence of family conversations about feeling states on the development of empathetic behavior, and thus moral understanding. But when and why do such family conversations arise with very young children? Are there empirical grounds for considering them to be developmentally important?

Analysis of the conversations between mothers and their children during the second year shows that feelings and inner states are discussed quite frequently by mothers and their young children (Dunn, Bretherton, and Munn 1987), and it is common for such discussions to focus on the feelings of people *other* than the child. Moreover, the mother's explanations of the cause of feeling states are often made in settings that are emotionally loaded. One context is that of maternal prohibition and punishment of the child; another is that of another person expressing distress. The explicit references by the two-year-olds to inner states, in contrast, are frequently made in a pretend play setting. The themes most often explored are tiredness, pain, pleasure, sadness or distress. The frequency of such references in pretend play demonstrates not only an interest in feeling states but a competence in enacting a feeling state other than their own current state.

Children, then, take part in conversations about others' feeling states in the second year; they play with and show interest in the cause of such feeling states; and their mothers discuss the causes in contexts that are far from affectively neutral. There are, moreover, striking individual differences between mothers in the frequency of such conversations about feeling states, and it appears likely that such differences are linked over time with differences in children's behavior. Four examples will illustrate the grounds for making such a claim.

First, in our initial sibling study we found that differences in the frequency with which mothers referred to the new siblings' feelings and wants were linked to differences in the affectionate, friendly and social behavior of both children fourteen months later (Dunn and Kendrick 1982). Second, differences in maternal comments to the older child about the second child's feelings during sibling conflict were linked to differences in the second child's appeals to the mother in subsequent sibling conflict six months later (Dunn and Munn 1985). Third, there was a significant positive correlation between the frequency of maternal references to inner states when the child was eighteen months old and the frequency with which the children made explicit reference to feeling states at twenty-four months ($r(42) = .62$) (Dunn, Bretherton, and Munn 1987). And fourth, in families in which the mother frequently referred to the feelings of the firstborn when intervening in sibling conflict, the secondborn was likely to show the relatively advanced behaviors of conciliation, reference to rules, and teasing at twenty-four months (Dunn and Munn 1986b).

Differences between families in the frequency of conversations about feeling states do appear to be related to differences in the children's behavior over time. We have no evidence, as yet, for links between such differences in discussion of feelings and differences in moral understanding later in development. However, one set of findings from the conversational analysis is particularly intriguing in relation to the development of moral understanding and judgment. Gender differences are evident in the frequency of conversations about feelings. On every measure in our current study, girls score more highly than boys. They are talked to more often about feeling states as eighteen-month-olds and as twenty-four-month-olds by both their mothers and their older siblings, and by twenty-four months they themselves talk more about feelings. Initiation of conversations about feelings by the mothers and discussion of causes of feelings are more common in families with girls than with boys. With the recent evidence for differences between women and men in the nature of their moral judgments (Gilligan, 1982)—with a far greater emphasis laid by women on the feelings of individuals—these gender differences in early conversations about feelings take on new importance.

## Social Understanding in the Second and Third Years: Implications for Theories of the Development of Moral Understanding

### Affect

Family life is highly emotional. But the ways in which affective experiences relate to developmental changes in the social understanding of very young children are far from clear. Some of the different theoretical possibilities are explored in Kagan's (1984) recent book, and two further caveats to his argument, raised by our observations, have already been outlined. In this concluding section five general points concerning the relation of affect and moral understanding will be summarized.

1. In the context of frustration over newfound independence, and conflict and rivalry with parents and siblings, the emotional experiences of the child are both frequent and intense. The anger and distress that the children express when their wishes are refused or when their sibling "wins" in a dispute demonstrate how important it is for the children to anticipate and understand the behavior of others in such situations, to grasp how other family members are likely to behave in order to make sure that their wishes are not frustrated. Both Sigmund and Anna Freud have emphasized that the sibling relation-

ship is, because of the intensity of emotions involved, central to the development of moral understanding (see for instance Freud and Dann 1951).

2. Although empathetic responses to others do become more frequent in the second and third years there is also an increase in diametrically different behaviors: actions that reflect a practical grasp of how to upset others. Not only does this sophisticated behavior depend on understanding the feelings and wishes of the sibling; it also suggests that the intense emotional experiences of rivalry within the sibling relationship may well lead to the learning or development of *immoral* behavior. Behavior that is specifically intended to hurt or upset others takes place at least as early as *moral* behavior. And the pleasure and interest that children show in breaking rules echo this point. The development and elaboration of unkind acts and transgression of rules is well worth our study. A focus on empathetic behavior alone would be unnecessarily narrow. If it is the development of moral understanding rather than moral judgment that we are attempting to describe, then the "immoral" behavior of teasing and the behavior of children when they carry out breaches of family rules should not be ignored. Such behaviors show us clearly that the children understand both how to hurt other people's feelings and also that such behavior is not acceptable to family members.

Others have argued that empathetic experiences do provide a motive for altruism and the development of morality; this approach, however, focuses on a relatively limited set of moral situations (Rest 1983). In fact some of the triadic interactions we have described here, in which a child witnesses a dispute between mother and sibling or a transgression by the sibling, present the child with interesting conflicts of interest and emotion—the dilemma of whom to support or help in situations in which helping one antagonist will annoy the other.

3. The emotional quality of particular relationships may well influence the route by which children grow to moral understanding. The link between a close sibling relationship and the role-taking skills apparent in joint pretend play highlights this point, an issue discussed more fully below.

4. The data make clear that by twenty-four months children's verbal comments show some grasp of the notion of responsibility and blame in relation to feelings and to social rules.

5. Finally, it is clear that many children grow up—at least in the United Kingdom—in a family world in which mothers continually articulate and discuss social and moral rules and others' feelings. Children are beginning to reflect on and articulate these issues as they

reach twenty-four months. Individual differences in mothers' discussion of feelings and rules even when addressing *others* in the family may be of some developmental importance.

## Peers and Adults

What are the implications of these findings for the theoretical arguments on the relative roles of peers and adults in fostering moral understanding? It appears that different family relationships may have relevance for different aspects of social and moral understanding. It is important to delineate these differences in the developmental implications of interaction with parents and with siblings and not to emphasize the importance of either one at the expense of the other. The correlational analyses from the observations suggest that the experience of a rivalrous sibling relationship is associated with the development of certain kinds of understanding: how to annoy and upset another person and how to enlist the aid of a parent against the sibling. The correlations indicate that the experience of a close and affectionate sibling relationship, in contrast, is linked to the early development of the ability to take part in role play, to conciliate and to cooperate with another (Dunn and Munn 1986a and 1986b). And the evidence from three of our studies and from that of Zahn-Waxler and Yarrow indicates that the experience of growing up with a mother who explains and is concerned about others' feelings is associated with the development of concilatory behavior, altruistic behavior, and the ability to discuss feeling states as early as two years.

What is striking is that even within the second and third years children are sensitive to the pragmatic implications of these differences. It is not only that children understand social standards but also that they understand the part that standards play in particular relationships. They tease mothers about politeness and about affection: "I don't love you Mummy," two of our twenty-four-month-olds said in triumph to their mothers. They tease siblings about possession, taking turns, and imaginary friends. Consider the following findings from our observations of these families when the children were three years old, with two questions in mind: Who initiates discussion of breaches of rules? Who draws attention to which kinds of breach? Figure 2.2 shows that three-year-old children are frequently responsible for initiating discussion of breaches. However, they initiate discussion of different kinds of breach with different family members. In parallel, these different family members themselves are concerned to draw the children's attention to different categories of breach.

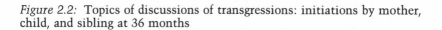

*Figure 2.2:* Topics of discussions of transgressions: initiations by mother, child, and sibling at 36 months

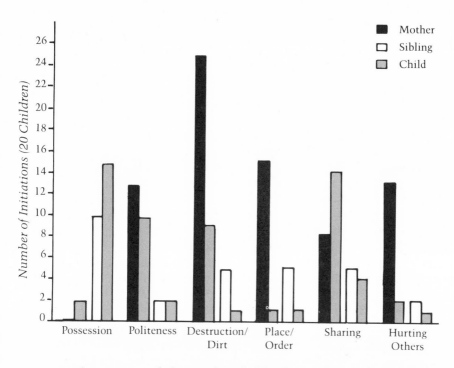

In the context of the mother-child relationship, politeness, destruction, and dirt are salient issues. In the context of the sibling-child relationship possession is discussed. By thirty-six months children are sensitive to these differences. It would surely therefore be a mistake to emphasize *either* the mother *or* the sibling as exclusively important in the development of children's understanding of cultural rules. The kinds of dichotomies that are put forward in theoretical discussions—for instance Piaget's dichotomy of the morality of constraint, experienced through interaction with an adult, and the morality of cooperation, experienced through interaction with peers—appear to be misleading. Our observations show that discussion and argument about what is allowed or forbidden—the morality of constraint—take place both with the sibling and with the mother. And the morality of cooperation can be experienced either with mother, with sibling, or with both.

Nevertheless the individual differences in the quality of these relationships with a parent or a sibling may well be important. In families in which the child is close to the sibling the child is likely to be involved in rather different exchanges over rules than the child who has no sibling or has an intense relationship with the mother and a relatively cool relationship with the sibling. How important such differences may be over time is an unexplored but intriguing question that deserves our attention. We need to examine the possible connections between the beginnings of social understanding and the quality of the relationships within the family in which the child grows up, a strategy taken in the research described in Dunn (1987). The recent review of research on moral development in Mussen's *Handbook of Child Psychology* (Rest 1983) concludes that "People generally change in the direction of making moral judgments on the basis of a better understanding of social relationships and social arrangements." The observations described in this chapter are of course concerned with moral understanding rather than moral judgment. But the point is equally apposite. I would argue further that it may well be in part *because* of the emotional urgency and significance of these relationships that children begin to attend to, explore, and exploit moral understanding. They are far from being able to make judgments about hypothetical moral dilemmas, but they are very close to being able to assign responsibility for family transgressions, to make choices about whom to support in family disagreements, and to use this understanding as a source of power and pleasure in their family relationships.

# References

Bower, G. 1980. Emotional Mood and Memory. Address to the American Psychological Association, Montreal.

Campos, J. J. and C. R. Sternberg. 1981. Perceptory Appraisal and Emotion: The Onset of Social Referencing. In M. E. Lamb and L. R. Sherrod, eds., *Infant Social Recognition*. Hillsdale, N.J.: Erlbaum.

Cheney, D. L. and R. M. Seyfarth. 1982. Recognition of Individuals within and between Free Ranging Groups of Vervet Monkeys. *American Zoologist* 22:519–29.

Cheyney, D., R. Seyfarth, and B. Smuts. 1986. Social Relationships and Social Cognition in Nonhuman Primates. *Science* 234:1361–66.

Dunn, J. 1987. *The Beginnings of Social Understanding*. Cambridge, Mass.: Harvard University Press.

Dunn, J., I. Bretherton, and P. Munn. 1987. Conversations between Mothers and Young Children about Feeling States. *Developmental Psychology* 23:132–39.

Dunn, J. and N. Dale. 1984. I a Daddy: 2-year-olds Collaboration in Joint Pretend with Sibling and with Mother. In I. Bretherton, ed., *Symbolic*

*Play: The Development of Social Understanding.* New York: Academic Press.

Dunn, J. and C. Kendrick. 1982. *Siblings: Love, Envy and Understanding.* Cambridge, Mass.: Harvard University Press.

Dunn, J. and P. Munn. 1985. Becoming a Family Member: Family Conflict and the Development of Social Understanding. *Child Development* 56:480–92.

———. 1986a. Sibling Quarrels and Maternal Intervention: Individual Differences in Understanding and Aggression. *Journal of Child Psychology and Psychiatry* 27:583–95.

———. 1986b. Siblings and the Development of Prosocial Behaviour. *International Journal of Behavioral Development* 9:265–94.

Freud, A. and S. Dann. 1951. An Experiment in Group Upbringing. *Psychoanalytic Study of the Child,* 4 London: Imago.

Garvey, C. 1977. *Play.* Cambridge, Mass.: Harvard University Press.

Gilligan, C. 1982. *In a Different Voice.* Cambridge, Mass.: Harvard University Press.

Goodenough, F. 1931. *Anger in Young Children.* Minneapolis: University of Minnesota Press.

Hoffman, M. L. 1976. Empathy, Role-taking, Guilt and Development of Altruistic Motives. In T. Lickona, ed., *Moral Development and Behavior: Theory, Research and Social Issues.* New York: Holt, Rinehart and Winston.

Kagan, J. 1981. *The Second Year.* Cambridge, Mass.: Harvard University Press.

———. 1984. *The Nature of the Child.* New York: Basic Books.

Klinnert, M. D., J. J. Campos, J. F. Sorce, R. N. Emde, and M. Svejda. 1983. Emotions as Behavior Regulators: Social Referencing in Infancy. In R. Plutchnik and H. Kellerman, eds., *Emotions in Early Infancy. Vol 2 of The Emotions.* New York: Academic Press.

Maccoby, E. E. and J. A. Martin. 1983. Socialization in the Context of the Family: Parent-Child Interaction. In P. H. Mussen, ed., *Handbook of Child Psychology. 4th ed.* Vol. 4. New York: John Wiley.

Martlew, M., K. Connolly, and C. McCleod. 1978. Language Use, Role and Context in a Five-year old. *Journal of Child Language* 5:81–99.

Much, N. C. and R. A. Shweder. 1978. Speaking of Rules: The Analysis of Culture in Breach. In W. Damon, ed., *New Directions for Child Development: Social Cognition.* San Francisco: Jossey-Bass.

Nucci, L. P. and M. S. Nucci. 1982. Children's Social Interactions in the Context of Moral and Conventional Transgressions. *Child Development* 53:402–12.

Nucci, L. P. and E. Turiel. 1978. Social Interactions and the Development of Social Concepts in Preschool Children. *Child Development* 49:400–407.

Piaget, J. 1965. *The Moral Judgment of the Child.* New York: Free Press.

Rest J. R. 1983. Morality. In P. H. Mussen, ed., *Handbook of Child Psychology. 4th ed.* Vol. 3. New York: John Wiley.

Turiel, E. 1983. Interaction and Development in Social Cognition. In E. T. Higgins, D. N. Ruble, and W. W. Hartup, eds., *Social Cognition and Social Development.* Cambridge: Cambridge University Press.

Zahn-Waxler, C., M. Radke-Yarrow, and R. C. King. 1979. Child Rearing and Children's Prosocial Initiations towards Victims of Distress. *Child Development* 50:319–30.

# Comment
## Language and the Beginnings of Moral Understanding
*Catherine Snow*

Judy Dunn's reflections, observations, and conclusions about situations that foster children's moral understanding and allow the sophistication of that understanding to be displayed aroused both great interest and a little frustration. The phenomena she describes are inextricably verbal, and therefore fascinating to anyone interested in child language. But Dunn presents and analyzes these phenomena using categories such as "incidents of conflict," "reference to social rules," "engagement in role play," and "display of empathy"—categories of social behavior that map only loosely onto the categories a conversational or linguistic analysis would generate. I wanted to know more about how both mothers and children talked in the situations described in order to assess how much of the meaning of the interactions resided in the language being used. The phenomena that Dunn has identified in her records of social interaction may or may not be equally identifiable from an analysis that focuses on the language used in the encounters.[1]

Developmental psycholinguists have a somewhat oversimplified, but nonetheless utilitarian view of the world which largely ignores how children feel or think about things in order to concentrate on what they say about them. The oversimplification represented by this view is, perhaps, forgivable since it seems that cognitive and linguistic development, at least for most children, are very closely connected. In the early stages of language development, linguistic and related cognitive capacities emerge more or less together, not in any standard order that would suggest that, for example, certain cognitive capacities are far in advance of the related linguistic achievements. Accordingly, developmental psycholinguists feel justified in acting as if what children say is equivalent to what they think. What we really want to know, then, about morality and its development is how it is talked about.

---

1. I am, of course, familiar with other work carried out by Dunn and colleagues in which a more specifically linguistic analysis of children's and mothers' talk about feelings was carried out (Dunn, Bretherton, and Munn, 1987).

This view may seem rather like an endorsement of a step *back* to methods of assessing moral judgment by looking only at verbal interview protocols, and a step *up* to children older than those we are concerned with in this book. Yet Dunn's observations show that such is not the case; she presents evidence that an enormous amount of talking about moral spheres occurs in natural contexts among very young children. Thus a linguistic analysis of children's talk about morality could be productive. Accordingly, I have undertaken a very small version of such an analysis in order to cast light on the issue of very young children's moral development from a slightly different angle, using perhaps the oldest technique of linguistic analysis—a lexical concordance.[2] Before presenting that analysis, though, I will summarize the major insights of Dunn's paper engendered for me.

First, her focus on moral *understanding* as distinct from moral *judgment* or action is salutary. Although Dunn limits her discussion to moral understanding explicitly because her subjects were too young for moral judgments, focusing on the issue of moral understanding is, in my opinion, precisely the right research strategy even for research on older children and adults.

Even though *understanding* and its prerequisites are her focus, Dunn does not pursue the relevance of what she terms "immoral development" to an analysis of early displays of morality. Dunn has pointed out that acting in a way that is intentionally cruel is a reflection of the ability to understand another's internal states just as being kind is, and thus that teasing is as much a manifestation of empathy as altruism is. She could have taken her reasoning a step further and claimed that unless a child has demonstrated the capacity to tease or to use empathy for negative ends in some other way, his or her display of altruism is not proof of empathetic capacities. Any particular altruistic act could be explained by some device other than empathy, but the display of both teasing and altruism by one child is more convincing evidence that the child has some understanding of the other's internal states.

The genesis of such an understanding remains mysterious. Trevarthen (1977), who called it "intersubjectivity," put its origins very early, at three months or so, and attributed its development to innate factors. Many of us would prefer to think of these early manifestations of intersubjectivity as a preparation for empathy rather than as empathy itself. Dunn has offered evidence in support of this skepticism by showing how environmental factors foster the development of the empathetic capacity. She found that hearing one's mother talking about people's wants and needs, especially those of one's siblings, contributes to one's own ability and willingness to talk about feelings, to the likelihood of having an affectionate

2. I would like to express my appreciation to Brian MacWhinney, both for allowing me to use the transcripts from his son Ross for the analysis and for running the analysis on the MacArthur Foundation-sponsored Child Language Data Exchange System.

sibling relationship, and to relatively advanced moral understanding at age two. The mechanism that might explain such a striking set of relations cannot be explicated from Dunn's data, but other phenomena she reports may provide a hint. She notes (following Kagan [1981]) children's interest in, curiosity about, and occasional distress at flawed objects or at events like breaking and spilling, and similar reactions to occasions of conflict between mother and sibling. Such interest may well identify "deviation" and "conflict" as an emerging domain of mystery for the child—what Karmiloff-Smith (1979) has referred to as a "problem space." Once the problem space is defined at twelve to eighteen months of age, the role of the environment (maternal discussion of rules, needs and wants; engagement in role play; the obligation to understand two alternative and conflicting points of view during intrafamilial arguments) is to provide the child with opportunities to work on the problem and culturally appropriate materials with which to solve it.

Dunn acknowledges the importance of cross-cultural comparisons for full understanding of the links between the social environment and the development of moral understanding, and between an appreciation of others' feelings, wants, and needs and the sphere of morality. To emphasize her point, let me suggest a few potentially valuable comparison cases.

1. According to Schieffelin's descriptions of mother-child interaction among the Kaluli, parents talk very little about the child's feelings and are unwilling to work hard (as American mothers do, using expansions and clarification requests) to ascertain the child's intentions when these are unclearly expressed (Schieffelin, 1979). Schieffelin claims that the Kaluli would see such behavior as inappropriate, in violation of their belief that we cannot know others' intentions unless they tell us. Thus, Kaluli children evidently do not have maternal discussion of their own and others' feelings as a resource when they encounter the problem space of moral understanding. How do they resolve issues of what constitutes kindness versus cruelty? How do Kaluli children develop empathy as a basis for moral understanding? It is interesting to note that, consonant with their unwillingness to interpret unclear intentions, the Kaluli relate the seriousness of a moral transgression not to the intention of the transgressor but rather to the enormity of the consequence (Schieffelin and Ochs 1983).

2. Lutz's description (1982) of residents of Ifaluk, an atoll in Micronesia, reveals a much greater concern with emotions as a topic of interest and of conversation than is typical in England. In Ifaluk people often "talk about our insides" and in so doing make no distinction between the affective and the cognitive dimensions. Dunn suggests that two-year-olds display similarly merged cognitive and affective spheres in their processing of information about flawed objects, conflict, and violations of rules.

3. Some societies rely on more subtle cues about the nature of the other's wants and needs than English or North American norms require or recognize. In Japan, for example, the "neutral" polite request form (i.e., the

level of mitigation considered appropriate for a request of minor importance to a social equal with whom one is acquainted but not intimate) is extremely indirect by Western standards. As hard as it is for American children to understand others' needs, Japanese children have an even greater problem because those needs are rarely expressed directly in Japan. Clancy (1985) has given a brilliant description of the ways in which Japanese mothers explicitly instruct their children in the true feelings that lie behind guests' polite, highly indirect requests and responses to offers. In a society like Japan, where the principles of moral action derive from feelings of obligation which are seldom publicly displayed by any sign on either side, studying the ontogenesis of moral understanding could be especially revealing.

4. Finally, the individual variation among the mothers (who were drawn from a spectrum of social classes) in their reliance on talk about feelings when dealing with conflict is reminiscent of the social class differences in styles of discipline reported by Hess and Shipman (1965). Working-class parents appealed to authority and threatened punishment in disciplining their children, whereas middle-class parents gave reasons that often involved reference to feelings—"because daddy will be upset if you break it," "because you'll be hungry later," and so on. Dunn makes no reference to social class differences in the frequency of her subjects' talk about internal states. But coupled with the usual finding that maternal education is related to use of praise (i.e., the invocation of positive feelings) rather than punishment as a behavior control technique (e.g., Laosa 1978), the Hess and Shipman findings suggest that the differential use of reference to internal states may be directing children into rather different worldviews— worldviews across which the basis for moral understanding differs in essential ways.

Dunn's most striking findings were the strong relations between maternal and child behavior. The correlations between frequency of maternal talk about feelings to eighteen-month-olds and children's talk about inner states at twenty-four months were high. They stand in contrast to the generally low correlations in the child-language literature between syntactic characteristics of maternal and child speech. Parents may influence what their children say more powerfully than how they say it.

Dunn's paper also aroused my interest in precisely how parents and their children talk about moral issues. Do parents or children introduce morality as a topic of conversation? How frequent are such conversations? Do parents provide children with much information on how to talk about issues of morality? I undertook a very preliminary analysis of conversations one child engaged in over a period of three-and-a-half years, with his parents (primarily his father, Brian) and occasionally his younger brother Mark. The period extended from the time the child, Ross, was two-and-a-half until he was six. The first step in the analysis was simply to search the transcripts, which represent a total of fifty-one hours, collected in thirty-second to fifteen-minute segments at irregular but frequent intervals, for instances of the words that I thought might be relevant to moral discussion.[3] The adjectives selected were:

| | |
|---|---|
| awful | nasty |
| bad | nice |
| good | right |
| mean | ugly |
| naughty | wrong |

In addition, three verbs were used as a basis for the search: hate, ought, should.

The utterance containing the target word was printed in the middle of a five-line "window" of text. Of the words selected, *good* and *bad* generated the most numerous examples. *Right, wrong,* and *pretty* generated many which were not of interest (i.e., not used in any way relevant to moral discussions), *mean* was most often used with its mental-verb meaning, and *ugly, nasty* and *naughty* occurred rarely or never.[4] *Ought* occurred only once in the entire corpus (used by a parent) and *should* or *shouldn't* were used deontically only twice per hour on average and only after age three-and-a-half with any frequency. *Good* and *bad* seemed like the most fruitful adjectives to submit to more detailed analysis, and *should* and *shouldn't* were maintained as a deontic comparison. In order to generate enough data per time point and yet allow the data to be analyzed developmentally, the thirty-four sessions were sampled so as to present data from ages two-and-a-half, three-and-a-half, four-and-a-half, and six (see table 2.4). Somewhat more sessions were sampled at the earlier ages and fewer at the later ages. The frequency data presented in table 2.4 have been adjusted to represent occurrence per six hours of recording time.

The first, perhaps most striking piece of information to emerge was how often the target words were used and yet how rarely, relatively speaking, they occurred in discussions of morals or standards. *Good* is a case in point. It is a highly polysemous word and is used in these interactions in many ways, more often to express approval ("good boy") or agreement ("good, we'll go later then") than to refer to the moral abstract notion of "good." In fact, only about 25 percent of the cases where *good* was used were relevant to the sphere of morality loosely defined, after uses like "good to eat," "tastes good," "good for one's health," "good friend," and "good machine" were excluded. In scoring uses, all which referred to hu-

3. This list is clearly not exhaustive. Consider the following example, from Ross aged four years, 8 months)
   *Brian:* I'm a good dad.
   *Ross:* No, you're a despicable dad.
   *Brian:* Where did you learn that?
   4. "Naughty" constitutes a clear case of North American/British dialect contrast. It was the standard term of disapproval in Dunn's data yet never occurred in the MacWhinney corpus.

**Table 2.4:** Use of "Should," "Bad," and "Good" in the Ross Corpus

| Sessions: | 24–30 | 40–43 | 51–54 | 57 |
|---|---|---|---|---|
| Age Range: | 2 yrs., 6 mos.– 2 yrs., 10 mos. | 3 yrs., 5 mos.– 3 yrs., 7 mos. | 4 yrs., 2 mos.– 4 yrs., 8 mos. | 6 yrs.– 6 yrs., 1 mo. |
| | *Total frequency per six hours* | | | |
| *should* | .6 | 11 | 21 | 16 |
| *bad* | 23.5 | 28 | 35 | 4 |
| *good* | 10.8 | 42 | 29 | 12 |
| | *Percentage of instances by child* | | | |
| *should* | 0 | 81 | 43 | 75 |
| *bad* | 51 | 53 | 49 | 0 |
| *good* | 37 | 48 | 41 | 0 |

man actions ("that was a good thing to do"), human spiritual state ("you're being a good boy," "I'm a good daddy") or products of the human mind ("those are bad ideas," "that's a good word") were included. *Bad,* on the other hand, though used less frequently than *good,* was much more likely to refer to the moral quality of persons or actions. Once expressions like "too bad" and "not bad" (as approval) were eliminated, *bad* was used morally about 80 percent of the time. One problem that arises for the child, then, is sorting out the semantic sphere relevant to morality from all the others which the vocabulary confounds with it.

The frequency data in table 2.4 suggest that whereas talking about "bad things" dominates moral discussions at two-and-a-half, the emphasis shifts to "good" at three-and-a-half, and increasingly at ages four-and-a-half and six to "should" and "shouldn't." Perhaps this is not surprising, for it parallels an increasing sophistication in the kinds of moral reasoning revealed in the discussions.

A first question one wants to ask of these data is "Who initiates discussions relevant to morality?" The answer is quite clear: parent and child share responsibility for introducing and for using the terms, at least during the time periods examined (see the last three lines in table 2.4). For most ages, and in cases where the frequencies are high enough for the percentages to be meaningful, child and parent split uses about fifty-fifty. This effect arises, of course, because most uses by both parties occur in conversations where, once the word is introduced, both go on to use it. However, first use within this conversational sequence was as likely to be by Ross as by his father.

The potential confusion, caused by the polysemy of *bad* and *good* is greatly mitigated by another characteristic in the occurrence of these words: the words rarely occur in isolation from other words of moral relevance. In at least half the cases, and particularly in cases where the term was being predicated of human beings and their actions, *good* and *bad* were used in conjunction with one another and with other key words for defining the moral sphere. *Bad* was associated with *punish, spank, hurt,* and *violence,* and *good* associated with *nice, sweet, kiss,* and *love.* These co-occurrences appear in fairly primitive "bad guys" versus "good guys" discussions on the early tapes:

> *Ross:* Marky not cry. Marky nice. Marky not bad boy. *(Two years, six months)*

> *Brian (father):* Tell me about tigers.
> *Ross:* Tigers are bad. *(Two years, nine months)*

> *Brian:* Is he nice? Is he real nice?
> *Ross:* Yeah. But he's growling.
> *Brian:* Is there anyone who's bad in there?
> *Ross:* Huh?
> *Brian:* Is anybody bad in there?
> *Ross:* No.
> *Brian:* No, they're all nice.
> *Ross:* But Star Trooper's bad.
> *Brian:* Yeah, he's the only one that's bad.
> *Ross:* But don't kiss him. *(Three years, six months)*

> *Brian:* They're not that bad.
> *Ross:* Do they hurt people?
> *Brian:* No. *(Three years, six months)*

> *Ross:* And that hulk said, "Where are putting this?" because that bad hulk was really mean. He would hurt boys and would hurt little people. But not you and Mommy and Marky and me. *(Three years, seven months)*

But they also appear in negotiations about what is bad, discussions of degrees of badness, and exploration of reasons, rules, and consequences in the moral sphere:

> *Brian:* What are you doing up there?
> *Ross:* I'm climbing up there.
> *Brian:* You know that's wrong. You know it's bad.
> *Ross:* Not bad!
> *Brian:* Sure it is.
> *Ross:* Good.
> *Brian:* Why is it good?
> *Ross:* 'Cause it's good. Ya, I won't slip.
> *Brian:* You know that's bad.
> *Ross:* Oh, I only doing it a little bit. *(Two years, ten months)*

*(Becky was going across the street.)*
**Brian:** Bad Becky, because she might get hit by a car.
**Ross:** No, good Becky *(meaning "Becky is really a good girl")*. *(Two years, nine months)*

**Ross:** Mean witch.
**Brian:** She's not real bad.
**Ross:** No?
**Brian:** No, she's not real bad.
**Ross:** She's a little bit bad?
**Brian:** Yeah, a little bit bad.
**Ross:** Oh.
**Brian:** A little bit bad.
**Ross:** Oh.
**Brian:** A little bit bad, but she's not real bad.
**Ross:** A little bit bad?
**Brian:** Just a little bit bad, yeah.
**Ross:** Not much bad?
**Brian:** No, not all bad. Not all bad.
**Ross:** Oh.
**Brian:** She's not really going to hurt you, she just says that she's going to. *(Two years, nine months)*

**Ross:** I have some bad ideas.
**Brian:** What are some of your bad ideas?
**Ross:** I want to be he-man.
**Brian:** That's not a bad idea.
**Ross:** Uh-huh. Marky and I are going to slap each other, and that's why he-man is bad. *(Four years, eight months)*

**Brian:** What do you have to do to get a punishment?
**Ross:** Be bad. *(Four years, eight months)*

**Ross:** We'll be good if you give us chocolate.
**Brian:** You better talk to Mommy.
**Ross:** I want to talk to YOU about chocolate.
**Brian:** How come?
**Ross:** Because we will be good.
**Brian:** You won't be good without it?
**Ross:** Because we WILL be good if you give us that. *(Three years, five months)*

*Bad* and *good* were linked not just to each other, but often to a limited number of semantic domains that seemed particularly salient for Ross in defining morality: bad guys versus good guys, bad ideas versus good ideas, and bad words versus good words. Constraining the discussions of bad and good to a few domains, and linking *bad* to *hurt* and to *violence* in those discussions, while *good* is linked to *nice,* clearly help the child to move from fairly concrete instantiations of the notions of badness and goodness to an elaborated, abstract, and more truly moral understanding of those terms.

How does this analysis supplement Dunn's on the ontogeny of moral understanding? First, it certainly supports her observations that talk about others' feelings and needs occurs frequently and is generated by children's growing interest in what is right and wrong, good and bad, as they move through the transition period. Secondly, it suggests that the issues of *good* and *bad, should* and *shouldn't* continue to occupy the child in increasingly sophisticated ways and to generate relevant input from both parent and siblings throughout the preschool years.

My view on the ontogeny of moral understanding, like Dunn's, emphasizes the crucial role of the child's social environment in offering a worldview in which feelings and principles are related and balanced. The role of the parent in promoting empathy undoubtedly begins well before the interactions discussed here. It may even begin with the first instances of adult-manufactured intersubjectivity early in infancy—the adult's interpretation of the child's emotion or attribution of intention to the child. These mirrorings of the child's state cannot be unambiguously seen as the product of a communicative event. Perhaps "communion" rather than communication is the right metaphor. Nonetheless, the intimacy achieved as a result may be an early stage of the empathy achieved a year or two later.

Two more precise mechanisms for the conversion of intimacy to empathy have been proposed. Stern (1985) suggests that parental *attunement,* or imitation of child action in another modality, provides a support to the child's discovery that another can know one's feelings. Dore (1983) argues that maternal prohibitions are occasions when the mother intervenes in the child's intentionality to generate, ultimately, a match between her view of what is prohibitable and his own of what is forbidden. The prohibitableness of some object or action is encoded in the word *no,* a word which the child adopts as a marker of his interest in undertaking the action.

The one-and-a-half to three-year-olds observed by Dunn and quoted in the analysis presented here are being subjected to equally powerful adult interventions. The children, by becoming interested in "rightness," "completeness," "wholeness," and "goodness" as a problem space provoke many occasions for the negotiation of the meaning of words and of acts. During such negotiations, parents exercise the right to define child behaviors as good or bad and to relate their goodness or badness to the intentions behind and the consequences of the acts. The effectiveness of the negotiation in producing a child who shares the parent's views on morality presupposes, in my opinion, the empathy, the like-mindedness, established earlier. In the absence of a basically trusting relationship with the parent there is no reason for the child to let the adult arbitrate the meanings of his words or acts.

Throughout this period, and into adolescence and adulthood, we must recognize the role of narrative in making both words and acts morally meaningful. Why is an act good or bad, after all? Because of the story that is told about it. Most acts are morally neutral if not viewed in the context of the intentions that led to them and/or the consequences that derived from them. The MacWhinney corpus demonstrates that, at least by age five, Ross understood that the moral status of an act is clarified by its consequences, such that a seemingly neutral act can be bad or a seemingly bad act good, depending on its effects:

> *Ross:* When you hit a person in the tummy, that's not bad, you know why? Because it gives them strength, in their tummy. *(Four years, eight months)*

> *Ross:* If I go out in the hallway with my blanket then they will get mad at me, so I shouldn't do that. *(Three years, eight months)*

> *Brian:* Why should't we eat it now, Ross?
> *Ross:* Cause if we can—if we DID eat it, Mom couldn't have any. *(Four years, seven months)*

Furthermore, Ross is capable of relating one act to another—of deriving moral principles from the existence of precedents—and of expressing rules about punishment as generic statements:

> *Brian:* *had declined to remove toy from younger sibling Mark.*
> *Ross:* Why not? They take them away from me at the mall.
> *Brian:* Well, so what?
> *Ross:* Well, that means you should take Marky's toy away. *(Four years, one month)*

> *Ross:* Bad boy is going to get a spanking. Mark's a bad boy, he is going to get a spanking. *(Three years, five months)*

Even before the age of three he understood that claims about the moral status of individuals (especially counterintuitive claims like "Mommy's a bad woman") need to be buttressed by a story that will justify them.

> *Ross, running to Brian:* Mommy's a bad woman. She tried to hurt ... she tried to hurt your little boy. *(Two years, ten months)*

Ross is beginning to recognize the degree to which morality is socially constructed. After his father asked if he was as good at home as he was at preschool, he answered, "What do you think? Whatever you think, is whatever I am" *(four years, eight months)*. The ultimate skill is, indeed, to treat good and bad as objects of contemplation by situating them in the realm of fantasy, and then to work out their principles of action. Dostoyevsky is a practitioner of this skill at its highest levels. But Ross at age four years, eight months, has made a good start:

*Ross:* At school we pretended we were bad guys, and I tickled the pretend bad guy.

## References

Clancy, P. 1985. The Acquisition of Japanese. In D. Slobin, ed., *The Cross-linguistic Study of Language Acquisition. Volume 1: The Data.* Hillsdale, N.J.: Erlbaum.

Dore, J. 1983. Feeling, Form, and Intention in the Baby's Transition to Language. In R. Golinkoff, ed., *The Transition from Prelinguistic to Linguistic Communication.* Hillsdale, N.J.: Erlbaum.

Dunn, J., I. Bretherton, and P. Munn. 1987. Conversations between Mothers and Young Children about Feeling States. *Developmental Psychology* 23:132–39.

Hess, R. D. and V. Shipman. 1965. Early Experience and the Socialization of Cognitive Modes in Children. *Child Development* 36:869–86.

Kagan, J. 1981. *The Second Year: The Emergence of Self-awareness.* Cambridge, Mass.: Harvard University Press.

Karmiloff-Smith, A. 1979. *A Functional Approach to Child Language.* Cambridge, Mass.: Cambridge University Press.

Laosa, L. 1978. Maternal Teaching Strategies in Chicano Families of Varied Educational and Socioeconomic Levels. *Child Development* 49:1129–35.

Lutz, C. 1982. The Domain of Emotion Words on Ifaluk. *American Ethnologist* 9:113–28.

Schieffelin, B. 1979. Getting It Together: An Ethnographic Approach to the Study of the Development of Communicative Competence. In E. Ochs and B. B. Schieffelin, eds., *Developmental Pragmatics.* New York: Academic Press.

Schieffelin, B. and E. Ochs. 1983. A Cultural Perspective on the Transition from Prelinguistic to Linguistic Communication. In R. Golinkoff, ed., *The Transition from Prelinguistic to Linguistic Communication.* Hillsdale, N.J.: Erlbaum.

Stern, D. 1985. *The Interpersonal World of the Infant: A View from Psychoanalysis and Developmental Psychology.* New York: Basic Books.

Trevarthen, C. 1977. Descriptive Analyses of Infant Communicative Behaviour. In H. R. Schaffer, ed., *Studies in Mother-Infant Interaction.* London: Academic Press.

# THREE

# Culture and the Construction of Moral Values: A Comparative Ethnography of Moral Encounters in Two Cultural Settings

*Carolyn Pope Edwards*

Moral values, or standards, constitute one of the most important aspects of social knowledge for children in any society. Standards are defined as conceptions of the "good," "right," or "obligatory" that influence choice in human action (Brandt 1954; Vogt and Albert 1966). The renewed interest in the emergence of standards is due in part to the realization that during the second year, children already show some comprehension of moral knowledge and commitment to standards (see Kagan 1981).

One issue that needs reexamination is the role of parents and other socializing agents. Is the acquiring or construction of early moral knowledge a largely self-guided process, as some recent cognitive-developmental theorists have argued? That is, is early moral knowledge "self-constructed" by young children on the basis of fundamental, universal, social experiences? This paper will critique that point of view, not by totally denying children's role as active reasoners but rather by suggesting that the strong version of the "self-construction" view underestimates the role of culture in moral development. Adults and other socializing agents always scaffold moral development for children by emphasizing those dimensions of moral situations that are important for the children to understand as they construct culturally appropriate moral knowledge. Comparative cultural research provides an especially valuable source of evidence about this scaffolding process, for without cultural comparisons we tend to overestimate the size of the child's maturational contribution and inflate the degree to which development is seen as universal, not strongly channeled by cultural forces.

All cultural groups have values that can be differentiated into at least four domains: *morality* (what one should do in order to be a good or virtuous person); *prudence* (what one should do to promote and protect self-interest); *aesthetics* (what one should do to protect and promote the beauty of the environment); and the *spiritual* or *religious* (what one should do because of the supernatural order of being) (Frankena 1963). The morality domain, some claim, consists of two separate subdomains—*morality proper* (centered on issues of justice, harm, and welfare) and *social conventions* (concerned with etiquette and other regulatory rules).

The basic questions addressed in this paper are these. What are the nature and content of the routine events and daily transactions that help young children to construct moral values? Are these events culturally patterned, that is, organized by the adults who set the stage for children's daily lives by assigning them to settings and activities of work and play (Edwards and Whiting 1980; Whiting 1980, 1983; Whiting and Edwards 1988)? Do these culturally patterned events affect children's understanding and commitment to standards?

In this paper I will not suggest full answers to these questions, but I will try to indicate why I believe we must integrate two traditionally opposed theoretical points of view. On the one hand, *cultural transmission theory* asserts that values are acquired by the individual through learning (or reconstructing) what Shweder (1982, 8) calls "previously organized, preregulated, prepacked 'collective representations.' " On the other hand, *self-construction theory* asserts that a receptivity to standards and a predisposition to construct certain kinds of value knowledge exist everywhere; value knowledge develops in culturally universal sequences tied to cognitive maturation and basic interpersonal experiences involving right and wrong.

The cultural transmission model has been a strong contender in the social sciences for a long time. A person taking the cultural transmission perspective would expect two things: (1) greater cultural differences than similarities in the basic organization of the routine events that surround the early learning of moral standards, and (2) a correlation between these events and the standards. For example, in a classic paper, John Whiting (1967) argued that the preservation of society requires that members of any group must be (unconsciously) motivated to obey the key rules, taboos, or laws. Whiting suggests that there are three independent systems worldwide that societies have developed for accomplishing this task: (a) "sorcery," the exaggerated and paranoid fear of retaliation from other humans; (b) "sin," the projected dread of punishment by gods or ghosts; and (c) "superego," the sense of guilt and readiness to blame the self that derives from a sense of personal responsibility for one's actions. Whiting presents empirical evidence to relate each of these motivational systems to a particular pattern of parental response to early moral transgression.

One of the most interesting proposals from the self-construction perspective—the one to be critiqued in this paper—comes from Turiel and his colleagues, Nucci and Smetana (see, e.g., Nucci 1982; Nucci and Turiel 1978; Turiel 1983; Smetana 1983, 1984). They have argued that all social standards belong to one of two basic types and that even very young children intuitively appreciate this fact. *Moral values proper* (centered on *interpersonal* issues of justice, harm, and welfare) are considered to be obligatory, objective, generalizable and context-independent (that is, not contingent on specific social roles, authority-dictates, or contextual considerations). These interpersonal norms are hypothesized to be constructed, *at a very early age,* on the basis of interactions that allow children to notice the *inherently harmful consequences* of moral transgression.

Conventional values (concerned with such matters as etiquette, dress, bearing, sex roles, and other customs) are said to be distinct from moral values. These *social system* norms serve regulatory, organizational, and communication functions and are contingent, contextual, and arbitrary. An understanding of their purpose is thought to appear *during the middle childhood years* as a result of interactions that help children to learn about their *normative status.* Such interactions would highlight dominant/subordinate relationships, order/disorder effects, contextual boundaries of rules, punishment/reward consequences, and the like.

Furthermore, rationales underlying morality are cognitively more accessible to young children. The "why" underlying the wrongness of hitting is intuitively more obvious than the "why" underlying the wrongness of swearing. Turiel and his colleagues believe that children's commitment to upholding moral rules consequently develops earlier than their commitment to conventional rules.

This paper discusses two corpora of observational data that have been examined ethnographically in order to probe the Turiel, Nucci, and Smetana theses. The purpose is to suggest specific ways in which this version of the "self-construction" model underestimates the scaffolding role of culture in moral development. The first corpus was collected in home settings in the community of Oyugis, Kenya; the

second in a toddler classroom in Poughkeepsie, New York. Both corpora of data lead me to doubt that the *boundaries* between moral and
conventional rules are so well defined. Rather, the data suggest that
all of the deeply held values in a community may involve merged
"moral" (obligatory/interpersonal) and "conventional" (regulatory/
organizational) foundations.[1] Furthermore, the interactions surrounding transgressions of various rule types may not necessarily be very
different; in all cases, authority figures may employ the types of responses that do *not* distinguish the domains—such as strong commands, threats, and sanctions.

Finally, the findings suggest that the rationales underlying social roles (task assignment) and social propriety can be made just as
salient and cognitively accessible to young children as the rationales
underlying control of aggression and care of others. The African children described in this study live in large, rural households that are
economic as well as social units; children are given responsibilities at
an early age that may increase their identification with social rules and
help them to appreciate their value. In such a cultural context,
the distinction between the obligatory/interpersonal and organiza-
tional/regulatory domains may be less prominent than in American
classrooms where "school rules" so clearly come "from outside." The
Oyugis children, consequently, demonstrate an early and strong commitment to such "conventional" rules that is not observably different
from their commitment to "moral" rules surrounding aggression and
care of others.

## The Emergence of Moral Concepts in Oyugis, Kenya

I am indebted to Carol Ember, professor of anthropology at Hunter
College, for use of a corpus of observational data that details the so-
cial-cognitive underpinnings of nurturant and prosocial behavior in
Kenyan children.[2] Ember studied twenty-eight children aged seven to

---

1. In their latest writings, Turiel and Smetana have also begun to consider
how specific rules relate both to moral and conventional underlying rationales (see
Smetana 1983; Turiel and Smetana 1983; Turiel and Davidson 1986). I am grateful
to Jerome Kagan, Edward Mueller, Larry Nucci, Richard Shweder, Judith Smetana,
and Elliot Turiel for thoughtful comments on an earlier version of this paper.

2. Carol Ember kindly allowed me to analyze her Oyugis observations for this
and an earlier paper. This paper refines and extends the conclusions presented in
Edwards (1986), using many of the same Oyugis observation excerpts. However, the
observations have been corrected using geneological information and children's
given names, provided by Ann Bookman. In Oyugis, most children have two given
names, one Christian and one Luo (Bookman and Ember, in press).

sixteen years in a Luo-speaking community of about 250 people in the South Nyanza district of Kenya (Bookman and Ember, in press; Ember 1973). This community, referred to as Oyugis (actually the name of the nearby market town), is one in which children grow up participating in economic, household, and child-care responsibilities. Households are large, ranging in size from two to twenty-four members (with an average of ten). Many households are polygynous and/or extended, so children often grow up living on a compound with siblings, half-siblings (children of their father's co-wife), and other relatives (e.g., nephews, uncles) close to them in age. Women bear the major responsibility for subsistence agriculture, housework, food preparation, and childcare. Their main helpers are their children over the age of five. These prominent features of the culture shape the drama of children's lives by organizing the cast of characters with whom children most frequently interact and constraining the types of scripts that unfold on the stage of daily living (see Edwards and Whiting 1980; Whiting and Edwards 1988).

Following the Whiting method (Whiting, 1980, 1983), Ember trained her observers, educated Luo-speakers, to collect fifteen-minute running record protocols on each child's behavior and interaction (see Edwards 1986 for a more complete description). My analysis has been based on 109 episodes excerpted from the observations in 1973 because they were seen as relevant to moral development. A reexamination of the data now reveals that each episode contains a moral situation—either a transgression or avoided transgression. We can tell that a transgression took place, or was opportunely avoided, because *one person intervened with a reprimand, correction, responsible suggestion, or prosocial command toward another.* The transgressor (or potential transgressor) in turn sometimes *cooperated or obeyed,* sometimes *offered an account or excuse,* and sometimes *refused or ignored the correction or suggestion.*[3]

The 109 episodes were classified according to the nature or cultural norm at issue, as follows: commands concerning *aggression toward small children* (twenty episodes); commands concerning *aggression toward animals* (eight episodes); suggestions related to

3. I took the fruitful idea of looking closely at moral "breaches" from Much and Shweder (1978). However, I have analyzed not only "transgression situations" (containing an accusation or account), but also nontransgression situations initiated by a responsible or prosocial command, because both types of situations reveal children's "moral reasoning-in-action."

Jean Briggs (1979), in a penetrating description of Inuit Eskimo socialization, demonstrates how even verbal teasing games can serve as moral encounters and reveal "moral reasoning-in-action."

*meeting the needs of others* (twenty-six episodes); conflicts over *turn-taking or sharing* (seven episodes); discussions about *task assignment* (thirty-four episodes); and commands concerning *proper social behavior* (fourteen episodes). The first four categories invoke Turiel's category of morality proper; the final two fit his category of social conventions. Together, the six categories appear to account for all of the episodes.

## Aggression Toward Small Children

Turiel, Nucci, and Smetana have claimed that moral rules prohibiting harm to others are constructed by children on the basis of social interactions in which pain or injury occurs. They suggest that one important type of information for the cognizing child is the victim's response, which suggests the intrinsic wrongness of hurting. They assume (see Hoffman 1983) that human beings are naturally empathic and distressed by injury to others.

It is not necessary to discount the motivating force of empathy in moral behavior to suggest that empathy can be reinforced by the wish to avoid punishment. To judge from the observations, Oyugis community values include strong prohibitions against the striking of small children by bigger ones. Adults make clear that infants and toddlers may not be beaten under any circumstances and that hitting or hurting small children is a punishable offense. (Wenger [1983], has described similar practices for a community on the Eastern coast of Kenya.)

How do adults communicate their values? Two examples were found in which mothers reasoned with their children about inhibiting aggression to babies. Such explanations focused in a direct way on the intrinsic wrongness of the aggression.

*(Example 1)*
**Jacob Opiyo** *(boy, three-and-a-half)* to mother: I can beat the infant.
**Mother:** Never do it, father *(By addressing her small son as*
    *"father," she flatters him in a culturally appropriate way and*
    *suggests that he is too mature to hurt an infant.)*
**Jacob:** Why is he destroying my book?
**Mother:** I'll buy you a new one.

*(Example 2)*
Infant, *Joash Okello (eight months old), urinates on the dress of*
    *Beatrice Adoya (sister, six), holding him. Beatrice takes a stick*
    *and hits him.*
**Mother,** *to Beatrice:* Don't beat him. He does not know.
*Moments later, infant urinates again and this time Beatrice simply*
    *reports it to mother.*

Many other examples suggest that adults most commonly use threatened or actual sanctions, with little or no discussion, on children who hit infants or toddlers.

*(Example 3)*
**Grandfather,** to Jomo Kenyatta *(boy, three-and-a-half, crying):* Who has beaten you?
**J.:** It was Gideon *(brother, five).*
**Grandfather:** Stop crying. I'll beat him in turn.
*Jomo stops.*

*(Example 4)*
**Jacob Opiyo** *(boy, three-and-a-half):* Father, Nabbath has hit me.
*Father whips Nabbath Atieno (half-sister, eight).*

Does this use of "power-assertive" techniques (unaccompanied by reasoning) result in the development of children who obey rules only to avoid punishment? Clearly not, because Oyugis children become early and stout defenders of these rules about aggression. This is seen in the following examples:

*(Example 5)*
**Simeon Okelo** *(boy, two-and-a-half)* to mother: Elizabeth *(sister, eight)* has been beating James *(brother, six).*
**Mother:** Why?
**Simeon:** I do not know.
*Mother drops the matter, probably because the six-year-old, James Odhiambo is considered able to defend himself.*

*(Example 6)*
**Elizabeth Atieno** *(girl, eight)* to Simeon Okelo *(brother, two-and-a-half):* Stop hitting the infant. *Simeon hits infant again.*
*A few days later, James Odhiambo (brother, six) hits Simeon and Simeon cries. Now Elizabeth protects little Simeon.*
**Elizabeth** to James: Stop beating that boy. *He stops.*

*(Example 7)*
*Beatrice Adoyo (girl, six) hits Gideon Magak (coresident cousin, three) on the head for no apparent reason. He cries.*
*Martin Otieno (Beatrice's brother, eight) hits Beatrice as a punishment.*
*Beatrice suppresses a tear.*

*(Example 8)*

*Jacob Opiyo (boy, three) comes up with a stick and hits Esron Juma*
*(brother, nine-and-a-half). Esron laughs and takes a long stick*
*and hits him back lightly. Jacob runs away and Esron misses*
*him four times. Finally, Esron's last stroke connects and Jacob*
*cries. Esron has hurt him unintentionally.*

*Micah Odhiambo (brother, seven-and-a-half) tells Esron not to hurt*
*Jacob.*

**Esron:** I did not mean to.

In each of these excerpts, the reader may notice that the offender "accepts" the correction of the intervener without protest, except in excerpt (8) where the offender makes the valid claim of unintentionality. The role of moral "sanctioning agent" in Oyugis is considered legitimate and desirable for older children. There are, nevertheless, "reasonable limits" to this power, and if children abuse it they may be reprimanded by their peers, as seen in the following observation:

*(Example 9)*

*Ayuby Nyaoke (boy, nine) sees Gideon Magak (co-resident nephew,*
*five) cutting the rails on the walls of the new house. Ayuby*
*beats Gideon and Gideon cries.*

*Ochieng' (Ayuby's nephew and Gideon's half-brother, seven) calls*
*Ayuby to come and see how Gideon damaged the house on*
*another occasion. Ayuby comes to look, and hits Ochieng',*
*saying,* Why did you pull the rails down?

*Ochieng' denies he did it, saying,* I didn't.

*Now a girl, Nabbath Atieno (Gideon's older sister, and Ayuby's*
*niece, eight), intervenes. She reprimands Ayuby, saying,* You're
bad to the children!

*Ayuby evades, saying,* They have to be taught.

## Aggression Toward Animals

Aggression toward animals is sharply distinguished in Oyugis from aggression toward human beings. Most Kenyans do not believe that animals should be carefully protected and treated with great consideration (B. Whiting, personal communication). However, needless cruelty to animals is considered reprehensible by the community.

In eight episodes, child sanctioning agents used commands or threats of sanctions to stop aggressive behavior. These are the kinds of responses that Nucci, Turiel, and Encarnacion-Gawrych (1983) say equally typify conventional and moral transgressions. Children did not display any of the responses that distinguish moral transgression and focus on the consequences of the act to the victim; they did not provide rationales, focus on the animal's pain, or evaluate the act as hurtful or unfair, for example.

*(Example 10)*
*Jacob Opiyo (boy, four) tries to throw a stone at the dog.*
**Micah Odhiambo** *(brother, seven-and-a-half):* Stop, or I'll beat you. *Jacob stops.*

*(Example 11)*
*Beatrice Adoyo (girl, six) pulls cat by the tail.*
**Gideon Magak** *(co-resident cousin, three):* Stop that or I'll beat you. *Instead, the older girl picks up a stick and chases Gideon away.*

*(Example 12)*
**Gideon Magak** *(boy, three) responds to an observed transgression of co-resident cousin, Lenet Achieng', by informing to his older brother, Jaob Juma:* Lenet is killing your grasshoppers.
**Joab** *(brother, nine) to Lenet:* Don't do that. I want to see them alive.
**Lenet** *(co-resident cousin, four):* Gideon is lying. I'm only touching them, not killing them.

What information do the commands, sanctions, and threats convey, unaccompanied as they are by statements that call attention to the effects of aggression on the victim? Do they highlight the "normative inappropriateness" or "inherent wrongness" of hurting? We cannot know, but I hypothesize that in the Oyugis cultural context, these strong responses suggest both: they are merged together. They emphasize the importance and overriding obligation of the moral rules. "You are (unconditionally) obliged to obey these rules" is the message conveyed by strong commands, sanctions, and threats of sanctions, when they come from loved and/or respected parents and older children in Oyugis.

## Positive Action to Meet Needs of Others

Children in Oyugis are often expected to help with the care of younger kin, and this deeply held value is backed up by moral sanctions. Children are reprimanded or punished if they are irresponsible about younger children in their care. In the following excerpt, a thirteen-year-old boy reminds his toddler nephew that if the toddler gets hurt, the bigger boy will be punished. The logic of this argument seems to be comprehensible and motivating to the two-year-old, because he immediately stops his dangerous play. The toddler shows himself to be an "empathic" and "reasonable" moral agent.

(Example 13)
A group of children are running along together and stop to examine a hole. A small boy Ben Guron Opiyo (age two), tries to look in too. Then Joseph Odhiambo (co-resident uncle, thirteen) says to him, Don't. You'll fall in, and mother will beat me. The small boy, Ben Guron, stops looking and slowly walks away.

Children are only rarely praised for responsible performance. In many parts of sub-Saharan Africa praise is believed to "spoil" children (Whiting and Edwards 1988). In one example found, a seven-year-old girl sought her mother's praise, and her mother honored her not with flattery but with the promise that she could take over the task from the mother.

(Example 14)
Elizabeth Aomo (girl, seven) helps her mother thresh millet: Am I not doing well?
Mother: Yes, my daughter. Nowadays, I'll be leaving this work for you to do in my stead. You are fit.
Elizabeth laughs when looking at Pares Opon (sister, three): I'm nicer and more helpful to mother than you are.
Pares ignores and doesn't reply.

What is the effect of the Oyugis training methods, including the use of punishments for irresponsibility? Though they do not focus on the consequences of transgression for the victim, they must in some way help children develop a self-regulated commitment to upholding the rules. Oyugis children often show an intense commitment to the value of concern for others, as seen in the following examples where one child spontaneously intervenes to try to help a third child:

(Example 15)
Jennifer Akinyi (girl, eleven) to Thomas Ager (brother, five): Go and take that baby because he's crying. Thomas laughs but doesn't go.
Jennifer: I'm telling you to go and you are just playing around with me. Go or else I'll beat you. Thomas runs to pick up the baby.

*(Example 16)*

**Janet Atieno** *(girl, eight, visiting)* to Elizabeth Aoma *(girl, seven),*
  *who is holding her baby sister:* Why is she crying?
**Elizabeth:** I do not know.
**Janet:** Tie her on your back and she will be all right. *Elizabeth does*
  *so.* Let us go and sit away from your mother. I think that will
  help the infant stop crying. *Elizabeth does so.*

*(Example 17)*

An infant, Judith Adhiambo *(girl, one) picks up a tin can being*
  *played with by Gideon Magak (brother, three). Gideon tells*
  *the infant,* Stop that.
**Beatrice Adoyo** *(co-resident cousin, six) to Gideon:* Give the baby one.
*Gideon does not comply.*
**Pamela Auma** *(sister, five-and-a-half) to Gideon:* Give the baby a
  tin. *Gideon does not.* Please give her one, my father. *Gideon*
  *complies.*

*(Example 18)*

Micah Odhiambo *(boy, seven-and-a-half) and Esron Juma (brother,*
  *nine-and-a-half) are walking along a path together.*
**Micah:** We better go home. The baby will cry. *Esron, the elder,*
  *ignores. Micah repeats the command. Esron still ignores.*

*(Example 19)*

Yucabet Adhiambo *(girl, thirteen) goes to fetch water from the*
  *waterhole with kids following near her.*
**Samson Ouma** *(brother, fifteen), reprimands her angrily:* Why have
  you taken those kids with you there? *Yucabet does not answer.*

*(Example 20)*

Visitor *(boy, five) holds a crying infant.*
**Levi Odhiambo** *(boy, three-and-a-half):* Why is she crying?
**Visitor:** I do not know.
**Levi** *(persisting):* Does she want food?
**Visitor** *(sarcastic):* I do not know because she doesn't talk.

## Conflicts over Turn-taking and Sharing (Positive Justice)

To the American observer, there is a striking paucity of conflicts over
turn-taking and sharing in Kenyan homesteads. We are used to
"fairness" being the centerpiece of children's moral concern. Western
theorists such as Piaget, Kohlberg, and Turiel have seen justice as the
necessary or natural center of moral reasoning. Yet of the 109 Oyugis
moral episodes, only seven involved conflicts over turn-taking or
sharing.

Oyugis adults rarely intervened in children's interactions in order to help them resolve justice disputes or to uphold a child's rights. Perhaps as a consequence, fairness does not seem a central moral value to the children.

In spite of the lack of emphasis on justice in turn-taking and the sharing of play materials, however, people are not oblivious to fairness concerns. The examples indicate that fairness is a moral value and that from a young age children are capable of understanding fairness issues and negotiating their rights. The "quality" of their disputes and discussions sounds "familiar" to us; it is only the quantity, the lack of emphasis, that seems surprising.

*(Example 21)*
*James Odhiambo (boy, six) asks Elizabeth Atieno (sister, eight) for a lemon. She tells James to go bring a knife. He goes. Simeon Okelo (brother, two-and-a-half) asks sister for a piece.*
**Elizabeth** *to youngest, Simeon:* It's James's turn now. You've had some.
**Simeon:** I haven't. *He has.*
**Elizabeth:** All right. *But shes does not give him any.*

*(Example 22)*
*Esron Juma (boy, nine-and-a-half) pulls Jacob Opiyo (brother, four) around on a "car" (really a wagon).*
**Esron to Jacob:** Get off. It is the baby's turn. *Jacob does not heed.* Then I won't let you ride again. *Jacob gets off, and Esron pulls the infant in the "car."*
**Jacob to Esron:** You come and pull me. It's my turn. *Esron does not heed. Jacob charges him with a stick, but Esron runs away.*

## Children's Discussions about Task Assignment

Task assignment (including issues about authority in commanding) is the most frequent of the six moral topics among Oyugis children (thirty-four episodes found). The research of Turiel, Nucci, and Smetana has generally found that young American children are more concerned with sharing and aggression transgressions than with breaches of conventional rules, such as task assignment and the social division of labor. The situation in Oyugis appears to be quite different.

This contrast may be related to cultural differences in the basic value hierarchies in the two societies. In addition, it probably reflects concrete differences in the children's everyday experience. At the time of Ember's research, Oyugis children typically spent a great portion of their time in mixed-age groups composed of kin and a large portion on their nonschool time working at responsible tasks. This learning environment would be expected to be one in which "prosocial commands" would be relatively frequent. That is to say, the older/younger age relations and responsible work activities would "elicit" or "encourage" a high frequency of commanding about work and proper social behavior (Whiting and Edwards 1988).

Perhaps the most interesting characteristic of the thirty-four episodes is the way in which they reveal the children to be "active moral reasoners," committed to their society's values and eager to discuss with one another the "rights and wrongs" of task assignment. The legitimacy of the *rationale* for a command and the *authority* of the commander are central issues to the children from a young age. They think about whether a task really needs to be done, whether it needs to be done urgently, and whether the commander has the right to command.

Although younger children are generally expected to obey the commands of older ones, the observations do not portray them as subservient or passively compliant. On the contrary, the children appear eager to extract the rationale for a command and are more likely to cooperate if convinced that the job is a necessary service that needs to be done immediately.

The following set of episodes illustrate instances in which younger children fairly quickly cooperated with older children's task commands. In all of them, the rationale for the command was either clearly stated by the older child or self-evident.

*(Example 23)*
*Two brothers are washing clothes.*
**Samson Ongyango** *(boy, thirteen-and-a-half):* Draw some more water.
**Thomas Ager** *(brother, five-and-a-half):* Why?
**Samson:** For the final washing.
*Thomas fetches the water.*

*(Example 24)*
**James Odhiambo** *(boy, six):* Why do you leave soap in the water? Don't you know it gets used up faster that way?
**Simeon Okelo** *(brother, two-and-a-half):* I never knew. *He takes the bar of soap out.*

*(Example 25)*
**Yucabet Adhiambo** *(girl, thirteen):* Collect the firewood and shelter it under the eaves before it rains.
*Thomas Okoth (brother, eight) complies. Sister stands by the door and examines the [threatening] weather.*

*(Example 26)*
**Samuel Okela** *(boy, fourteen) to Micah Odhiambo (brother, eight):*
Stop playing now. You better go fetch firewood right away.
*Micah does not go, so* **Samuel** *continues:* Collect the blankets
before you go fetch firewood.
*Micah does comply, gathering up the blankets that had been spread
out to sun in the yard.*
**Samuel** *now says to Micah:* Let us all go to get wood. *He sets off
and Micah picks up a panga knife and follows.*
*As they walk along, younger* **Micah** *asks older Samuel:* What would
we do if it starts raining right away, before we can get any
wood.
**Samuel:** We would return home. *They walk on.*

*(Example 27)*
**Nabbath Atieno** *(girl, eight) commands Gideon Magak (brother,
three), in a flattering style:* Come here, Mr. Chief. *Gideon
doesn't go. She then explains:* Come and take the baby because
I want to go for water at the pond. There is no water in our
house. *Gideon complies.*

*(Example 28)*
**Nabbath Atieno** *(girl, eight) sees Jomo Kenyatta (brother, three)
picking at the charcoal in the hearth. She commands:* Stop
that because the baby will watch and copy you. *Jomo stops.*

Contrast those episodes with the following set, in which the
younger, commanded children put up strong resistance—more or less
successfully—to the authority of elder children.

*(Example 29)*
**Sophia Okech** *(girl, fifteen):* Go home and find out whether the hens
are feeding on the corn spread out in the sun.
*Lorna Auma (sister, ten) doesn't take heed but goes on playing.*
**Sophia** *to Lorna:* What are you doing? Do you mean to say you
haven't heard my words? Go quickly, otherwise I'll cane you.
*She picks up a stick.*
*Lorna runs away, then stands by watching elder sister and looking
at her angrily.*
**Sophia:** I'll be satisfied if only you'll go where I've sent you.

*(Example 30)*
**Samuel Okela** *(boy, fourteen) is making rope for weaving a mat. He
tells brother to divide the sisal in little pieces for him.*
**Micah Odhiambo** *(brother, eight):* Certainly not. Don't think I've
come here to work for you. *Samuel backs down, doesn't reply.*

*(Example 31)*
**Lusi** *(girl, eleven):* What are you still doing? Come quickly and help me do this cloth, quickly. *(She has been waiting four minutes.)*
**Odhiambo** *(brother, nine, rudely):* You have no right to hurry me up.

*(Example 32)*
*Isdora (girl, ten, visiting the household) calls Ochieng' (boy, eight) to come get the baby because it's crying. Ochieng' tries to come but on the way is deliberately blocked by his little half-brother, Gideon Magak (five). The girl canes Gideon to let Ochieng' go by.*
**Gideon** *(complaining, wittily):* Can't you remember what I've done for you? I brought the baby from the other house for you and now you're caning me!
**Nabbath Atieno** *(Gideon's sister, eight) offers comfort to Gideon:* If she can't remember what you did for her, then never help her anymore. *The cousin leaves and withdraws into the house.*

The final episode above clearly illustrates how skillful a child as young as five can be in reasoning about a moral principle (reciprocity), interpreting a situation to his own advantage, stating his case, and successfully challenging the authority of an older child.

## Commands Concerning Proper Social Behavior

The last group of episodes to be considered focuses on proper social behavior. Americans emphasize the equality of persons and tend to think of etiquette or manners as "mere conventions," outside of the true moral domain. Moral philosophers Ladd (1957) and Frankena (1963) exclude etiquette from the "institution" of morality.

African cultures, in contrast, attach great importance to proper social behavior—respectful address, dignified bearing, table manners, cleanliness, and other matters related to etiquette and correct presentation of self. These cultures emphasize age and sex hierarchies in interpersonal relations and rely upon social rules to facilitate the flow of interpersonal interaction (LeVine 1973).

Do the people of Oyugis view the rules of etiquette and proper social behavior as "mere conventions," distinct from morality proper? Or do they consider them to be part of the true moral domain? Our data cannot provide a direct answer to this question, but they do suggest two relevant facts.

First, young Oyugis children construct a working knowledge of the social conventions and demonstrate a "commitment" to the rules.

They both spontaneously enforce the rules and (often, not always) comply when themselves corrected.

*(Example 33)*
*Two girls, aged four and four-and-a-half, examine the observer's raincoat.* **Gideon Magak** *(boy, 3) to co-resident cousin, Lenet Achieng' (girl, four):* Stop touching the visitor's possessions. *Lenet stops.*

*(Example 34)*
**Pamela Auma** *(girl, five-and-a-half):* Ogodo is coming here. Don't come outside unless you put on your dress. *Beatrice Adoyo (co-resident cousin, six) doesn't answer. She does not dress but sits in the bedroom.*

*(Example 35*
**Jomo Kenyatta** *(boy, three) to Jacob Opiyo (half-brother, three-and-a-half):* Get off my father's chair. *Jacob ignores him.*

Second, as with other types of rules, Oyugis children readily use physical sanctions to back up their commands. In three examples found, the sanctioning agents were the older children and the younger, sanctioned children accepted the others' authority.

*(Example 36)*
*Ayuby Nyaoke (boy, nine) hits Nabbath Atieno (co-resident niece, eight) for letting the infant defecate on his mother's bed. Nabbath cries.*

*(Example 37)*
**Nabbath Atieno** *(girl, eight):* Clean your nose. *Jomo Kenyatta (brother, three) ignores. Nabbath repeats command, picking up a cane. Jomo still ignores. Nabbath repeats, trying to hit him. Jomo goes off unwillingly and comes back.* **Nabbath:** It's not very clean. *Again Jomo goes to clean his nose and comes back. A few minutes later, sister Nabbath tells little brother to go wash his face. He refuses, mimicking her rudely.*

*(Example 38)*
**Jomo Kenyatta** *(boy, three) tries to uproot a pumpkin in the family garden.*
**Perce Akinyi** *(sister, 11-and-a-half):* Don't or I'll beat you. *Jomo runs away.*

Why are the children in Ember's observations so committed to rules of proper social behavior? I claim that it is due to the conditions of their daily experience. These conditions serve to make salient and comprehensible the rationales underlying the rules. For example, by the time they reach middle childhood most have spent many hours in the company of infants and toddlers. They have experienced countless occasions in which it seemed necessary to deal with a small child who was annoying, dirty, or out of control. They have both dispensed and received rude and disrespectful behavior. In sum, they have had many concrete opportunities to observe how rules of politeness, respect, etiquette, and modesty are necessary for pleasant relations within the social system of the large African household.

## Summary of Findings on Oyugis Children

Turiel's theory is a valuable contribution to understanding the development of moral concepts because of its focus on the kinds of routine social encounters that lead the child to construct rules and standards. However, on the basis of material on Kenyan children, I claim that the distinction between moral and conventional transgressions may not be as distinct as Turiel implies. The social encounters surrounding the rules may not be observably different, at least in some cultural communities.

It is clear that young Kenyan children around the age of two or three have already begun to "enforce" many kinds of rules by making prosocial suggestions and by complying more readily when provided explanations. Why do they show as strong a commitment to rules delineating social roles and proper social behavior as to rules concerning justice, aggression, and care of others?

I would claim that it is a matter of the salience of the social benefits connected to cooperation with the rules. The "good purposes" or "reasons for" many kinds of rules can be made comprehensible to young children. Just as a child who receives a hit or kick can directly experience the purpose of rules prohibiting aggression, so too a child who experiences a delay in her supper because her older sibling did not collect the firewood can see for herself the "inherent rightness" of rules about obedience to parents. Similarly, just as a child who cares for an infant can apprehend the purpose of moral rules prescribing nurturance, so too a child who tries to control an unruly, unhygienic, and unmannerly toddler can construct the inherent need for cleanliness and etiquette standards. I claim that Oyugis children do not see one type of rule as more "necessary" than the other. The logical rationales for the existence of both types are clear and obvious, even to

young children. Oyugis parents do not need to preach to children
about the rationales underlying any of these rules because the routines of children's lives amply contain the evidence.

It is interesting to note that Chinese children also seem to differ
from Americans in their commitment to "conventional" rules. Navon and Ramsey (in preparation) have recently described the behavior
of preschool children observed in eight preschools in the city of
Nankung. A comparison of the Chinese data to American observations suggests that the Chinese and American children differ in the
readiness with which they defend their rights to property. The Chinese children were less likely than the Americans to react when a
peer removed an object from their work space, and they allowed
building materials to flow more freely from child to child around the
play table. In addition, the Chinese and American children differed in
their commitment to the social conventions regarding "clean-up
time." The Chinese children, but not the Americans, cleaned up ea-
gerly and even fought with others to get access to the job of putting
away materials at the end of the play period. The Chinese teachers
were observed to intervene and to treat seriously children's disputes
regarding clean-up but to simply "laugh off" and disregard children's
disputes about rights to toys.

**The Emergence of Moral Standards in a Toddler Classroom in
Poughkeepsie, New York**

In order to put the Oyugis material into comparative perspective, I
have performed a similar kind of ethnographic analysis of a corpus of
observational material that I collected at the Vassar College Nursery
School in the spring of 1975.[4] Again, there are two main questions: (1)
Are sharp distinctions necessarily made between moral and conventional transgression-situations? (2) Do young children show a
stronger and earlier commitment to "moral" than to "conventional"
rules? While the answer to these questions was "no" for the Oyugis
material, it might be expected to be "yes" for this U.S. material, given
the previous empirical findings of Turiel, Nucci, and Smetana.

I observed a group of four two-year-olds and their teacher in an
"experimental" classroom (toddler classrooms being very unusual
then) that met twice a week for a ninety-minute period. A parent

4. I wish to thank the former director (Dorothy Levens), staff, parents, and
children of the Vassar College Nursery School for allowing and encouraging me to
conduct these observations. (The names of the four Vassar children have been
changed here.)

(usually but not always the mother) remained present. The parents typically sat together and chatted while the children participated in the activities. Children and parents did interact, but for the purposes of this analysis I have excluced social interactions involving parents.

At the time that I collected these observations I was fresh from fieldwork in Kenya. I remember thinking how uninteresting the Vassar observations were. Nothing ever seemed to happen; there were no aggressive conflicts between children, no disciplinary actions by teachers, no rules stated, no arguments by children. I put them away in a drawer for nine years.

Now, knowing a good deal more about early childhood education, I look at the material from a more informed perspective. I can now see that the teacher, though young, was experienced and skillful according to the cultural standards of her reference group, professional early-childhood educators. She had planned the environment and activities with specific goals in mind. She wished to minimize the possibility of "time-wasting" conflicts arising between children and maximize the time spent by each child in "purposeful," self-initiated, and self-directed activity. She knew how to get the children to do what she wanted by means of requests and invitations. She never used reprimands, rule-statements, strong commands, or sanctions.

While there are few "transgression" situations, that is, situations of accountability containing an accusation or an account, we can nevertheless see the emergence of value concepts in the children and relate these processes to adult behavior. The analysis is based on sixty-eight "moral episodes" excerpted from the observations. As with the Oyugis material, each episode contains either a moral transgression or an "opportunity."

The sixty-eight episodes (see table 3.1 below) were coded according to the type of teacher response. Typically the teacher exerted what educators call "positive guidance" and maintained a smooth, conflict-free flow of activity by (a) suggesting or inviting a desired action. Occasionally, she (b) interrupted an undesired action, usually by suggesting a positive alternative. Sometimes, she (c) simply noticed and/or praised a spontaneous occurrence of a desired behavior. Finally, in some cases, she (d) allowed undesired behaviors to continue or to be corrected by the children themselves.

The episodes were further coded according to the norm at issue. Like Turiel and colleagues, I found, first, that the "justice/harm/welfare" cluster is strongly enforced in the classroom setting (twenty episodes). In this classroom, this cluster of values could be accurately summed up by the following principle: "Don't interfere with someone else's activities, but do facilitate the sharing of food, space, and other resources."

The second norm enforced is one that is not even mentioned by Turiel and colleagues as either a moral value or a convention. That omission is odd, because the "work ethic" is a central moral value in North America, deeply embedded in the goals of industry, science, and technology (Vogt and Albert 1966). In the case of the preschool classroom, where "play is the business of childhood," the work ethic assumes concrete form as "Keep busy, be purposeful" (eleven episodes), and "Do as much as you can for yourself, without teacher assistance" (seven episodes).

Finally, two types of "conventional" values are enforced: "Follow the routine schedule of the day" (twenty-one episodes), and "Keep the classroom neat and orderly" (nine episodes). No other major type of moral or conventional rule was enforced in this classroom.

## Justice/Rights/Welfare Encounters

Turiel and colleagues have theorized that knowledge of moral values surrounding justice, harm, and the welfare of others is constructed by children on the basis of social encounters in which they themselves can see the intrinsic consequences of transgression.

The teacher at the Vassar Nursery School directed her behavior with children as if she shared the same theory about child development. She deemphasized sanctions (and never threatened or punished by means of ridicule, anger, deprivation of privileges). Instead, she sometimes allowed the children to explore the negative consequences of transgression (such as making someone else cry) and sometimes suggested an alternative way to solve the problem (such as finding another toy to use). When a child sought praise or information about his actions, the teacher described and evaluated any "correct" action of the child. Here is an episode that illustrates these processes.

> *(Example 1)*
> *The children are doing water play. Katie tries to take the bottle that Jimmy is using.*
> **Jimmy:** No. *He begins to cry.*
> **Katie:** I want dat! *The teacher now hands her a similar bottle which she accepts.*
> *A moment later, Katie points to the cup that Jimmy is now using and which she was using before.*
> **Katie:** I want dat!

**Teacher** *(calmly):* Go get another one. *Katie runs to nearby cabinet and gets a cup. She plays for a long time pouring water from a teapot over and over into the cup.*
**Jimmy** *(pointing to teapot):* I want dat! *Katie allows Jimmy to take it.*
**Katie** *(to teacher):* I give that to Jimmy.
**Teacher:** Yes, you gave that teapot to Jimmy. That was nice of you.

Here are two other episodes in which the teacher guided the children through concrete experiences of moral behavior ("asking, not grabbing," and "sharing resources").

*(Example 2)*
*At the water table on another day, Katie grabs for her doll, lying next to Jimmy's hand.*
**Teacher:** Can you ask Jimmy to give you your baby?
**Katie:** Jimmy, can I have the baby? *Jimmy hands her the doll.*
**Teacher:** Thank you, Jimmy. *She looks meaningfully at Katie as if expecting Katie to imitate.*
**Teacher** *(repeats):* Thank you, Jimmy. *Katie still ignores.*

*(Example 3)*
*Jimmy walks around the snack table carrying the bowl full of pretzels. He eats one.*
**Teacher:** Pass them.
*Jimmy gives a piece to Nina.*

In none of these episodes do we see the teacher making a general rule-statement, such as, "It's good to share," or "It's wrong to grab." Such abstractions are probably too complex to be processed as useful information by young two-year-olds. Instead the teacher focuses on concrete acts and their consequences. (These consequences presumably *could* have included sanctions, as in Oyugis, but did not at Vassar because they were considered "unprofessional" teacher behavior.)

## The Work Ethic

The work ethic was not explicitly preached to the children at Vassar but instead was implicit in the carefully planned environment, an example of Whiting, Chasdi, Antonovsky, and Ayres's (1966, 83) central principle: "Certain aspects of the child rearing process seem to have the effect of, if not creating, at least strengthening values far beyond the conscious intents of the agents of socialization."

The Vassar nursery classroom elicited purposeful play with its attractive and careful arrangement of materials. This environment provided the necessary backdrop for the explicit teacher interventions designed to foster the children's version of "hard work," namely, busy, purposeful play.

Eighteen episodes (see table 3.1) were found in which a teacher fostered hard work. She never reprimanded a child for not keeping busy, for seeking help, or for quitting a project. However, she did initiate desired actions, and she described and praised hard work and independent effort. She did not state values in the form of rules; rather, she offered concrete choices and described and praised the children's actions in words. In general, she sought to help children experience the intrinsic, desirable consequences of the prescribed behavior in a way that probably helped them to construct for themselves the rationale underlying the work ethic, namely, that it leads to culturally defined "competence."

*(Example 4)*
*Nina takes a set of fitting boxes off the shelf and dumps them out.*
    *She struggles to put a few of them back together, then shows*
    *what she has done to the teacher.*
*The teacher congratulates her greatly.*

*(Example 5)*
*Jimmy walks toward the sandbox carrying two pots for the play*
    *shed.*
**Teacher:** Can you climb in, Jimmy? *Jimmy does so.*
**Teacher:** You climbed in all by yourself.

*(Example 6)*
*William enters the classroom and takes off his coat with help of*
    *teacher.*
**Teacher:** Do you want to paint?
**William:** Yes. *She puts a bib on him.*
**Teacher:** Wanna paint with blue paint?
**William:** Yes. *She hands him a brush.*
*Fifteen minutes later, William is still working on his picture.*
**Teacher:** See what William's making. Wow. It's all with blue. *She*
    *comes over and studies his painting intently. William*
    *continues to paint.*
*After another fifteen minutes, William is still working at the easel.*
**Teacher:** You've really worked on this picture, William. *William*
    *now paints with great energy.*

**Table 3.1** Classification of 67 Moral Episodes (Poughkeepsie, New York) (Observations Conducted at Vassar College Two-year-old Program)

| Type of Rule/Norm at Issue | Number of Episodes | Teacher Initiates Correct Action | Teacher Interrupts Incorrect Action Suggests Alternative | Child Complies Immediately with Teacher Suggestion | Teacher Notices, Praises Correct Action | Teacher Allows Incorrect Act to Self-Correct or Continue |
|---|---|---|---|---|---|---|
| *Justice/Rights/Welfare* | | | | | | |
| Don't interfere with others' activities; do facilitate sharing of food, space, materials | 20 | 8 (40%) | 6 (30%) | 10 (67%) | 1 (5%) | 5 (25%) |
| *Work Ethic* | | | | | | |
| Keep busy, be purposeful | 11 | 4 (36) | 0 | 4 (100) | 7 (64) | 0 |
| Do as much as possible for yourself | 7 | 5 (71) | 0 | 5 (100) | 2 (29) | 0* |
| *Conventions* | | | | | | |
| Children should follow schedule of day, including appropriate dress | 21 | 15 (67) | 4 (19) | 15 (79) | 1 (10) | 1 (5) |
| Children should help keep the classroom neat and orderly | 9 | 5 (56) | 1 (11) | 3 (50) | 1 (11) | 2 (40) |

*In fact, parents did often help children with things they could probably have done themselves. However, because parent interactions were excluded from this analysis, they are not counted here.

## Conventional Rules: The Schedule

In the Vassar classroom, as in most American preschools, the day follows a set routine, including the wearing of appropriate dress for specific activities such as messy art work or outdoor play. These rules, regulating the children's and teacher's behavior, can be considered as partly moral (instead of purely "conventional") because the rules are intended to serve the welfare of the children as much as the convenience of the teachers. Predictability and order are thought by teachers to reduce young children's separation anxiety and free their energies for purposeful activity.

There were twenty-one episodes in which the Vassar teacher enforced the specific rules related to her schedule. As with the other values, however, she avoided sanctions, strong commands, and rule-statements. Instead she invited or requested children to perform the desired action. This behavior probably encouraged them to feel that they were "choosing" the desired act and focused their attention on the rewarding consequences of moving along into the next activity. Thus, as with other important values, the teacher fostered social encounters that allowed children to focus on the "inherent" consequences, that is, the rationale underlying the rules. Here are some typical examples:

> *(Example 7)*
> **Teacher:** Shall we start cleaning up for snack? *Katie ignores and keeps on doing waterplay.*
> **Teacher** *(looking meaningfully at the water tray):* There's a lot of water in there.
> **Katie:** I all done. *She allows teacher to remove bib. Then she plays with a ball and studies the gerbil in its cage.*
> **Teacher:** Katie. *Pause.* Katie. *Pause.* Katie. *Pause. Katie looks up.*
> **Teacher:** Will you put the pegboard away? *Katie comes over and gets it. She walks with it around the room, eventually putting it on the shelf.*
> **Teacher:** That's right. *Katie comes to the table and is immediately given food and drink.*

> *(Example 8)*
> *The children are washing down the table for snack.*
> **Teacher:** We're through wiping now.
> *The children run to the refrigerator and each is given something to carry to the table.*

## Conventional Rules: Neatness and Order

Finally, the Vassar teacher apparently felt it was within her moral authority to enforce norms related to the order and cleanliness of the environment. Several episodes showed that she was not concerned with children keeping themselves clean while playing or eating, but she did encourage them to put toys back after playing with them, to avoid spills, to pick up food dropped on the floor, and the like. The order and neatness of the classroom are seen by professionally trained teachers as necessary to help children focus their attention—to prevent them from becoming distracted and to help them see the materials and choices available.

Her manner of "teaching" of these norms was consistent with her approach to the other norms. She generally modeled and invited the desired action, and described and praised cooperative responses. In the case of episode 13 below, she used humor to divert the child from completing an undesirable act: she "suggested" a ridiculous alternative behavior.

*(Example 9)*
*Nina drops playdough on the floor.*
**Teacher:** Can you pick it up?
*Nina ignores and goes off.*

*(Example 10)*
*During snack, Katie spills her juice.*
**Teacher:** Oopsy. *Teacher starts to wipe it up, but William darts over and does it.*

*(Example 11)*
*Nina sits on teacher's lap pretending to "read" a book. Finished, she drops it on the floor.*
**Teacher:** Can you put it back on the shelf.
*Nina ignores and goes off.*

*(Example 12)*
*Jimmy plays with a truck, then pushes it aside.*
**Teacher:** Shall we put this one back on the shelf? *Jimmy nods, watches her do it.*
**Teacher:** Which one do you want now?
**Jimmy:** Dat! *He takes blocks off the shelf.*

*(Example 13)*
*William playfully goes toward his teacher holding out a paint brush, full of blue paint. He tries to paint her, but she laughs and tells him to paint me (the observer). He heads toward me.*
**I:** Paint my paper.
**William:** Yeah. *He paints blue on my notes.*

Summary of Findings on Poughkeepsie Children

The Vassar toddler observations echo the Oyugis observations in two key ways. First, they suggest that young children show an emerging sensitivity and commitment to adult standards. In the Vassar material, this commitment is evidenced by the children's ready cooperation with teacher suggestions. They seem compliant with suggestions related to all four value norms (see table 3.1). The numbers involved are small but suggest that the two-year-olds complied most readily with prosocial suggestions related to "keeping busy" and "following the schedule." They appear to have had more trouble adhering to norms related to "justice/harm/welfare" and "mess/disorder."

Second, the observations suggest the strong role of culture in determining a patterned approach by authority figures to moral transgression and "opportunity" situations. The teacher in the Vassar classroom showed a consistent way of providing guidance related to all four moral/conventional norms. Supportive of a larger goal of promoting rational, autonomous, moral problem solving, she deemphasized sanctions and her authority role. Instead, she emphasized the rationale or underlying "purpose" for each type of value norm.

## Conclusion

The findings suggest that there are fundamental cultural differences in the organization of social encounters surrounding rules and their transgression. In some cultural (or subcultural) communities, adults sharply distinguish justice/harm/welfare rules from "conventional" regulations. The American settings studied by Turiel, Nucci, and Smetana seem to present examples. In other communities adults do not divide the central rules into separate domains and do not treat encounters surrounding them differently. Such a pattern was found for the Oyugis, Kenya community and, in a different way, for the model toddler classroom of Poughkeepsie, New York. The findings suggest that it is the learning environment (culturally variable), not the child, that subdivides morality into separate domains, such as "morality proper" versus "other conventions." It is the culture, not the child, that decides what normative and regulatory rules and standards are most important, necessary for social life, and obligatory.

We should not abandon our search for fundamental differences in the way that moral motivation is activated and maintained (B. Whiting 1950; J. Whiting 1967). Cultural groups do differentially employ such techniques of persuasion as sanctions, reasoning, teasing, and shaming, perhaps thereby creating children "committed" to morality for different conscious and unconscious reasons.

These findings do not indicate that moral knowledge is entirely "culturally transmitted." Quite the contrary. Both sets of observations reveal young children to be rational beings—active moral reasoners—fully engaged with the people around them in trying to understand what is right and wrong. Their cooperation and noncooperation, their questions and arguments, their attempts to persuade and willingness to "do battle" to enforce the rules, suggest that young children are not passive receivers of adult wisdom. Children do not simply "receive" knowledge of standards, nor do they autonomously "construct" it without cultural assistance. Rather they "reconstruct" or "re-create" culturally appropriate moral meaning systems. That is, with increasing age and experience, children apply progressively more complex and mobile logical schemas to cultural distinctions and categories; they transform what they are told and what they experience into their own self-organized realities. These realities are idiosyncratic to each individual child and yet bear witness to extensive cross-cultural commonalities in early moral reasoning (Miller 1986). Although self-construction and social transmission seem to be opposed and incompatible theories about development, they must be coexistent, complementary empirical processes. Development involves and requires both processes at every level, and researchers must appreciate both simultaneously rather than habitually focusing on only one of them and ignoring the other.

# References

Bookman, A., and C. Ember. In press. *Luo Child and Family Life.* New Haven, Conn.: Human Relations Area Files.

Brandt, R. B. 1954. *Hopi Ethics.* Chicago: University of Chicago Press.

Briggs, J. L. 1979. *Aspects of Inuit Value Socialization.* Ottawa: National Museum of Canada, Canadian Ethnology Service, paper no. 56.

Edwards, C. P. 1986. Another Style of Competence: The Caregiving Child. In A. D. Fogel and G. F. Melson, eds., *Origins of Nurturance.* New York: Erlbaum.

Edwards, C. P., and B. B. Whiting. 1980. Differential Socialization of Girls and Boys in the Light of Cross-cultural Research. In C. M. Super and S. Harkness, eds., *Anthropological Perspectives on Child Development.* New Directions for Child Development, no. 8. San Francisco: Jossey-Bass.

Ember, C. R. 1973. Feminine Task Assignment and Social Behavior of Boys. *Ethos* 1:424–39.

Frankena, W. K. 1963. *Ethics.* Englewood Cliffs, N.J.: Prentice-Hall.

Hoffman, M. L. 1983. Empathy, its Limitations, and its Role in a Comprehensive Moral Theory. In W. M. Kurtines and J. L. Gewirtz, eds., *Morality, Moral Behavior, and Moral Development.* New York: John
Wiley.

Kagan, J. 1981. *The Second Year: The Emergence of Self-Awareness.* Cambridge, Mass.: Harvard University Press.

Ladd, J. 1957. *The Structure of a Moral Code.* Cambridge, Mass.: Harvard
University Press.

LeVine, R. A. 1973. Patterns of Personality in Africa. *Ethos* 1:123–52.

Miller, J. 1986. Early Cross-cultural Commonalities in Social Explanation.
*Developmental Psychology* 22:514–20.

Much, N., and R. A. Shweder. 1978. Speaking of Rules: The Analysis of
Culture in Breach. In W. Damon, ed., *Moral Development.* New Directions for Child Development, vol. 2. San Francisco: Jossey-Bass.

Navon, R., and P. G. Ramsey. In preparation. A Comparison of Chinese
and American Children's Possession and Exchange of Materials. University of Massachusetts—Amherst.

Nucci, L. P. 1982. Conceptual Development in the Moral and
Conventional Domains: Implications for Value Education. *Review of
Educational Research* 52:93–122.

Nucci, L., and E. Turiel. 1978. Social Interactions and the Development of
Social Concepts in Preschool Children. *Child Development*
49:400–407.

Nucci, L., E. Turiel, and G. Encarnacion-Gawrych. 1983. Children's Social
Interactions and Social Concepts: Analyses of Morality and Convention in the Virgin Islands. *Journal of Cross-Cultural Psychology*
14:469–87.

Shweder, R. A. 1982. Beyond Self-constructed Knowledge: The Study of
Culture and Morality. *Merrill-Palmer Quarterly* 28:41–69.

Smetana, J. G. 1983. Social-Cognitive Development: Domain Distinctions
and Coordinations. *Developmental Review* 3:131–47.

_____. 1984. Toddlers' Social Interactions Regarding Moral and Conven-
tional Transgressions. *Child Development* 55:1767–76.

Turiel, E. 1983. *The Development of Social Knowledge: Morality and Convention.* Cambridge: Cambridge University Press.

Turiel, E., and P. Davidson. 1986. Heterogeneity, Inconsistency and Asynchrony in the Development of Cognitive Structures. In I. Levin, ed.,
*Stage and Structure.* Norwood, N.J.: Ablex.

Turiel, E., and J. G. Smetana. 1983. Social Knowledge and Action: The Co-
ordination of Domains. In W. M. Kurtines and J. L. Gewirtz, eds.,
*Morality, Moral Behavior, and Moral Development.* New York: John
Wiley.

Vogt, E. Z., and E. M. Albert. 1966. *People of Rimrock: A Study of Values
in Five Cultures.* Cambridge, Mass.: Harvard University Press.

Wenger, M. 1983. Gender Role Socialization in an East African Community: Social Interaction between 2–3-Year-Olds and Older Children in Social Ecological Perspective. Ed.D. diss., Harvard University.

Whiting, B. B. 1950. *Paiute Sorcery.* New York: Viking Fund Publications in Anthropology, no. 15. (Johnson Reprint Corporation, 1971).

———. 1980. Culture and Social Behavior: A Model for the Development of Social Behavior. *Ethos* 2:95–116.

———. 1983. The Genesis of Prosocial Behavior. In D. Bridgeman, ed., *The Nature of Prosocial Development: Interdisciplinary Theories and Strategies.* New York: Academic Press.

Whiting, B. B., and C. P. Edwards. 1988. *Children of Different Worlds: The Formation of Social Behavior.* Cambridge, Mass.: Harvard University Press.

Whiting, J. W. M. 1967. Sorcery, Sin, and the Superego: A Cross-cultural Study of Some Mechanisms of Social Control. In C. S. Ford, ed., *Cross-Cultural Approaches: Readings in Comparative Research.* New Haven, Conn.: Human Relations Area Files Press.

Whiting, J. W. M., E. H. Chasdi, H. F. Antonovsky, and B. C. Ayres. 1966. The Learning of Values. In E. Z. Vogt and E. M. Albert, eds., *People of Rimrock: A Study of Values in Five Cultures.* Cambridge, Mass.: Harvard University Press.

# Comment
## Alternative Approaches to Moral Socialization
*Edward Mueller*

This chapter is filled with rich and provocative detail on transgression-sanction encounters among the Luo children of Kenya and American toddlers. The cultural differences reported ring true and add significant and interesting detail to our discussions of moral development. However, Carolyn Pope Edwards's interpretation of the moral socialization process could profit from amplification.

First, Edwards considers only two of the possible theoretical origins of morality—cultural transmission and self-construction—and implies that they are exhaustive. Second, although the evidence presented is interpreted as supporting cultural transmission, a self-construction model is retained but its status is left in doubt. Finally, the chapter could profit from additional justification for using transgression-sanction encounters as the primary basis for inferences about moral development.

I will now consider each of these points and then introduce a different view on cultural transmission. The chapter should not oppose the viewpoints of those who favor cultural transmission, like Whiting and Quine, to those who favor cognitive construction, like Kohlberg and Turiel, as if they were the only two possibilities. The contemporary followers of Hume, among them Kagan and Campos, believe that much of principled morality rests on the generation of emotions that are biologically prepared reactions to violations of standards. The role of emotion is absent both from cultural transmission and cognitive construction models.

The chapter does not indicate how cultural transmission and self-construction processes might be integrated. At the beginning, the two models are opposed. Edwards asks whether morality is culturally transmitted by "authority figures" who scaffold routine events so that their moral meaning is understood, or whether morality is a species-general, inevitable product of general cognitive growth and universal social experience. Later, Edwards interprets her data as supporting social transmission—in the sense of cultural scaffolding—although on the last page she implies that elements of self-construction are also present because children interpret socialization models with their own "mobile logical schemes." This conclusion leaves the reader unsure how to integrate the two points of view. Perhaps what is crucial in model development is the child's recreation of culture in "self-organized realities." Such a conclusion points directly to self-construction.

A third problem is that the Luo observations were limited to situations broadly classifiable as "transgression-sanction" encounters. A child does or does not do something that is ordered or requested by an older child or adult. The latter then teaches, admonishes, or punishes the younger child. One mother responded to her three-year-old son's wish to hit his infant brother with the admonition, "Never do it, father." Among the Luo this response flatters the child by implying that he is too mature to strike a helpless infant. Yet, one can not imagine an American mother addressing her three-year-old son this way.

If we assume that most of the transgression instances cited relate to moral standards, it is unclear whether the young child is acquiring such standards in these encounters and if so how. The most familiar version of cultural transmission is a social reinforcement model. It states that transgression-sanction encounters are social reinforcement trials, where children are punished for moral mistakes and directly tutored in the right thing to do. Edwards sees the adult's role in socialization as one of "structuring routine event," like the interactive scaffolding approach derived from Vygotsky rather than the direct reinforcement approach. But at the same time it is easy to equate her operational choice of transgression encounters with a punishment-teaching model.

I believe it is useful to consider a different view of cultural transmission in which transgressions play a different role. I suggest that learning standards is more often a consequence of identification with others, especially emotionally significant authority figures and friends, than it is the result of scaffolding or reward and punishment. Although this view is sympathetic to the role of culture, it holds that observers can not literally "see" moral development in concrete social interactions because the child's identifications are abstract representations and internal constructs.

Morality is self-constructed through culture but not through casual, public encounters. Many developmental psychologists believe that in order to understand the growing child we must understand these inner models of the self and of significant others (Bretherton, in press). While the existence of such models is universal, the content learned is culturally specific and dependent on the actual values of the particular persons to whom children are emotionally attached.

Edwards uses transgression-sanction encounters as index of a culture's moral commitments. American children are often corrected for their transgressions over turn-taking, sharing, and fairness because Americans care about these behaviors. By contrast, the Luo sanction behavior surrounding obedience to authority and division of tasks because those are their areas of daily concern. Thus, in my view, sanctions from others reflect those standards that a society is having difficulty socializing. If a moral standard is completely internalized and generates no ambivalence, it will not be sanctioned because children will rarely violate it. American teachers must say repeatedly, "Children you must share," because America is a culture whose values and economy promote acquisitiveness and competition rather than sharing and cooperation. Americans view peers as agents against whom one will ultimately compete. American parents tell their children they should share, while they promote self-interest with greater intensity. The American child, sensing the contradiction, tests the moral limits for the weaker standard on sharing.

By contrast, among the Luo, useful, friendly work relations among children are a central part of daily life, and personal property is less important. Thus, sharing between children is well socialized and few transgressions are observed. However, the necessities of a manual labor economy dictate a different dilemma in peer relations among the Luo. Children who direct younger ones in the completion of daily chores may be in conflict as to whether peer interaction should be essentially egalitarian play relations or authority work relations. The younger child involved in such interactions, perhaps seeking clarity on this theme, does not always submit willingly to being ordered about by the older child. Thus, transgressions occur and threats and punishments become necessary.

In one Luo protocol (no. 29, p. 136), the child would rather play than go home as ordered to find out whether or not the chickens are eating the corn that was put out to dry. The child's older sister, lacking the pure authority of a parent, resorts to the threat of a caning, but that threat receives only partial compliance.

In sum, I suggest that transgression encounters are a good index of a culture's socialization problems, the standards over which there is ambivalence, rather than of the deepest standards that have pure acceptance. Thus, we do learn something about a culture's economic necessities and their relation to standards when we code transgressions and sanctions, but we learn less about how a culture's deepest standards are acquired. We can now see why the African mother addresses her three-year-old son as "father." On the one hand it affirms the important identification with the father that developmental theory claims is emerging at this time; on the other, it reaffirms symbolically where ultimate authority rests. In this frame the American mother might be expected to address her young son as friend. We are indebted to Carolyn Edwards for providing such rich detail and a perspective that is necessary if we are to gain insights into the growth of a child's morality.

## References

Bretherton, I. In press. New Perspectives on Attachment Relations in Infancy: Security, Communication and Internal Working Models. In J. Osofsky, ed., *Handbook of Infant Development.* 2d ed. New York: John Wiley.

# Morality: Its Structure, Functions, and Vagaries

*Elliot Turiel, Melanie Killen, and Charles C. Helwig*

Leo Lowenthal, sociologist, proponent of critical theory, and sole sur-
vivor of the Frankfurt School originated at the Institute of Social Research in pre-Nazi Germany, recently asserted that "relativism has
always been the enemy of political progressive movements—political
in the widest sense of the word. Don't forget it was Mussolini who
said, 'I am a relativist.' "[1] At the age of eighty, Lowenthal is concerned that contemporary university students maintain a utopian
spark and not surrender to the "spirit of relativism."

The issue of relativism has been of intense concern and debate
among students of morality for a long time. Many influential philosophers advocate nonrelativistic positions (e.g., Brandt 1959; Dworkin
1978, 1983; Frankena 1963; Fried 1978; Gewirth 1978; Nagel 1970,
1982; Rawls 1971; Scheffler 1982, 1984). In contrast to them and to
Lowenthal, who views relativism as the enemy of progressive political movements, social scientists have often associated relativism

We wish to thank Carolyn Hildebrandt, Jerome Kagan, Peter Kahn, Marta Laupa, Larry
Nucci and Richard Shweder for their comments on an earlier draft of this chapter. The
preparation of the chapter was supported by Spencer Foundation Funds, provided by
Bernard R. Gifford, Dean of the School of Education at the University of California,
Berkeley.

1. Reported in an interview by Martin Jay in *California Monthly*, December,
1984.

with tolerance, freedom, and antiimperialism (Hatch, 1983; Wester-marck 1932). Relativism is dominant particularly among anthropol-ogists and sociologists because it supports their perspective that the learning of standards, patterns, frames, scripts, or practices of one's society or culture is the primary basis for moral values, cognitive schemes, and social behaviors. There are other reasons for its domi-nance in social scientific circles. (For an excellent review see Hatch's [1983] treatise on *Culture and Morality*.) These include biases favor-ing behaviorism, the malleability of persons, top-down explanations that render the group, culture, and society as entities that dominate individual psychology, and a minimal role for thought or rationality in social realms.

The issue of moral relativism has been anything but in equilib-rium in social scientific thought. It has been and remains a persistent source of critical analysis, controversy, and contradiction. For exam-ple, during the relativistic heyday of cultural anthropology (e.g., Be-nedict 1934; Boas 1938, and Herskovits 1947, as cited in Hatch 1983), the shortcomings of relativism were cogently and insightfully noted by the Gestaltists (e.g., Asch 1952; Duncker 1939; Wertheimer 1935). Nor did relativism come without its ambiguities and internal contra-dictions. One particular contradiction was that relativistic views were often motivated by (nonrelativistic) moral concerns of tolerance for other groups and equality in the status of varying cultural sys-tems. As noted by Hatch (1983, 64), the relativism of early twentieth-century cultural anthropologists "contains a more or less implicit value judgment in its call for tolerance; it asserts that we *ought* to respect other ways of life."

Westermarck's (1912) treatise on relativism illustrated these in-ternal contradictions. He argued for relativism on the grounds that because moral concepts are based on emotions, which are subjective, they lie outside the categories of truth or objectivity. Yet, in defend-ing against the charge that ethical relativism and subjectivism is "a dangerous doctrine, destructive to morality, opening the doors to all sorts of libertinism," Westermarck asserted that

> ethical subjectivism seems to me more likely to be an acquisition for moral practice. Could it be brought home to people that there is no ab-solute standard in morality, they would perhaps be somewhat *more tol-erant in their judgments*, and more apt to listen to the voice of *reason*. . . . We have, indeed, no reason to regret that there are men who rebel against the established rules of morality; it is more deplorable that the rebels are so few, and that, consequently, the old rules change so slowly. Far above the vulgar idea that the right is a settled something to which everybody has to adjust his opinions, rises the conviction that it

has its existence in each individual mind, capable of any expansion, proclaiming its own right to exist, and, if need be, venturing to make a stand against the whole world. Such a conviction makes for *progress*. (19–20, emphasis added)

Westermarck's defense of relativism paradoxically includes a call for adherence to the value of tolerance and invokes reason and progress.

Beyond these seemingly nonrelativistic moral arguments advocating relativism,[2] there exists what some consider the compelling empirical basis of variations in moral practices supporting the idea of relativism. Variations in behaviors, attitudes and social practices are taken as direct evidence of moral relativism and a reflection of the societal determination of individual socialization (with social transmission as the mechanism for development). As extensively discussed elsewhere (Asch 1952; Duncker 1939; Hatch 1983; Schmidt 1955; Spiro 1984, 1986; Wertheimer 1935), however, variations in social practices should neither be taken as "proof" of relativism nor automatically translated into an explanatory mechanism (transmission and incorporation) for moral acquisition. Findings of variations constitute data requiring explanation of the nature and sources of social behaviors.

In this chapter, it is not our aim to deal with the issue of relativism directly but to consider antecedent questions regarding possible sources of variations in social behaviors and practices. The starting point of our discussion is the proposition that variations in social judgments and practices are not solely determined by societal differences; they exist within societies and, moreover, within individuals. First, we discuss data pertaining to this proposition and ways of explaining the bases for variations of social judgments and behaviors in our society. Then we consider possible explanations of cross-cultural variations and commonalities in social practices. This is followed by discussion of the relation of variations to explanations of processes of

2. Debates over relativism, situational specificity, absolutism, and universalism have been highly tinged with accusations and counteraccusations essentially based on moral positions. For example, the relativism of the cultural anthropologists was in part a reaction to earlier orderings of (one's own) Western culture as superior or more advanced than other cultures. Relativistic anthropologists found fault with the implication of inequality inherent in such a position and with its justification of external impositions to "improve" cultures deemed inferior or less advanced. Moral relativism, in turn, has been criticized for its ostensible acceptance of any social practice, conservation of the status quo, and the failure to recognize its own moral positions of tolerance and freedom. Clearly, value-laden moral considerations underlie *all sides* of the debate.

development. We consider the role of varying types of early childhood experiences in the development of social judgments and actions.

It should be stated at the outset that we do not question that variations in social practices exist. In fact, it is not difficult to list empirical observations of such variations. The most dramatic and frequently cited examples pertain to fundamental issues of physical harm and survival. For instance, variations exist in cultural practices regarding the taking of life. Infanticide is practiced in some societies; in others it is the practice to kill or allow one's elderly parents to die. Variations are also evident regarding issues of freedom and equality. Whereas some societies may place emphasis on equality, others are hierarchically structured with rigid differentiations in castes, social classes, or racial groups. Further examples are evident in the sacredness attached to cultural and religious practices. Attitudes toward sexual activities also vary, especially concerning premarital sex and homosexuality.

Variation is found within societies as well. In our own culture there is much heated disagreement over issues like premarital sex, homosexuality, and abortion. Variation is apparent even with regard to physical harm. In most places there are exceptions to the prohibition against inflicting physical harm, such as self-defense or war. Moreover, there are striking historical examples of seeming heterogeneity within Western culture. In the not too distant past, slavery was practiced and the lynching of blacks was acceptable in certain regions of the United States. At around the time of World War II, Nazi society accepted the premise of racial superiority and the value of annihilating the Jewish race. Apartheid is currently practiced in South Africa.

As already noted, observations of variations in social practices, in themselves, do not provide an explanation of social behaviors. In our view, variations can stem from a number of sources, including nonmoral social realms and the ways conflicting goals are resolved. Variations may also stem from the ways in which moral prescriptions are applied in different settings. This suggests that societies and their individual members cannot be characterized through the template of a general, homogeneous, or even predominant orientation. In such a case, it would be necessary to examine possible distinctions in types of social judgments and behaviors, and to determine the extent to which variations exist within and between individuals. In particular, it is essential to conduct *comparative* analyses of different components of the individual's judgments and actions, accounting for different domains of social reasoning, including concepts of morality, societal organization, religious systems, and judgments about individual or personal jurisdiction. Furthermore, analyses of social judgments should account for the assumptions individuals make about the universe; that is, their premises about biological, psychological, natural, and supernatural phenomena. There is also need to examine the role of coordination and conflicts among different types of social considerations—moral and nonmoral—in social decisions.

We are arguing for an expanded view of social domains, based on the proposition that there is typically heterogeneity in the social behaviors of individuals stemming from the *coexistence* of different social orientations, motivations, and goals. It is our assumption, therefore, that variations in social behaviors exist to an even greater extent than generally assumed in discussions of cross-cultural variability. Moreover, this proposition has implications for explaining development. One implication is that there is not a unitary experiential source of acquisition and change in children's social development. Different types of social experiences must be accounted for in explanations of social development; it is not solely a top-down process of society to adult (older person, authority) to child.

## The Coexistence of Social Orientations

Insofar as general templates are used to characterize and contrast given cultures or societies, they sometimes vary from one researcher to another. One familiar scheme for distinguishing among social-moral systems, including the orientations acquired by individuals in those systems, is the dichotomy between collectivistic and individualistic orientations (Hogan 1973; Hogan, Johnson, and Emler 1978; Sampson 1977). Our own culture is often characterized as primarily oriented to individualism, emphasizing personal liberties and rights of citizens. Various public sources for this characterization can be found. For example, the U.S. Constitution stresses individual liberties and rights and there is public concern (in the courts, legislatures, and the media) with independence, self-determination, and autonomy. Furthermore, successful adaptation to the capitalist economic system requires at least some measure of competitiveness and individual initiative.

These facts, however, do not necessarily mean that members of the society can be characterized as oriented to individualism. The content of official documents or public statements may not reflect individual members' attitudes and behaviors. In addition to official and public pronouncements (which themselves may not be of one kind), there are other influences upon individuals, including the specific, concrete interactions and conflicts of everyday experience. Moreover,

individuals may interpret and transform the messages contained
within official and public doctrines.

Data of adequate scope from developmental or social psychology
are difficult to come by and rarely used to support propositions of predominant social orientations. Survey research, though often lacking
the desired depth of cognitive analyses, does provide findings with
some scope. A set of striking and particularly informative findings are
available from recent (late 1970s) large-scale surveys of attitudes
toward civil liberties (McClosky and Brill 1983). Using national cross-
sectional samples of the general population, the surveys included
nearly three thousand randomly chosen adult Americans. The two
surveys had 590 questions, with each survey containing items tap-
ping attitudes toward civil liberties: freedom of speech, press, assembly, association, religion, dissent, due process, privacy, and lifestyle.
The majority of these items dealt with various aspects of civil liberties as applied in particular contexts or situations. A number of other
items posed questions about freedoms or civil liberties, in general.

The findings show that there is heterogeneity of social orientations within the society and individuals, and they are thus at variance
with the characterization of this culture as predominantly individualistic. While members of this society support freedom, liberties, and
individuality on some items, they do not on other items. To convey
the nature of the heterogeneity, in tables 4.1 and 4.2 we present a
sampling of the survey items and results dealing with the areas of
freedom of speech, freedom of religion, due process, and privacy. Table 4.1 contains questions presented in general, abstract terms (e.g., "I
believe in free speech for all no matter what their views might be"),
while table 4.2 contains questions posed with regard to particular situations (e.g., "A community should allow the American Nazi party
to use its town hall to hold a public meeting"). A comparison of the
results in these two tables demonstrates variation between respondents' attitudes toward abstract concepts and their application in certain specific situations.

Very high levels of acceptance of the rights to freedom of speech
and religion as well as to due process and privacy are evident from
table 4.1. Especially striking are the data regarding freedom of speech.
If one were only to look at results based on the general questions, it
would indeed appear that persons in our society are oriented toward
individualism, independence, and autonomy. Table 4.2 shows otherwise! In each of the specific areas, the extent of endorsement of freedom or civil liberties is considerably lower than for the general items
(in most cases only a *minority* of respondents endorsed liberties in
the contextualized situations). A similar pattern holds for freedom of

religion, due process, and privacy. Whereas these freedoms and rights are endorsed, they are not always applied when in conflict with, for example, the desire to prevent crime or to ensure that criminal activity not go unpunished.

Correspondingly, it was found (see McClosky and Brill 1983, 116–30) that rights of assembly and association are not upheld in various situations, like those with the possibility of violence or disorder or when the purpose is opposed by the community. Other findings, pertinent to the purported individualistic orientation in the society, bear on the issues of civil disobedience and adherence to alternative lifestyles. The researchers found a predominant orientation toward upholding laws and subordinating personal decisions and conscience to the maintenance of the collective legal system. The conclusions drawn from the data on lifestyle are that the public has a distinct preference for "conventional values and traditional modes of conduct," and that there is *both* tolerance and intolerance of alternative lifestyles. (Again, there were variations in accordance with type of question posed.) For the most part, freedom of sexual conduct among consenting adults is accepted in the abstract. However, some specific forms of sexual conduct, such as homosexuality, are not accepted.

We have detailed the McClosky and Brill findings in order to provide a sense of the range of issues that lead individuals to qualify or subordinate their attitudes toward liberties and rights. The majority of survey items entailing the application of liberties to particular situations essentially placed liberties in conflict or competition with other considerations of importance to the respondents. These included issues pertaining to harm, general welfare, prejudice toward minority groups, national security, and the disruption of daily life. Furthermore, individuals' attitudes toward liberties and rights are attenuated when they do not serve to maintain the legal system, or are perceived to be in opposition to consensus and dominant views (radicalism, deviance). These findings do not by any means stand in isolation. They are consistent with surveys (Zellman and Sears 1971) of the attitudes of children and adolescents (ages nine to fourteen years), and with several other surveys dating back to the 1930s, including the well-known Stouffer (1955) study (for a review, see Zellman 1975). Apparently, social science stereotypes are difficult to shake.

These survey findings also buttress the viewpoint articulated in a series of essays by Shweder (1979a, 1979b, 1980). Focusing primarily on evidence from research on culture and personality, Shweder argued against generalized descriptions of individual traits or cultures. In line with this position, the McClosky and Brill findings do not support the notion of individual consistency (generalized traits).

**Table 4.1:** Selected Survey Items of the General or Abstract Type

| | Percent endorsing civil liberties response[a] |
|---|---|
| *Freedom of speech* | |
| I believe in free speech for all no matter what their views might be. | 89 |
| People who hate our way of life should still have a chance to talk and be heard. | 82 |
| We could never be free if we gave up the right to criticize our government. | 89 |
| Unless there is freedom for many points of view to be presented, there is little chance that the truth can ever be known. | 86 |
| The idea that everyone has a right to his own opinions is being carried too far these days. | 81 |
| *Freedom of religion* | |
| Freedom to worship as one pleases applies to all religious groups, regardless of how extreme their beliefs are. | 69 |
| *Due process* | |
| All systems of justice make mistakes, but which do you think is worse? | |
| —To convict an innocent person. | 60 |
| —To let a guilty person go free. | |
| When police catch a violent gangster, they should: | |
| —treat him humanely, just as they should treat everyone they arrest. | 78 |
| —be allowed to be a bit rough with him if he refuses to give them the information they need to solve a crime. | |
| If someone is caught red-handed beating and robbing an older person on the street: | |
| —the suspect should still be entitled to a jury trial and all the usual legal protections. | 72 |
| —it's just a waste of taxpayer's money to bother with the usual expensive trial. | |
| In order for the government to effectively prosecute the leaders of organized crime: | |
| —it should stick strictly to the rules if the government wants other people to respect the law. | 68 |
| —it may sometimes have to bend the rules if there is no other way to convict them. | |
| In enforcing the law, the authorities: | |
| —should stick to the rules if they want other people to respect the law. | 62 |
| —sometimes have to break the rules in order to bring criminals to justice. | |

**Table 4.1:** *(continued)*

| | Percent endorsing civil liberties response[a] |
|---|---|
| *Privacy* | |
| Searching a person's home or car without a search warrant: | |
| —should never be allowed. | 59 |
| —is sometimes justified in order to solve a crime. | |
| If the police suspect that drugs, guns, or other criminal evidence is hidden in someone's house, should they be allowed to enter the house without first obtaining a search warrant? | |
| —Yes. | |
| —No. | 66 |
| Do you think the police should have the right to stop anyone on the street and demand to see some identification even if the person is not doing anything illegal, or shouldn't they have this right? | |
| —should not have this right. | 72 |
| —should have this right. | |
| An American citizen: | |
| —is entitled to have his privacy respected, no matter what he believes. | 72 |
| —shouldn't mind having his record checked by patriotic groups. | |

*Source:* Based on McClosky and Brill 1983.

[a]For some items respondents indicated agreement or disagreement with a statement (e.g., I believe in free speech for all no matter what their view might be). Other items were of a sentence-completion type requiring the respondents to choose one or two alternatives. The percentages presented reflect choices of the alternative favoring civil liberties.

We interpret the responses to the general, abstract questions as representing genuinely held views which may be applied in many situations. It is possible, however, to take a more extreme position by interpreting the findings to actually reflect the irrelevance of general, abstract concepts like civil liberties for the real-life decisions people make (which would be a further argument against the stereotype of individualism). The line of reasoning would be that the discrepancies between responses to the general and contextualized questions show that espousal of a commitment to civil liberties does not translate into decisions that account for concrete events. Yet, in our view, the validity of a general concept should be taken into account in explaining decisions about situations that include other competing social (moral and nonmoral) considerations.

Several social psychological experiments provide evidence that general concepts like welfare, truthfulness, and justice *do* guide be-

**Table 4.2:** Selected Survey Items in Context or Specific Situations

|  | Percent endorsing civil liberties response[a] |
|---|---|
| *Freedom of speech* | |
| *Attitudes toward free speech under various conditions* | |
| Free speech should be granted: | |
| —to everyone regardless of how intolerant they are of other people's opinions. | 58 |
| —only to people who are willing to grant the same rights of free speech to everyone else. | |
| Should government authorities be allowed to open the mail of people suspected of being in contact with fugitives? | |
| —No, it would violate a person's right to correspond with his friends. | 50 |
| —Yes, as it may help the police catch criminals they have been looking for. | |
| Should a community allow the American Nazi party to use its town hall to hold a public meeting? | |
| —Yes. | 18 |
| —No. | |
| If a group asks to use a public building to hold a meeting denouncing the government, their request should be: | |
| —granted. | 23 |
| —denied. | |
| | |
| *Free speech and academic freedom* | |
| When a community pays a teacher's salary, it: | |
| —doesn't buy the right to censor the opinions she expresses in the classroom. | 29 |
| —has the right to keep her from teaching ideas that go against the community's standards. | |
| Refusing to hire a professor because of his unusual political beliefs: | |
| —is never justified. | 29 |
| —may be necessary if his views are really extreme. | |
| If it is discovered that an elementary school teacher is a lesbian: | |
| —she should be able to go on teaching because sexual preference should not be a ground for dismissal. | 44 |
| —she should not be allowed to continue teaching. | |
| | |
| *Freedom of the press / Press censorship* | |
| Selling pornographic films, books, and magazines: | |
| —is really victimless crime and should therefore be left unregulated. | 23 |
| —lowers the community's moral standards and therefore victimizes everyone. | |
| Censoring obscene books: | |
| —is an old-fashioned idea that no longer makes sense. | 29 |
| —is necessary to protect community standards. | |
| Which of these comes closer to your own view? | |
| —The government has no right to decide what should or should not be published. | 30 |
| —To protect its moral values, a society sometimes has to forbid certain things from being published. | |

164

**Table 4.2:** *(continued)*

| | Percent endorsing civil liberties response[a] |
|---|---|
| *Freedom of the press in advocacy of radical views* | |
| Should groups like the Nazis and the Ku Klux Klan be allowed to appear on public television to state their views? | |
| —Yes, they should be allowed no matter who is offended. | 29 |
| —No, because they would offend certain racial or religious groups. | |
| Books that preach the overthrow of the government should be: | |
| —made available by the library, just like any other book. | 32 |
| —banned from the library. | |
| Books that could show terrorists how to build bombs should be: | |
| —available in the library like any other book. | 14 |
| —banned from public libraries. | |
| *Freedom of religion* | |
| The freedom of atheists to make fun of God and religion should be legally protected no matter who might be offended. | 26 |
| *Due process* | |
| In dealing with muggings and other serious street crime, which is more important? | |
| —To protect the rights of suspects. | 10 |
| —To stop such crimes and make the streets safe even if we sometimes have to violate the suspect's rights. | |
| When the country is at war, people suspected of disloyalty: | |
| —should be fully protected in their constitutional rights. | 28 |
| —should be watched closely or kept in custody. | |
| A person suspected of serious crimes: | |
| —should have the right to be let out on bail. | 16 |
| —should be kept safely in prison until the trial. | |
| *Privacy* | |
| If the leaders of organized crime meet in a private home or office to discuss their criminal activities: | |
| —they should be free to hold such a meeting without interference. | 15 |
| —the police should be able to "bug" their meeting place to collect evidence against them. | |
| Tapping of telephones of people suspected of planning crimes: | |
| —should be prohibited as an invasion of privacy. | 36 |
| —is necessary to reduce crime. | |
| When undercover police agents secretly join far right or far left political groups to keep an eye on them: | |
| —they are violating the rights of the group's members. | 8 |
| —they are only doing what is necessary to protect our society. | |
| Is it: | |
| —a bad idea for the government to keep a list of people who take part in protest demonstrations. | 25 |
| —a good idea. | |

*Source:* Based on McClosky and Brill 1983.

[a]For some items respondents indicated agreement or disagreement with a statement (e.g., I believe in free speech for all no matter what their view might be). Other items were of a sentence-completion type requiring the respondents to choose one of two alternatives. The percentages presented reflect choices of the alternative favoring civil liberties.

havior (Asch 1956; Haney, Banks, and Zimbardo 1973; Milgram
1974). Consider the moral concept of human welfare and the associated prescription that it is wrong to inflict physical harm on an innocent person. When posed with general questions about inflicting
harm, most would endorse the position that it is categorically wrong
to do so (in fact, this has been found in research with children and
adolescents: Killen 1985; Turiel 1983). Nevertheless, we cannot be
led to the conclusion that people always avoid inflicting harm, as is
evident from various sources including social-psychological experiments. In certain experimental conditions (Milgram 1963) the majority of subjects did inflict what they assumed to be intense physical
harm to another person in obedience to the commands of an experimenter in authority. This particular finding might appear to demonstrate the lack of relevance of the moral precept when it comes to its
application in concrete situations. However, in several other experimental conditions that varied the salience of the harm or authority
components the majority of subjects (sometimes all subjects) defied
the experimenter and refused to inflict harm on another person. In
those conditions the welfare concept was applied. Moreover, separating the different moral (harm) and social (authority and social organization of the experiment) considerations allows for an explanation
of behavioral choices in the various experimental conditions (see Turiel and Smetana 1984 for an analysis). In fact, even when subjects did
not defy the authority their concerns with avoiding harm were relevant since they were highly conflicted about their actions (Milgram
1974). There is a useful analogy to be drawn between the McClosky
and Brill findings on attitudes and the behavioral findings in the social-psychological experiments, since in both cases responses varied
in accordance with type of stimuli.

The distinction between espousing a general moral concept and
advocating its application in context has a bearing on the nonrelativistic philosophical perspectives mentioned earlier. In those perspectives, morality is defined by the criteria of obligatoriness and inclusiveness (Dworkin 1978; Fried 1978; Gewirth 1978; Scheffler
1982). It could be argued that variations in the application of general
moral concepts to contextual situations contradict these philosophical criteria. Such a position, however, would both fail to take into
account psychological realities and would constitute an overly stringent interpretation of the moral criteria (Williams 1981).

The criteria are meant to define morality in the abstract (the all
other things being equal case). Although individuals believe a moral
concept is important and generalizable, psychological reality is such
that there are strongly competing nonmoral claims in life. An indi-

vidual's actions sometimes may be discrepant with moral concepts when the situation implicates other strongly held motives or beliefs. The issue of variation has been addressed by philosophers adhering to the view that morality is generalizable. Two potential sources of variation are exceptions to "categorical" norms and the role of significant personal considerations in moral obligation (especially when moral and personal considerations conflict). The classic example of an exception is the case of self-defense, which can involve inflicting harm that is legitimate from the moral point of view. Exceptions of this sort, based on situational factors, do not invalidate the generalizability criterion in that the concepts underlying the exceptions are consonant with moral criteria (Fried 1978, 44).

Philosophers have also discussed the relations between morality and significant personal goals. We cannot detail the issues and debates revolving around this question (see Nagel 1982; Scheffler 1984; Williams 1981). However, it is important to note that there are ways of maintaining the philosophical criteria of generalizability and inclusiveness, along with the recognition that there may be legitimate conflicts between morality and personal goals.

## Coexistence, Heterogeneity, and Social Domains

Findings of variation in social judgments and practices are not in themselves indicative of the validity of any particular position on the nature or sources of morality but do require explanation. They constitute a descriptive starting point that has its basis in the particular patterns of variation obtained. The conclusion we draw from the pattern of findings discussed in the previous section is that it is useful— and we further maintain, necessary—to study and explain both (a) individuals' general social concepts (i.e., their understandings of the abstract manifestations of concepts like civil liberties, welfare, or justice) and (b) the application of those concepts in contextualized situations. A research strategy to accomplish these aims involves first separating variables and then examining their interrelations (Turiel and Davidson 1986). In doing so, at least two types of assessments of social reasoning can be made. One entails the use of stimuli representing what Wertheimer (1935) has referred to as "pure" or prototypical cases, which he maintained allow for assessment of the parameters of general concepts in their abstract manifestations. These stimuli pose problems or tasks designed to elicit one type of general concept. As examples, the McClosky and Brill items in table 4.1 are of this kind in that they represent stimuli regarding an issue (e.g., civil liberties) that is not in conflict with other considerations.

The second type of assessment entails the use of what can be referred to as multifaceted or mixed situations (Turiel 1983; Turiel and Smetana 1984), which include components bearing on more than one type of concept. The contextualized items in table 4.2 are of this kind in that they include conflicts between moral concepts (e.g., welfare in conflict with civil liberties), as well as conflicts between moral and nonmoral considerations (e.g., welfare or liberty in conflict with conventionally accepted modes of behavior). The use of prototypical stimuli allows for study of basic categories of social judgments, which in turn provides a basis for study of the application of those judgments in situations with a mixture of categories. (See Turiel and Davidson 1986, for a discussion of the logical fallacies in the argument [e.g., as put forth by Rest 1983] that examples of category mixture invalidate the separation of the categories.)

Research with children and adolescents has investigated general concepts of morality and social convention, and the coordination of those concepts in multifaceted situations. This research, which is part of what has come to be referred to as a "domain" approach to cognitive and social cognitive development (Damon 1977; Feldman 1980; Keil 1986; Nucci 1981; Smetana 1982; Turiel 1975, 1983), provides a basis for understanding variations in social judgments and actions—including the sort found in the survey studies. Although surveys provide a wealth of information, a shortcoming of this methodology is that it does not allow for direct study of reasoning processes underlying attitudes. Research on domains of social judgment assesses conceptual criteria and entails the identification of epistemological categories of social judgment. In line with the strategy of separating variables prior to examining their coordinations, there has now accumulated a body of data on general concepts in the moral and conventional domains derived through the use of stimuli of the prototypical or abstract type (e.g., Much and Shweder 1978; Nucci 1981; Pool, Shweder, and Much 1983; Turiel 1979). More recent research has focused on judgments and actions in contextualized situations with components from more than one domain (Killen 1985; Smetana 1982, 1983; Turiel 1983; Turiel and Smetana 1984; Turiel and Davidson 1986).

Research with prototypical situations explored the different social knowledge systems (domains) developed by children on the assumption that the functions and aims of systems of social interaction are not of one kind. For example, functions and aims of efficiency and coordination in social organization may differ from functions and aims of justice and welfare in social relations. One central task is taxonomic. Whereas developmental researchers traditionally have focused on taxonomies for age-related levels of thought (vertical organization in development), it is also necessary to identify and describe those conceptual systems that coexist and which are not developmentally ordered (referred to as horizontal organization in Turiel and Davidson 1986). Three general social knowledge systems have been investigated. Most of the research has dealt with morality and social convention, but some studies examined children's developing knowledge of persons or psychological systems. In addition to the epistemological task of classifying domains of social knowledge, a goal of these studies is to determine how individuals conceptualize and distinguish the domains.

The general strategy has been a recursive one: using definitions of domain to inform data-gathering procedures and data to inform the descriptions insofar as they apply to individuals' judgments. As stressed elsewhere (Turiel and Davidson 1986), these procedures must be regarded as efforts based on working hypotheses, since the range and boundaries of domains are still not precise. The working definitions for the domains have also been partly guided by philosophical treatments (for detailed analyses the reader can consult Duncan and Fiske 1977; Lewis 1969; Searle 1969, for convention, and Dworkin 1978; Gewirth 1978; Rawls 1971; Scheffler 1984 and numerous others for morality). The application of philosophical definitions and criteria in our research has been extensively discussed in other places (see especially Shweder, Turiel, and Much 1983; Turiel 1983; Turiel and Davidson 1986; Turiel and Smetana 1984). Those sources also present the rationale for the criteria and an explanation of the relations among criteria within each domain.

Stated most generally, the domain distinction is based on the proposition that understandings of social systems, including sociocultural institutions ranging from families to government, are analytically distinguishable from abstracted concepts of how persons ought to relate to one another. In brief, conventions are part of constitutive systems and are shared behaviors (uniformities, rules) whose meanings are defined by the constituted system in which they are embedded (Searle 1969). Adherence to conventional acts is contingent on the force obtained from socially constructed and institutionally embedded meanings. Conventions are thus context-dependent and their content may vary by socially constructed meanings (Lewis 1969). While morality also applies to social systems, it is not constitutive or defined by existing social arrangements (Gewirth 1978). In this perspective on morality (Brandt 1959; Dworkin 1978; Fried 1978), prescriptions are characterized as unconditionally obligatory, generalizable, and impersonal insofar as they stem from concepts of

welfare, justice, and rights (Dworkin 1983; Rawls 1971). There are
ways in which moral prescriptions intersect with socially constructed meanings and constitutive systems. This issue is addressed
directly in a later section after a summary of some of the research on
children's reasoning within each domain.

A consistent finding from studies examining morality and convention is that, for prototypical situations, children at early ages form
general concepts distinguishable by domain (extensive reviews of the
research are available in Nucci 1982; Smetana 1983; and Turiel 1983).
They judge moral issues to be obligatory, applicable across like situations, not contingent on specific social rules or authority-dictates,
and not alterable on an arbitrary basis. They judge conventions as
contingent on social organization—such as rules, authority, and existing arrangements. Insofar as they distinguish moral from conventional issues, children and adolescents display variation and heterogeneity in their social orientations.

This heterogeneity of social orientations reflected in the coexistence of domains points to the existence of organized systems of
thought within individuals. Our interpretation of the findings is that
children generate understandings of the social world by forming intuitive theories regarding experienced social events. This proposition
does not by any means exclude the emotional features of individuals'
moral and social orientations. In fact, recent research (Arsenio 1985;
Arsenio and Ford 1985) has begun to explore childrens' emotional attributions in moral and conventional evaluations. In our perspective,
however, children's judgments and conceptual transformations
(which have been the major focus of the research) are a central aspect
of morality and social convention. This formulation, in turn, has implications for the proposed relations between domains. Given the emphasis on conceptual transformations and constructions, we do not
take the position that domains are unrelated to each other—as seems
to be the case in Fodor's (1983) formulation of innately determined
modularity. It is our position, instead, that the different domains, although analytically distinct structures, are related in multifaceted
situations that include moral and nonmoral components (Turiel and
Davidson 1986). In addition, components of events like available information, the specific situational circumstances, and assumptions
about reality (e.g., the natural order, biology, psychological states) all
have a bearing on the ways domains of judgment are accessed (Asch
1952; Duncker 1939). These particulars may vary by society and by
communities within societies.

In subsequent sections we explain our position on interrelations
among events, assumptions about reality, and domains of judgment.

First, we provide some background regarding the findings on how children in our culture conceptualize prototypical events. Tables 4.3 and 4.4 contain a comprehensive list of studies conducted in the United States (a total of twenty-eight studies) and a listing of events found to be associated with convention and morality, respectively. Table 4.3 shows that a large number of specific conventions have been used, that the conventions applied to several contexts (e.g., school, family, religion), and that in most cases the specific conventions were used in more than one or two studies. From these tables it should be evident that within our culture there is a correspondence between certain kinds of events and the domain of reasoning applied by children and adolescents. However, this finding and the above-mentioned finding of domain specificity at an early age require further interpretation and elaboration.

In the first place, it is notable that many of the events classified as conventional (table 4.3) may appear to be of lesser importance or entail lesser consequences than the events classified as moral (table 4.4). Such an impression is in line with findings that moral rules are generally evaluated as more important than conventional rules (Nucci 1981; Smetana 1981; Turiel 1978). This may appear to be a confounding factor in the research in the sense that the distinction may be determined primarily by differences in the perceived importance or seriousness of the items presented (a quantitative dimension). However, this is not necessarily a confound because morality may be *conceptually* distinct from convention and, at the same time, generally (but not exclusively) of greater importance (Gewirth 1978; Rawls 1971). Accordingly, differences between moral and conventional events in ratings of importance would not necessarily mean that the distinction can be attributed solely to differences in perceived importance.

Since it is not always the case that conventions are rated as of lesser importance than moral issues (the distributions probably overlap), it is possible to separate the use of conceptual criteria for each domain from perceived importance. As indicated in table 4.3, high levels of importance are attributed to several conventional items, including cross-gender activities (Carter and McCloskey 1983–84; Carter and Patterson 1982; Stoddart and Turiel 1985), nudity (Turiel 1983; Weston and Turiel 1980), and religious rules (Nucci 1986). For instance, it was found (Stoddart and Turiel 1985) that sex-role deviations, which were conceptualized as violations of social conventions, were rated as seriously as moral transgressions. (This was not the case at all ages, as there is a U-shaped curve in ratings by five- to thirteen-year-olds.) Moreover, it has been found that adolescents who

**Table 4.3:** Stimulus Events Classified as Conventional in Domain-Distinction Studies

| Event Type | Studies | Examples of Event Type |
|---|---|---|
| School Rules | Arsenio and Ford 1985; Dodsworth-Rugani 1982; Nucci 1981, 1982; Nucci and Herman 1982; Smetana 1981, 1985a, 1985b; Smetana, Bridgeman, and Turiel 1983; Smetana, Kelly, and Twentymen 1984; Stoddart and Turiel 1985. | Chewing gum in class; boy entering girls' bathroom*; eating in class; talking without raising hand; a child not participating in show and tell; a child not sitting in designated place during story time; a child not placing his/her belongings in the designated place; talking during nap time; standing during snack; child undressing on the playground*; leaving the classroom without permission; coming into class late; not lining up in the schoolyard after recess; talking back to the teacher; leaving assigned seat in classroom. |
| Forms of address | Davidson, Turiel, and Black 1983; Nucci 1981; Nucci and Herman 1982; Nucci, Turiel, Encarnacion-Gawrych 1983; Smetana 1982, 1985b; Smetana, Bridgeman, and Turiel 1983; Stoddart and Turiel, 1985; Turiel 1978. | Calling a teacher by his/her first name; not addressing a judge as "Your Honor." |
| Conventions governing attire and appearance | Arsenio and Ford 1985; Davidson, Turiel, and Black 1983; Shantz 1982; Smetana 1985b; Smetana, Bridgeman, and Turiel 1983; Tisak and Turiel 1985; Turiel 1978, 1983. | Baseball player doesn't wear uniform to game; not wearing school uniform; dressing casually in a business office; public nudity*; a boy not combing hair. |
| Game rules | Dodsworth-Rugani 1982; Lockhart, Abrahams, and Osherson 1977; Nucci, Turiel, and Encarnacion-Gawrych 1983. | Hide and seek rules; game rules generated by subject. |
| Family rules | Davidson, Turiel and Black, 1983; Dodsworth-Rugani 1982; Smetana 1981; Tisak 1984. | Not clearing one's dishes from the table after dinner; not saying grace before snack. |

172

**Table 4.3:** *(continued)*

| Event Type | Studies | Examples of Event Type |
|---|---|---|
| Customs (e.g., etiquette) | Arsenio and Ford 1985; Carter and Patterson 1982; Damon 1977; Davidson, Turiel, and Black 1983; Lockhart 1980; Lockhart, Abrahams, and Osherson 1977; Nucci 1981, 1982; Nucci and Herman 1982; Smetana 1982, 1985b; Smetana, Bridgeman, and Turiel 1983; Stoddart and Turiel 1985; Turiel 1978. | Not using utensils; drinking soup out of a bowl; swearing; girl wearing a skirt sits with her knees apart; husband adopts wife's surname after marriage. |
| Sex-role conventions | Carter and McCloskey 1983–84; Carter and Patterson 1982; Damon 1977; Stoddart and Turiel 1985; Turiel 1978, 1983. | Boy wears barrette to keep his hair out of his eyes while playing football*; boy wears fingernail polish*; girl gets a crew-cut*; girl wears boy's suit*; a boy wants to become a nurse caring for infants when he grows up*; a boy wears a dress to school*; boy or girl uses toys meant for opposite sex*; boy or girl tries to cross gender occupation boundaries*; sex role conventions provided by subject. |
| Sexual conventions | Nucci 1986; Smetana 1982. | Premarital sex*; masturbation*; birth control ("the pill"); homosexuality*; divorce*; marital sex solely for pleasure. |
| Religious conventions | Nucci 1986. | Not attending Mass on Sunday*; eating fifteen minutes before communion*; receiving communion without confession*; going a year without communion*; not attending Mass on Easter or Christmas*; ordaining women*; day of worship*; work on Sunday*; head covering*; baptism*; interfaith marriage, women preaching*; premarital sex.* |
| Other conventions | Davidson, Turiel, and Black 1983; Lockhart, Abrahams, and Osherson 1977; Smetana 1982; Smetana, Bridgeman, and Turiel 1983. | Meaning of words; greetings (girl greets her friends by bowing rather than customary greeting); celebrating holidays and birthdays by sending cards. |

*Conventional events viewed as important.

explicitly state that they do not consider sex-role deviations as morally wrong nevertheless express a strong personal commitment to sex-role maintenance (Carter and McCloskey 1983–84).

A similar pattern of findings emerges from studies specifically designed to examine relations between domain of judgments and at-

**Table 4.4:** Stimulus Events Classified as Moral in
Domain-Distinction Studies

| Event Type | Studies | Examples of Event Type[a] |
|---|---|---|
| Physical harm and welfare | Arsenio and Ford 1985; Brendemeier 1984; Davidson, Turiel, and Black 1983; Dodsworth-Rugani 1982; Nucci 1981, 1982, 1986; Nucci and Herman 1982; Nucci, Turiel, and Encarnacion-Gawrych 1983; Shantz 1982; Smetana 1981, 1982, 1985b; Smetana, Bridgeman, and Turiel 1983; Smetana, Kelly, and Twentymen 1984; Stoddart and Turiel 1985; Tisak and Turiel 1984, 1985; Weston and Turiel 1980. | Hitting, pushing, killing. |
| Psychological harm | Brendemeier 1984; Nucci 1986; Smetana 1985a; Smetana, Kelly, and Twentymen 1984. | Hurting feelings, name-calling, ridiculing a cripple. |
| Fairness and rights | Arsenio and Ford 1985; Davidson, Turiel, and Black 1983; Dodsworth-Rugani 1982; Lockhart 1980; Lockhart, Abrahams, and Osherson 1977; Nucci 1981, 1982, 1986; Nucci and Herman 1982; Nucci, Turiel, and Encarnacion-Gawrych 1983; Shantz 1982; Smetana 1981, 1982, 1985a, 1985b; Smetana, Bridgeman, and Turiel 1983; Smetana, Kelly, and Twentymen 1984; Stoddart and Turiel 1985; Tisak 1984; Tisak and Turiel 1984, 1985; Turiel 1983. | Stealing, destroying other's property, breaking a promise, slavery, turntaking. |
| Positive "prosocial" moral behaviors | Nucci 1980; Nucci and Herman 1982; Shantz 1982; Smetana 1981, 1982, 1985b; Smetana, Bridgeman, and Turiel 1983; Weston and Turiel 1980. | Donating to charity, sharing, helping others in distress. |

[a]Given the numerous scenarios used to present the moral events to subjects, space limitations require that they be stated here in general terms. In the actual studies these events were presented to subjects in concrete situations comparable to the presentation of the conventional events. For instance, in Davidson, Turiel, and Black (1983), "stealing" was presented in a story describing a school setting in which one student took a dollar from another student who had earned it performing chores.

tributions of importance. In one study (Turiel 1983) judgments were elicited regarding conventional transgressions that children might regard as highly deviant, disruptive, or resulting in strong reactions from others (i.e., a child wearing pajamas to school, a boy wearing a dress), and moral transgressions with lesser (stealing a pencil) and greater (stealing five dollars) consequences. Children conceptually distinguished the moral and conventional events, even though they sometimes rated the conventional transgression to be of equal or greater seriousness than the minor moral transgressions.

An interesting age difference emerged in the attributions of importance. Younger children (about six years of age) generally rated the conventional transgressions (e.g., wearing pajamas to school) as more serious than a moral transgression with minor consequences (stealing a pencil), while older children (about ten years of age) rated the moral transgression as more serious. However, as demonstrated in another study (Tisak and Turiel 1985), the older children do attribute importance to those particular conventional transgressions. In that study, subjects (from seven to eleven years) were posed with a task requiring a forced choice (if one of two acts had to be committed) between a minor moral transgression and a conventional transgression with major consequences. On the one hand, subjects stated that children would choose to engage in the minor moral transgression (which is indicative of their perception of these conventions as consequential). On the other hand, they stated that the conventional transgression *should* be chosen rather than the minor moral transgression (which is indicative of their domain conceptualization of the events). It appears that for the older children importance can have two meanings. One stems from the perceived severity of consequences and the other from perceived importance of the moral status of the act.

Further evidence that the domain distinction is not based solely on importance comes from Nucci's (1986) insightful analysis of relations between morality and religious prescriptions or rules. A series of well-designed studies examined the judgments of subjects with strong religious affiliation (fundamentalist Mennonite and Amish Christians) regarding the alterability and universality of moral and conventional rules strongly endorsed in the religion. The sequence of questions posed to subjects was designed to test the limits of authority attributed to the rules or prescriptions. The issues presented, the questions posed, and results obtained are summarized in table 4.5, which is reproduced from Nucci (1986). First, subjects were asked if it would be all right for religious authorities or the collective membership (the congregation) to eliminate or change the rule. The majority of subjects at each age stated it would be wrong to do so for

**Table 4.5:** Percentages of Amish/Mennonite Children Responding "It Would Be Wrong" to Rule Alterability, Act Universality, and God's Word Contingency Questions for Moral and Nonmoral (Conventional) Issues

| Issue: | Rule Alterability | | | | Act Universality | | | | God's Word Contingency | | | |
|---|---|---|---|---|---|---|---|---|---|---|---|---|
| | 10–11 | 12–13 | 14–15 | 16–17 | 10–11 | 12–13 | 14–15 | 16–17 | 10–11 | 12–13 | 14–15 | 16–17 |
| *Nonmoral/Convention:* | | | | | | | | | | | | |
| Day of worship | 44 | 47 | 50 | 36 | 25 | 27 | 18 | 09 | 0 | 0 | 0 | 0 |
| Work on Sunday | 100 | 93 | 94 | 82 | 67 | 60 | 44 | 27 | 6 | 0 | 0 | 0 |
| Head covering | 75 | 50 | 75 | 82 | 13 | 27 | 12 | 09 | 0 | 0 | 0 | 0 |
| Baptism | 71 | 79 | 88 | 82 | 25 | 57 | 18 | 27 | 0 | 0 | 0 | 0 |
| Interfaith marriage | 53 | 40 | 44 | 27 | 31 | 20 | 12 | 09 | 6 | 0 | 0 | 0 |
| Women preaching | 53 | 36 | 44 | 91 | 19 | 07 | 18 | 30 | 6 | — | 12 | 11 |
| Premarital sex | — | — | 75 | 90 | — | — | 25 | 45 | — | 0 | 11 | 14 |
| M̄ Nonmoral* | 66 | 58 | 66 | 67 | 30 | 33 | 20 | 18 | 3 | 0 | 2 | 2 |
| *Moral:* | | | | | | | | | | | | |
| Stealing | 100 | 100 | 100 | 100 | 81 | 93 | 94 | 91 | 81 | 70 | 88 | 91 |
| Hitting | 94 | 100 | 94 | 91 | 88 | 86 | 100 | 100 | 81 | 70 | 88 | 82 |
| Slander | 88 | 100 | 100 | 100 | 81 | 100 | 88 | 100 | 75 | 78 | 88 | 89 |
| Damaging property | 88 | 93 | 98 | 98 | 88 | 87 | 88 | 100 | 88 | 83 | 94 | 100 |
| M̄ Moral | 92 | 98 | 98 | 98 | 85 | 92 | 93 | 98 | 81 | 75 | 90 | 90 |

*Source:* Taken from Nucci 1986.

*Note: Rule Alterability,* "Would it be all right for the congregation to remove or alter the rule?" *Act Universality,* "Is it all right for members of another religion which has no rule about the act to engage in the act?" *God's Word Contingency,* "If God had made no rule about the act, would it be all right to engage in the act?"

*Calculated without premarital sex item.

either the moral or nonmoral rules. As table 4.5 shows, a greater differentiation between the two rule types was made in judgments as to whether members of other religions could legitimately engage in the act. The clearest source for the distinction is with regard to what Nucci refers to as "God's word contingency." Whereas virtually all subjects considered it permissible to engage in the nonmoral behaviors in the absence of biblical injunctions, the majority of them judged it wrong to engage in the moral transgressions even in the absence of biblical prescription or directive from God. These findings reveal the coexistence of different social orientations in nonsecular settings; even among certain devout persons living in Western society religious and moral prescriptions are not equated.

The coexistence of social orientations has been demonstrated in adolescents and young adults (as in Nucci's study) and, as noted earlier, in young children as well. This still leaves open the question of the scope and generality of the distinction across age and situations. Two hypotheses are plausible from the initial findings of a domain distinction. The strong set of hypotheses is that the distinction is made in early childhood, maintained over age and across situations, and that there is a minimal interaction between moral and nonmoral social judgments in multifaceted (mixed) situations. Alternatively, it may be that (a) the distinction is made at an early age but is less stable at younger than older ages; (b) the distinction interacts with situational parameters, such that it is unstable for certain issues even at older ages; and (c) there is an interaction between moral and nonmoral social judgments in mixed situations.

The large body of evidence now accumulated points to the validity of the latter set of hypotheses. First, it appears that the distinction is less stable and less generalized at younger than at older ages. Some studies show that young children have the competence to distinguish moral from conventional issues in fairly clear-cut ways, but older children do so more consistently. The age differences are of two types. One is that at younger ages (up to about eight or nine years) children are not as consistent in the dimensions they apply to the distinction (Lockhart 1980; Lockhart, Abrahams, and Osherson 1977; Shantz 1982; Smetana 1981). Further, younger children's domain distinctions are limited to familiar issues (Davidson, Turiel, and Black 1983). It has been found that six-year-olds apply domain-appropriate reasoning to familiar but not unfamiliar issues. In contrast, by about the age of ten years, children apply distinctively moral and conventional judgments to both familiar and unfamiliar issues. With age, children are able to abstract common elements in events and, thereby, generalize their judgments from familiar to unfamiliar situations.

The emergence, with age, of a stable and comprehensive domain distinction for prototypical cases does not mean it is then applied to all social situations, nor that the domains are completely segregated in mixed situations. First consider the judgments of adolescents and adults regarding a set of social issues that in our culture are domain-ambiguous. Current research (Turiel and Hildebrandt, in preparation) examined four such issues: abortion, homosexuality, pornography, and incest (for convenience's sake, to be referred to here as "ambiguous"). These particular issues have an "ambiguous" status in some important respects: they are not clearly classifiable as part of the moral domain but are often treated as categorically unacceptable; at cultural or subcultural levels they are highly charged issues with strong social sanctions; and, with the exception of incest, there are strongly held varying attitudes regarding their permissibility.

The study was designed to allow for comparative analyses of reasoning within individuals. A central aim was to examine how reasoning about the ambiguous issues, on the part of subjects who appear to treat them as categorically wrong (i.e., have a moral orientation toward them), compared with their reasoning about prototypical moral issues. If moral judgments can be distinguished from reasoning about social conventions, how do individuals reason about those issues that are "hard cases?" By hard cases we mean issues that may not result directly in injustices or harmful consequences, but do come with strong cultural endorsements and sanctions.

Comparisons were drawn among (a) ambiguous issues, (b) prototypical moral issues (i.e., rape, unprovoked killing), and (c) issues of a conventional nature treated by some of the subjects in the study as within the jurisdiction of personal choice (i.e., males wearing make-up, marijuana use, nudity). Although the analyses (based on the responses of over two hundred high school and college-age subjects) are still underway, some early results are informative for the present purposes. First, not surprisingly it was found that there are variations between individuals in attitudes toward the ambiguous issues. Some subjects regarded the acts as acceptable, judging them to be within personal jurisdiction and out of the jurisdiction of societal or legal control.[3] Other subjects evaluated the acts as wrong. Subjects' vary-

3. In judging these acts as acceptable and under personal jurisdiction, subjects were referring to contexts free of coercion or exploitation. With regard to homosexuality, the judgments pertained to the acceptability of the behavior between consenting adults and not to the moral implications of imposing restrictions on it. Insofar as subjects considered incest an issue under personal jurisdiction, it was with reference to consenting adults. Similarly, pornography was considered acceptable under noncoercive conditions.

ing attitudes toward the ambiguous issues stemmed from differing assumptions about aspects of reality and its natural order. A variety of sometimes uncertain and contradictory assumptions were made by most subjects regarding biological, psychological, sociological, or religious systems that structured judgments about the ambiguous issues. In contrast with these individual differences, there was consensus regarding the prototypical moral issues, with virtually all subjects regarding those acts as categorically wrong in a generalizable way and within the jurisdiction of societal and legal control. A second finding was that individuals manifested a coexistence of domains of reasoning. While they reasoned in unequivocal, consistent, and what could even be viewed as inflexible ways with regard to the prototypical moral issues, for certain conventional issues these same subjects accepted the legitimacy of personal choice, expressing a liberal, relativistic, and flexible social orientation.

A third finding stems from comparisons of subjects' reasoning about the ambiguous issues with their reasoning about the prototypical issues among those who regarded those acts as wrong. The two types of issues were conceptualized differently. Judgments about the prototypical issues were consistent across a set of dimensions (such as whether the act should be regulated by law, or if its status is contingent on the existence of law or common practice in this country and other countries) and consistently justified by reasons of harm and general welfare. Judgments about the ambiguous issues took several forms, reflecting similarities to the moral issues when subjects assumed the acts to produce harm and differences from the moral issues when judgments were based on assumptions about an aspect of reality and its natural order. Inconsistencies and internal contradictions were also prevalent in the subjects' judgments about the ambiguous issues but not about the prototypical moral issues.

In contrast with judgments about prototypical moral issues (e.g., killing, rape), those concerning certain "ambiguous" social issues show variation and are often inconsistent and self-contradictory. While a fuller description of such reasoning awaits further analyses, a general hypothesis drawn from these results is that individuals' conceptual structures bearing on prototypical issues can be in tension with understandings of strong tacit or explicit cultural norms that are, on the one hand, presented as obligatory and, on the other hand, do not have a direct link to harm, justice, or rights. The tension to which we refer, it must be stressed, is not necessarily of a conscious nature but is evident in analyses of the inconsistencies and contradictions in reasoning about the ambiguous issues (types of inconsistencies that generally do not appear with regard to the prototypical issues). Hence, for some subjects, the ambiguous issues are not clearly categorized in the domains of reasoning manifested with regard to other issues.

There is another sense in which social situations are not prototypical and not classifiable in one domain. These are the types of situations, referred to earlier in the context of the McClosky and Brill (1983) survey findings, that include multiple components potentially requiring the coordination of domains of judgment. In proposing that individuals form differentiated domains of social judgment it is necessary not only to explain reasoning within the domains but also to account for relations between domains. As noted earlier, domain analyses allow for the separation of variables as a basis for study of their coordination in contextualized situations entailing domain mixtures.

An emerging body of research is attending to domain coordinations in multifaceted situations. Analyses have been conducted of domain coordinations in judgments (Smetana 1983; Turiel 1983, chap. 6) and behavioral decisions (Turiel and Smetana 1984). A methodological advantage to the strategy of separating domains for analyses of their coordinations is that it provides a basis for task analyses of the parameters of situations or stimuli. For example, task analyses of the Milgram (1974) experimental situations served as a basis for interpreting behaviors in different experimental conditions as significantly determined by the ways domains of judgment intersect with situational parameters (for details, see Turiel and Smetana 1984).

A recently completed study (Killen 1985) provides an analysis of domain coordinations in children's judgments. This study has interesting parallels with the general and contextualized items in the McClosky and Brill survey. The study, however, explored conceptual criteria and supports a domain separation and mixture interpretation of the variations and inconsistencies evident in the survey data.

In the Killen study children (ages six to twelve years) were presented with prototypical moral situations (pertaining to harm and distributive justice), as well as with situations that included components similar in form to some of the contextualized survey items. The general situations contained a straightforward moral component, such as a child hitting another. Other situations were multifaceted in that the moral component was placed in conflict with social-organizational or personal considerations. For instance, choices were posed between preventing harm and continuing a task necessary to the maintenance of a group activity (i.e., a member of a team insuring that a game activity is not terminated; the maintenance of classroom order). Multifaceted situations also posed choices between preventing harm to a stranger or to a close personal relation.

The findings of this study, too, show that variations in social orientations stem from domains of judgment and efforts at coordinating domains in multifaceted situations. In the prototypical situation pertaining to harm, all children in each age group put forth the view that hitting is wrong. Moreover, their justifications for this evaluation were based on concepts of welfare and a perceived obligation to avoid inflicting harm on persons. This unanimity was not evident in the multifaceted, contextualized situations. For instance, 33 percent of the children did not give priority to preventing harm over the maintenance of a team activity. In addition, there was variation in judgments as to whether priority should be given to preventing harm to a stranger or close relative. In the multifaceted situations, regardless of the action choice endorsed, the large majority of children at all ages took into account both moral and nonmoral components in the decision-making process (see figure 4.1 for an example of these findings). Only a minority of children focused solely on nonmoral features. (Similar patterns were obtained for situations dealing with distributive justice.)

These findings further demonstrate that evaluations of moral actions can vary by situational context. Whereas the reasons or jus-

*Figure 4.1:* Mean percentage of coordinated responses (focusing on more than one component) for each age, for Social/Moral (SM) and Personal/Moral (PM) conflict situations (Source: Killen 1985)

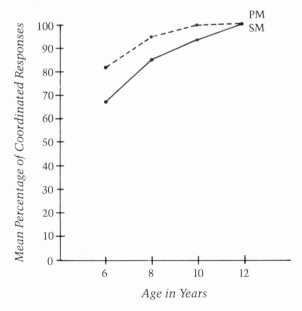

tifications given for evaluations in the prototypical situations were of the moral type (e.g., welfare, justice), in the multifaceted situations the justifications generally included moral and nonmoral reasons. Since the children brought their moral concepts to bear upon the contextualized situations, it can be said that the moral concepts clearly evident in the prototypical situations are relevant to decisions in the multifaceted, contextualized situations. Given that moral considerations were not the only judgments relevant to the multifaceted situation, it can also be said that the coordination (in conflictful or non-conflictful ways) of different types or domains of judgment is an important aspect of social decision making. To understand variations in social judgments, therefore, multiple classification systems are needed for both situational variables and person variables. Task analyses are required to identify the components implicated in particular situations.

## Domains of Judgment and Social Events

We have proposed that the findings of variation in attitudes or judgments between general, abstract situations and contextualized situations do not simply reflect disconnected differences in the ways external stimuli elicit responses from persons. We propose that judgments of persons are *interactive* with situations and that, in part, response variations stem from the application of different types or domains of social judgment in a given situation. Therefore, another aspect of the enterprise is specification of the parameters of situations through task analyses.

In an interactive model of this sort, a relationship is proposed between stimuli (events, situations) and individuals' conceptualization of them as moral or conventional (and, of course, as mixed or multidimensional). More generally, there is a relation between the structure of judgments (subject) and the structure of the environment (object). One aspect of this relation pertains to the influences of experienced events on the development of social judgments. This developmental aspect is considered in a later section. A second aspect pertains to the relation of events to domains, given that judgments have been formed. In actuality, these two aspects are not easily disentangled since any interaction has the potential for stimulating changes in judgments. Nevertheless, it is necessary to accept this ambiguity for purposes of empirical investigations of domains of social judgment.

Specifying relations between events and conceptual domains is a difficult and important problem requiring a great deal of additional theoretical and empirical work. It is also a problem that, in our view, has not been adequately formulated by any of the extant perspectives. The earliest investigations of children's moral and conventional concepts represented an effort not only to identify epistemological categories (the domains of judgment) but also to provide a basis for specifying elements and categories of stimuli. It was pointed out (see especially Turiel 1978) that, for the most part, the stimuli in experimental and interview studies of children's moral behaviors and judgments were chosen without explicit analyses of their criteria and morally relevant features. We will resurrect an example used at the time to illustrate the point: "Suppose that in order to investigate moral reasoning a researcher used a series of mathematical problems with subjects of different ages. Such a procedure would be questionable because we could not be confident that subjects in the study had engaged in moral reasoning at all" (Turiel 1978, 35).

As also noted at the time, the example of a mathematical task is a simplification of the issue that illustrates the problem. Normally, research on moral development utilized social situations as stimuli, sometimes with implicit assumptions about their morally relevant features. (See Turiel 1978, 38–45 for a listing of the variety of stimulus events that had been used in research on moral development.) A more adequate strategy is to provide explicit criteria for the events used as stimuli. This proposition obtains greater weight from the assumption that not all social events are in the moral domain. If the sole proposed criterion for morality were that it involves social interaction, then a simple distinction between "social" and "nonsocial" situations might be sufficient, although explicitly specifying the criteria for social situations is desirable. Most researchers of moral development, however, have not assumed that all social events are equivalent to moral events.

The task is twofold. One aspect concerns the methodological requirement that criteria for stimulus events be specified and synchronized with the topic under investigation. It can be safely assumed that this requirement is noncontroversial, but its importance needs to be reiterated. The other aspect is theoretical and pertains to explanations of relations between domains of judgment and the elements of social stimuli or events. Criteria for stimuli are, of necessity, guided by the theoretical perspective on the domain in question.

In addition to formulating an explanation of the relations between domains and events, research on morality and convention has aimed at practicing what was preached (a message that still needs to be preached) through specification of criteria for choices of stimuli in the studies. A perusal of tables 4.3 and 4.4, which list the prototypical events used in the research, shows at least that there is an empirical basis (in this culture) for separating events in accordance with domains. The event distinctions are generally consistent with the proposition that morally relevant events have features like consequences to persons, injustice, and benevolence, and that conventionally relevant events are, in themselves, arbitrary or neutral and obtain their nonneutral status by the contexts that give them their meanings.

The source for the empirically obtained relation is, however, open to further interpretation. At one pole, it may be maintained that there is no necessary intersection between events and domains because judgments or attitudes are determined by factors outside of the particular features of actions. For example, social actions may be said to obtain their meaning for individuals mainly from particular cultural judgments, ideologies, or worldviews. Hence, any event can be primarily and in a first-order sense part of the moral domain insofar as it is treated as such by the culture. (This appears to be the position taken by Shweder [1986] and Shweder, Mahapatra, and Miller [this volume] in their "social communication" theory of moral development.) At the other pole, it may be maintained that there is a direct mapping of the content of events to domains, such that a domain of judgment is given in the event itself. In this view, an event would have an independent, objective status deterministic of domain. It appears that Shweder, Mahapatra, and Miller (this volume; also Shweder 1980) attribute this interpretation to our approach and that of our coworkers (e.g., Nucci 1981; Smetana 1983). Such an attribution is a misconception that probably has its source in our concern for specifying criteria for stimulus events. The idea that events have an objective status deterministic of judgments is actually in contradiction with the interactive model we have proposed, which emphasizes the construction of structures of judgment stemming from individuals' actions and experiences.

A third interpretation of the relations between events and judgment, consistent with our approach, is that they are interactive. This means that the relation between events and domains of judgment is neither arbitrary nor *solely* determined by meanings imposed upon social interactions (e.g., by cultural judgments or ideologies). The relation is interactive in that the domain of judgment is not given in the event, but features of the event do contribute to judgments constructed by individuals. As stated by Turiel and Davidson (1986, 116–17):

This analysis makes use of the distinction between the media of interaction and the object of interaction. By media, we refer to the materials a subject interacts with, as they might be recorded by an objective observer (without access to the subject's interpretation.) By object, we refer to the epistemological significance of the materials, which is determined by the specific type of knowledge the subject brings to bear on these materials. . . . The principal strategy for domain identification involves distinguishing types of subject-object interactions. The assumption is that there are different types of theorizing (the subjective side) appropriate to different objects of thought (the objective side). . . . The object of thought is not given directly by the medium of interaction; it is partially determined by the type of theorizing applied. Accordingly, it is possible to describe this strategy of domain identification as one of distinguishing the fundamentally different ways that media can be construed, interpreted or treated as objects of thought.

From an interactive and interpretative perspective the elements of events are not in an arbitrary relation with individuals' domains of judgment, as evidenced by the common features of acts classified as moral (table 4.4). The stimulus events used in the research share a number of features central to individuals' moral reasoning: they are intentional (i.e., nonaccidental) acts having negative consequences for others (e.g., physical or psychological harm, injustice) and the victim is an unwilling participant. The descriptions of events presented to subjects were constructed to be clear cases of an agent intentionally harming (or behaving unfairly toward) an unwilling victim. That subjects interpreted the acts this way is evidenced by data on subjects' justifications; subjects made reference to these features of the acts in their responses. Furthermore, in research that explicitly posed questions about acts with different intentions (Davidson, Turiel, and Black 1983), it was shown that subjects took intentionality into account in their moral judgments.

The criteria characterizing moral judgments (generalizability, impersonality) apply to acts including these features (harmful consequences, intentionality) and not solely to the behavioral act per se. The domain identification of events, therefore, should not be taken in a positivistic or overly literal fashion. Because many acts with moral implications have consequences inextricably bound up with them (e.g., stabbing someone with a sharp object) there is a tendency to interpret our domain classifications of acts in an overly literal fashion. To classify events, however, it is necessary to examine their component features, since the specifics of a situational context have a bearing on the classification. Assumptions about reality or the natural order, and cultural definitions also may have a bearing on the subject's domain interpretation of events, given that the assimilation of events to domain of judgment is not a static process and can be conceptually transformed. A class of events can be accessed from the point of view of varying domains (Turiel and Davidson 1986).

## Applications and Extensions of Social Concepts in Situational Contexts

It is also necessary to distinguish between *applications* and *extensions* of knowledge in the types of conceptual transformations made by individuals. Once acquired, moral concepts can be applied (or not applied) to various contexts and situations. In our interpretation of the McClosky and Brill survey findings, for example, moral concepts pertaining to rights and civil liberties were clearly applied in some situations (the general items) but not always in others (the specific items). The extension of moral knowledge refers to cases where a moral concept (e.g., avoidance of harm) is extended to encompass actions or types of harm that originally may not have been part of the concept's immediate experiential source. For example, moral concepts governing actions that harm other persons in one's immediate environment can be extended to cover actions believed to be harmful to unobservable entities (e.g., souls of deceased ancestors, supernatural beings, etc.).

The following examples illustrate the application of moral concepts in context and the extension of moral concepts in cases of mediating beliefs about unobservable phenomena. Scheffler (1984) makes use of the following example in the context of a philosophical discussion. At issue is the moral status of an act like brushing one's teeth in the morning. In Scheffler's treatise moral judgments differ from other normative judgments in that they are inclusive, and an act like brushing one's teeth could be regarded as apart from moral assessment (e.g., the act can be regarded as a personal one pertaining to health and prudence.) As Scheffler argues, however, the same action, under certain circumstances, is subject to moral assessment. The scenario is that the person who is about to start brushing his teeth observes another in the next room trying desperately to dislodge a piece of food stuck in his windpipe; further, the toothbrusher is an expert in the use of the Heimlich maneuver and the only one in a position to help, and so on. To simply continue brushing his teeth would be morally unacceptable, asserts Scheffler ("indeed, morally quite awful"). A literal construal of the classification of events by domain would be that an act like brushing one's teeth is always nonmoral and that, therefore, this example is in contradiction with the classification. It would have been patently wrong for us to propose such a literal system and it was not our intention to do so. The example provided by Scheffler illustrates a distinction similar to the general and contextualized instances discussed earlier. The classifications are reasonable under the assumption that individuals make inferences about events and can draw upon the circumstances and context to conceptually transform them. In this example, brushing one's teeth, per se, does not become a moral issue. The context changes the event by introducing a new element (preventing harm).

A second example pertains to the infliction of physical harm. Suppose we saw a person putting a sharp object into the abdomen of an "innocent," defenseless person who is prone and unconscious. Would that be an example of a prototypical moral transgression? Again, these issues cannot be approached literally because the context has a bearing on the classification. For instance, the person using the sharp object may be a surgeon operating on a patient to insure his well-being. When working with the assumption that individuals can conceptually transform events, the level of analysis is not solely in the literal description of events; it includes context, with the goals of the activity and its consequences. There are other examples of "infliction" of harm that entail other relevant goals (e.g., a parent disciplining a child, self-defense, and preventing greater harm).

Similar considerations apply to the classification of events as conventionally relevant. Conventions do not have features like intentional harm or injustice but rather are behavioral uniformities which function within a network of shared meanings and serve to facilitate the attainment of social ends. The relativity of conventional arrangements is one of the features distinguishing them from moral ones. Conventions are alterable and relative to the extent that (a) the goals and functions they serve vary across groups; (b) other conventional arrangements replace existing conventions and still serve the same goals; and (c) the salience of goals changes within groups, necessitating the formation of new conventional arrangements.

Before an event may be classified as conventional, it is important to take into account the goals and functions of the act in particular social situations. As an example, we consider a straightforward convention like "shaking hands," which may serve as a greeting. It is relative across contexts; in many societies people do not greet one another by shaking hands, and the convention may operate only in specific contexts within those societies where it is found. Moreover, another convention could replace shaking hands and still serve the same function. In our research, shaking hands would thus serve as a prototypical example of a social convention. However, prototypical conventional events can also be transformed by the situational circumstances so that moral considerations apply to them. Consider the case of a society where people generally greet each other by shaking hands, the act serving its standard conventional functions. Now, suppose there were an individual within this society with a fatal disease, readily communicable through physical contact. Let us further suppose that this person is aware of his disease, and knows that it is easily transmitted. Let us also say he happens to have a grudge against his previous employer. Imagine a scenario where this individual arranges a meeting with his exboss in order to shake hands with him so as to transmit his fatal disease. Of course, this is not a "social-conventional" act. Its application has morally relevant features (i.e., intentionally inflicting harm on an unwilling victim). The fact that an otherwise conventional act has been transformed into a moral one by the addition of certain features does not mean that the act of shaking hands is not generally functioning as a social convention in this context. The act simply does more than serve the usual conventional function in this example.

Now consider another example bearing on the "conventional" content of dress. The example is fanciful and certainly implausible, but it has ramifications for our subsequent discussion of the role of variations in cultural contexts. Suppose one were to learn that each time he wore yellow socks (he does this infrequently) his neighbor experienced a nonfatal heart attack (the neighbor was not necessarily aware when the individual was wearing yellow socks). A cautious person might be led to avoid wearing yellow socks for "moral" reasons. If a causal connection were determined between the two events, it might be seen as a moral imperative (especially by the sufferer of the heart attacks) that this person not wear yellow socks. There might exist two somewhat different types of causal links. One is that the sight of person A wearing yellow socks produces great emotional upset in person B, which results in a heart attack. This link makes for what has been referred to as a second-order phenomenon (Turiel 1983). A second (fanciful) causal link is that wearing yellow socks has some direct physical effect upon other persons. Such events and facts (i.e., that person A wearing yellow socks is causally linked to heart attacks in person B) are of obvious relevance to judgments about avoiding harm to persons and serve to transform the conceptualized status of the act (e.g., arbitrary to nonarbitrary from a moral viewpoint).

Introducing a bit of ambiguity into the example, suppose we were told, without any opportunity for firsthand observation, that each time someone in a certain city in the United States wears yellow socks it results in heart attacks among persons in some distant land. Accepting the validity of the information could very well result in the community prohibiting a form of dress for moral reasons. Similarly, a community may have the belief that there is an afterlife and that those who have died from heart attacks experience negative consequences whenever their living relatives wear yellow socks. Accepting this belief in an afterlife and the validity of the information regarding the negative consequences could result in the community prohibiting forms of dress in certain persons for moral reasons. This is a case of the extension of preexisting moral concepts (that one should avoid inflicting harm) to actions influencing the welfare of unobservable entities. The reader may have noticed that the example has become less fanciful since beliefs do exist regarding the afterlife and possible connections between earthly activities and unobserved consequences. Moreover, the examples point to the relevance of beliefs and information regarding matters that are not of direct access or based on firsthand judgments of validity. These examples are intended to illustrate the importance of separating moral judgments from factual or informational assumptions about events.

## Domains of Judgment and Cultural Contexts

The relevance of accepted facts, sources of information, and beliefs regarding the natural order and the supernatural for moral judgments and conclusions was considered a number of years ago (Asch 1952; Duncker 1939). More recently an anthropologist (Hatch 1983, 67) put it as follows: "For the anthropologist to establish the claim about the radical differences in values among the world's populations, they would have to eliminate these differences in factual belief and compare pure moral values uncontaminated by existential ideas."

From a Gestaltist perspective, Asch and Duncker earlier had called for consideration of the role of available knowledge and accepted assumptions about persons, reality, and the universe (natural and supernatural, observable and unobserved) in research on moral judgment and behavior. Asch suggested that beliefs regarding the nature of the afterlife have a bearing on how a society treats its elderly. In one society, for example, a son was obligated to kill his parents while they were still in good health because of "the belief that people continue to lead in the next world the same existence as in the present and that they maintain forever the condition of health and vigor they had at the time of death" (Asch 1952, 377). Similarly, moral judgments may be associated with beliefs or knowledge regarding the sources and cures of illness (e.g., that illness is produced by germs and viruses or by spirits; Asch 1952, 563). Class, race, and caste distinctions, with their associated hierarchies, are other aspects of social relations often associated with assumptions and accepted knowledge (sometimes purportedly with a scientific data base) regarding psychology, physiology, and heredity (Gould 1981). As mentioned earlier in this chapter, research with adolescents and young adults revealed that intuitive psychological, biological, and natural-order assumptions were associated with their evaluative judgments of issues like abortion, incest, pornography, and homosexuality (Turiel and Hildebrandt, in preparation).

The sources of laypersons' assumptions about the different realms and disciplines of knowledge are varied. Although many assumptions are derived from generally accepted knowledge in the community, laypersons also form theories of the sort that have led to their characterization as intuitive psychologists and social scientists (Nisbett and Ross 1980; Ross 1981; Shweder 1979b, 1980; Turiel 1979). Reliance on assumptions, information, and knowledge not derived firsthand is not restricted to the layperson, however. Even experts (e.g., professional scientists) must rely on knowledge derived from a relevant community. As Polanyi (1964, 163) put it:

> The knowledge comprised by science is not known to any single person. Indeed, nobody knows more than a tiny fragment of science well enough to judge its validity and value at firsthand. For the rest he has to rely on views accepted at secondhand on the authority of a community of people accredited as scientists. But this accrediting depends in its turn on a complex organization.

Polanyi went on to explain that the commitment to the scientific community is not accepted unconditionally. Existing scientific opinion is viewed as a competent but not supreme authority. Although individual scientists are regarded as competent, the possibility remains that they may be mistaken in many ways. Perhaps the "intuitive" social scientist operates under similar conditions and qualifications.

The role of information, knowledge, and assumptions regarding persons, physical or social causality, and the natural or supernatural order in evaluative judgments is largely unexplored territory. Research on the issues of incest, pornography, and homosexuality provides a beginning. Comparing judgments in different cultural context may prove to be a fruitful approach to the study of this problem. Some research on morality and convention has been conducted in non-Western contexts (Carey and Ford 1983; in Indonesia; Hollos, Leis, and Turiel 1986, in Nigeria; Song, Smetana, and Kim, in press, in Korea). A cross-cultural study conducted by Shweder, Mahapatra, and

Miller (reported in this volume) is the most extensive to date; their findings have the potential for illuminating the relations among domains of judgment, assumptions about natural order, and events. The research reported by Shweder, Mahapatra, and Miller is part of a more general "social communication" theory of moral development (Edwards 1985; Edwards, this volume; Shweder 1986; Shweder and Miller 1985) that includes postulates in agreement and disagreement with the approach on domains presented here. We will discuss their work at some length in order to address issues raised by social communication theory regarding the domain approach, as well as to consider general theoretical and methodological issues raised by cross-cultural findings. One of the stated aims of the Shweder, Mahapatra and Miller essay in this volume is to evaluate our approach (which they label "social interactional"). Just as they point to strengths and limitations in our approach we find strengths and limitations in theirs. Their theory, too, raises as many conceptual and empirical issues as it resolves (which, we hasten to add, is not meant as a criticism, as it would apply to most scholarly enterprises).

## Moral Judgments, Ideologies, and Divergent Rationality

An extensive account of social communication theory is unnecessary since much of it is presented in this volume. It would be useful to highlight some main points, and, as a means of best understanding their position, to make reference to views presented elsewhere on social construction (Shweder and Miller 1985) and divergent rationalities (Shweder 1986). A major proposition is that morality is acquired by children through communications of cultural judgments and ideology. Moral evaluations and judgments are transmitted to children by those referred to as "local guardians of the moral order" (especially parents) in the context of routine practices (especially within family life). The routines that make up regular practices and convey the organization of the family and society reflect the moral order. Since culture determines which practices are moral, events are classifiable as moral or nonmoral solely in reference to cultural practices and ideology.

In their view, moral ideologies are socially constructed in the sense that different moral realities can be constituted and the different realities are equally rational or reasonable. Systems of moral judgment in varying cultures represent different frameworks stemming from fundamentally different conceptions of self, society, and nature. It is proposed that like other systems of thought, including religion and science, cultural differences in morality represent divergent—incommensurable—rationalities. Neither reason nor evidence allows judgments of comparable adequacy between moral systems since they constitute divergent rationalities (Shweder 1986).

However, constraints are placed on the idea of divergent rationality. Although cultures vary in their worldviews, there are certain mandatory features of morality, in contrast with discretionary features, that appear to be common across cultures and thus candidates for universality. Nevertheless, the moralities of cultures, especially those of the secular United States and the orthodox Hindu temple town of Bhubaneswar, are primarily divergent. The divergence is characterized by a distinction between rights-based and duty-based moral codes. The rights-based morality of the United States is fundamentally related to a free-contract ideology and the belief in a "social order that is built up out of self-interested individuals in the pursuit of their wants and preferences." According to social communication theory, conventionality exists in individually oriented cultures which separate social order from the natural moral order. In duty-based Indian culture natural moral order is fundamentally related to social roles and arrangements. Shweder, Mahapatra and Miller (p. 3) assert that the duty-based approach to morality

> . . . is to start with the assumption that social arrangements are primary or fundamental, and to attribute moral significance to the universal fact of role differentiations (for example, within the family) and the unequal distribution of health, wealth, status, beauty and intelligence across individuals. That view argues that a differentiated social morphology is part of the natural order of things, that the moral value of a person is dependent on the position occupied within a system of particularistic interpersonal relationships, and that the moral value of a person can be measured by reference to the skills, talents and psychological qualities that are his or her just desert. It judges as fair whatever actions ensure that the proportions between differentiated social functions and social roles are adapted to the society as a whole.

This sketchy account of the general theory put forth by Shweder, Mahapatra, and Miller aims to highlight some main points pertaining to an evaluation of its strengths and limitations and to how it relates to our own approach. It is difficiult to do justice to the approach in such short space, especially since the range of the discussion is sometimes breathtaking. In fact, that wide range is both a strength and a shortcoming. It is a strength in that it opens up new areas of investigation and starts to account for cultural assumptions, information, and knowledge about "reality." The shortcoming is that the theory attempts to encompass a great deal with only a few constructs: communication and transmission are seen as the basic sources and mechanisms for development; culture is the primary source of morality and explanatory basis for rationality; and morality is seen to encompass a wide range of social practices.

Cross-cultural research is always of value in the study of social development, but not only because it reveals variations in social practices. As noted earlier, findings of variation require explanation. One of the contributions of the cross-cultural research reported by Shweder, Mahapatra, and Miller is that it serves to draw additional distinctions regarding moral orientations. These include the distinctions between mandatory and discretionary aspects of morality, as well as between context-independent and context-dependent moral obligations. The idea that there are discretionary features of morality is useful and needs to be incorporated into empirical investigations. However, the proposition brings with it some difficult conceptual problems calling for epistemological criteria to distinguish the mandatory from the discretionary. As far as we can tell, it is only the presence or absence of consensus among moral philosophers and cultures that serves to distinguish the mandatory (consensus-based) from the discretionary. The problem is that a presumed consensus can change if one were to talk to other philosophers or include additional cultures. Would findings of cross-cultural variability on a feature now in the mandatory category shift it to the discretionary category?[4] The distinction helps delineate how moral concepts of the general, abstract type may be applied in contexts with particular assumptions about reality (the "facts" of situations) and in varying social arrangements or organizations. Without the defining criteria, however, the distinction is slippery. Similarly, the distinction between universalistic context-independent moral thinking and context-dependent moral thinking requires explanation. In the Shweder, Mahapatra, and Miller analysis it is mainly presented as an empirically based distinction. We make a similar distinction and approach it through analyses of separate moral and nonmoral variables and their intersection in

---

4. Issues revolving around racial distinctions and discrimination provide interesting examples regarding the status of discretionary features of morality. For instance, there are variations between and within societies regarding the rights of minority groups, as is evident in recent history by the practice of slavery in the United States and in contemporary times by various manifestations of unequal treatment of certain racial groups. It is not clear to us how the idea of discretionary features of morality would apply to variations in these types of practices. More generally, the extent to which consensus or variability relate to mandatory or discretionary features requires further specification.

mixed-domain situations. This issue is considered further in our rein-terpretation of the Shweder, Mahapatra, and Miller data.

Shweder, Mahapatra, and Miller also use cross-cultural compar-isons as a vehicle for identifying assumptions about different aspects of reality, the natural and psychological world. In this respect, their research begins to uncover areas called for by Asch (1952), Duncker (1939), and Hatch (1983). The ethnographic accounts of traditional Hindu views of the individual, the social order, and the natural order (Shweder and Miller 1985) as well as the empirical data from Indian subjects provide a wealth of information on assumptions and theories about realms like the natural, supernatural, biological, psychological, and sociological. These accounts also point to similar and discrepant assumptions in Western cultures. On this issue, there is some con-vergence between our approach and social communication theory. Specifying such variables is consistent with our emphasis on the dif-ferences between prototypical and contextualized cases. Moreover, as noted earlier, the work on concepts of incest, pornography, and ho-mosexuality examines the intersection of evaluative judgments and knowledge of, or assumptions about, similar variables.

## Global Morality versus Heterogeneity in Social and Moral Orientations

In our view, identifying, disentangling, and drawing relations among religious, natural, biological, and psychological concepts is necessary for a more comprehensive analysis of moral and social evaluations. A limitation of the Shweder, Mahapatra, and Miller approach is that in-sufficient attention is given to distinctions of this sort. This is in part a consequence of their implicit proposition of interrelatedness of varying aspects of individuals' judgments within worldviews. The proposition that natural, social, and psychological orders are all formed by moral ideology is not the limitation to which we refer. We wish to state explicitly that its limitation lies not in the fact that it is an alternative hypothesis to our proposition of the coexistence of domains of judgment. The limitation is in the failure to make the type of separation of variables needed to provide evidence for the hy-pothesis.

However, the Shweder approach to the integration of varying as-pects of judgments includes two premises that require scrutiny in light of the type of data we have presented thus far. These are the as-sumption of homogeneity in cultural orientations and a perspective on morality that globally encompasses most, if not all, social prac-tices. Shweder, Mahapatra, and Miller appropriately argue for the compatibility of diversity and rationality. Their search for diversity does not go far enough in that it seems to stop with diversity in comparisons between cultures. In their analysis diversity between cultures implies a homogeneity in the social-moral-natural worldviews within cultures. Insofar as a culture embodies a homogeneous orientation there is little room for coexisting domains of judgment or for diverse concerns in the culture or its individual members and the conflicts that may result. In our view of coexisting domains of judgment, diversity in rationalities spreads further than variations between cultural orientations. In this regard, we find ourselves in substantial agreement with the postulates, persuasively presented by Shweder (1979a, 1979b, 1980) in earlier writings, that individuals do not possess general traits or orientations and that there is no compelling evidence for the proposition of cultural integration.

A central contrast drawn by Shweder, Mahapatra, and Miller in cultural orientations is the distinction between the duty-based morality of India and the rights-based morality of the United States. The prepublication draft of the Shweder and Miller (1985) essay contained excerpts from an interview with a temple priest, which were provided to illustrate the duty-based morality of India and its associated role-centered features. Here we reproduce that dialogue:

> "Do all people have the right to speak?" The question is put to a temple priest in the old town of Bhubaneswar. The priest replies: "All have the right to speak. Even children have the right." The question is pressed further: "Standing on the Bada Danda (the "main road" leading to the Temple of Juggernath in Puri, Orissa) a man boldly announces over a loudspeaker that widows should eat meat and fish, wear colored saris and ornaments, use vermilion and eye make-up and put color on their feet, and that sons should address fathers by their first names. Will you defend his right to speak even if everyone wants to beat him?" Replies the priest: "He has a right to speak, but there are things that should not be said. First, we should try to make him understand. If that fails, all will beat him. Even if you have a right to speak you should not say such things."

The comments of the temple priest may be of surprise to McClosky and Brill (1983) or other survey-takers in the West for their *consistency* with the findings on attitudes toward civil liberties in the abstract and in contextualized situations. As previously discussed (see table 4.1), in American samples most state that "all have a right to speak." Put the question in various contexts and the number of respondents supporting the right decreases dramatically (see table 4.2). Often, the right to free speech is subordinated to social duties and social goals. The similarities between the responses of the Hindu priest and Westerners regarding rights and duties are striking. This is not to deny the differences. Westerners are not likely to endorse restrictions on free speech because one is speaking in favor of widows eating meat and fish. However, Westerners do often subordinate rights to "duties." More generally, the findings we discussed in the previous sections argue for the coexistence of rights and duties, as well as for the coexistence of judgments about harm, justice, social roles, and social order.

Moreover, a concern with rights is not absent among Hindus in India. In a public address in New Delhi, Rajiv Ghandi, prime minister of India, recently spoke to the issue of the rights of women in his country. Ghandi asserted that women are the most disadvantaged and discriminated against persons in the society, a situation which he referred to as shameful and reflecting backwardness in thinking. Indeed, the issue of women's status in the society is prevalent in the social communication approach to social practices in India. Many of the social issues used by Shweder (1986) and Shweder and Miller (1985) to illustrate a duty-based morality in India and to contrast it with rights-based morality bear on the differential role of women and their special obligations (see esp. Shweder 1986, 188–89). It should also be noted that while in India there is public concern with rights, in the United States there is public concern with the types of issues defined by Shweder as duty-based. As examples, two recent Supreme Court opinions used "duty-based" arguments in upholding restrictions on individual rights to speech (Bethel School District v. Fraser, 84-1667, U.S. 1986) and homosexual activities (Georgia v. Hardwick, 85-140, U.S. 1986).

The emphasis on cultural homogeneity in social communication theory appears to be the basis for its global and encompassing view of morality. This is perhaps the most significant point of divergence with our position and, in this respect, Shweder's position has interesting commonalities with that of Kohlberg (1969, 1971) and his colleagues. In comparing the domain approach with Kohlberg's formulation of three major levels of moral judgment, Shweder, Mahapatra, and Miller state that the domain approach has turned the Kohlberg three-level scheme on its side. Instead of a developmental moral sequence that progresses from egoistic-personal to conventional to true moral understanding, it is stated, we have proposed that each of these three forms of understanding constitutes a domain that undergoes a separate course of development. This characterization of our approach is an oversimplification. Insofar as we have turned the three-level scheme on its side, it is from the perspective of domain specificity and toward the aim of explaining structures of moral and social judgment and practices. We propose that coexisting with morality are the individual's intuitive psychological and sociological understandings.

Shweder, Mahapatra, and Miller are in agreement with most of these distinctions but wish to apply them mainly to Western cultures (and perhaps to some other cultures). In other respects, however, their approach is consonant with Kohlberg's conceptualization of the realms of prudence, psychology, and convention as all part of morality. In social communication theory these presumably moral concepts are not ordered developmentally. In keeping with the emphasis on cultural determination and homogeneity, the morality of any of these concepts is structured by culture. That is, culture dictates the form and content of morality, such that most social practices, including those characteristic of each of the levels proposed by Kohlberg and many more, can be part of morality. The form and content of what may be conveyed as moral by a given culture seems boundless.

One manifestation of this all-encompassing view of morality is that importance of social practice is equated with morality. This equation is manifest in their methodology (which is considered below). It is also evident in their interpretation of Murdock's cross-cultural survey of the types of infractions of rules and taboos that are considered directly to cause illness in 139 societies (Murdock 1980, as cited in Shweder, Mahapatra, and Miller). These include food (e.g., a Muslim eating pork) and sexual taboos, as well as violations of rules of etiquette. Moreover, those violations are higher on Murdock's list of cross-cultural frequency of causes of illness than are violations like theft or inflicting physical harm. The line of reasoning advanced by Shweder, Mahapatra, and Miller (not by Murdock) is that the view that a transgression causes illness is an indication of its perceived seriousness, which in turn is an indication that it is considered to be a moral transgression.

An alternative view of the association between social infractions and illness is that it reflects a variety of factors. In the cultures surveyed by Murdock, food, sex, and etiquette taboos are higher on the list of causes of illness than theft or killing. The Shweder, Mahapatra, and Miller interpretation leads to the implausible conclusion that in those societies food, sex, and etiquette are of greater moral relevance than theft or murder. An alternative speculation is that non-socially administered sanctions (illness, disease) have been theorized within cultures to explain taboos regarding practices that are not directly related to actions with harmful consequences to persons. In that case, Murdock's listing would indicate a general recognition of differences between acts associated with morality and convention. Another obvious factor relevant to the Murdock analysis is that health, illness, and prudential matters are important to most peoples. Therefore, a theory (whatever its source) associating illness with a particular act will treat the avoidance of the act as important. Hence, the perceived seriousness of a rule violation would not necessarily be an indication of its moral status. Otherwise, it would have to be said that the "taboo" communicated to children in the West that they avoid people with measles is a moral one.

Shweder, Mahapatra, and Miller do not sufficiently account for prudential sources of significant social practices. As an example, in Bhubaneswar the taboo on contact with a menstruating woman appears to be prudential. Shweder and Miller (1985, 48) assert that it is natural for a menstruating woman to be prohibited from sleeping in the same bed with her husband. This is apparently related to the view that menstrual blood is poisonous. The consequences of a husband coming into contact with this "poison" are grave: "His beauty will vanish. He will become ill and after some days he will die." Indeed, a wisely self-protective husband would avoid poison for reasons of prudence. Of course, a wife who does not avoid contact with her husband can be faulted on the moral ground of inflicting great harm. These two sides of the issue parallel the injunction that children should not play with sharp objects. Prudence dictates that a child avoid playing with knives so as not to cut himself or herself. Morality dictates that a child avoid using a knife to cut someone else.

Also open to question is the assumption that perceived seriousness reflects a moral orientation. We reviewed studies (see table 4.2) showing that certain social practices considered important or serious are judged through nonmoral criteria. More generally, a global view of morality as encompassing a wide range of social practices risks overlooking significant nonmoral social concepts by assimilating them to the moral template. Shweder, Mahapatra, and Miller give examples of significant practices they assume to be moral, such as those entailing social hierarchies, exclusion of classes of persons, condoned infliction of harm, legitimized restrictions of liberties, and so on. There may be, however, nonmoral institutional, prudential, and sociological functions to such practices that make them important for individuals and societies. In economic contexts, for instance, social practices promoting hierarchies and exclusion of classes of persons may be tied to profit and efficiency. Exclusionary practices may also serve to maintain harmony and cohesion among those included. Under certain conditions parents may discipline children not solely as an expression of moral blame but also as a means of shaping behavior based on an implicit or explicit theory of the psychology of development. Similarly, punishments administered to adults may reflect an intuitive sociological perspective on the maintenance of roles and organization. The potential conflict between social organizational functions and moral goals is brought out by Berlin's (1981) consideration of the concept of equality in an orchestra. Berlin points out that in the organization of an orchestra inequality in the distribution of authority is accepted to achieve musical goals. In the community of musicians and music lovers the maintenance of roles and hierarchical organization is important.

## Assumptions, Facts, and Domains in India: A Critique and Reinterpretation from an Alternative Paradigm

At this juncture, we trust it is evident that our theoretical perspective on domain specificity and developmental processes represents an alternative paradigm to the perspective on cultural determination through social transmission of generalized forms of moral ideology. It appears that this is a classic case of paradigm clash; there is a difference in, shall we say, worldviews. Moreover, the empirical methods, procedures, and modes of data interpretation are also divergent in many ways. It is our intent to consider the methodology of Shweder, Mahapatra, and Miller and to reinterpret some of their findings from the domain perspective. Before doing so, however, Shweder's intriguing notion of divergent rationality bears further commentary, for it is the case that social communication theory does not allow for an evaluation of alternative theoretical systems (such as ours) without contradicting itself.

The position taken by social communication theory on culture and morality is guided by the more general proposition of divergent rationality—for example that duty-based morality is a rationality divergent from rights-based morality. Because there are rationally based frameworks with differing premises, assumptions, rules of evidence, and means of assessing and interpreting data, divergent frameworks are not comparable. In Shweder's (1986) view, divergent rationalities are evident in religious frameworks, as well as among theoretical perspectives in the natural and social sciences. Rational discussion can be had within perspectives, paradigms, or traditions, but not across them. For Shweder, the inability to cross paradigms is evident in many realms. For instance, it is evident in the divergent rationalities of creationist and evolutionary views of the origin of life, and in diverse schools of thought in the social sciences (e.g., divergences between behaviorism and psychoanalysis, or classical and Marxist economics). According to Shweder, the relative adequacy or truth of any of these perspectives cannot be settled by reason or evidence.

While maintaining that reason and evidence cannot be used to compare divergent schools of thought, Shweder argues, using reason, logic, and empirical evidence, that social communication theory is more adequate than alternative paradigms, such as our domain approach (implying we should relinquish our worldview and embrace his). This has the makings of a vicious circle. If Shweder is correct in his use of reason and evidence and in his claims of greater adequacy, then his premises regarding divergent rationality cannot be right—they would be disconfirmed by his own use of reason and evidence. If Shweder is correct in his view of divergent rationality and incommensurability, then his use of reason and evidence to argue for greater adequacy would be invalid. In that case, it would have to be accepted that the cultural-anthropological paradigm of social communication theory and its general worldview represent a rationality divergent from other theories and worldviews, such as Freud's psychoanalytic-biologistic worldview, or Skinner's behaviorist-environmentalistic worldview, or Piaget's structuralist-interactional worldview. If our analysis of this contradictory state of affairs is correct, a fundamental modification in social communication theory is needed to break the circle. (A more general discussion of paradoxes and internal contradictions in the analyses of proponents of social constructionism is in Turiel, in press.)

As we do not completely adhere to the view of divergent rationality or incommensurability, we would not assert that the data presented by Shweder, Mahapatra, and Miller can be ignored.[5] However, it is important to recognize that their data were gathered from the perspective of a particular set of assumptions and views that in many important respects resulted in different procedures from those used in research conducted from the domain perspective.

## General Methodological Considerations

Shweder, Mahapatra, and Miller present comparisons of the social judgments of middle-class and upper middle-class secular subjects

5. In part, the clash is between paradigms reflecting the disciplines of anthropology and developmental psychology. In several respects, the two disciplines start with very different assumptions, address different questions, and attempt to explain different phenomena of human experience. Accordingly, efforts at crossing the two disciplines confront the problem of coordinating divergences in paradigms. The not too successful efforts of the past forty or fifty years at combining the two disciplines indicate that this is a hazardous enterprise.

from Hyde Park, Chicago (an elite university setting) and subjects from the orthodox Hindu temple town of Bhubaneswar in India (subjects were from Brahman and Untouchable families). By comparing secular and orthodox groups, the research mixes categories in that subjects differ in nationality, culture, and religiosity.[6] A more adequate design would have been to include secular and nonsecular samples from each national/cultural setting. Since the design confounds religiosity with nationality and cultural variables, the application of the findings to general psychological and developmental processes is not demonstrated. To illustrate, Shweder, Mahapatra, and Miller con-

6. The limitations of solely using subjects from an orthodox temple town are evident in the ways some Indians now living in the United States responded to the items in the Shweder, Mahapatra, and Miller interview. These responses were obtained through pilot work, in which questions were posed to Indians regarding a set of the Shweder, Mahapatra, and Miller items. Several of the respondents spontaneously offered negative comments regarding the appropriateness of the items for the religion. This indicates that the types of controversies and diverse interpretations of social practices familiar to Westerners may also exist among Hindus. The following informative commentary comes from an administrator in a Northern Californian Hindu temple and cultural center:

> Before we go any further, I want to ask you a question. What's your objective? Do you want to find out about Hinduism, or you are talking about social customs that some of the Hindus observe? What you have done, you have picked up some social customs of a very, very tiny minority of Hindus, here and there. . . . All your questions, except the last, they are about very superfluous customs of some sects of Hindus. . . . They are all social customs. And there are certain social customs which have a basis on religion and there are some which have a basis on environment, or some sectarian beliefs. . . . I have studied Christianity, I have studied Islam, so in every religion according to me, there are three things: one is the basic or the fundamental principles, the other is what we call the rituals. I think you understand what I mean by rituals. Say you baptize a child. Now how a Roman Catholic baptize the child and how the Protestant baptize a child? There is a difference. So likewise there are rituals in every religion. And then the third thing is what we call mythology. . . . So if we concentrate on fundamental principles of religion and if we concentrate only on rituals or mythology, there will be world of difference. And there will be terrible, terrible, terrible misunderstandings because you know the rituals, their interpretations are different, their meanings are different. Mythology is different, mythology sometimes you believe in something, sometimes you don't. But if you only concentrate on the principles, fundamental principles of religion, which are eternal, they don't change; rituals change. Mythology can be interpreted. For instance, you take any religion—speaking truths. No religion says that you should not speak, uh, you should tell lies. No religion says that honesty is not the best policy. No religion says that man should hate man. Love is the theme of every religion. So if we don't, if we completely ignore the fundamentals and we only concentrate on mythology or rituals, then we are in trouble.

clude that findings of variability between the two groups support the developmental propositions of transmission, social communication, and replication of cultural ideology. It may be, however, that transmission, communication, and replication are processes of acquisition in orthodox nonsecular contexts while some other processes hold in other contexts. (This is not, we want to be clear, a hypothesis we are currently prepared to endorse.) The confounding of nationality and religiosity does not allow for analysis of these kinds of issues. As discussed below, the confounding also has a bearing on conventionality.

The Shweder, Mahapatra, and Miller data come primarily from three types of questions regarding thirty-nine items. These were the perceived seriousness of each transgression, evaluation of the act (is it right or wrong?), and the alterability and perceived relativity or universality of the practice. A subject's judgment about a given item was considered conventional only if the practice was judged both relative and alterable within one's group. Responses of relativity and unalterability within the group were considered to meet the criterion for "context-dependent moral obligation." Using these criteria, Shweder, Mahapatra, and Miller reported a paucity of conventional judgments in the two samples. The Indian sample showed hardly any conventional judgments. The American sample showed a greater, although still low, frequency of conventional judgments than did the Indian sample (especially at older ages). The general conclusions drawn from their findings are that the distinction between morality and convention is culturally specific and that in India all events have a moral basis and conventionality is virtually nonexistent.

Shweder, Mahapatra, and Miller's conclusions are overstated and not as firmly established as implied. There are shortcomings in the way stimulus items were classified and in their assessment procedures. There is also a divergence from the methods used in our domain approach since Shweder, Mahapatra, and Miller do not report subjects' reasons or justifications for their responses. In research from the domain approach, coding of justifications (e.g., Davidson, Turiel, and Black 1983) is an important complement to assessments of importance, evaluations of acts, and the criteria of alterability and relativity.

In the Shweder, Mahapatra, and Miller analyses there is an overreliance on subjects' attributions of importance or seriousness of transgressions as indicating a moral orientation. Assessments of justifications help distinguish importance ratings from domain of reasoning (Tisak and Turiel 1985; Turiel 1983). Correspondingly, Shweder, Mahapatra, and Miller use evaluations of acts (is the act wrong?) without subjects' justifications. In the research in the United

States (i.e., many of the studies summarized in tables 4.3 and 4.4) individuals typically evaluated conventional and moral transgressions as wrong. Among other measures, subjects' justifications for their evaluations serve to distinguish different conceptual bases for similar "gross" evaluations. There are several possible nonmoral perspectives for differing evaluations of right or wrong, such as religious, prudential, or informational. Perhaps the clearest examples come from the studies including sex-role transgressions, where it was found that subjects used different kinds of reasons in evaluating acts as wrong (Carter and McCloskey 1983–84; Stoddart and Turiel 1985). Shweder, Mahapatra, and Miller's analysis, relying solely on cultural comparisons of items evaluated as right or wrong, renders their findings ambiguous. Whereas the patterns of disagreement and agreement on evaluations of items are of interest, they do not directly assess domain differences or similarities. Analysis of justifications in conjunction with epistemological criteria is a requisite methodology for comparative study of domains in social reasoning.

Another problem associated with the lack of justification data is that elements of moral and natural-order conceptions are not sufficiently separated. In the Shweder, Mahapatra, and Miller analysis, descriptive statements about natural order (e.g., nonarbitrary conceptions of causality) are not separated from statements pertaining to obligatory moral ends. It is asserted that for Indian subjects the natural order *is* a moral order. In part, this assertion stems from findings that certain social practices tied to natural (earthly or unearthly) phenomena are not viewed as alterable or contextually relative and are not based on social sanctions.

It is necessary, however, to separate conceptions of natural order as a moral order from conceptions of natural order as a set of assumptions or theories about the world. Natural order may influence judgment either (a) by virtue of beliefs about consequences automatically ensuing from an act, or (b) by virtue of a prescriptive orientation toward laws of nature, psychology, biology, and so on. From the perspective of a subject who believes that harmful consequences will naturally result from engaging in an act, social consensus, cultural practices, and whether or not the act is done in private will have no relevance for the moral judgment. In a similar fashion, for the subject who believes the act violates a natural law, social consensus and the criteria of conventionality will not bear upon the subject's judgment, insofar as these considerations do not influence natural-law conceptions.

Analyses of underlying justifications can help distinguish the two conceptions of the natural. Where judgment is based on a belief about harmful consequences ensuing from the act, the justifications will generally take the form of moral and prudential concerns, and the act's rightness or wrongness will be *contingent* on the occurrence or nonoccurrence of these consequences. However, where judgment is grounded on a conception of the act as a natural law, the justifications will reference this law, and the rightness or wrongness of the act will be contingent *upon the law itself* and not upon the occurrence of morally or prudentially relevant consequences.

Research in the United States (Turiel and Hildebrandt, in preparation) shows that both of these orientations to natural-order conceptions are applied to contested issues like incest, pornography, and homosexuality. Individuals sometimes reason from assumptions about the act's inherent harmfulness, and in those cases their reasoning resembles that exhibited in the prototypical moral issues. Reasoning about these issues also reflects a fusion of natural-order and prescriptive moral judgments that often contains inconsistencies, contradictions, and qualifications. That individuals in India do not solely view the natural order as an inherently prescriptive moral order is evident from the limited information on justifications provided (usually in the form of sketchy quotations from protocols). Individuals reference prudential concerns, moral concerns, and social-organizational concerns throughout the rationales and "argument structures" provided by the researchers. It has not been demonstrated that, among Indians, natural-order based moral and prudential judgments (i.e., judgments based on unearthly, biological, or psychological theories about cause and effect relationships) differ from moral and prudential judgments (of earthly observable events). We are not suggesting that Indians *never* conflate descriptive natural-order and prescriptive judgments in their reasoning. Our hypothesis is that Indian subjects do so for certain issues, just as has been found with American subjects. Without a detailed examination of justifications it is not known for which events this phenomenon occurs.

Similar considerations hold for the use of the criteria of unalterability/alterability and universality/relativity. For Shweder, Mahapatra, and Miller, the judgment that an act is both unalterable and universal constitutes a criterion for morality (a criterion with which we generally agree). It is necessary, however, to be able to distinguish moral from nonmoral judgments of nonalterability and universality. As an example, Lockhart, Abrahams, and Osherson (1977) found that by a certain age children judge a "physical law" (i.e., specific gravity of rocks) as unalterable by consensus and applicable across social settings (universal). Accordingly, without task analyses of stimulus items and justification responses, it can be difficult to discriminate what may be different types of judgments. This is particularly relevant when considering judgments related to natural order. It may be that some judgments of unalterability and universality stem from the conception that a person-related (social or psychological) event is simply fixed by nature (as in the conception that the law of gravity is "fixed" by nature).

The way Shweder, Mahapatra, and Miller classify items represents a fundamental divergence from our approach. They attribute to us the view that events have an objective status, in the sense discussed earlier, and on that basis classify items in a literal and positivistic fashion. The implication is that we would classify events by their "objective" content, without consideration of context, circumstances, or interpretations and meanings given to them by individuals. On that basis, Shweder, Mahapatra, and Miller attribute to us a conventional classification ("morally resistant" events) of any event dealing with content like food, clothing, terms of address, greetings. In turn, any items dealing with direct or observable harm are in the moral category ("morally prone" events).

As detailed earlier, these attributions are based on a misconception of our position. In attributing to us a "literal" classification of stimulus items, Shweder, Mahapatra, and Miller mistakenly consider our viewpoint to ignore the premises, beliefs, and factual assumptions surrounding events (as illustrated by the "yellow socks" example). In addition, many of the stimulus items appear to involve domain mixtures and conflicts between competing moral considerations. The failure of Shweder, Mahapatra, and Miller to account methodologically for the distinction between prototypical events and those involving conflicts or multiple domain components is consistent with their assertion that observations of domain-mixed events cast doubt on the distinction between domains. They imply that a separation of domains would be valid only if there were not instances of domain overlap or ambiguity. In our view, this represents both a logical fallacy (see Turiel and Davidson 1986) and a positivistic bias in the construal of categories. The nature of such a bias regarding category distinctions, in general, was aptly put by Searle (1983, 79) in discussing what he viewed as a pervasive philosophical proposition in literary theory derived from logical positivism:

> . . . there is the assumption that unless a distinction can be made rigorous and precise it isn't really a distinction at all. Many literary theorists fail to see, for example, that it is not an objection to a theory of fiction that it does not sharply divide fiction from non-fiction, or an objection to a theory of metaphor that it does not sharply divide the

metaphorical from the nonmetaphorical. On the contrary, it is a condition of the adequacy of a precise theory of an indeterminate phenomenon that it should precisely characterize that phenomenon as indeterminate; and a distinction is no less a distinction for allowing for a family of related, marginal diverging cases.

In any event, since the distinction between prototypical and mixed events is an important aspect of our taxonomy of stimulus events, it cannot be ignored in analyses purporting to examine that taxonomy cross-culturally.

## Task Analyses and Categorization of Stimulus Events

Since we do not fully accept the classifications attributed to us, we have undertaken task analyses and reinterpreted the stimulus events using ethnographic material from the Shweder, Mahapatra, and Miller essay (this volume), as well as from Shweder (1986) and Shweder and Miller (1985). Where possible, we took into account available information regarding the assumptions, premises, and accepted facts relevant to the judgments of subjects from India. The task analyses presume a distinction between knowledge stemming from direct experience and mediated knowledge regarding phenomena that are not experienced by individuals directly. The analyses also accounted for the previously noted distinction between the direct experiential origins of knowledge and their application or extension. Our task analyses are limited because the information provided is at times sparse. Nevertheless, we were able to construct at least preliminary classifications for many of the stimulus items. We classified twenty-eight of the thirty-nine events (the remaining eleven could not be classified without further information on Indian beliefs and/or social organization) into the following categories summarized in table 4.6: (a) *direct moral events*, (b) *unearthly-belief-mediated moral events*, (c) *multidimensional events*, and (d) *social-conventional events*. Table 4.6 also provides a listing of events in each category and a brief description of the event's parameters relevant to the task analysis.

The category of *direct moral events* encompasses actions with directly or immediately inferred consequences involving harm, injustice, or violation of rights. In these events the effects of an action are readily available and typically require only a minimum of inferential activity to deduce that harm or injustice has occurred. The "directness" of these events is a function of certain basic human features (e.g., the capacity for persons to experience physical or psychological harm irrespective of cultural definitions and shared meaning systems), as well as of the observable nature of the cause and effect relationships for these acts. These events are of the prototypical type in that harmful consequences or injustice are salient and there are no competing moral or social-organizational components. Because of the direct and nonconflicted nature of these events, there should be a considerable degree of cross-cultural similarity in evaluations. Indeed, all eight events classified as *direct moral* were considered transgressions in both cultures.

Other events in the study bear on mediated knowledge of harmful consequences to which children have no direct access. These are events that, because they pertain to matters like food or dress, Shweder, Mahapatra, and Miller assume we would classify as conventional. We would not do so—as indicated earlier by the examples regarding shaking hands and wearing yellow socks. One variant of the latter example dealt with the acceptance of an afterlife and the community belief that those who have died from heart attacks experience negative consequences whenever their living relatives wear yellow socks. Given those two premises, an otherwise neutral act would be conceptually transformed into one with moral (harmful) implications.

Several of the presumed conventional items (listed in table 4.6) are of precisely this type. They fall under the category of *unearthly-belief-mediated moral events*, which refers to events that implicate the existence of nonobserved entities (e.g., souls, deceased ancestors) who either suffer harm from earthly actions or serve as intermediaries between an act and harmful earthly consequences. Some examples derived from Shweder's ethnography of such beliefs in India are as follows: that if a son were to eat chicken the day after his father's death it would result in his father's soul not receiving salvation (Shweder and Miller 1985, 48); that if a widow were to eat fish regularly it would cause her great suffering and offend her husband's spirit (Shweder, Mahapatra, and Miller, this volume, 1–82); that if a menstruating woman were to enter the kitchen it would result in the deceased ancestors leaving the household for several generations—an event that would bring various misfortunes on the family (Shweder and Miller 1985, 48).

The data from items in this category yield evidence for the validity of the distinction between moral judgments and assumptions about the nature of reality (Asch 1952; Hatch 1983). Among the Indian subjects assumptions are made about nonobserved entities that can experience harm from the performance of earthly activities. Such knowledge is mediated since children do not have direct access to the experiences. In turn, moral injunctions regarding the prevention of harm are *extended* to nonobserved entities.

.

**Table 4.6:** Task Analyses and Category Classifications of Shweder-Type Events[a]

| Events | Elements Determining Classification |
|---|---|
| ***Direct Moral Events.*** *Events with directly observable and immediately inferred consequences (i.e., causing harm, producing injustice, violating rights).* | |
| In school a girl drew a picture. One of her classmates came, took it, and tore it up. (32) | Destruction of another's property: violation of property rights. |
| While walking, a man saw a dog sleeping on the road. He walked up to it and kicked it. (20) | Infliction of physical harm. |
| A father said to his son, "If you do well on the exam, I will buy you a pen." The son did well on the exam, but his father did not give him anything, spending the money on a carton of cigarettes. (24) | Breach of promise: violation of trust. |
| There was a rule in the hotel: Invalids and disfigured persons are not allowed in the dining hall. (29) | Discriminatory treatment of a class of persons. |
| Two people applied for a job. One of them was a relative of the interviewer. Because they were relatives, he was given the job although the other man did better on the exam. (21) | Unfairness in the form of partiality. |
| You went to a movie. There was a long line in front of the ticket window. You broke into line and stood at the front. (30) | Unfairness in the form of not taking proper turn. |
| You meet a foreigner. He is wearing a watch. You ask him how much it cost and whether he will give it to you. (31) | Violation of respect for persons and or property. |
| A poor man went to the hospital after being seriously hurt in an accident. At the hospital they refused to treat him because he could not afford to pay. (15) | Failing to alleviate serious physical harm. |

***Unearthly-Belief-Mediated Moral Events.*** *Events in which mediating beliefs about unearthly entities play a part in the event's status as a moral transgression. The classification of these acts as "moral" is based on the kinds of consequences believed to ensue—i.e., harm to others, violation of rights, unfairness, etc. In some cases the moral feature of the event is unobservable (e.g., harm to souls of the deceased), while in other cases unearthly entities intercede between the act and harmful earthly consequences.*

| | |
|---|---|
| The day after his father's death, the eldest son had a haircut and ate chicken. (1) | Harmful consequences: deceased father's soul would not receive salvation if proscription against eating chicken is not observed. |

**Table 4.6:** *(continued)*

| Events | Elements Determining Classification |
|---|---|
| One of your family members eats beef regularly. (2) | Harm to the cow, believed to be a sacred being. |
| A widow in your community eats fish two or three times a week. (4) | Harmful consequences: act will offend husband's spirit and cause the widow to suffer greatly. |
| Six months after the death of her husband the widow wore jewelry and bright colored clothes. (5) | Violation of marital trust, based on (1) the belief that the widow will have sex if she makes herself attractive, and (2) the belief in an afterlife and a continuing bond between husband and wife. |
| A woman cooks food for her family members and sleeps in the same bed with her husband during her menstrual period. (7) | (1) Harmful consequences: it is believed that if a menstruating woman enters the kitchen the deceased ancestors will not come to the home for several generations, resulting in various calamities and misfortunes for the family. (2) Harmful consequences: it is believed that menstrual blood is poisonous and if the husband comes into contact with his wife during menses he will be destroyed. |
| After defecation, a woman did not change her clothes before cooking. (8) | Harmful consequences: it is the wife's duty to offer food to returning spirits of dead ancestors, and for this purity is required. Were she not to do this duty it is believed the deceased ancestors would not eat, and the goddess of wealth would leave the house. This would result in ruin for the family. |
| A widow and an unmarried man loved each other. The widow asked him to marry her. (11) | Violation of marital trust (infidelity), based on a belief in an afterlife and the continuing bond between husband and wife. |

*Multidimensional Events. Three types of events with more than one dimension: (1) domain mixtures, (2) conventional violations with potential second-order moral effects, and (3) conflicts between competing moral considerations.*

| | |
|---|---|
| A letter arrived addressed to a fourteen-year-old son. Before the boy returned home, his father opened the letter and read it. (34) | Domain Mixture. Moral component: violation of privacy rights. Social-conventional component: authority jurisdiction. |

*(contd. on next page)*

**Table 4.6** *(continued)*

| Events | Elements Determining Classification |
|---|---|
| A boy played hooky from school. The teacher told the boy's father and the father warned the boy not to do it again. But the boy did it again and the father beat him with a cane. (37) | Domain Mixture. Moral component: infliction of harm. Social-conventional component: violation of commands of an authority. Also may include an explicit or implicit theory of child discipline practices. |
| A father told his son to steal flowers from his neighbor's garden. The boy did it. (19) | Domain Mixture. Moral component: violation of property rights. Social-conventional component: authority jurisdiction. |
| A young married woman went alone to see a movie without informing her husband. When she returned home her husband said, "If you do it again, I will beat you black and blue." She did it again; he beat her black and blue. (35) | Domain Mixture. Moral component: infliction of harm. Social-conventional component: violation of the commands of an authority. |
| A wife is waiting for her husband at the railway station. The train arrives. When the husband gets off, the wife goes and kisses him. (28) | Conventional violation with potential *second-order* moral effects in the form of psychological harm or offense. |
| Two men hold hands with each other while they wait for a bus. (39) | Conventional violation with potential *second-order* moral effects in the form of psychological harm or offense. |
| It was the king's order, if the villagers do not torture an innocent boy to death, twelve hundred people will be killed. The people killed the innocent boy. So the king spared the life of the twelve hundred people. (14) | Moral conflict. Act of physical harm to one person is pitted against potential physical harm to many persons. In addition, there is also a social-conventional component of authority jurisdiction. |
| A father, his eldest son and youngest daughter traveled in a boat. They had one life jacket. It could carry one person. The boat sank in the river. The father had to decide who should be saved. He decided to save his youngest daughter. The father and the eldest son drowned. (33) | Moral conflict. Forced choice of saving one life. |

**Table 4.6** *(continued)*

| Events | Elements Determining Classification |
|---|---|
| **Social Conventions.** *Acts that may be conventional insofar as they constitute behavioral uniformities within the social context (tentative classification; see text).* | |
| A man had a wife who was sterile. He wanted to have two wives. He asked his first wife and she said she did not mind. So he married a second woman and the three of them lived happily in the same house. (9) | Act may violate a convention governing marriage relationships. |
| In a family, a twenty-five-year-old son addresses his father by his first name. (13) | Act may violate a convention governing forms of address. |
| A woman is playing cards at home with her friends. Her husband is cooking rice for them. (18) | Act may violate sex-role conventions. |
| In a family, the first-born son slept with his mother or grandmother till he was ten years old. During these years he never slept in a separate bed. (36) | Act may constitute adherence to convention governing sleeping arrangements. |
| A man does not like to use a fork. Instead he always eats rice with his bare hand. He washes it before and after eating. He does this when he eats alone or with others. (38) | Act may constitute adherence to convention governing table manners. |

[a]Numbers in parentheses refer to Shweder et al.'s numbering system. Ethnographic information for the classification comes from the following sources: Shweder, Mahapatra, and Miller (pp. 1–82); Shweder and Miller (1985); Shweder (1986).

The Shweder, Mahapatra, and Miller findings show there are cultural differences in assumptions about reality and similarities in moral injunctions regarding harm. For example, a separation needs to be made between moral concepts and assumptions about an afterlife. If one accepts the assumption that there is an afterlife and that certain earthly actions affect the well-being of a person in the afterlife, then that action can be regarded as moral. If one assumes, in contrast, that there is no material or spiritual afterlife, then one's actions would not be seen as having direct harmful consequences to a person who has died. All the moral events (in our classification) have in common a concept of welfare (avoiding harm to others) and an understanding of a causal relation between actions and harmful consequences. As the findings show, for the Indian subjects judgments about the *unearthly-belief-mediated* variety are akin to their judgments about other instances of actions producing harm. In contrast, subjects from the United States did not consider these events transgressions. This cultural variability is to be expected since the assumptions, premises, and accepted facts differ for Indians and Americans.

It may appear from the category of *belief-mediated* events that by our analysis *any* event can become part of the moral domain if the subject believes that harm or injustice will follow from the act. In one sense this is true—that is, from the viewpoint of the subject's reasoning. However, the attribution of harmful consequences to particular acts and entities is dependent on verification of factual knowledge in ways that are applicable cross-culturally. For instance, consider the proposition that eating chicken the day after one's father's death has harmful consequences for the father's soul. If it were somehow verified that there is an afterlife and that eating chicken has harmful consequences, then it is likely the event would take on moral significance in Western culture. Similarly, if the nonexistence of an afterlife were verified to the satisfaction of most Indians, then it is likely the act would lose its moral significance there.

In table 4.6, a number of items are grouped under the general category of *multidimensional events*. This category includes three types: domain mixtures, conventions with the potential for second-order effects, and conflicts between competing moral demands.

Some of the items include components from more than one domain (e.g., moral considerations in conflict with social-organizational considerations) and are clearly events of the contextualized type in the McClosky and Brill survey and the experimental conditions of the Milgram study. As already discussed extensively, the domain of judgment individuals apply to these events may vary by situational parameters (e.g., salience of components) and type of relation between domains (e.g., in conflict or synchrony). One simple example of a mixed-domain event in table 4.6 is the case of a father who orders his son to steal flowers from a neighbor's garden. In this event the conflict between the social-organizational (authority) and moral (stealing) components resembles the Milgram experiments, in which an authority (the experimenter) orders the subject to inflict harm on an innocent person. This is a mixed event in India *and* the United States since in both cultures fathers are authority figures and stealing is a moral transgression.

It is not always the case that mixed events in one culture should also be classified as mixed events in another culture (e.g., persons in authority may differ cross-culturally). A number of the examples are mixed events in India (i.e., have both moral and social-organizational concerns) but are single-domain events in the United States. An example is the event in which a young married woman repeatedly disobeys the orders of her husband by going to see a movie without first obtaining his permission, and in consequence he "beats her black and blue." In India, there is a social-organizational concern (the hierarchical division of roles and authority within the family) that does not hold in the same way in the United States (authority is more evenly distributed between husband and wife). By repeatedly disobeying her husband, the woman in the story was intentionally contravening the commands of an authority figure. It is likely that Indian subjects view the maintenance of familial role differentiations as a matter of great importance, permitting the use of corporal punishment to ensure its enforcement. Although the absence of justification data does not allow us to determine with certainty how Indian subjects conceptualized this event, the finding that Indians did not view the act as a transgression suggests they judged the moral feature of physical harm as subordinate to the social-organizational consideration of authority and maintenance of sex-role differentiations. These social-organization considerations, it should be reiterated, apply to marriage as a social institution in India; marriages in the United States are typically less stratified and role-differentiated. Therefore, what might be a purely moral transgression in the United States is a mixed-domain event in India. The event does have its counterparts in the United States, as evidenced by the results of the Milgram experiment. In the United States, legitimized punishment is administered for violations of important social-organizational rules. In military or school settings, for example, hierarchical authority distinctions are a central part of the social order, and punishment of violators is often severe (although at present corporal punishment is probably rarely practiced).

A similar case from Shweder's examples is the event in which a father uses corporal punishment to discipline his son for playing hooky from school. In addition to the moral component of harm (the father beats the boy with a cane) and the social-organizational considerations of maintaining obedience and hierarchical authority in the family, the event may be evaluated on the basis of naive theories of child-rearing and discipline practices. It may be seen as in the child's best interest, ultimately, to suffer the punishment.

Another type of event grouped within the multidimensional category pertains to second-order moral consequences. These are conventional violations that may be regarded as having moral implications insofar as they may cause offense to persons. The second-order effect has been documented in the United States through adolescents' judgments regarding nudity at a public beach (Turiel 1983). Public nudity was conceptualized by most subjects as a breach of social convention. However, some of those subjects negatively evaluated the act if it were to offend bystanders (hence the second-order effect). Two of the Shweder, Mahapatra, and Miller items are of this type (a couple kissing in public, and two men holding hands while waiting for a bus).

A third type of multifaceted event involves dilemmas with two conflicting moral considerations. The inclusion of these events is likely due to Shweder, Mahapatra, and Miller's concern with Kohlberg's (1969) theory and methodology, which relies on moral dilemmas. (Judgments regarding conflicting moral considerations have not yet been a focus of research in the domain approach.) However, one of the events embodying a moral dilemma may also be a mixed-domain event. In this event a king orders the villagers to put to death an innocent boy or else twelve hundred people will be killed; the villagers kill the boy and the lives of the people are spared. This event is similar to the "disastrous consequence" examples employed by Utilitarians to argue the limitations of deontological moral reasoning. Deontological moral reasoning would evaluate the act negatively, while a strict utilitarian (consequence-based) evaluation might view killing the boy as the necessary alternative, since it results in the "greatest good" given the circumstances. Furthermore, the presence of an authority command raises the possibility of social-organizational concerns entering into individuals' judgments as well.

We cannot draw specific implications for findings on this set of items because relative salience of the components would influence responses. In part, salience is determined by cultural factors. We would expect, however, to find variations within cultures on some multidimensional events. In fact, it was only on these events that within-culture variation was obtained in India (these are, in the Shweder, Mahapatra, and Miller numbering system, 14, 28, 33, and 34, presented in table 4.6). More generally, on multidimensional items there were findings of commonalities and differences between cultures. For example, in both cultures it was considered wrong for a boy to steal on his father's orders—suggesting that the moral component was more salient than the authority component.

Before considering the final category, we note that two of the events we did not task-analyze have interesting implications for cross-cultural research. These are events reflecting differences in social arrangements that produced different judgments in the two cultures. One pertains to marriage arrangements. For Americans, marriage is generally conceived to be a union based on mutual affection and within the jurisdiction of the two parties. Consequently, Americans judge as acceptable the item in which a doctor's daughter marries a garbage man against her father's will. In contrast, in India marriage is a "social" institution carrying with it consequences for the status and power of the families of husband and wife. Marriages in India have many more "concerned parties," and it may be seen as unjust for one person to decide on a matter that affects many (as suggested by Shweder, Mahapatra, and Miller's "distilled argument structure" for Hindu informants). The institution of marriage differs in important respects for the two cultures, serving different functions and affecting people in dissimilar ways. However, the underlying fairness notions of Indians and Americans do not seem incommensurable. On many matters Americans would accept the basic postulate that it is unfair for one (or two) individual(s) to decide on issues seriously affecting the lives of many. While this example demonstrates important cultural differences in the social-organizational considerations implicated in the institution of marriage, it demonstrates similarities in moral reasoning as well.

A related example is found with respect to cultural differences regarding inheritance patterns. One item concerns the unequal distribution of inheritance, whereby the son receives most of the father's property while the daughter is only entitled to a small portion. From a strictly egalitarian viewpoint the act seems unfair. However, Indians reportedly justify this form of distribution on the grounds that the son is required to take care of his parents in their old age and to pay their funeral expenses (Shweder and Miller, 1985). This justification reflects a consideration of the way the particulars of a situation can enter into moral judgments of fair distribution. The rationale given for why the son should inherit more shows an attempt to take into account relative need and to compensate for previous obligations— concerns that might also enter into issues of distributive justice in Western culture.

In table 4.6, we are left with only five events classified as social conventions. (Recall that we have reclassified items Shweder, Mahapatra, and Miller assumed we would consider conventional.) Ethnographic information for these events was particularly sparse in contrast to the other categories. The events were classified primarily on the basis of the conventional nature of the categories they represented (e.g., forms of address, customs, table manners). The classification of items in this category should be seen as tentative; further information about Indian beliefs, premises, and assumptions could necessitate a reclassification. Of these events, three were evaluated negatively in India, while two of them were not considered transgressions.

## Convention in India?: Still an Open Question

The task analyses and reinterpretations of the Shweder, Mahapatra, and Miller items have an important bearing on their propositions that the moral/conventional distinction is specific to cultures which are oriented to individualism and that convention is absent in cultures oriented to natural-moral order. We do not believe that Shweder, Mahapatra, and Miller have documented their proposition that conventional judgments are absent in orthodox Hindu culture. In the first place, according to our task analyses very few conventional items were used in their research. Furthermore, the primary criterion for conventional judgments—alterability and relativity—is applied in overly stringent ways and the assessment questions are ambiguous.

The criterion for conventional judgments of alterability *and* relativity is overly stringent because its application would mean that any practice that is considered unalterable within one's culture, yet relative, would be classified as moral. To apply the criterion adequately it is necessary to ascertain the basis by which unalterability is combined with relativity. One way of doing so is to test the limits of the authority for altering a rule or social practice—as was done by Nucci (1986) in assessments of concepts of religious conventions (see table 4.5). The two judgments of unalterability by consensus within the society and relativity for other societies may indicate that the perceived authority for alterability lies somewhere other than in consensus. Alternatively, it may indicate instances in which individuals access an event in two ways, reflecting the coexistence of domains of judgments. That is, individuals may see an event as having moral ramifications with regard to their own society and conventional ramifications with regard to another society. It is interesting to note that the proportion of Indian subjects stating that certain social practices are relative ranges between 19 percent and 30 percent (adding the "context-dependent moral" and "conventional" responses in table 1.7 of Shweder, Mahapatra, and Miller). Again, justification data would be useful in clarifying the issue.

On the basis of the available data, we do not know whether (or to what extent) responses combining unalterability and relativity reflect context-dependent moral reasoning. The idea of context-dependent moral obligation is useful, but the conceptual basis for the distinction between universally binding and context-dependent moral obligations needs specification. We have pursued a similar distinction (Smetana 1983; Turiel 1983) in analyses of situations of moral and conventional domain mixture and of "second-order" moral effects. The hypothesis is that one source of context-dependent moral obligation is the intersection of morality and convention. There may be other sources.[7]

Moreover, the specific questions used by Shweder, Mahapatra, and Miller to assess the relativity dimension bear scrutiny. Subjects were asked if another society would be a *better place* if a particular practice were stopped. They were not asked relativity questions of the type used in other studies (e.g., is it all right not to have a rule; or is it all right for the society to engage in a practice). Asking subjects whether another society would be a better place if it abolished a social practice is highly ambiguous with regard to criteria for morality because of the question's many connotations. A subject could state that abolishing a practice would result in a "better place" because it provides a smoother way of coordinating interactions, or leads to greater harmony and social order, or is more expedient or efficient. There are still other possible nonmoral sources for the response, including one's beliefs. If one is convinced of the existence or nonexistence of a God, for instance, then it might be thought better, for various reasons, if others knew it. If one believed that the world is round or that Darwinian evolutionary theory is correct, then perhaps it would be concluded that another country is better off knowing it. Closer to home, if one believes that "social communication" theory is correct, then it

---

7. One source of "context-dependent" morality is in assumptions about "reality". An example offered by Shweder, Mahapatra and Miller of a context-dependent moral obligation is a Brahman who reasons that it is wrong for a widow to eat beef (a "hot" food) in India because it will stimulate her sexual appetite, but all right for American widows to eat beef because America's cold climate counteracts the effects of "hot" foods. This subject's argument includes a consideration of the ways in which climatic factors interact with biological and unearthly processes in producing the relevant consequences; this additional component allows exceptions to the general "law of nature" governing the effects of hot foods on widows. The prescriptive basis of the judgment—prudence and possibly moral concerns stemming from the act's effects on the spirit of the deceased husband—is the same for a subject who reasons about the eating of "hot" foods by widows as a universal moral obligation and for this subject's context-dependent moral reasoning. *Universal* and *context-dependent* moral reasoning are differentiated, in some cases, by "factual" beliefs (e.g., whether climate is a causally relevant variable to include in a consideration of the effects likely to result from eating "hot" foods). A distinction reflecting differences in conceptions of reality (e.g., cause and effect relationships) is different from distinctions in systems of prescriptive thought (moral judgment systems). Epistemologically significant context-dependent moral thinking would demonstrate contextuality in the *prescriptive* ground of individual's moral judgments. A case of this would be an individual who reasoned that moral concerns (e.g. justice, preventing harm) are important considerations for judgments pertaining to the social interactions within one culture but do not apply to judgments of the practices of all cultures. It is reasoning of the latter variety that Shweder, Mahapatra, and Miller have not demonstrated.

might be thought that other places (e.g., other laboratories) would be better off if they recognized it (we assume this to be a "nonmoral" position taken by Shweder, Mahapatra, and Miller). A relevant empirical finding is that (a) on the one hand adolescents consider certain gender-related behaviors as appropriate, better than deviations from them, and would want to avoid places which do not adhere to them, and (b) on the other hand, the same adolescents do not evaluate such deviations as morally wrong (Carter and McCloskey 1983–84; Stoddart and Turiel 1985).

A sound indication that the items used by Shweder, Mahapatra, and Miller do not adequately meet criteria for convention and that the assessment procedures are imprecise is the finding of only a small amount of conventional reasoning in the American sample. Using the Shweder, Mahapatra, and Miller criteria, the so-called morally resistant events elicited only 20 percent conventional reasoning in the adults, a significant increase over the amount shown by the youngest subjects (5- to 7-year-olds). These findings are discrepant with results from many studies of United States samples showing substantially more conventional reasoning (even at the youngest ages). The Shweder, Mahapatra, and Miller findings, therefore, underestimate young children's understanding of the distinction between morality and convention.

We trust that Shweder, Mahapatra, and Miller would agree that underestimating young children's competence is indicative of methodological variations. They have argued (also see Shweder 1982) that features of tasks are importantly related to the thinking elicited from subjects and that variations in task characteristics produce variations in judgments. Young children's competencies are often underestimated because of task characteristics and by the way questions are posed ("it is easy to devise tasks which confuse the young child"; Shweder 1982, 358). By this line of reasoning, it would have to be said that the Shweder, Mahapatra, and Miller task characteristics and modes of questioning serve to underestimate the young child's understanding of convention. Similarly, task characteristics produced lower frequencies of conventional judgments among older subjects in the Shweder, Mahapatra, and Miller sample than in other studies.

We can also point to two specific task characteristics contributing to the low frequency of conventional judgments. One is the unfamiliarity of several Hindu social practices for American subjects. In addition, from the perspective of young Americans who are unaware of the religious or spiritual underpinnings of the events, some of the social practices may have appeared discriminatory because a subset of the population (e.g., widows, women) is singled out for special treatment. Hence the finding that "morally resistant" events were moralized by American subjects.

Perhaps Shweder, Mahapatra, and Miller also underestimated the presence of conventional reasoning in the Indian subjects because of task characteristics, as reflected in the choice of items and questions posed (it may be easy to devise tasks that serve to weight responses toward one type of thinking or another). As Shweder and others have stressed, the failure of individuals or groups to display a type of judgment on certain tasks does not mean that the type of judgment is unavailable or nonexistent. Thus, the proposition that conventional judgments are not made within orthodox Hindu culture remains undocumented. It is especially important to use tasks more closely associated with potentially nonreligious aspects of systems of social interactions (or at least to determine if such interactions exist).

Nevertheless, it is conceivable that conventional judgments do not exist in Hindu and other orthodox cultures. Were that the case, there are plausible alternative explanations to the one presented by Shweder, Mahapatra, and Miller. We have proposed that individuals form judgments about conventions and an understanding of constitutive systems out of their social interactions. The metaphor is of a developing intuitive social scientist cognizant of social organizations. In nonsecular settings the metaphor of an intuitive theologian and/or naturalist may be applicable. Individuals may show a degree of specialization in their intuitive understandings, and perhaps in some orthodox comunities specialization in intuitive theology overwhelms the intuitive social science side of things.

These speculations require further research. We do know, however, that conventional judgments are not restricted to Western settings. Three separate studies conducted in non-Western settings yield evidence of conventional reasoning and its distinction from moral reasoning. In one study (Song, Smetana, and Kim, in press) the subjects were from Busan, Korea (the second largest city in the country) and ranged from five to eighteen years of age. Using four separate transgressions for each domain, assessments were made of evaluations of transgressions, justifications, rule contingency, and relativity. Moral and conventional transgressions were judged differently on most dimensions.

Another study (Hollos, Leis, and Turiel, 1986) included eight to eighteen-year-old subjects from a village in Southern Nigeria. With regard to two transgressions (stealing, violation of greeting rule), assessments were made of evaluations, justifications, sanctions, and alterability. As in some studies conducted in the United States, the distinction was not clearly made by the youngest subjects (eight- to eleven-year-olds). Older subjects, however, justified each transgression type differently; they also regarded the conventional rule as alterable and the moral rule as unalterable.

The third study (Carey and Ford 1983) was conducted in Indonesia and only included ten- to eleven-year-olds (mainly Christians and Moslems). Subjects evaluated three transgressions (stealing, talking loudly in a classroom, not wearing shoes to school) for degree of wrongness and provided reasons for their rankings. The moral transgression was ranked as more serious than the conventional transgressions and the justifications for the rankings corresponded with domain of the events. The patterns of justifications provided by Indonesians for the nonmoral transgressions differed somewhat from those found in comparable studies in the United States (Nucci 1981). Subjects in both settings used justifications based on social organization (rules, authority, social order) and personal jurisdiction. There were differences in the specific nonmoral transgressions associated with each type of justification. Those differences support the proposition that conventions function in a network of shared meanings that may vary from one social setting to another.

## Social Experiences and Development

As stated earlier, the issue of variations in social practices has important implications for explanations of the process of development. Focusing on cross-cultural variations, Shweder, Mahapatra, and Miller and Edwards propose that children acquire social judgments through cultural messages communicated mainly by parents, and, especially in early childhood, in the context of social practices. On the basis of the proposition that variations stem from the coexistence of domains of judgment, we propose that children form inferences out of varied experiential sources. As detailed shortly, research on early childhood experiences supports this contention. First, we consider ways of using cross-cultural findings to inform explanations of development.

Although there have been numerous efforts over the years to integrate the disciplines of anthropology and developmental psychology, it appears to us that for the most part their potential joint contributions have not been realized. One reason for this is the understandable tendency to lapse into unresolved nature-nurture debates. Whereas some anthropologists have collaborated with psychologists of an environmentalist bent (especially learning theorists), others have forged links with those of a nativistic bent (such as ethologists and sociobiologists). The former have obtained findings of cross-cultural differences in support of nurture, while the latter have found cross-cultural similarities in support of nature. Cross-cultural comparisons are used more for the purpose of estimating the influences of environment or heredity than to explain processes of acquisition.

To explain development it is necessary to elucidate specific propositions regarding processes of acquisition and examine those propositions through close analyses of changes in children's judgments and actions. It is also important to avoid a common pitfall in this kind of work, which we refer to as the "exposure fallacy." The simplest form of this fallacy is the assumption that if children were exposed to that which they acquire, then it was acquired through direct learning or internalization. A more complex version is as follows: If some children (say in one group) were exposed to $X$ while other children (say in another group) were not, and those exposed develop $X$ while the others do not, then that is evidence for (a) the proposition that $X$ is acquired through the mechanism of internalization or replication, and (b) the validity of a general developmental theory of internalization. The use of evidence is as follows: if development is due to nature (heredity, nativism), then differential exposure would not matter; if differential exposure matters, then nurture (meaning internalization or replication) explains development. Such propositions focus exclusively on nature or nurture, without inclusion of alternative developmental processes like assimilation and construction through the child's interpretive activities. The fallacy is in translating differential exposure into an explanation of developmental processes. Exposure can both serve to stimulate the interactive process and provide material for cognitive processing and comprehension—which, in turn, can lead to its acceptance, partial acceptance, or rejection on the part of the child.

A brief example from the realm of science illustrates the fallacy and the potential role of experience and exposure in conceptual constructions. Prior to the discovery or formulation of certain theoretical explanations (e.g., Einstein's theory of relativity, Darwin's theory of evolution) working scientists had not acquired those propositions. Subsequent to their formulation (i.e., after exposure to them) many of those same scientists and new cohorts understand and accept the concepts. Solely using differences in exposure as the basis for ascertaining the acquisition process, it would be said that scientists internalize or replicate content to which they are exposed. It is more plausible that the exposure provides material by which the scientists are able to understand and construct for themselves a new perspective. Moreover, the development of prior concepts is a necessary basis for the comprehension of new concepts. Indeed, scientists who may not have discovered the concepts themselves are nevertheless able to apply them creatively and in ways that lead to additional formulations.

We are not proposing that the development of children's thinking necessarily parallels transformations in the thinking of professional scientists. The example merely illustrates that while exposure is an important source, internalization is not the only explanation. Moreover, in order to explain the influence of exposure to concepts, ideas, frameworks, and so forth, it is necessary to account for the intersection of the child's existing concepts or judgments and the environmental content.

The example suggests that exposure as one source of ideas, theories, or values is compatible with an acquisition process based on the individual's actions upon the environment, including inferences and interpretations of experienced events. Children's social environments contain varied elements of interaction, which can be analyzed from the perspective of the child's interpretations of experiences. Included are significant interactions with adults in positions of authority (parents and other familiar and unfamiliar adults), as well as with other children (Piaget 1932; Youniss 1980). Children are likely to learn a great deal from their relations among themselves. A frequently overlooked source of social knowledge is in the reactions of the self and others to experienced events (e.g., experienced or observed emotional reactions to an event like one person harming another; see Turiel 1983 for an extensive analysis of the role of elements of social interactional events in the development of social judgments). Another aspect of the social environment includes social institutional elements, such as rules and authority relations in systems of social organization (Damon 1977; Laupa and Turiel 1986).

As a means of investigating individual-environment interactions, systematic observations have been conducted in day-care center classrooms (Smetana 1984), preschools (Much and Shweder 1978; Nucci and Turiel 1978; Nucci, Turiel, and Encarnacion-Gawrych 1983), elementary and junior high school classrooms and playgrounds (Nucci and Nucci 1982a), and unsupervised playgrounds (Nucci and Nucci 1982b). These studies demonstrate that children's social interactions are indeed multifaceted (for reviews of the findings, see Nucci 1982 and Turiel 1983). *Patterns* of interaction and communication revolving around moral transgressions differ from those revolving around conventional transgressions. Since these studies mainly assessed interactional patterns, they did not yield data regarding children's interpretations of those interactions or the effects of the experiences on development. The studies show heterogeneity in children's experiences and differential patterns of social interaction associated with domains of social judgment.

The implications we draw from our observational studies differ from those drawn by Edwards (1985, this volume) from observations of social interactions among children and adults in a community in Kenya. The various observational examples presented by Edwards mainly focus on statements made by parents or older siblings to children. It is presumed that observations of parental discipline methods and communications are evidence both of how children acquire morality and of the content of the moral codes acquired (which has the makings of the "exposure fallacy"). As one example, Edwards points to observations in which sanctions or threats of sanctions by a parent or older sibling result in the child ceasing to commit a transgression like hitting another. Such examples demonstrate immediate behavioral control but are not evidence for influences on children's moral development. In fact, there is a good deal of evidence that physical punishment as a child-rearing method is ineffective in promoting moral development (Hoffman 1970, 1977; Kohlberg, 1963). Moreover, recently it has been found (Patterson, 1982) that parental punishment increases the amount of aggressive behavior in boys who have already demonstrated aggressive tendencies. (An additional ambiguity is that Edwards's presentation of the observational material does not include a coding system to categorize responses. The interpretations do not always derive in an obvious way from the protocols.)

Edwards misconstrues our position regarding the social interactional basis for the development of moral and conventional judgments. In keeping with the proposition that children attend to and interpret various aspects of their environment, we hypothesized that elements of social-interactional events are important components of children's experiences that contribute to the formation of their judgments. We further hypothesized that the relevant elements of events serving to stimulate moral judgments differ from elements serving to stimulate concepts of convention. It has been proposed that elements of the events themselves should be taken into account, in addition to communications from others. We did not propose that moral events or transgressions are free of communications, directives, or discipline from adults.

The observational studies on morality and convention referred to earlier have shown that elements of events along with commands or instructions are involved in children's social interactions. As noted, the patterns of interaction and communications differed by domain of transgression. Most of the studies were conducted in school settings and the conventional transgressions involved institutional rules and expectations. In those cases, it was found that the youngest children (toddlers and preschoolers) rarely reacted spontaneously to conventional transgressions. With age, children's responses to school-related conventions increased (Nucci and Nucci 1982a). In the unsupervised playground settings children (from seven to fourteen years of age) responded to both types of transgressions, but with greater frequency to moral transgressions (Nucci and Nucci 1982b). In these settings children of all ages frequently responded to moral transgressions. In their reaction and communications the children related to elements of events, including consequences to persons; they also responded with direct and unelaborated commands to other children. Insofar as children (older ones and especially in playground settings) responded to conventional transgressions, it was by communicating the importance of maintaining rules and social order, reacting with social disapproval, and giving direct commands.

Of course, adults also formed a significant part of the social interactions with regard to both moral and conventional transgressions. Adults, too, communicated about elements of moral events. Adult communications in the context of conventional transgressions focused on institutional features like rules and social order and thereby provided rationales for convention that differed from the rationales provided for morality. While to a substantial extent adults responded with sanctions and commands to both transgression types, adult commands and sanctions were more common for conventional than moral transgressions.

Perhaps the major misunderstanding is that both Edwards and Shweder, Mahapatra, and Miller have taken our propositions to mean (a) that morality is associated *only* with elements of events and that convention is associated with sanctions and commands, and (b) that rationales are presented and understood for moral and not conventional transgressions. For instance, Edwards attributes to us the idea that adult sanctions, prohibitions and commands are not associated with children's moral transgressions. On that premise, examples from the observations in Kenya of the use of sanctions, prohibitions, and commands are regarded as evidence disconfirming our position. This line of reasoning, it should now be evident, is not consistent with our position on both empirical and conceptual grounds. Edwards's analysis fails to distinguish the corroboration of knowledge from its source. Adult commands may serve to corroborate knowledge derived from other sources (e.g., the child's own experiences and judgments). In our research adult sanctions and commands were observed in the context of moral transgressions. However, adult sanctions and commands were combined with both explicit adult com-

munications regarding elements of the events and chidren's own reactions to the events. At issue is not whether adults provide
sanctions or commands (they do, of course), but how children relate
to those experiences and how those experiences intersect with other
experiences. Whereas a variety of adult efforts at social control and
instruction can, in important ways, stimulate processes of acquisition and change, it does not follow that the process itself is given in
the environmental event or that it results in children's direct incorporation of transmitted content.[8]

In related fashion, Shweder, Mahapatra, and Miller imply that
we propose that moral thinking "is free of social communication."
Again, at issue is not whether adults communicate with children
about social issues but the form of those communications, as well as
the nature of the effectiveness of their influence. In fact, it has been
maintained (Turiel 1983, chap. 8) that analyses of parent-child interactions need to include broadened conceptions of social communication. Conceptions of social communication can be expanded in at
least two respects. One is to account for the implicit communications in parental discipline methods (such as physical punishment
and love-withdrawal). The second is to account for reciprocity in the
interactions and children's comprehension in the communication
process. Our view of social communication is part of the general position that development stems from an interactive process entailing
interpretations, inferences, abstractions, and constructions of social
understandings. The individual's interactions are varied and include
different types of social relations, exposure to rules and prohibitions,
structured social systems, direct experiences of social events, and
transmitted information about different components of perceivable
and unperceivable aspects of the environment. Therefore, a construc-
tivist position does not imply, as is sometimes mistakenly assumed,
that all or even most of a child's acquisitions occur "in solitary" or in

8. Several other misconceptions of our position are evident in Edwards's presentation. For example, it appears she incorrectly assumes we regard conventions as
unimportant ("mere" conventions). She also has us classifying task assignments as
conventions. Insofar as we have discussed task assignments and rules (as in a study
by Dodsworth-Rugani [1982], discussed in Turiel 1983), they were not grouped with
conventional rules. Edwards also misrepresents our position when stating we have
proposed that an understanding of convention does not appear until middle childhood. Some studies (e.g., Nucci and Turiel 1978) do indicate that preschool children
do not respond to violations of conventional school or institutional rules. We do
not, however, draw the implication that young children have no understanding of
convention or that such understandings emerge later than moral understandings. In
fact, it has been explicitly stated that preschool children may very well form understandings of conventions in other contexts (Turiel 1983, 46).

a social vacuum. Rather, it implies that development is not simply a top-down process of accommodation and that, therefore, a variety of experiential sources are implicated in social development.

Cross-cultural researchers would avoid the "exposure fallacy" through direct investigations of processes or mechanisms of acquisition in children of varying ages. From our perspective, cross-cultural research would best serve to explain development by exploring the varied types of individual-environment interactions, their relative emphases within given cultural contexts, and possible conflicts (Malinowski 1926) engendered by different sources of judgments or knowledge. The cross-cultural research presented by Shweder, Mahapatra, and Miller and Edwards is especially useful for an understanding of how children interpret and assimilate different aspects of communications (e.g., about the observable and unobserved; about what can and cannot be manipulated by the child; about the conceptual and informational; about the secular and the nonsecular). Their procedures, however, are inadequate in this regard. Whereas they focus on possible external sources of acquisition, the mechanisms by which the external content is formed in children are insufficiently elaborated. Explanations are not provided for how communications from the local guardians of the moral order (e.g., parents) influence children. (The traditional mechanisms of reinforcement, imitation, modeling, or identification do not seem to be their candidates.)

In the absence of detailed explanations of the acquisition process we cannot evaluate the Shweder, Mahapatra, and Miller position. However, a focus on parental communications and practices in the early years of childhood as the source of morality includes the general expectation that children's early acquisitions have predictable consequences for later life, that parental practices have consequences for children's later life, and that there would be a high level of agreement between the social orientations of parents and their offspring. The available evidence does not provide support for these expectations. Negative conclusions have been drawn from periodic reviews (e.g., Hoffman 1977; Kohlberg 1963, 1969; Maccoby and Martin 1984; Shweder 1979a) of research on the question of how early childhood attainments carry into later life and on the influences of parental child-care practices on later judgments and behavior. In reviewing culture and personality research bearing on relations of early experiences and development ("to what extent does the past influence the present?"), Shweder concluded that little evidence existed for consistency in the individual's behavior over time or for the influence of early parental child-care practices on later behavior. These conclusions confirmed earlier reviews of relations between child-rearing practices and various indices of moral development by Hoffman (1977) and Kohlberg (1963, 1969). Studies conducted in naturalistic settings have yielded low correlations and inconsistent results from study to study. These studies included measures of the degree and methods of discipline (such as reinforcement, physical punishment and love-withdrawal) and parental attitudes, as well as measures of children's guilt, resistance to temptation, character traits, and conscience.

More recently, Maccoby and Martin (1983) have drawn similar conclusions regarding discipline practices and children's behaviors. They further argue that the research suffers from the lack of explicit theoretical links between parental practices and the acquisition of values, judgments, or behaviors. Along these lines, they maintained that parenting practices and orientations are not homogeneous (e.g., restrictive or permissive) across situations and contexts. Even the family environment itself cannot be characterized as a unitary experiential source in children's social development. Parents report using multiple child-rearing methods that vary by situation and the response of the child (Grusec and Kuczynski 1980).

The expectation of parent-child agreement is unsupported by findings from several studies. On a number of dimensions there are discrepancies or only weak correspondences between the values or attitudes of parents and their children. Studies by Furstenberg (1967, 1971) assessed a variety of attitudes toward social issues (e.g., educational and occupational values, achievement, mobility) and generally found low levels of agreement between parent-child pairs. In Furstenberg's studies higher levels of agreement were obtained when children perceived their parents' attitudes correctly. The pattern of low level of agreement in most parent-child pairs along with higher levels of agreement when children accurately perceive parental attitudes is evident in other studies, including assessments of political attitudes (Tedin 1974), educational goals (Smith 1982), and values and occupational aspirations (Cashmore and Goodnow 1985). This pattern is of particular relevance to the study of developmental processes because it indicates not only that children do not always replicate parental attitudes but also that they interpret and misinterpret communications from parents. It cannot simply be assumed that judgments communicated to children will be understood in the ways intended by parents. In an extensive study of moral, conventional and personal concepts, Smetana (in press) has demonstrated that there are many areas of both agreement and disagreement between adolescents and their parents.

The political socialization literature indicates that there is a fair degree of agreement between parents and children in political party identification and religious affiliation (Jennings and Niemi 1968). However, weak correspondences have been found between parents and adolescents or young adults in their attitudes toward specific political or religious issues (Acock and Bengston 1980; Jennings and Niemi 1968; Middleton and Putney 1963). The specific issues surveyed, to give some examples, pertained to school integration, communists in public office, speaking against the church, interpretations of the bible, and attitudes toward social, religious, and ethnic groups.

Studies of levels of parent-offspring agreement suggest that children may interpret and conceptually transform parental communications. If parents, as cultural agents, are the primary source of children's judgments, then higher levels of agreement would be expected. It could be maintained, however, that in this society the agents for transmission of attitudes or values are not as much the parents as others in public leadership positions. However, the McClosky and Brill (1983) data indicate discrepancies between the responses of the general population sampled and those in leadership positions. Particularly with regard to the contextualized items, the leaders were more supportive of the civil liberties positions than the general public (even after controlling for age, sex, education, religiosity, income, and place of residence). Insofar as community leaders provide cultural messages to the general public, these findings indicate that the messages often go unheeded. The findings also raise a related problem for analyses of the cultural basis of development: insofar as there is heterogeneity of social orientations it is difficult to determine the locus of cultural ideology and to ascertain who serve as "agents" of society or "guardians" of the moral order. Also, insofar as there is heterogeneity in social orientations, it is necessary to account for the role of conflict in the developmental process.

We have drawn negative implications for models of social transmission from studies of child-rearing practices, levels of agreement between parents and their offspring, and discrepancies in attitudes of community leaders and the general public. However, this body of research has positive implications for explanations of developmental process that entail multifaceted and reciprocal interactions of the individual and environment. We do not suggest that early experiences are irrelevant to development. Nor do we suggest that parents play an unimportant role in children's development (nor that peers necessarily have greater influence than adults). Further, we are not suggesting that cultural ideologies or community leaders have no influence on attitudes and judgments. We propose that early experiences establish foundations for later development, but not that they are deterministic of later development. Parents play significant and diverse roles but not causal or deterministic ones in children's social development. Moreover, we propose that interactions with persons other than parents are significant and that, in later years especially (e.g., adolescence and early adulthood) the role and influence of parents may decline (Smetana, in press). There are discontinuities as well as continuities between social and moral judgments in early childhood and social and moral judgments in later years. Hence judgments formed in early childhood serve as foundations for later transformations and are not deterministic.

These propositions regarding individual-environment interactions are supported by recent research on early social development, focusing on parent-infant and parent-toddler interactions, as well as peer interactions among toddlers. One of the first arguments to counter the view that early social interactions are primarily determined by parents came from Bell's (1968) classic reinterpretation of socialization findings. He demonstrated that parents and adults modify their behavior to accommodate to infant dispositions and temperaments; the implication was that parents are not solely responsible for determining the outcome of communicative interactions. Subsequent investigations began to focus on the role of infants in social interactions, particularly the extent to which they are actively engaged in social exchanges and in structuring social communicative interactions (see Uzgiris 1985, for a recent review).

The goal of some studies has been to analyze joint activities that are part of the parent-infant interactive system (Bretherton and Bates 1979; Bullowa 1979; Collis and Schaffer 1975; Fafouti-Milenkovic and Uzgiris 1979; Kaye 1977; Newson 1977; Schaffer, Collis, and Parsons 1977; Stern 1977; Trevarthen 1979). In general, the studies have shown that infants respond to communications from parents and that they develop schemes for structuring interactions. Although the behaviors observed are simple, such as eye gaze or hand gestures, the patterns of interaction that emerge when analyzing these behaviors in social exchanges are fairly complex (actions that reflect joint activities include vocal interaction, interpersonal gaze, deictic gaze, gaze and gesture, gaze and vocalizing; Collis 1979). Of most relevance is the documentation of mutual regulation in mother-infant interaction (Brazelton et al. 1975; Tronick, Als, and Adamson 1979). As described by Tronick, Als, and Adamson (1979, 368–69),

> These performances by the infant are organized and appropriate. They clearly indicate that the infant is not simply exhibiting a rigid and unmodifiable pattern of behavior into which the mother fits herself. Rather the infant is adjusting his responses appropriately to the actions

of his partner. . . . All of these examples give evidence that the infant is aware of his partner's communication. . . . In normal face to face communication, the joint possession of rules accounts for the synchronous movement of caregiver and infant through different phases. Never is one partner causing the other to do something. One musician does not cause the other to play the next note. In the same manner neither the mother nor the infant causes the other to greet or to attend. They are mutually engaged in an activity.

The analogy is informative. Just as musicians coordinate their activities, so do mothers and infants. Other studies on mother-infant interaction that have examined turn-taking sequences in face gazing (Bakeman and Brownlee 1977; Brazelton 1977) and early conversations (Schaffer, Collis, and Parsons 1977) also show that infants and parents develop structured, reciprocal social routines.

These data suggest that conventions or rituals for organizing interactions have their foundation in mother-infant dialogues. Findings of the kind reported by Tronick, Als, and Adamson constitute precursors to later social conventional interactions, in our view, since infants demonstrate awareness of violations in mother-infant interactions. Some researchers have proposed a framework for tracing the early development of conventions. According to Kaye (1982), for instance, a hallmark of early social development is the formation of conventional interactions. Kaye maintains that shared meaning may be absent in very early interactions but does find evidence for the first shared meanings soon after twelve months of age. He concludes that mother-child interactions are reciprocal and systematic and that "the infant is an active partner having definite effects upon the behavior of caretakers" (1982, 52).

From a developmental perspective, achievements during infancy are relevant to later attainments in that they form a foundation for social interactions in subsequent years. While detailed studies of the developmental transitions from infancy have not yet been done, information is available from studies of shared understandings in toddlers and preschoolers. In addition, the research with toddlers demonstrates that heterogeneity in social experiences and social orientations can be traced to early childhood. Viewing the findings on toddler interactions from the perspective of coexisting heterogeneous orientations explains some of the seemingly contradictory findings obtained by different researchers.

Studies that examine parent-child interactions generally portray the toddler as socially oriented and as displaying early forms of moral behaviors (e.g., helping, sharing). For example, in a study by Hay (1979) children between twelve and twenty-four months were observed participating in cooperative interchanges or sharing episodes with their parents; the large majority of these interchanges were initiated by the children. Similarly, Rheingold, Hay, and West (1976) found that the majority of toddlers observed in interaction with a parent or another adult in a homelike laboratory setting shared objects. In contrast, some of the studies of peer interaction portray toddlers as lacking social abilities with respect to establishing reciprocal relations in object-sharing situations. Bronson (1981), in a review of toddler-peer interaction studies, concluded that positive (i.e., nondisputatious) social reciprocity is possible but rare in toddler social interaction. She also concluded that instances of prolonged contact and mutual understandings were found mainly in possession-related conflicts.

Part of this diverse picture of toddler sociability may be due to the history of interactions established in parent-child interaction, which is only just emerging in toddler-peer interaction. Acquaintance among peers enhances the degree of social reciprocity in peer interaction (Becker, 1977; Mueller and Brenner, 1977). In Mueller and Brenner's (1977) observations of playgroups meeting over a period of six months it was found that with time toddlers' social interactions increased significantly. Becker (1977) observed pairs of children of ages nine to ten months in homes over the course of two to four weeks and compared their behavior with pairs (controls) who only met for the first and last observation times. Reciprocal interactions increased for the pairs who met over time but not for the control pairs. These studies suggest that acquaintance and the establishment of a common interactive history facilitates social reciprocity among toddlers. Furthermore, familiarity may explain the discrepancy between parent-child and peer interaction findings. This is evidenced by the findings of Fafouti-Milenkovic and Uzgiris (1979), where infants (at three-and-a-half months of age) encountering an unfamiliar woman responded less to her overtures to communicate than they did to overtures from their own mother.

We have seen that by the preschool years children do make distinctively moral judgments. That preschoolers act on those judgments is evidenced by Sawin's (1980) observations of children (three to seven years) in playgrounds at child-care centers. Even in the absence of adult supervision, most children responded to the distress of other children. It also appears that by the preschool years children actively create and maintain stable social organizations and devise strategies and procedures for resolving conflicts among themselves independent of adult directives or mandates. In a recent investigation (Killen and Turiel 1985) of preschoolers' strategies for resolving conflicts, observations were made of social interactions in two settings. One was relatively unstructured and included a fair amount of adult supervision (children at free play in the preschool playground). The second setting was relatively structured and had little adult supervision; small groups of children participated in peer sessions meeting at regular intervals for about six months.

The study showed that children's social interactional patterns varied by setting. In the free play setting children spent little sustained time with others and when conflicts arose they generally relied on adults to resolve them. In addition, many conflicts revolved around children's attempts to test the limits and boundaries of rules established by adults. By contrast, in the absence of adult intervention during structured peer group sessions, children negotiated methods for sharing, adhering to game rules, and resolving conflicts. During these sessions, children engaged in relatively complex exchange offers (e.g., offering desired toys for promises of friendship), and in discussions regarding the distribution of toys. Further, they attempted to structure group cohesion over the six-month period through methods of including and excluding others in group activities.

The two social orientations observed in this study among preschoolers parallel findings from other studies. Children appear cooperative and social in some contexts and uncooperative or asocial in other contexts. Variables like the history of interaction, setting constraints, and age of peers play a role in determining types of sociability manifested by children. Research on early social development presents a heterogeneous rather than homogeneous view of social experience. Early social behavior is not guided solely by adults; infants, toddlers, and preschoolers have been found to initiate diverse types of social interchanges.

The research on early social interactions begins to elucidate the foundations of later social development. These findings are consistent with the propositions of coexistence and heterogeneity in individuals' social orientations. The proposition of commonality or consistency of social behavior and judgment across social settings needs to be balanced by examination of the qualitatively different kinds of social interactions experienced by individuals. Developmental analyses of age-related changes in both conceptual systems *and* patterns of social interaction need to be undertaken. The aim of such a strategy is to delineate classes of social interaction and to examine their relationship to qualitatively different systems of social judgment (i.e., domains of reasoning). Our discussion of the cross-cultural findings of Shweder, Mahapatra, and Miller stressed the importance of considering, as a means of explaining variations in judgment between cultures, how experiences are interpreted and conceptually trans-formed. A similar consideration holds for explanations of age-related variations in reasoning. Developmental research needs to consider simultaneously potential age-related differences in how children in-terpret social experiences and how they conceptualize and organize their social knowledge, as well as potential differences with age in the types of social interactions themselves.

## Conclusion

Morality is of indisputable importance to individuals and serves as a guide for organizing social life. Morality should be given its due, but it should also take its place among other aspects of social life, social regulation, and social organization. Similarly, culturally defined judg-ments or ideologies are an important influence on social development that should be placed in the broader context of a varied social envi-ronment constituting elements of the developing child's interactions. Because a child's environment is not restricted to one class of inter-action, social development must ultimately be explained as entailing systematic changes, over many years, stemming from interactions with a variety of dimensions of the social world. In our view, the het-erogeneity manifest in social life does not represent randomness or incoherence in the behaviors or judgments of individuals but is asso-ciated with systematic and coherent structures of judgment and re-flects the formation of different social epistemological categories.

   As stated at the outset, variation in social practices is often as-sociated with the idea of moral relativism. This association stems from the assumptions that cultural orientations represent homoge-neous systems and that differences between cultures account for vari-ations in social practices. Yet there are more sources of variation than only cultural differences. Broadening the sources of variation beyond cultural differences is consistent with the proposition (Asch 1952; Hatch 1983; Schmidt 1955) that findings of variations in social prac-tices are not evidence for relativism. In the context of an exchange dealing with political theory and moral philosophy, this issue was re-cently addressed by Dworkin ("Letters to the Editor," *New York Re-view of Books*, 21 July 1983):

> The idea that the world is divided into distinct moral cultures, and that it should be the goal of politics to foster the value of "community" by respecting the differences, has for a long time been associated with po-litical conservatism and moral relativism. It is once again fashionable in political theory, but its proponents have paid insufficient attention

to their central concepts. Moral traditions are not clubs into which the peoples of the world are distributed so that everyone carries a membership card in one but only one. On the contrary, these traditions can be defined at different levels of abstraction, and people who belong to a common tradition at one level of abstraction will divide at another, more concrete, level.

Dworkin's point is twofold. He maintains that "we cannot leave justice to convention" and perhaps more importantly, that there are different levels of abstraction for social orientations. When this is taken into account individuals cannot be readily characterized by membership in "clubs." Dworkin's contention is consistent with much research evidence and most obviously with the survey data on attitudes toward civil liberties. People who might seem, by the survey data, to belong to the club of individualism with regard to some of the prototypical items do divide up with regard to the contextualized items. Moreover, there are two dominant traditions in American society—capitalism and democracy—that in several respects present conflicting values and goals (McClosky and Zaller, 1984). We would especially stress that the individual can be seen as divided among "traditions."

We believe there is reason to assume that implicit in some of this century's major social scientific analyses of social and moral development is a recognition of heterogeneity of social orientations, in societies and individuals, reflecting distinct epistemological concerns. Notable examples are Baldwin (1897), Durkheim (1925), and Mead (1934), who, in their different ways, were extremely influential thinkers about the role of social context in thought and behavior. To be sure, there were some major differences in their positions. Yet each stressed that thought and action are embedded in contexts of social interaction. Each stressed that social life involves shared meanings, collective sentiments and goals, symbolic systems, and differences in constituted social arrangements. For these theorists, self, thought, and action are formed within shared or symbolic systems of social relations.

These perspectives on the constitutive bases of society, however, were not always in accord with explanations of the origins of morality. Durkheim, who took the strongest position on the societal source of morality, struggled with issues of autonomy and the relation of the community or nation-state to humanity. Durkheim attempted to reconcile his central proposition that morality has its source in the group with the idea that morality should concern all of humanity by asserting that the goal of the state should be to realize "among its own people the general interest of humanity—that is to say, committing itself to an access of justice, to a higher morality, to organizing itself in such a way that there is always a closer correspondence between the merit of its citizens and their condition of life with the end of reducing or preventing individual suffering" (1925, 77).

Both Baldwin and Mead carried the relation of morality and the individual a little further by granting the individual some measure of independence from society. For Baldwin (1897, 540), the moral can show progress through individual practice: "In the ethical realm the individual may rule himself by rules which are in advance of those which society prescribes, and also exact them. This is common not only with the moral seer, but in the life of us all." A reciprocal relation of individual and society was proposed by Mead (1934, 168) as well: "We can reform the order of things; we can insist on making community standards better standards. We are not simply bound by the community." A common theme in social scientific analyses is the dialectic between shared meaning in constituted social systems and moral prescriptions that are not solely determined by social arrangements. In our view, this is also a dialectic common to social life.

# References

Acock, A. D., and V. L. Bengston. 1980. Socialization and Attribution Processes: Actual versus Perceived Similarity among Parents and Youth. *Journal of Marriage and the Family* 42:501–15.

Arsenio, W. F. 1985. Affective Component of Social Cognition and the Relation to Behavior. Ph.D. disser., Stanford University.

Arsenio, W. F., and M. E. Ford. 1985. The Role of Affective Information in Social-Cognitive Development: Children's Differentiation of Moral and Conventional Events. *Merrill-Palmer Quarterly* 31:1–17.

Asch, S. E. 1952. *Social Psychology.* Englewood Cliffs, N.J.: Prentice-Hall.

———. 1956. Studies of Independence and Conformity: A Minority of One against a Unanimous Majority. *Psychological Monographs* 70, no. 9.

Bakeman, R. and J. Brownlee. 1977. Behavioral Dialogues: An Approach to the Assessment of Mother-Infant Interaction. *Child Development* 48:195–203.

Baldwin, J. M. 1897. *Social and Ethical Interpretations in Mental Development: A Study in Social Psychology.* New York: MacMillan.

Becker, J. M. T. 1977. A Learning Analysis of the Development of Peer-Oriented Behavior in Nine-month-old Infants. *Developmental Psychology* 13:481–91.

Bell, R. A. 1968. A Reinterpretation of the Direction of Effects in Studies of Socialization. *Psychological Review* 75:81–95.

Benedict, R. 1934. *Patterns of Culture.* Boston: Houghton Mifflin.

Berlin, I. 1981. *Concepts and Categories: Philosophical Essays.* New York: Penguin Books.

Brandt, R. B. 1959. *Ethical Theory.* Englewood Cliffs, N.J.: Prentice Hall.

Brazelton, T. B. 1977. Evidence of Communication in Neonatal Behavioral Assessment. In M. Bullowa, ed., *Before Speech: The Beginning of Interpersonal Communication.* Cambridge: Cambridge University Press.

Brazelton, T. B., E. Tronick, L. Adamson, H. Als, and S. Wise. 1975. Early Mother-Infant Reciprocity. In *Parent-Infant Interaction,* CIBA Foundation Symposium, no. 33. Amsterdam: Associated Scientific Publishers.

Brendemeier, B. J. 1984. Moral Reasoning and the Perceived Legitimacy of Intentionally Injurious Sports Acts. Unpublished manuscript. University of California, Berkeley.

Bretherton, I., and E. Bates. 1979. The Emergence of Intentional Communication. In I. C. Uzgiris, ed., *New Directions for Child Development.* Vol. 4, *Social Interaction and Communication During Infancy.* San Francisco: Jossey-Bass.

Bronson, W. C. 1981. *Toddler's Behaviors with Agemates: Issues of Interaction, Cognition and Affect.* Norwood, N.J.: Ablex.

Bullowa, M. 1979. *Before Speech: The Beginning of Interpersonal Communication.* Cambridge: Cambridge University Press.

Carey, N. and M. Ford. 1983. Domains of Social and Self-regulation: An Indonesian Study. Paper presented at the meeting of the American Psychological Association, Los Angeles.

Carter, D. B., and L. A. McCloskey. 1983–84. Peers and the Maintenance of Sex-typed Behavior: The Development of Children's Conceptions of Cross-gender Behavior in their Peers. *Social Cognition* 2: 294–314.

Carter, D. B., and C. J. Patterson. 1982. Sex-roles as Social Conventions: The Development of Children's Conceptions of Sex-role Stereotypes. *Developmental Psychology* 18:812–24.

Cashmore, J. A., and J. J. Goodnow. 1985. Agreement between Generations: A Two-process Approach. *Child Development* 56:493–501.

Collis, G. M. 1979. Describing the Structure of Social Interaction in Infancy. In M. Bullowa, ed., *Before Speech: The Beginning of Interpersonal Communication.* Cambridge: Cambridge University Press.

Collis, G. M., and H. R. Schaffer. 1975. Synchronization of Visual Attention in Mother-Infant Pairs. *Journal of Child Psychology and Psychiatry* 4:315–20.

Damon, W. 1977. *The Social World of the Child.* San Francisco: Jossey-Bass.

Davidson, P., E. Turiel, and A. Black. 1983. The Effect of Stimulus Familiarity on the Use of Criteria and Justifications in Children's Social Reasoning. *British Journal of Developmental Psychology* 1:49–65.

Dodsworth-Rugani, K. J. 1982. The Development of Concepts of Social Structure and their Relationship to School Rules and Authority. Ph.D. disser., University of California, Berkeley.

Duncan, S., and D. Fiske. 1977. *Face-to-face Interaction*. Hillsdale, N.J. Erlbaum.

Duncker, K. 1939. Ethical Relativity? (An Inquiry into the Psychology of Ethics). *Mind* 48:39–53.

Durkheim, E. [1925] 1961. *Moral Education*. Glencoe, Ill.: Free Press.

Dworkin, R. 1978. *Taking Rights Seriously*. Cambridge, Mass.: Harvard University Press.

_____. 1983. To Each His Own. *New York Review of Books*, April 14.

Edwards, C. P. 1985. Another Style of Competence: The Caregiving Child. In A. D. Fogel and G. F. Melson, eds., *Origins of Nurturance*. New York: Erlbaum.

Fafouti-Milenkovic, M., and I. C. Uzgiris. 1979. The Mother-Infant Communication System. In I. C. Uzgiris, ed., *New Directions for Child Development*. Vol. 4., *Social Interaction and Communication during Infancy*. San Francisco: Jossey-Bass.

Feldman, D. H. 1980. *Beyond Universals in Cognitive Development*. Norwood, N.J.: Ablex.

Fodor, J. 1983. *The Modularity of Mind*. Cambridge, Mass.: MIT/Bradford Press.

Frankena, W. K. 1963. *Ethics*. Englewood Cliffs, N.J.: Prentice-Hall.

Fried, C. 1978. *Right and Wrong*. Cambridge, Mass.: Harvard University Press.

Furstenburg, F. F., Jr. 1967. Transmission of Attitudes in the Family. *Dissertation Abstracts International* 28 (10-A), 4295. University Microfilms No. 68-55899.

_____. 1971. The Transmission of Mobility Orientation in the Family. *Social Forces* 49:595–603.

Gewirth, A. 1978. *Reason and Morality*. Chicago: University of Chicago Press.

Gould, S. J. 1981. *The Mismeasure of Man*. New York: W. W. Norton.

Grusec, J. E., and L. Kuczynski. 1980. Direction of Effect in Socialization: A Comparison of the Parent's vs. the Child's Behavior as Determinants of Disciplinary Techniques. *Developmental Psychology* 16:1–9.

Haney, C., C. Banks, and P. Zimbardo. 1973. Interpersonal Dynamics in a Simulated Prison. *International Journal of Criminology and Penology* 1:69–97.

Hatch, E. 1983. *Culture and Morality: The Relativity of Values in Anthropology*. New York: Columbia University Press.

Hay, D. F. 1979. Cooperative Interactions and Sharing between Very Young Children and their Parents. *Developmental Psychology* 15:647–54.

Hoffman, M. L. 1970. Moral Development. In P. H. Mussen, ed., *Carmichael's Manual of Child Psychology*. Vol. 2. New York: John Wiley.

_____. 1977. Moral Internalization. In L. Berkowitz, ed., *Advances in Experimental Social Psychology*. Vol. 10. New York: Academic Press.

Hogan, R. 1973. Moral Conduct and Moral Character: A Psychological Perspective. *Psychology Bulletin* 79:217–32.

Hogan, R., J. Johnson, and N. P. Emler. 1978. A Socioanalytic Theory of Moral Development. In W. Damon, ed., *New Directions for Child Development*. Vol. 2., *Moral Development*. San Francisco: Jossey-Bass.

Hollos, M., P. Leis, and E. Turiel. 1986. Social Reasoning in Ijo Children and Adolescents in Nigerian Communities. *Journal of Cross-Cultural Psychology* 17, 352–74.

Jennings, M. K., and R. G. Niemi. 1968. The Transmission of Political Values from Parent to Child. *American Political Science Review* 62:169–84.

Kaye, K. 1977. Toward the Origin of Dialogue. In H. R. Schaffer, ed., *Studies in Mother-Infant Interaction*. London: Academic Press.

_____. 1982. *The Mental and Social Life of Babies*. Chicago: University of Chicago Press.

Keil, F. 1986. On the Structure Dependent Nature of Stages of Cognitive Development. In I. Levin, ed., *Stage and Structure: Reopening the Debate*. Norwood, N.J.: Ablex.

Killen, M. 1985. Children's Coordination of Moral, Social and Personal Concepts. Ph.D. disser., University of California, Berkeley.

Killen, M., and E. Turiel. 1985. Conflict Resolutions in Preschoolers' Social Interactions. Paper presented at 15th Annual Meeting of the Jean Piaget Society, Philadelphia.

Kohlberg, L. 1963. Moral Development and Identification. In H. W. Stevenson, ed., *Child Psychology*. 62d Yearbook of the National Society for the Study of Education. Chicago: University of Chicago Press.

_____. 1969. Stage and Sequence: The Cognitive-developmental Approach to Socialization. In D. A. Goslin, ed., *Handbook of Socialization Theory and Research*. Chicago: Rand McNally.

_____. 1971. From Is to Ought: How to Commit the Naturalistic Fallacy and Get Away with It in the Study of Moral Development. In T. Mischel, ed., *Psychology and Genetic Epistemology*. New York: Academic Press.

Laupa, M., and E. Turiel. 1986. Children's Conceptions of Adult and Peer Authority. *Child Development* 57:405–12.

Lewis, D. 1969. *Convention: A Philosophical Study*. Cambridge, Mass.: Harvard University Press.

Lockhart, K. L. 1980. The Development of Knowledge about Uniformities in the Environment: A Comparative Analysis of the Child's Understanding of Social, Moral and Physical Rules. Ph.D. diss., University of Pennsylvania, Philadelphia.

Lockhart, K. L., B. Abrahams, and D. N. Osherson. 1977. Children's Understanding of Uniformity in the Environment. *Child Development* 48:1521–31.

Maccoby, E. E., and J. A. Martin. 1983. Socialization in the Context of the Family: Parent-Child Interaction. In P. H. Mussen, ed., *Handbook of Child Psychology.* 4th ed. Vol. 4, *Socialization, Personality and Social Development.* New York: John Wiley.

Malinowski, B. [1926] 1976. *Crime and Custom in Savage Society.* Totowa, N.J.: Littlefield, Adams and Co.

McClosky, H., and A. Brill. 1983. *Dimensions of Tolerance: What Americans Believe About Civil Liberties.* New York: Russell Sage Foundation.

McClosky, H., and J. Zaller. 1984. *The American Ethos: Public Attitudes toward Capitalism and Democracy.* Cambridge, Mass.: Harvard Univeristy Press.

Mead, G. H. 1934. *Mind, Self, and Society.* Chicago: University of Chicago Press.

Middleton, R., and S. Putney. 1963. Student Rebellion against Parental Political Beliefs. *Social Forces* 41:377–83.

Milgram, S. 1963. Behavioral Study of Obedience. *Journal of Abnormal and Social Psychology* 67:371–78.

_____. 1974. *Obedience to Authority.* New York: Harper and Row.

Much, N., and R. Shweder. 1978. Speaking of Rules: The Analysis of Culture in Breach. In W. Damon, ed., *New Directions for Child Development.* Vol. 2, *Moral Development.* San Francisco: Jossey-Bass.

Mueller, E., and J. Brenner. 1977. The Origins of Social Skills and Interaction among Playgroup Toddlers. *Child Development* 48:854–61.

Murdock, G. P. 1980. *Theories of Illness: A World Survey.* Pittsburgh: University of Pittsburgh Press.

Nagel, T. 1970. *The Possibility of Altruism.* Princeton, N.J.: Princeton University Press.

_____. 1982. The Unreasonable Demands of Morality. Unpublished manuscript, New York University.

Newson, J. 1977. An Intersubjective Approach to the Systematic Description of Mother-Infant Interaction. In H. R. Schaffer, ed., *Studies in Mother-Infant Interaction.* London: Academic Press.

Nisbett, R., and L. Ross. 1980. *Human Inference: Strategies and Shortcomings of Social Judgment.* Englewood Cliffs, N.J.: Prentice Hall.

Nucci, L. P. 1981. The Development of Personal Concepts: A Domain Distinct from Moral or Societal Concepts. *Child Development* 52:114–21.

_____. 1982. Conceptual Development in the Moral and Conventional Domains: Implications for Values Education. *Review of Education Research* 52:93–122.

_____. 1986. Children's Conceptions of Morality, Social Conventions, and Religious Prescription. In C. Harding, ed., *Moral Dilemmas: Philosophical and Psychological Reconsiderations of the Development of Moral Reasoning.* Chicago: Precedent Press.

Nucci, L. P., and S. Herman. 1982. Behavioral Disordered Children's Conceptions of Moral, Conventional and Personal Issues. *Journal of Abnormal Child Psychology* 10:411–26.

Nucci, L. P., and M. Nucci. 1982a. Children's Social Interactions in the Context of Moral and Conventional Transgressions. *Child Development* 53:403–12.

———. 1982b. Children's Responses to Moral and Social Conventional Transgressions in Free-play Settings. *Child Development* 53:1337–42.

Nucci, L. P., and E. Turiel. 1978. Social Interactions and the Development of Social Concepts in Preschool Children. *Child Development* 49:400–407.

Nucci, L. P., E. Turiel, and G. E. Encarnacion-Gawrych. 1983. Children's Social Interactions and Social Concepts: Analyses of Morality and Convention in the Virgin Islands. *Journal of Cross-cultural Psychology* 4:469–87.

Patterson, G. R. 1982. *Coercive Family Process.* Eugene, Oreg.: Castalia Press.

Piaget, J. 1932. *The Moral Judgment of the Child.* London: Routledge and Kegan Paul.

Polanyi, M. 1964. *Personal Knowledge: Towards a Post-critical Philosophy.* New York: Harper and Row.

Pool, D. L., R. A. Shweder, and N. C. Much. 1983. Culture as a Cognitive System: Differentiated Rule Understandings in Children and Other Savages. In E. T. Higgins, D. N. Ruble, and W. W. Hartup, eds., *Social Cognition and Social Development: A Socio-Cultural Perspective.* Cambridge: Cambridge, University Press.

Rawls, J. 1971. *A Theory of Justice.* Cambridge, Mass.: Harvard University Press.

Rest, J. R. 1983. Morality. In P. H. Mussen, ed., *Handbook of Child Psychology.* 4th ed., Vol. 3, *Cognitive Development,* ed. J. H. Flavell and E. Markman. New York: John Wiley.

Rheingold, H. L., D. F. Hay., and M. J. West. 1976. Sharing in the Second Year of Life. *Child Development* 47:1148–58.

Ross, L. 1981. The "Intuitive Scientist" Formulation and Its Developmental Implication. In J. Flavell and L. Ross, eds., *Social Cognitive Development: Frontiers and Possible Futures.* Cambridge: Cambridge University Press.

Sampson, E. E. 1977. Psychology and the American Ideal. *Journal of Personality and Social Psychology* 35:767–82.

Sawin, D. B. 1980. A Field Study of Children's Reactions to Distress in their Peers. Unpublished manuscript, University of Texas at Austin.

Schaffer, H. R., G. M. Collis, and G. Parsons. 1977. Vocal Interchange and Visual Regard in Verbal and Pre-verbal Children. In H. R. Schaffer, ed., *Studies in Mother-Infant Interaction.* London: Academic Press.

Scheffler, S. 1982. *The Rejection of Consequentialism: A Philosophical Investigation of the Considerations Underlying Rival Moral Conceptions.* Oxford: Clarendon Press.

———. 1984. The Reasonableness of Morality. Unpublished manuscript, University of California, Berkeley.

Schmidt, P. H. 1955. Some Criticisms of Cultural Relativism. *Journal of Philosophy* 52:780–91.

Searle, J. 1969. *Speech Acts.* London: Cambridge University Press.

———. 1983. The World Turned Upside Down. *New York Review of Books,* Oct. 27.

Shantz, C. V. 1982. Children's Understanding of Social Rules and the Social Context. In F. C. Serafica, ed., *Social-cognitive Development in Context.* New York: Guilford Press.

Shweder, R. A. 1979a. Rethinking Culture and Personality Theory. Part I: A Critical Examination of Two Classical Postulates. *Ethos* 7:255–78.

———. 1979b. Rethinking Culture and Personality Theory. Part II: A Critical Examination of Two More Classical Postulates. *Ethos* 7:279–311.

———. 1980. Rethinking Culture and Personality Theory. Part III: From Genesis and Typology to Hermeneutics and Dynamics. *Ethos* 8:60–94.

———. 1982. On Savages and Other Children. *American Anthropologist* 84:354–66.

———. 1986. Divergent Rationalities. In D. W. Fiske and R. A. Shweder, eds., *Metatheory in Social Science: Pluralism and Subjectivities.* Chicago: University of Chicago Press.

Shweder, R. A., and J. G. Miller. 1985. The Social Construction of the Person: How Is It Possible? In K. J. Gergen and K. Davis, eds., *The Social Construction of the Person.* Springer Verlag International Series in Social Psychology.

Smetana, J. G. 1981. Preschool Children's Conceptions of Moral and Social Rules. *Child Development* 52:1333–36.

———. 1982. *Concepts of Self and Morality: Women's Reasoning about Abortion.* New York: Praeger.

———. 1983. Social-Cognitive Development: Domain Distinctions and Coordinations. *Developmental Review* 3:131–47.

———. 1984. Toddlers' Social Interactions Regarding Moral and Conventional Transgressions. *Child Development* 55:1767–76.

———. 1985a. Preschool Children's Conceptions of Transgressions: Effects of Varying Moral and Conventional Domain-Related Attributes. *Developmental Psychology* 21:18–29.

———. 1985b. Children's Impressions of Moral and Conventional Transgressions. *Developmental Psychology* 21:715–24.

———. In press. Adolescents' and Parents' Conceptions of Parental Authority. *Child Development.*

Smetana, J. G., D. L. Bridgeman, and E. Turiel. 1983. Differentiation of Domains and Prosocial Behavior. In D. L. Bridgeman, ed., *The Nature of*

*Prosocial Development: Interdisciplinary Theories and Strategies.*
New York: Academic Press.

Smetana, J. G., M. Kelly, and C. T. Twentymen. 1984. Abused, Neglected
and Nonmaltreated Children's Conceptions of Moral and Social-conventional Transgressions. *Child Development* 55:277–87.

Smith, T. E. 1982. The Case for Parental Transmission of Educational
Goals: The Importance of Accurate Offspring Perceptions. *Journal of
Marriage and the Family* 44:661–74.

Song, M., J. G. Smetana, and S. Kim. In press. Korean Children's Conceptions of Moral and Conventional Transgressions. *Developmental Psychology.*

Spiro, M. E. 1984. Some Reflections on Cultural Determinism and Relativism with Special Reference to Emotion and Reason. In R. A. Shweder
and R. A. LeVine, eds., *Culture Theory: Essays on Mind, Self, and
Emotion.* New York: Cambridge University Press.

———. 1986. Cultural Relativism and the Future of Anthropology. *Cultural Anthropology* 1:259–86.

Stern, D. 1977. *The First Relationship: Infant and Mother.* Cambridge,
Mass.: Harvard University Press.

Stoddart, T., and E. Turiel. 1985. Children's Concepts of Cross-gender Activities. *Child Development* 56:1241–52.

Stouffer, S. 1955. *Communism, Conformity and Civil Liberties.* New
York: Doubleday.

Tedin, K. L. 1974. The Influence of Parents on the Political Attitudes of
Adolescents. *American Political Science Review* 68:2579–92.

Tisak, M. S. 1984. Children's Conceptions of Authority within Different
Systems of Social Rules. Ph.D. disser., Stanford University.

Tisak, M., and E. Turiel. 1984. Children's Conceptions of Moral and Prudential Rules. *Child Development* 55:1030–39.

———. 1985. Variations in Seriousness of Transgressions and Children's
Conceptions of Moral and Conventional Events. Unpublished manuscript, University of California, Berkeley.

Trevarthen, C. 1979. Communication and Cooperation in Early Infancy: A
Description of Primary Intersubjectivity. In M. Bullowa, ed., *Before
Speech: The Beginning of Interpersonal Communication.* Cambridge:
Cambridge University Press.

Tronick, E., H. Als, and L. Adamson. 1979. Structure of Early Face-to-face
Communicative Interactions. In M. Bullowa, ed., *Before Speech: The
Beginning of Interpersonal Communication.* Cambridge: Cambridge
University Press.

Turiel, E. 1975. The Development of Social Concepts: Mores, Customs and
Conventions. In D. J. DePalma and J. M. Foley, eds., *Moral Development: Current Theory and Research.* Hillsdale, N.J.: Erlbaum.

———. 1978. The Development of Concepts of Social Structure: Social
Convention. In J. Glick and A. Clarke-Stewart, eds., *The
Development of Social Understanding.* New York: Gardner Press.

_____. 1979. Distinct Conceptual and Developmental Domains: Social Convention and Morality. In C. B. Keasy, ed., *Nebraska Symposium on Motivation, 1977. Social Cognitive Development*. Vol. 25. Lincoln: University of Nebraska Press.

_____. 1983. *The Development of Social Knowledge: Morality and Convention*. Cambridge: Cambridge University Press.

_____. In press. The Social Construction of Social Construction. In W. Damon, ed., *Child Development Today and Tomorrow*. San Francisco: Jossey-Bass.

Turiel, E., and P. Davidson. 1986. Heterogeneity, Inconsistency, and Asynchrony in the Development of Cognitive Structures. In I. Levin, ed., *Stage and Structure: Reopening the Debate*. Norwood, N.J.: Ablex Press.

Turiel, E., and C. Hildebrandt. In preparation. Judgments about Controversial Social Issues. University of California, Berkeley.

Turiel, E., and J. Smetana. 1984. Social Knowledge and Action: The Coordination of Domains. In W. M. Kurtines and J. L. Gewirtz, eds., *Morality, Moral Behavior and Moral Development: Basic Issues in Theory and Research*. New York: John Wiley.

Uzgiris, I. C. 1985. The Social Context of Infant Imitation. In M. Lewis and S. Feinman, eds., *Social Influences and Behavior*. New York: Plenum.

Wertheimer, M. 1935. Some Problems in the Theory of Ethics. *Social Research* 2:353–67.

Westermarck, E. 1912. *The Origin and Development of the Moral Ideas*. Vol. 1. London: Macmillan and Co.

_____. 1932. *Ethical Relativity*. London: Routledge and Kegan Paul.

Weston, D., and E. Turiel. 1980. Act-Rule Relations: Children's Concepts of Social Rules. *Developmental Psychology* 236:417–24.

Williams, B. 1981. Persons, Character and Morality. In B. Williams, ed., *Moral luck*. Cambridge: Cambridge University Press.

Youniss, J. 1980. *Parents and Peers in Social Development*. Chicago: University of Chicago Press.

Zellman, G. L. 1975. Antidemocratic Beliefs: A Survey and Some Explanations. *Journal of Social Issues* 31:31–53.

Zellman, G. L., and D. O. Sears. 1971. Childhood Origins of Tolerance for Dissent. *Journal of Social Issues* 27:109–36.

# The Do's and Don'ts of Early Moral Development: Psychoanalytic Tradition and Current Research

*Robert N. Emde, William F. Johnson, and M. Ann Easterbrooks*

In the encyclopedic four-volume fourth edition of Mussen's *Handbook of Child Psychology*, the "moral development" chapter is found not in the volume entitled "Socialization, Personality and Social Development," nor in "Infancy and Developmental Psychobiology," nor in the volume devoted to theory. Instead, it appears within "Cognitive Development," if not suggesting that moral development is a matter of developing judgment and rationality, then at least implying that recent moral development research derives primarily from the cognitive theories of Piaget and Kohlberg. Such research, for the most part, begins with the school-age child and often involves verbal responses obtained from children queried using a standard set of moral dilemmas.

There has been less research on preschool-age children, but in this research cognitive approaches have also been preeminent. By virtue of what the toddler shows us, it is difficult to accept this "purely

This work was supported by NIMH project grant #MH22803 and Research Scientist Award #5 K02 MH36808. During the year this was written, Dr. Emde was a Fellow at the Center for Advanced Study in the Behavioral Sciences and received partial support from the John D. and Catherine T. MacArthur Foundation. The authors would like to acknowledge the critical commentary provided by the editor and by Drs. Mardi Horowitz, Joy Osofsky, and L. Alan Sroufe.

245

cognitive" approach. In order to tell a more sensible story we must extend our interests into other domains.

This chapter is directed to a consideration of what psychoanalysis may have to offer research in early moral development. We should acknowledge, first, that the psychoanalytic tradition shares a history of concerns and commitments with the cognitive tradition. Both psychologies are interested in the meaning of experience, and both are committed to understanding the individual's activity in organizing developmental experience. Piaget acknowledged his debt to psychoanalysis in devising his probing technique for uncovering the child's active strategies of problem solving, that is, paying as much attention to the child's errors as to successes. But psychoanalysis began as a psychology of conflict and, unlike cognitive psychology, has given central emphasis to a number of areas that can inform today's research in moral development. The areas include (1) relationships, (2) motives, (3) affect, (4) individuality, and (5) psychopathology.

Our plan is to review the classic psychoanalytic formulation concerning early moral development, for it can serve as a framework for viewing changes in the theory and for evaluating our current research needs. Following this, we will consider some problem domains that recent observations bring to the fore.

## The Psychoanalytic Tradition

Most researchers outside of psychoanalysis consider "internalization" as central to moral development. Moral internalization was used in one recent review to describe how individuals increasingly come to regulate inevitable conflicts between personal needs and social obligations (Hoffman 1983) and in another review to describe how individuals increasingly are governed by internal standards in the absence of external reinforcers (Rest 1983). Psychoanalysts have thought of the problem in similar terms, asking how, in the course of development, external conflict (i.e., a conflict of intentions between parent and child) becomes internal conflict (i.e., a conflict of intentions within the child; see A. Freud 1980; Kennedy and Yorke 1982).

One form of internalized regulation is the superego. Freud wrote that the superego was heir to the Oedipus complex. During the age period of four to six years, there is a change in conscience development in which the child encounters a very specific conflict with external authority. Because of the child's libidinal desires for the parent of the opposite sex and rivalrous and aggressive feelings toward the parent of the same sex, unpleasant affects and thoughts emerge. These include a fear of bodily harm (castration anxiety) and a sense of powerlessness and of being excluded. The child deals with these powerful and unpleasant feelings through the development of a new regulatory apparatus. According to Freud, who formulated the prototype of this theory in 1923, there is a major transformational event; the child identifies with the powerful parent of the same sex and thereby internalizes the external authority. This internalized authority is the superego, a new mental structure that emerges around six years of age. As a result of superego formation, the child copes with conflicts over intentions, desires, and fantasized actions, along with their anticipated consequences. Most of this activity occurs beyond awareness, but its themes are reenacted repeatedly in play and in favorite stories (Bettelheim 1977).

Rather than going into the complexities of the psychoanalytic understanding of this process, its unconscious dynamic elements, and its normative variations, we choose to highlight several points about its outcome. First, the child's sense of morality is now more independent of others. It no longer requires the presence of the parents and is no longer based on the child's prediction of parental response. Second, the outcome is such that external conflict has become internal conflict. According to the theory, the chief source of self-esteem is no longer the parents but, instead, the new mental structure (i.e., the superego); correspondingly, what was previously experienced as parental disapproval now becomes experienced as guilt (Sandler 1960). Finally, it is worth noting that this process mainly concerns the don'ts of experience—prohibitions and restraints on what one wants to do—and is as much affective as cognitive. The superego is both aggressive and punitive.

From the beginning of his formulation about the superego, Freud was also concerned with what was transmitted to the child as ideal by the parents and the culture. Conflict with impulses was seen to occur as a result of the child's private assessment of self against an ideal in which a gain could come from narcissistic gratification (Freud [1914] 1957; [1920] 1955; Sandler 1960). Even after formulating the idea of the superego, Freud ([1923] 1961) felt there was a vital aspect of conscience that was structured from early (pre-oedipal) identifications with parents and included positive or admired aspects of the relationship. Although there is little conceptual clarity on this subject, the "ego ideal" is often treated in psychoanalysis as the mental structure regulating morality according to internalized ideals relating to what one ought to do. These ideals are generally based on love rather than threats of retaliation or hostility. Some have indicated that this form of moral regulation has its roots in the natural everyday experience of the young child with his or her parents, and especially with the guiding, comforting, and protective aspects of such interactions (Sandler 1960; Schafer 1960).

Within this psychoanalytic conception of the development of morality, problems have particularly arisen with the theory that the superego is a product of the resolution of the Oedipus complex. The inability to distinguish superego identifications from early ego identifications before superego formation was acknowledged as a theoretical inconsistency (Rappaport 1957). Clinicians began to conceptualize particular ego functions without referencing the more global superego concept. Sandler dramatized this set of circumstances in 1960 by referring to the "apparent conceptual dissolution" of the superego in psychoanalysis. Other problems, empirical in nature, presented specific challenges to the postulated linkage between superego formation and the resolution of the Oedipus complex. Research from the Hampstead Index Study Group found cases of school-age (latency) children with clear, unresolved oedipal struggles who nonetheless experienced guilt and other superego phenomena (Holder 1982).

Even more to the point, psychoanalytic observations documented significant pre-oedipal features of morality. Psychoanalysts observed that before age five, children developed quite complex modes of coping with conflict. These behaviors seemed to have a degree of independence from parents and implied some degree of internalization. Clearly, these observations were inconsistent with any simple notion of a conscience which emerged suddenly and full-blown at five or six.

### Early Forms of Moral Development

Psychoanalytic theory has pointed increasingly to the implications of early structures that are related to later superego development. Ferenczi (1927) described "sphincter morality," implying the existence of a general mode of compliance with parental demands during the period of toilet training. Anna Freud ([1936] 1960), based on her observations, expanded the notion of psychiatric defenses to include coping with pain arising from the outside world (as compared with the inside world); as part of this perspective, "identification with the aggressor" occurs when the child handles the anxiety resulting from the threat of punishment by adopting the behavior of the punitive parent. Because the child internalizes the adult criticism but does not accept it as self-criticism, Anna Freud considered this defense a precursor of the superego.

Spitz (1957, 1958) used his infant observations to propose a specific early moral structure which emerges during the second year. A new level of organization was indicated by the child's acquisition of the "semantic no," which Spitz considered a milestone in the early development of conscience, and which usually appeared around fifteen months of age. Toward the end of the first year, when the child is developing an understanding of prohibitions and commands, a form of primitive "identification with the gesture" occurs, along with a mirroring of the adult's gesture. The child hears "no" repeated many times, and the prohibition has an invariant quality across occasions, with considerable affect expressed in voice, face, and gesture. The child experiences repeated frustrations associated with hearing "no" and, because these actions are uncompleted, the "no" comes to have additional power. (Spitz hypothesized the Zeigarnik effect would apply here, in which incomplete actions are better recalled.) The child then makes an "identificatory link" and takes the "no" from the parent in gesture and word. Because of unpleasant memories, the "no" then becomes a vehicle for expressing aggression—in this case, against the parent.

For Spitz, the acquisition of the semantic no is a complex cognitive and psychobiological process, and the resultant structure of negation is viewed as the beginning of a capacity for judgment; it will eventually form the basis for self-criticism. In a next step, the child begins to turn the internalized mechanism against himself or herself in play; the role of the grown-up is assumed, and the child says "no, no" to himself or herself. Spitz, following Freud, emphasizes the acquisition of mastery in this process: a passive experience is converted into an active one. Sandler (1960), borrowing from cognitive psychology, proposed that early moral internalizations were best thought of in terms of organizing activity in which inner models were constructed—that is, schemata. During infancy these schemata are organized around experiences of need satisfaction in the midst of activities with the care-giver. Initially, these need-satisfying experiences are not differentiated from the self, but later, separate, inner models of mother (and father) are constructed. These models become a source of expectations in which the activities of the parents can be recognized and interpreted; moreover, such models are used to estimate which classes of behavior will lead to parental approval and which to parental disapproval. What Sandler refers to as "preautonomous superego schemata," however, only operate under the eyes of the parents. In other words, this form of early moral regulation is based on the child's prediction of parental reaction and not on internal conflict or guilt. More recent psychoanalytic discussions (Holder 1982; Kennedy and Yorke 1982) have emphasized the important role of care-givers as auxiliary superegos during this phase.

In summary, psychoanalytic theoreticians have found it useful to postulate early structures that enable the child to learn standards and rules. In general, guidelines for action (do's) are thought to be learned before prohibitions (don'ts), and a major period for internalization is highlighted, spanning the end of the first year through the middle of the second year. The structures are both cognitive and affective; furthermore, they involve internalizing aspects of parental relationships within the context of need satisfaction. These formulations are descriptive, and, while plausible, they require research linking them to other sectors and evaluating the ways that individual differences in development and socialization impact upon internalization.

## Psychoanalytic Areas of Special Emphasis

Somewhat paradoxically, the psychoanalytic tradition points to major gaps in our knowledge—to what we don't understand and need to investigate. This is particularly true when we look at islands of recent research that need to be connected within what we call "psychoanalytic areas of special emphasis."

### Relationships

Psychoanalysis pointed to the importance of the infantile loving relationship with the parent as a basis for internalizing rules and standards (Freud [1914] 1957; Nunberg [1932] 1955) and implied that the quality of later relationships with mother and father was important for internalizing prohibitions and constructing a conscience. Unfortunately, the constructs of identification and narcissism which were postulated as mediators of this process have not yielded to theoretical or empirical clarification. Such has not been the case with another psychoanalytically inspired construct, that of the "attachment system."

Bowlby (1958, 1969) introduced the concept of attachment to refer to a psychological organization which operates according to control principles of goal correction. The set goal, from the outside view, is to gain or maintain proximity and contact with the attachment figure. From the inside view, the set goal is to maintain felt security (Sroufe and Waters 1977). Bowlby emphasizes that attachment systems are biologically important and are primary motives, rather than secondary to other systems. It is particularly during the second six months of infancy that proximity and interaction-promoting behaviors become organized around a small hierarchy of familiar caretaking figures (Ainsworth 1973; Bowlby 1969; Bretherton in press). Recently, Bretherton (in press) has argued cogently for the increased use of Bowlby's concept of "internal working models" in thinking about the developing attachment system. Internal working models of the world, of significant persons, and of self are continually being constructed and modified by the child but, once organized, they tend to function outside of awareness and become resistant to change.

Largely as a result of the work of Ainsworth and her students (Ainsworth et al. 1978), these ideas have become operationalized, and an experimental assessment paradigm, the "strange situation," has led to a remarkably productive line of research. When the "strange situation" is used, infants can be classified reliably according to patterns of attachment as early as one year, and there is now a considerable body of research indicating that such patterns are related not only to ratings of earlier maternal sensitivity and responsiveness in the home (Ainsworth et al. 1978; Egeland and Farber 1984) but also to patterns of observed interactions with teachers and peers in the preschool and early school years (Main and Weston 1981; Sroufe 1983). The longitudinal observations of Sroufe (1983) provide evidence for security of attachment in infancy being linked with empathy and control of aggression in the preschooler.

We now need research that explicitly links early moral development with individual differences in attachment patterns. The construct of "internal working models" of self and others seems a promising one for ultimately describing such linkages. As Bretherton points out, the construct has the virtue of being representational, but affective as well as cognitive, and involving the internalization of relationships (Bretherton, in press). There are already intriguing indications of research directions. It has been observed all too often that the abused or rejected child tends to perpetuate a pattern of rejection across care-giving relationships. At a finer level, could we not predict that an attachment figure's repeated rejection of the child's attempts for comfort during stress will have an effect on the child's inner working model? As Bretherton puts it, this rejection could have an effect not only on the working model of the parent (seen as rejecting) but on the working model of the self (seen as not worthy of help and comfort). Correspondingly, might we not predict that such children would be less likely to comfort or to help others in distress?

Other features of internal working models have to do with a particular form of moral behavior, namely parenting. Several studies (see review by Bretherton 1985; Main, Kaplan, and Cassidy 1985; Ricks 1985) indicate cross-generational effects of patterns of infant-parent attachment. In other words, it looks as though the internal model constructed in early childhood may influence how the parent performs with his or her own child.

Other research questions have to do with the specificity of early working models of relationships. We now know that previous psychoanalytic notions about a general care-giving relationship or a singular relationship with the mother in infancy were wrong. Toward the end of the first year, attachment relationships are specifiably different for mother, father, and other care-givers (Lamb 1978; Main and Weston 1981; Owen 1981). How are individual differences in working models of these relationships integrated? Are they related to individual differences in moral development or to seeming inconsistencies in the activation of early moral structures? Bowlby (1980) postulates that multiple models of a single figure may coexist from earlier and current phases of development along with correspondingly different models of the self; in pathological conditions, models with incompatible interpretations of experience may become defensively dissociated (as cited in Bretherton, in press). Could such a process also be the source of structuralized inconsistencies of conscience (for example, as in so-called superego lacunae, described by Johnson and Szurek 1954)? Could certain aspects of self, when activated, be immoral as compared with other aspects which are generally moral?

There are other questions. What about gender differences? To what extent, as Gilligan (1984) suggests, is a moral sense based more on loving relationships for girls than for boys? If the suggestion holds, one would predict more of an interaction between attachment and early moral development in girls than in boys.

Up to now, attachment research (and psychoanalysis in general) has not paid sufficient attention to reciprocity in early care-giving relationships. Our longitudinal studies corroborate what others have noted: the predominant parental concern of the first year, nurturing, changes toward the end of the first year to a concern with discipline. Early parental declarations of "no" seem to be used as alerting signals in situations of danger, such as when the crawling infant is about to approach an electrical outlet or the edge of the stairs. A loud adult utterance causes the infant to pause and allows time for protective intervention. Toward the end of the first year, however, parents typically hold their child accountable, and teaching the meaning of prohibitions becomes a parental preoccupation. This seems to be a finely tuned adaptive system wherein parents intuitively know their child's readiness for understanding and for communicating about intentionality. More research needs to be done on individual differences in the emergence of intentional communication within parent-child dyads and on the consequences of disjunctures for the learning of prohibitions and standards. This is a time when shared plans and shared meaning (cf. Bretherton 1985; Mueller 1985) become increasingly important for the inner working models of discipline and of self.

## Motives

Psychoanalytic theories of early moral development have focused on a conflict of motives. At first, the conflict involves opposing intentions between parent and child; later it involves opposing intentions within the child. But we now appreciate that the infant learns "rules" before there is conflict. Early "rules" undoubtedly have a strong basis in innate organized structures and would be encompassed in the domain of what psychoanalysis, following Hartmann ([1939] 1958), has referred to as the "conflict-free sphere" of ego development. Well-studied examples are found in turn-taking, in face-to-face gaze behavior, vocalizing, and play with mother (see discussions in Brazelton and Als 1979; Bruner 1982; Stern 1977; Tronick 1980). Rules about how to communicate—about how to engage, maintain, and terminate social interaction—are operative well before language. These rules probably reflect developmental functions that are strongly cannalized or buffered against deviation so that one might not expect individual differences of major consequence (McCall 1979). Still, one might ask, are there short-term consequences of deprivation of dyadic play and of turn-taking experiences such that later learning about cooperation and prohibition is adversely influenced?

Early motivational conflict is seen to involve the child's impulses on one side and constraining motives on the other side. Aggression has been foremost among impulses considered in early motivational conflict. Because of the child's normal frustration of needs and innate tendencies, Freud felt the experience of aggression toward the parents was inevitable and that aggression eventually became turned against the self. Freud also observed (also see Sandler 1960) that the severity of the child's conscience was often much greater than could be accounted for by the child's actual treatment by the parent. In other words, the child was actively contributing more than he or she was responding to. There are many research questions which could be asked about these formulations. Are individual differences in the amount of the child's (and the parent's) aggression related to the quality and strength of the child's development of conscience? Are there normative and optimal amounts of frustration? Earlier versions of psychoanalytic theory assumed that too little frustration of needs (overindulgence) or too much frustration (deprivation) would predispose to a faulty conscience (Fenichel 1945). More recent formulations have emphasized questions about the appropriateness and meaning of frustration experiences at different ages and in different family contexts. After the developmental acquisition of restraints or countermotives (i.e., after conflict is "internalized"), one might assume that repeated temptation experiences could have adverse consequences for further conscience development.

The clinical literature has noted variations in aggression around times of teething, weaning, and toilet training, but there has been no systematic research linking these to variations in conscience development. The same could be said for variations in "erotic" impulses. It is striking that psychoanalysis has given less emphasis to the role of erotic impulses in early moral development (as contrasted with their central role in the oedipal configuration). Additionally, it has hardly been noticed that there is less concern expressed today than in earlier times about constraining and prohibiting autoerotic activities (such as masturbation, smearing of feces, etc.).

In contrast to the dearth of research on erotic motivation, interest in mastery motivation has been strong. Freud ([1915] 1957) originally saw mastery in terms of a drive "vicissitude" in which a passive experience was turned into an active one. Spitz (1958) emphasized that a gain in mastery occurred for the child when the parental "no" was internalized and used against others. Following the theoretical elaboration of mastery by White (1963), the work of Yarrow and his colleagues operationalized the assessment of mastery motivation and has now traced its development into the second year (see review of Morgan and Harmon 1984). Do children with more mastery motivation have earlier or qualitatively different forms of conscience development? Current research may provide some answers.

Exploration as a motive to be restrained is not a part of psychoanalytic theory. Still, it is obviously important, as everyday observation would indicate. The infant, becoming a toddler, increasingly "gets into things," and, in our longitudinal studies, this area is probably the major source of parental prohibitions. In Bowlby's theory, exploration is seen as important and is presumably activated when there is felt security in the attachment relationship. But as we have already discussed, exploratory motivation is not based solely on felt security within an attachment relationship. Clearly, there is considerable room for theoretical and empirical work in this area.

Now we turn to the other side of the motivational conflict, the constraining side. In addition to motivation arising from love for the parent (early forms of wanting to be like the parent; Freud [1914] 1957; Nunberg [1932] 1955; Rappaport 1957), classical psychoanalysis saw constraining forces in terms of drive vicissitudes, not only for aggression (aggression turned against the self), but for the libidinal drive (fear of loss of the parent, fear of loss of the parents' love, and later, fear of body mutilation in retaliation for erotic wishes). Increasingly, however, psychoanalysis has become disenchanted with the usefulness of abstract metapsychological constructs relating to vicissitudes of instinctual drives and, at the same time, has come to appreciate the role of maturation and cognitive factors. Accordingly, current thinking postulates the activation of structures impelling toward completion and of self schemata in social interaction that carry with them not only imitation and internalization of gestures (Mead 1934; Spitz 1957) but also a tendency toward balanced communication, cooperation, and even altruism. Recently Kagan (1984) has suggested that there may be a maturational basis for constraint against aggression and for helping others in distress. Observations of the normative emergence of such functions during the second year, as systematically described by Radke-Yarrow and Zahn-Waxler (Radke-Yarrow, Zahn-Waxler, and Chapman 1983; Zahn-Waxler and Radke-Yarrow 1982) and others, form the basis for this inference. Other observations of comforting, sharing, and helping before three years (Dunn and Kendrick 1979; Mahler, Pine, and Bergman 1975; Radke-Yarrow, Zahn-Waxler, and Chapman 1983; Rheingold, Hay, and West 1976; Zahn-Waxler and Radke-Yarrow 1982) point to an independent source of motivation for prosocial behavior in the normal child. Perhaps, as Kagan indicates, motivation could reside in the maturational emergence of responsive feeling states.

This brings us to our next psychoanalytic area of special emphasis, that of affect.

## Affect

Throughout its history, psychoanalysis has held that moral development is an intensely emotional affair. Still, there is probably no area of psychoanalytic emphasis that has undergone greater change than the area of affect theory. Originally conceptualized as drive derivatives and as reactive, intermittent, and often disruptive states, emotions are now thought of in terms of adaptive, ongoing, and active processes (see review in Emde 1980b). Emotions serve evaluation, providing incentives for particular courses of action. At any moment, emotions allow us to monitor ourselves, our states of being, and our engagement with the world, and they allow us to monitor others, their intentions, their needs, and their states of well-being and engagement. This dramatic change in viewpoint can be traced in the clinical theory of psychoanalysis, beginning with Freud's theory of signal anxiety ([1926] 1959) and continuing with theories of other signal affects (e.g., Brenner 1975; Engel 1962) as well as other, more general formulations (e.g., Emde 1980b; Schur 1969). Emotions are regarded as the center of clinical work, where it is necessary to monitor the feelings of another in order to provide understanding and help. Beyond this, empathy—in the sense of appreciating and responding to another's feelings—is considered essential for the operation of general processes quite relevant for morality including intimacy, cooperation, and parenting.

Within this context, psychoanalysis has come to regard emotions as central regulators of moral activity. For psychoanalysis, in the protypical situation the child's intentions call forth an emotion which signals a sense of impending punishment or approval. As we have discussed, the psychoanalytic theory of conscience began with the superego and with guilt as the "moral" emotion. Presumably, guilt arose in the four to six year age period and included a sense of the need for self-punishment and a lowered self-esteem. Psychoanalytic ideas about earlier moral development have also postulated moral emotions as regulators and, following the guilt model, have cast them almost entirely on the side of displeasure. Forerunners of guilt have been hypothesized to occur in anticipation of parental punishment or disapproval—in other words, in response to the don'ts or prohibitions of the toddler's experience (Fenichel 1945). Shame has been hypothesized as a feeling state that signals that one is not living up to the expectations, values, or ideals of the parents, first, and then of the self (i.e., in connection with the ego ideal and the do's of experience—see Piers and Singer 1953).

From a critical standpoint, one would have to say that although these notions may be intuitively compelling, psychoanalytic descriptions of forerunners of guilt and shame in the toddler and preschool period have been unclear, and no systematic research observations are available. It also seems striking that psychoanalysis (indeed, like other psychologies) has hardly considered the role of positive emotions in relation to the internalization of moral standards. Recent emotion research, including evidence for discrete emotional structures, social referencing, and early "moral emotions," will be discussed later under "Reformulations."

## Individuality; Psychopathology

The final areas of special psychoanalytic emphasis will be mentioned briefly. Individuality has been a preoccupying concern of psychoanalysis. For children and adults, this concern has usually taken the form of understanding the meaning of experience and the uniqueness of a "life story." For infants and toddlers, a concern with individuality involves a different kind of challenge, namely, taking into account a sufficient variety of behavior so that one can understand the complexity and uniqueness of organized experience without relying on language (Escalona 1968). Curiously, there is little psychoanalytic speculation about the role of individuality in early moral development. Perhaps this is due to the overwhelming challenge of constructing even a general "story" in the one- or two-year-old, but it may also be due to the interactional nature of the relevant processes. After all, one would not expect different subtypes of temperament based on moral development (and, indeed, there seem to be none). It is unclear what direction research will take in this area, but the study of shared meaning, of "intersubjectivity," and of matches and mismatches between parent-child partners may prove to be fruitful.

The area of psychopathology reminds us that psychoanalytic theory is fueled by clinical concerns. Psychoanalytic theorists have postulated various "moral pathology" syndromes of older children and adults, describing impoverishment in the three areas of (1) relationships, (2) motivational conflict, and (3) affect organization (Bowlby 1944; Goldfarb 1943). Questions remain regarding the coherence between these three domains, and it is unclear at present how research on these syndromes would inform specific hypotheses about early moral development.

Perhaps a word can be said, however, about the psychoanalytic construct of repression and psychological defense. Repression was originally conceptualized in connection with the Oedipus complex when, in the midst of internal conflict and painful affect, a part of experience (fantasy or memory) was excluded from awareness and in fact was not susceptible to recall under most circumstances. This concept became the prototype for defense mechanisms in general and was later broadened to include pre-oedipal children and defenses against the outside world as well (A. Freud [1936] 1960). From a developmental view, repression might be understood metaphorically as follows. It is as if a part of the personality becomes walled off and ceases to participate in development. From a systems point of view, it is as if boundaries to the outside are thickened so that a part of the personality functions as a closed system while the rest is open, growing and exchanging information with the environment (Emde 1980a).

As recent observations of abused and neglected children (Fraiberg 1980) and of children of depressed parents (Zahn-Waxler et al. 1984) seem to show, defensive operations in toddlerhood can be prominent in extreme circumstances and so are in need of study.

Clinical research might answer the question of whether particular varieties of defensive constellations might predispose one to specific moral pathologies when interacting with particular stressful environments. In these circumstances, one could easily imagine outcomes of disorders in which conscience does not figure, or where there is a protection against painful affects. Is it possible that particular early defensive operations lead to a sequestering of experience from the self? Psychoanalytic clinicians have postulated early "splitting" operations, such as those which Kohut (1977) described in cases of narcissism (as "horizontal" splits in self). Others have discussed such operations in terms of "false" and "real" or "good" and "bad" selves (cf. Jacobson 1964; Sullivan 1953; Winnicott 1965). Furthermore, there is now considerable psychoanalytic literature on adult borderline personality syndromes where early dissociation or splitting operations are postulated (Kernberg 1975; Rinsley 1978).

## Reformulations

The large-scale issues involved in reformulating psychoanalytic "metapsychology" (no longer generally considered useful either scientifically or metaphorically) will not be commented on here (see, e.g., Gill and Holtzman 1976). Suffice it to say that most psychoanalytically oriented developmental researchers have replaced a drive-reduction framework with an adaptive regulatory-systems framework.

In the area of early moral development, however, we can offer some particular commentary. There seems to be an emerging consensus on the need for reformulating the theory which had given almost exclusive emphasis to the four to six year oedipal age period. The psychoanalytic areas of special emphasis reviewed—developing relationships, motivational conflict, and affect—give the clear impression of intensive moral development before four years of age. In fact, there seems little reason to assume that this early age period is of less importance than the later one. Thus, a first reformulation can be stated in a straightforward, descriptive way. From a psychoanalytic point of view, the one to three year age period is a time when motivational conflict is first internalized and when affectively meaningful rules and standards are formulated within the context of specific caregiving relationships. From the point of view of the family, the toddler becomes willful and acquires the use of negation; correspondingly, parents become increasingly concerned with teaching discipline in addition to nourishing.

A second reformulation is more speculative, and its clarification awaits further research. There may be at least two streams of early moral development centered on emotions, each with the potential for promoting cooperative or prosocial behavior—one arising outside the arena of conflict and the other arising within the arena of conflict. Because this kind of reformulation encompasses current research and may contain exciting opportunities for discovery, we will review current thinking about it in more detail.

## Empathy Emergence

The first stream, that which arises outside the arena of conflict, may have to do with the emergence of empathy. The importance of empathic arousal as a prosocial motivator (e.g., feeling distressed at another's discomfort and wanting to help or comfort) has been emphasized by Hoffman (1977), who originally postulated its importance in early moral development. The emergence of comforting responses during the middle of the second year, along with helping and sharing behaviors, has been demonstrated in the studies of Radke-Yarrow, Zahn-Waxler, and their colleagues (e.g., Radke-Yarrow, Zahn-Waxler, and Chapman 1983; Zahn-Waxler and Radke-Yarrow 1982) and has provided considerable evidence for empathy as a normative developmental acquisition. Kagan (1984), following Hoffman, has proposed that empathy, with its strong maturational basis, may act as a natural constraint on the toddler's aggression against others. Beyond this, Kagan speculated on the basis of his studies that the human potential for certain feeling states may be "a non-relativistic platform upon which a set of universal, or principled, moral standards can be built" (Kagan 1984, 123).

The implications of these ideas is that there may be a maturational basis for early moral development that does not require "discipline" or learning within a context of conflict. Still, it would seem likely that additional components of this proclivity would be influenced by the quality of empathy experiences with primary caregivers. We are reminded of the Freudian assumption, restated by Ekstein (1978), to the effect that good mothering makes for good empathy (also see discussion in Radke-Yarrow, Zahn-Waxler, and Chapman 1983). This proposition not only has clinical plausibility but receives empirical support from two sources, the observations of Zahn-Waxler, Radke-Yarrow, and King (1979) and the findings of cross-generational continuities in attachment security (Ricks 1985) . We also know that in the latter part of the first year, the infant learns a considerable amount about "rules" of social interaction, turn-taking, and participating in discourse. Although such "rules" do not involve empathy in the strict sense, they may involve "affect attunement" (cf. Stern 1985) of infant with care-giver, and they generally arise outside the arena of conflict. Kaye (1982) and Bruner (1982) have described how this form of internalization depends on consistent care-giving interactions, increasingly involves shared intentions (intersubjectivity), and forms an important scaffolding for the later form of communication involving the social exchange of symbols—that is, for language.

## The Early Moral Emotions

A second stream of early moral development also begins without conflict; however, it develops a new level of organization in the midst of conflict. Like the first stream, it is centered on emotions and has a strong biological basis. Early in infancy, organized patterns of emotion provide a means for signaling to care-givers, indicating states of need, satisfaction, and engagement. Research evidence indicates, for example, that discrete facial expressions of emotion are linked to motivational states and to care-giving responses; these include joy, fear, sadness, anger, surprise, disgust, pain, and interest (Emde, Kligman, Reich, and Wade 1978; Hiatt, Campos, and Emde 1979; Izard et al. 1980; Stenberg 1982; Stenberg, Campos, and Emde 1983). Furthermore, patterns of infant facial expressions correspond to those found to be universal in cross-cultural studies of adults (Ekman, Friesen, and Ellsworth 1972; Izard 1972). Because emotions are biologically patterned, with a similar organization throughout the lifespan, we have speculated that they also reflect something deeper in the infant's structuring of experience. Emotional patterning may provide a basic sense of continuity in the midst of developmental change—or an "affective core" for early self-experience (Emde 1983). By the last quarter of the first year, the infant seeks out emotional signals from others and makes use of such expressions in situations of uncertainty in order to regulate his or her behavior accordingly, a phenomenon which has been designated as "social referencing" (Klinnert et al. 1983). Social referencing has been investigated not only in experimental situations of uncertainty but also in more naturalistic situations of parental prohibition. Beginning early in the second year, the child checks back either after or before the prohibited act; presumably, the child is seeking resolution of the uncertainty or some sort of confirmation for a decision in the emotional signal of the parent.

The role of discrete emotions in the formation of the child's internal working models of self and others is not yet understood. We do know that the middle of the second year is a nodal time for the emergence of self-awareness. This knowledge is based on evidence of the child's self-recognition in mirrors and video images, of the child's emotional responses to his or her own acts in the midst of a demonstrated awareness of the intentions of others, and on the use of personal pronouns by the end of the second year (Amsterdam 1972; Kagan 1981; Lewis and Brooks-Gunn 1979; Schulman and Kaplowitz 1977). Does the emergence of self-awareness bring with it a new level of emotional organization? We tend to think so. A new set of patterned emotional responses, which might be referred to as "the early moral emotions," seems to emerge at this time. These responses occur under the watchful eye of the care-giver and imply the child's awareness of uncertainty, of a problem, and, increasingly, of conflicting intentions. In our view, these "early moral emotions" include (1) positive affect-sharing and pride, (2) shame, and (3) "hurt feelings" (a possible forerunner of guilt).

The early moral emotions are in need of systematic research. We believe they have the following characteristics. First, they are more complex than discrete emotions and do not have any simple correspondence with emotional expressions in face, voice, or posture. Second, they are based on relationships—on a past history of experience with particular individuals in particular contexts. Third, they are based on some sense of struggle, dilemma, or conflict. Fourth, they are anticipatory. They are "signal affects" and portend the consequences of an intended outcome. Finally, moral emotions, by their nature, are necessarily embedded in knowledge structures of self and other. Since morality involves social cooperation, one would expect early forms of it to involve scripts about self and other, along with simple rules.

Positive affect-sharing may be regarded as a harbinger of the moral emotions. Although there is considerable individual variation, positive affect-sharing becomes prominent at about one year of age. Many children will share their smiles and sparkling-eyed pleasure with care-givers, not only as part of a general state of well-being but after specific actions that have involved effort. The activity, with a smile searching for the return of another's smile and then an amplification of the original expression of pleasure, is what is striking, and it may give one the impression of pride. Pride itself is a moral emotion in which a standard or rule has been successfully applied in a given situation and in which there is a positive self-evaluation in relation to another who approves. Although systematic research needs to be done, there are indications that pride emerges in the second year.

Correspondingly, shame is a moral emotion in which a rule has been violated and in which there is a negative self-evaluation in relation to another. The child has an awareness of having done something wrong. There is an aversion of gaze, an expression of unpleasure, and there may be a postural limpness in the context of carrying out a prohibited act. In the presence of a significant other, shame presumably takes on anticipatory functions that will guide the regulation of future decisions. Few would argue the point that shame is central in early moral development, but the behaviors of relevance for shame and the conditions under which it is regularly elicited require study.

The investigation of early morality scripts is likely to be vigorous during the next few years. As early as twenty-four months, many children are aware of transgressions and expected feelings of others in particular situations (Bretherton et al. 1985; Dunn 1985). It seems likely that by the third year, the child has role reversal capacities (something also indicated by our observations of child play) and that these capacities will enter into constructed units involving moral emotions. Horowitz (1981) has postulated a simple morality script in which the self is perceived as criticized and the other as scornful, with the individual either experiencing scorn or shame, depending on which pole of the role-relationship model is designated as the self at any given time.

"Hurt feelings" is a response which often occurs in the context of a prohibition from a parent, particularly when the prohibition is delivered in an angry tone. The child "looks hurt," with a facial expression which is experienced by the observer as "pained," involving elements of sadness, anger, and/or "pouting." Is such a response a forerunner of guilt? Only longitudinal research will cast light on this question. As will be discussed below, self-criticism during the second year is probably limited to events "under the watchful eyes of the care-giver."

## Under the Watchful Eyes of the Care-giver—The Internalization of Do's and Don'ts during the Second Year

Recent observations of infants and their parents suggest some steps in the early internalization of do's and don'ts, steps that occur under the watchful eyes of the care-giver. Most of the observations come from a longitudinal study of middle-class families with normal infants seen in both the home and laboratory at six-month intervals. Although individual differences were considerable, we believe our observations portray a meaningful sequence leading to a developmental outcome. By twenty-four months, all of our infants presented evidence of internalized rules for don'ts as well as for do's as long as a parent was present and could be referenced. Because our interest is in what leads up to this outcome, most of the observations cited below are at twelve and eighteen months.

## Internalizing the Do's

During the first year, parents are primarily concerned with meeting their child's needs, and the child develops an expectation that needs will be reliably met. As documented in the research literature on the development of attachment (see reviews in Bretherton and Waters 1985; Maccoby and Martin 1983) and as confirmed in our observations, the child comes to experience security through the availability of his or her parents. This is manifested by a balance of interest, curiosity, and exploration of the environment when in the presence of the care-givers (Emde, Gaensbauer, and Harmon 1982).

During the latter half of the first year, parents increasingly guide their child's activities so that the child is able to fulfill parental goals, and parents give approval to desired behaviors (also see Kaye 1982). Thus, the child experiences mastery not only in relation to his or her own goals but also in relation to parental goals.

*Observations*

Parents of twelve-month-olds in our sample frequently attempted to get their child to help in putting away the toys at the conclusion of their visit to our playroom. They often instructed their child to say "thank you" or "goodbye" upon leaving.

While in our playroom, twelve-month-old children were frequently noted to interrupt their solitary play with a toy to look to their parents and even to approach a parent and demonstrate their play activity. This was often accompanied by an exchange of smiles.

One mother suggested to her eighteen-month-old daughter that she "get the book and sit in the chair and read it to the doll baby," and as the child accomplished that feat, she looked at her parents and they smiled proudly at her. She smiled back at them.

At twelve and eighteen months, mutual referencing and sharing of positive affects occurred frequently. These phenomena occur in the midst of particular activities and may facilitate imitation and identification with the parents. The child and the parental model appear to share the joy of mastery, which results in part from the child's striving to do what the parents do and approve. The child's smile may be the beginning of the emotion of pride.

*Observation*
In our social referencing experiments, twelve-month-old infants in
our laboratory are positioned beside their mothers while
playing with a female tester. As a small toy robot emerges into
view, the infant typically looks puzzled and then looks toward
the tester (more often than toward the mother) for information
to guide subsequent behavior. If the tester shows a happy face,
the infant approaches the robot; if the tester shows a fear face,
the child avoids the robot and goes to mother (who has been
instructed to maintain a neutral expression).

In this circumstance, the infants seem to have internalized a
rule related to context. Their awareness that this is the tester's playroom seems to lead them to expect the tester to be the relevant source
of information as to whether the situation is permissive. Therefore,
the infants look more to the tester than to the mother in order to obtain guidance about what to do.

*Observations* (all at eighteen months)
During their visit, a mother described how her son had behaved after
he had spilled some milk the previous day. She had been
talking on the telephone and had simply said "uh-oh"; he
repeated the word and then, without prompting, retrieved paper
towels from the kitchen and cleaned up the mess.
A girl was observed in our playroom to approach a box of facial
tissues, take a single one, blow her nose, and look for a garbage
can, saying "trash?" The parents confirmed that she knows the
word and used it at home.
Another set of parents described how their daughter had built a
tower of blocks and had excitedly brought her grandmother
from another room to show off the construction, smiling
broadly.
In our playroom, an eighteen-month-old took several tissues and
proceeded to dust the room. The parents praised him and he
beamed; they smilingly told the interviewer that he often
imitated his mother as she did housework.
After a mother had warned "careful," a girl was observed to hand
over a clock that she had picked up from the coffee table. Later,
in response to a parental request that she return the clock to
the table, she hugged it close to her and carried it back to its
rightful place. She then returned smiling to her parents who
were talking with the interviewer.

In these examples, parents often characterized their child's smiles as
illustrations of "pride."

The internalization of the do's may begin earlier than the internalization of the don'ts, presumably because of participation and sharing with the parent and because of imitation and identification in the midst of parental guidance. The don'ts may require a sense of separateness from the parents and of conflicting goals.

## Internalizing the Don'ts

*Observations*
Parents of a twelve-month-old girl report that their child will not stop a behavior when told "no." They need to remove the child's hand from the object, and she may repeatedly "test them."

In our playroom, an eighteen-month-old boy played with a hammer on the pounding bench. When he hammered the chair, both parents said, "no," and mother unsuccessfully attempted to take the hammer. The child hammered the chair again, and the parents at first ignored this; mother later grabbed the hammer and laid it on the floor. The child took the hammer again and hit the chair. Mother then retrieved the hammer.

In another example, parents report that when they say, "no" to their eighteen-month-old daughter, she ignores them, stares at them, occasionally will smile, and usually repeats the prohibited behavior.

Parents initially attempt to reduce opportunities for undesired activities or give verbal disapprovals. Parents structure the child's environment to decrease "no-nos" and, in any given instance, may remove the child or the prohibited object. Toward the end of the first year, a parental "no" may interrupt the child's action if the "no" is intense and if it carries an angry tone. For other children, or on other occasions, a parental "no" may have minimal effect on the child's behavior, and the parents may need to remove the child or object in order for the action to cease. In these instances, the child may be distracted or may return to the object without understanding that it is forbidden on every occasion.

A variety of affective responses may result from early parental prohibitions, including anger, surprise, or a puzzled pause. Occasionally, there will be smiles or even laughter. (In the latter instance, some infants seem to experience the interruption as a "game"; others may be beginning to use their smiles instrumentally, as if to convince the parents to say "yes.")

*Observations*

Parents report that their twelve-month-old boy will stop a forbidden
behavior when told "no," look at the parents with curiosity,
but will continue it later.

In our playroom, an eighteen-month-old boy repeatedly returned to
the tape recorder after having been told "no" by father and
mother. Father initially directed the child to a set of toys. Later
in the session, the child returned to the recorder and then
complied with mother's prohibition as she directed him once
more to the toys. He returned to the tape recorder two more
times and was distracted once more; the second time, he
merely approached the tape recorder and looked, smiling. The
parents report that he frequently looks "frozen" and crushed if
someone is angry at him.

Soon, the parental "no" will suffice to stop the child but only
briefly. Furthermore, verbal prohibitions are typically accompanied
by parental substitute actions (such as toy play). It is as if parents attempt to substitute a "do" for a "don't." A rudimentary internal control is first demonstrated when the child is obviously interested in
something, hesitates, and looks back at the parents. The social referencing of the parents' behavior and facial expressions reinforce the
child's impression that a prohibition situation exists (if the parents
look stern or shake their heads). Gradually, the parental "no" will
have a more sustained effect than just during the initial minutes.
Even under the eyes of the parents, however, the prohibited behavior
is apt to recur on the next day.

The child may respond with anger or distress (even sadness)
when prohibited or prevented from reaching his or her goal. Initially,
the distress or anger occurs on each occasion of prohibition. As the
child comes to accommodate to the parents and match their goals,
anger and distress occur only when the child is tired, ill, or frustrated.

*Observations*

An eighteen-month-old girl looked to the parents as she approached a
coffee table in our playroom with "prohibitable" objects on it
(facial tissues, clock, vase with flowers).

A twelve-month-old boy approached and gently touched the tape
recorder, while looking at the interviewer, and then went back
to the tape recorder. He pointed to the tape recorder, looking at
the interviewer again, then pointed to the tape recorder again,
no longer touching it (the interviewer looked interested but
tried not to either encourage or discourage the act).

Parents report that another twelve-month-old boy seems to know a
number of acts that are forbidden; however, he is uncertain. In

father's words, "when he suspects he is doing something
wrong, he will make sure he catches your eye and points to it,
and then he will start doing it."
Finally, another eighteen-month-old boy was observed in our
playroom to approach a vase, look back toward his parents, and
smile. The parents said, "You know you're not supposed to do
that, don't you?" Several minutes later, he again approached
the table, this time touching the vase gently before looking
toward the parents (who happened to be busy and not looking
at him on this occasion); he then pulled his hand away with an
expression of apparent satisfaction.

If the child has partially internalized a prediction of the parental
response, there may be a look to the parents as if for reassurance of
the correctness of the act (as if to say, "This seems bad, and I must
restrain myself—have I got it right?"); the child may or may not carry
through the action with the forbidden object. The external presence
of the parent is apparently still required for control. The child may
respond with sobering or interest when prohibited or with "hurt feelings" at the violation of an externally imposed parental standard. An
interesting area for future research is the suggested sequence of uncertainty followed by the mastery involved in "having got it right," as
suggested by the above observation of the eighteen-month-old boy.

*Observations*
An eighteen-month-old girl approached our playroom table with
prohibitable objects, stared at them, reached toward them, then
passed by with a smile of satisfaction.
Parents of an eighteen-month-old boy describe instances in which
"we can't even see what he is doing, and he will run into the
room we are in and say 'no,' and drag us back into the room,
wanting confirmation that he did something wrong."
On a home visit, another eighteen-month-old girl was fascinated by
the video taping equipment brought into her home. She
remained near it, saying "no, no, no, no," to herself but did not
touch.
Another child at eighteen months approached a tape recorder in our
playroom and said, "hot," a reference to his babysitter's word
for prohibited objects, according to the parents.

During this phase, internalization of the don'ts is more stable,
but the child still requires parental presence for control. The "no" is
often not necessary for restraining behavior when the parents are
present. When parents are not present, however, the child will engage
in prohibited behaviors. In the prior phase, some children look to

their parents' eyes as though in need of reassurance in the midst of an uncertain schema for a rule about the prohibition; in this phase, some children appear to do something similar. Concerned with whether the rule holds in the absence of the parents, they will seek out the parents and "tell them" about the "no-no," as though needing reassurance of the existence of the standard in the parents' absence.

The ability to repeat the "no" or to imitate the gesture of prohibition marks further progress toward internalization of parental standards. Spitz referred to such actions as reflecting both the child's having made an identificatory link with the prohibiting care-giver and the child's expressing aggression against the parents as well as experiencing mastery. Clearly, such gestures as head shaking and repeating the words "no, no" can reflect an attempt to master the meaning of the "no" schema prior to full internalization of a particular standard.

*Observations*

Three eighteen-month-old children each responded to a gentle parental prohibition in different ways. One girl put her hands in her pockets with her head (somewhat) drooped. Another girl turned away from her parents, covered her eyes with her hands, and whined softly. A boy quickly withdrew his hand from the prohibited object and somewhat sheepishly returned to his mother's side to play with the toy in her lap.

One eighteen-month-old boy banged on the radiator when reminded by dad not to touch the tape recorder. Another eighteen-month-old boy in our playroom hit a baby's doll in his mother's lap following his parents telling him to replace the magazines on the table. Still another eighteen-month-old, after replacing a vase on the table, subsequently banged on the table vigorously with the toy hammer.

An eighteen-month-old boy in our playroom became fascinated by the tape recorder and approached it many times. On one occasion he said, "pretty," before reluctantly touching it and moving it slightly. He then turned back toward his parents, saying "Daddy," in a plaintive manner and laying his head in his father's lap.

Another eighteen-month-old boy frequently returned to the tape recorder in our playroom. After the first prohibition from mother, the child moved toward her somewhat sheepishly. He later returned to the tape recorder, touching it gently while looking at father, and then ceased touching when told "no." He returned twice more, saying "pretty" on one occasion. On another occasion, there was again a prohibition, and he looked "hurt."

The first set of observations may indicate the beginnings of the moral emotion of shame. The child, independently of the care-givers' action but under their watchful eyes, has a sense that he or she has done something wrong. The second set of observations apparently reflects the child's frustration in the midst of a conflict between his or her own intention and the wish for parental approval; in other words, it would appear that restraint can lead to frustration and then aggression, which is displaced to another activity. Finally, one wonders if the sustained effect on the mood of the last child noted above, which followed a transgression, might not be a forerunner of guilt.

These emotional responses, which occur under the eyes of the watchful parent, are not well understood. Much research needs to be done concerning their relation to particular circumstances, their developmental fate in individual children, and their roles in regulating behavior at this age.

*Observations*
A twenty-four-month-old girl is observed by her parents to say "no, no" to a workman's tools that she sees for the first time. An eighteen-month-old boy is prohibited by his mother when he approaches a tape recorder with the phrase "it's the doctor's." Later he applies the word "doctor's" to the tape recorder and restrains himself from touching it; he also applies this word to a clock he is told he cannot have.

Further progress in the internalization of don'ts occurs when children show the ability to generalize from one prohibited object to another. Overall, there was considerable individual variation in the phases of internalization among the thirty-two children observed at twelve and eighteen months. One child may show at eighteen months what another child exhibited at twelve months of age. Maturational factors are surely involved, as well as parental style of discipline. By twenty-four months, however, there is a dramatic developmental change in competence. Very few children touched prohibitable objects, although many looked longingly toward them. The parents also reported that their children's tantrums had decreased.

Our observations of the child, in both playroom and home, took place in the presence of the parent. We observed the internalization process during the second year "under the watchful eyes of the care-giver." Clearly, full mastery of the existence of behavioral standards for the don'ts is present only when the child will restrain prohibited behaviors without the parents present. We do not, as yet, have observations concerning this more advanced "outcome," but we know it is not a full accomplishment of the two-year-old and that it continues to develop during the third year. Observations of the child's play and of peer interaction during parental absence will be particularly important in order to understand this higher level of internalization. It is helpful to recall the comment of Spitz in this matter: the meaning of the "no" experience can be considered mastered when the child actively uses a schema involving "no" in play, assumes a parental role, and prohibits in the play activity (Spitz 1957).

### Summary and Conclusion

Although early psychoanalytic notions of moral development (superego formation) stressed the four to six year age span and the internalization of the don'ts (prohibitions), subsequent analytic theorizing about internalizations has expanded to include infancy and toddlerhood and the do's. Psychoanalytic concerns with relationships, motives, and affects contribute to the researcher's quest for knowledge about early moral development. Two streams of moral development have been hypothesized to occur during toddlerhood. One involves the emergence of empathy; the other involves the internalization of prohibitions (social referencing and the experience of conflict). Our observations during the second year have highlighted how internalizations first occur under the watchful eyes of the care-giver, and we have paid particular attention to the emergence of what we might consider the "moral emotions." We can only assume that these processes become consolidated and increasingly autonomous as selfawareness grows during the child's third year.

# References

Ainsworth, M. D. S. 1973. The Development of Infant-Mother Attachment. In B. M. Caldwell and H. N. Ricciuti, eds., *Review of Child Development Research.* Vol. 3. Chicago: University of Chicago Press.

Ainsworth, M. D. S., M. Blehar, E. Waters, and S. Wall. 1978. *Patterns of Attachment.* Hillsdale, N.J.: Erlbaum.

Amsterdam, B. K. 1972. Mirror Self-Image Reactions before Age Two. *Developmental Psychology* 5:297–305.

Bettelheim, B. 1977. *The Uses of Enchantment.* New York: Vintage Books.

Bowlby, J. 1944. Forty-four Juvenile Thieves: Their Characters and Home Life. *International Journal of Psychoanalysis* 25:19–52 and 107–27.

———. 1958. The Nature of the Child's Tie to His Mother. *International Journal of Psychoanalysis* 39:350–73.

———. 1969. *Attachment and Loss*. Vol. 1, *Attachment*. New York: Basic Books.

———. 1980. *Attachment and Loss*. Vol. 3, *Loss: Sadness and Depression*. New York: Basic Books.

Brazelton, T. B., and H. Als. 1979. Four Early Stages in the Development of Mother-Infant Interaction. *Psychoanalytic Study of the Child* 34:349–69.

Brenner, C. 1975. Affects and Psychic Conflict. *Psychoanalytic Quarterly* 44:5–28.

Bretherton, I. 1985. Attachment Theory: Retrospect and Prospect. In I. Bretherton and E. Waters, eds., *Growing Points in Attachment Theory and Research*, in Monographs of the Society for Research in Child Development, vol. 50, nos. 1–2 (serial no. 209): 3–35. Chicago: University of Chicago Press.

Bretherton, I., J. Fritz, C. Zahn-Waxler, and D. Ridgeway. 1985. The Acquisition and Development of Emotion Language: A Functionalist Perspective. Submitted for publication.

Bretherton, I., and E. Waters, eds. 1985. *Growing Points in Attachment Theory and Research*, in Monographs of the Society for Research in Child Development, vol. 50, nos. 1–2 (serial no. 209). Chicago: University of Chicago Press.

Bruner, J. 1982. *Child's Talk: Learning to Use Language*. New York: W. W. Norton.

Dunn, J. 1985. *The Transition from Infancy to Early Childhood*. Paper presented at the meetings of the Society for Research in Child Development, Toronto.

Dunn, J., and C. Kendrick. 1979. Interaction between Young Siblings in the Context of Family Relationships. In M. Lewis and L. A. Rosenblum, eds., *The Child and Its Family*. New York: Plenum.

Ekman, P., W. Friesen, and P. Ellsworth. 1972. *Emotion in the Human Face: Guidelines for Research and an Integration of Findings*. New York: Pergamon Press.

Ekstein, R. 1978. Psychoanalysis, Sympathy, and Altruism. In L. G. Wispe, ed., *Altruism, Sympathy, and Helping: Psychological and Sociological Principles*. New York: Academic Press.

Egeland, B., and E. Farber. 1984. Infant-Mother Attachment: Factors Related to Its Development and Changes over Time. *Child Development* 55:753–71.

Emde, R. N. 1980a. A Developmental Orientation in Psychoanalysis: Ways of Thinking about New Knowledge and Further Research. *Psychoanalysis and Contemporary Thought* 3, no. 2, 213–35.

———. 1980b. Toward a Psychoanalytic Theory of Affect: I. The Organizational Model and Its Propositions. In S. Greenspan and G. Pollock, eds., *The Course of Life: Psychoanalytic Contributions toward Un-*

*derstanding Personality Development.* vol. 1, *Infancy and Early Childhood.* Washington, D.C.: U.S. Government Printing Office.

_____. 1983. The Prerepresentational Self and Its Affective Core. *Psychoanalytic Study of the Child* 38:165–92.

Emde, R. N., T. Gaensbauer, and R. J. Harmon. 1982. Using Our Emotions: Principles for Appraising Emotional Development and Intervention. In M. Lewis and L. Taft, eds., *Developmental Disabilities: Theory Assessment and Intervention.* New York: S. P. Medical and Scientific Books.

Emde, R. N., D. H. Kligman, J. H. Reich, and T. Wade. 1978. Emotional Expression in Infancy: I. Initial Studies of Social Signaling and an Emergent Model. In M. Lewis and L. Rosenblum, eds., *The Development of Affect.* New York: Plenum.

Engel, G. 1962. Anxiety and Depression-Withdrawal: The Primary Affects of Unpleasure. *International Journal of Psychoanalysis* 43:89–97.

Escalona, S. K. 1968. *The Roots of Individuality. Normal Patterns of Development in Infancy.* Chicago: Aldine.

Fenichel, O. 1945. *The Psychoanalytic Theory of Neurosis.* New York: W. W. Norton.

Ferenczi, S. 1927. Psycho-analysis of Sexual Habits. In E. Glover, trans., *Further Contributions to the Theory and Technique of Psychoanalysis.* London: Hogarth Press.

Fraiberg, S. 1980. *Clinical Studies in Infant Mental Health: The First Year of Life.* New York: Basic Books.

Freud, A. [1936] 1960. *The Ego and the Mechanisms of Defence.* Trans. C. Baines. New York: International Universities Press.

_____. 1980. Personal communication.

Freud, S. [1914] 1957. On Narcissism: An Introduction. In J. Strachey, ed. and trans., *The Standard Edition of the Complete Psychological Works of Sigmund Freud.* Vol. 14. London, Hogarth Press.

_____. [1915] 1957. Instincts and Their Vicissitudes. In J. Strachey, ed. and trans., *The Standard Edition of the Complete Psychological Works.* Vol. 14.

_____. [1920] 1955. Beyond the Pleasure Principle. In J. Strachey, ed. and trans., *The Standard Edition of the Complete Psychological Works.* Vol. 18.

_____. [1923] 1961. The Ego and the Id. In J. Strachey, ed. and trans., *The Standard Edition of the Complete Psychological Works.* Vol. 19.

_____. [1926] 1959. Inhibitions, Symptoms, and Anxiety. In J. Strachey, ed. and trans., *The Standard Edition of the Complete Psychological Works.* Vol. 20.

Gill, M. M., and P. S. Holtzman, eds. 1976. *Psychology versus Metapsychology: Psychoanalytic Essays in Memory of George S. Klein.* Psychological Issues, Monograph 36. New York: International Universities Press.

Gilligan, C. 1984. The Conquistador and the Dark Continent: Reflections on the Psychology of Love. *Daedulus* 113:75–95.

Goldfarb, W. 1943. Infant Rearing on Problem Behavior. *American Journal of Orthopsychiatry* 13:249–65.

Hartmann, H. [1939] 1958. *Psychoanalysis and the Problem of Adaptation.* New York: International Universities Press.

Hiatt, S., J. Campos, and R. N. Emde. 1979. Facial Patterning and Infant Emotional Expression: Happiness, Surprise, Fear. *Child Development* 50:1020–35.

Hoffman, M. L. 1977. Moral Internalization: Current Theory and Research. In L. Berkowitz, ed., *Advances in Experimental Social Psychology.* Vol. 10. New York: Academic Press.

_____. 1983. Affective and Cognitive Processes in Moral Internalization. In E. T. Higgins, D. N. Ruble, and W. W. Hartup, eds., *Social Cognition and Social Development: A Sociocultural Perspective.* New York: Cambridge University Press.

Holder, A. 1982. Preoedipal Contributions to the Formation of the Superego. *Psychoanalytic Study of the Child* 37:245–72.

Horowitz, M. J. 1981. Self-righteous Rage and the Attribution of Blame. *Archives of General Psychiatry* 38:1233–38.

Izard, C. 1972. *Patterns of Emotion: A New Analysis of Anxiety and Depression.* New York: Academic Press.

Izard, C., R. Huebner, D. Risser, G. C. McGinnes, and L. Dougherty. 1980. The Young Infant's Ability to Produce Discrete Emotional Expressions. *Developmental Psychology* 16, no. 2, 132–40.

Jacobson, E. 1964. *The Self and the Object World.* New York: International Universities Press.

Johnson, A. M., and A. Szurek. 1954. Etiology of Antisocial Behavior in Delinquents and Psychopaths. *Journal of the American Medical Association* 154:814–17.

Kagan, J. 1981. *The Second Year.* Cambridge, Mass.: Harvard University Press.

_____. 1984. *The Nature of the Child.* New York: Basic Books.

Kaye, K. 1982. *The Mental and Social Life of Babies: How Parents Create Persons.* Chicago: University of Chicago Press.

Kennedy, H., and C. Yorke. 1982. Steps from Outer to Inner Conflict Viewed as Superego Precursors. *Psychoanalytic Study of the Child* 37:221–28.

Kernberg, O. 1975. *Borderline Conditions and Pathological Narcissism.* New York: Jason Aronson.

Klinnert, M. D., J. J. Campos, J. F. Sorce, R. N. Emde, and M. Svejda. 1983. The Development of Social Referencing in Infancy. In R. Plutchik and H. Kellerman, eds., *Emotion in Early Development.* Vol. 2 of *Emotion: Theory, Research and Experience.* New York: Academic Press.

Kohut, H. 1977. *The Restoration of the Self.* New York: International Universities Press.

Lamb, M. E. 1978. Qualitative Aspects of Mother- and Father-Infant Attachments. *Infant Behavior and Development* 1:265–75.

Lewis, M., and J. Brooks-Gunn. 1979. *Social Cognition and the Acquisition of Self.* New York: Plenum.

Maccoby, E., and J. Martin. 1983. Socialization in the Context of the Family: Parent-Child Interaction. In P. H. Mussen, ed., *Handbook of Child Psychology.* 4th ed. Vol. 4, *Socialization, Personality, and Social Development,* ed. E. M. Hetherington. New York: John Wiley.

Mahler, M. S., E. Pine, and A. Bergman. 1975. *The Psychological Birth of the Human Infant.* New York: Basic Books.

Main, M., K. Kaplan, and J. Cassidy. 1985. Security in Infancy, Childhood, and Adulthood: A Move to the Level of Representation. In I. Bretherton and E. Waters, eds., *Growing Points in Attachment Theory and Research,* in Monographs of the Society for Research in Child Development, vol. 50, nos. 1–2 (serial no. 209):66–104. Chicago: University of Chicago Press.

Main, M., and R. Weston. 1981. The Quality of the Toddler's Relationship to Mother and Father: Related to Conflict Behavior and the Readiness to Establish New Relationships. *Child Development* 52:932–40.

McCall, R. B. 1979. The Development of Intellectual Functioning in Infancy and the Prediction of Later IQ. In J. Osofsky, ed., *Handbook of Infant Development.* New York, John Wiley.

Mead, G. 1934. *Mind, Self, and Society.* Ed. C. Morris. Chicago, University of Chicago Press.

Morgan, G. A., and R. J. Harmon. 1984. Developmental Transformations and Mastery Motivation: Measurement and Validation. In R. N. Emde and R. J. Harmon, eds., *Continuities and Discontinuities in Development.* New York: Plenum.

Mueller, E. 1985. Shared Meaning in Prelinguistic Communication. In J. Danks and I. Kurcz, eds., *Knowledge and Language.* New York: North-Holland.

Nunberg, H. [1932] 1955. *Principles of Psychoanalysis.* New York: International Universities Press.

Owen, M. T. 1981. Similarity between Infant-Mother and Infant-Father Attachments. Ph.D. diss., University of Michigan.

Piers, G., and M. B. Singer. 1953. *Shame and Guilt.* Springfield, Ill.: Charles C. Thomas.

Radke-Yarrow, M., C. Zahn-Waxler, and M. Chapman. 1983. Children's Prosocial Dispositions and Behavior. In P. H. Mussen, ed., *Handbook of Child Psychology.* 4th ed. Vol. 4, *Socialization, Personality and Social Development,* ed. E. M. Hetherington. New York: John Wiley.

Rappaport, D. 1957. A Theoretical Analysis of the Superego Concept. In M. M. Gill, ed., *The Collected Papers of David Rappaport.* New York: Basic Books.

Rest, J. R. 1983. Morality. In P. H. Mussen (ed.), *Handbook of Child Psychology.* Vol. 3, *Cognitive Development,* ed. J. H. Flavell and A. M. Markman. New York: John Wiley.

Rheingold, H., D. F. Hay, and M. J. West. 1976. Sharing in the Second Year of Life. *Child Development* 47:1148–58.

Ricks, M. H. 1985. The Social Transmission of Parental Behavior: Attachment across Generations. In I. Bretherton and E. Waters (eds.), *Growing Points in Attachment Theory and Research,* Monographs of the Society for Research in Child Development, vol. 50, nos. 1–2 (serial no. 209):211–27. Chicago: University of Chicago Press.

Rinsley, D. B. 1978. Borderline Psychopathology: A Review of Aetiology, Dynamics and Treatment. *International Review of Psychoanalysis,* 5:45–54.

Sandler, J. 1960. On the Concept of Superego. *Psychoanalytic Study of the Child* 15:128–62.

Schafer, R. 1960. The Loving and Beloved Superego in Freud's Structural Theory. *Psychoanalytic Study of the Child* 15:163–88.

Schulman, A. H., and C. Kaplowitz. 1977. Mirror-image Response during the First Two Years of Life. *Developmental Psychobiology* 10:133–42.

Schur, M. 1969. Affects and cognition. *International Journal of Psycho-Analysis* 50:647–53.

Spitz, R. 1957. *No and Yes: On the Genesis of Human Communication.* New York: International Universities Press.

_____. 1958. On the Genesis of Superego Components. *Psychoanalytic Study of the Child* 13:375–404.

Sroufe, L. A. 1983. Infant Caregiver Attachment and Patterns of Adaptation in Preschool: The Roots of Maladaptation and Competence. In M. Perlmutter, ed., *Minnesota Symposium in Child Psychology* 16:41–81. Hillsdale, N.J.: Erlbaum.

Sroufe, L. A., and E. Waters. 1977. Attachment as an Organizational Construct. *Child Development* 48:1184–99.

Stenberg, C. 1982. The Development of Anger Expressions in Infancy. Ph.D. diss., University of Denver.

Stenberg, C., J. Campos, and R. N. Emde. 1983. The Facial Expression of Anger in Seven-month-old Infants. *Child Development* 54:178–84.

Stern, D. N. 1977. *The First Relationship: Mother and Infant.* Cambridge, Mass.: Harvard University Press.

_____. 1985. Affect Attunement. In J. Call, E. Galenson, and R. Tyson, eds. *Frontiers of Infant Psychiatry—II.* New York, Basic Books.

Sullivan, H. S. 1953. *The Interpersonal Theory of Psychiatry.* New York: W. W. Norton.

Tronick, E. 1980. The Primacy of Social Skills in Infancy. In D. B. Sawin, R. C. Hawkins, L. O. Walker, and J. H. Penticuff, eds., *Exceptional Infant.* Vol. 4. New York: Brunner/Mazel.

White, R. W. 1963. *Ego and Reality in Psychoanalytic Theory.* Psychological Issues, Monograph No. 11. New York: International Universities Press.

Winnicott, D. 1965. Ego Distortion in Terms of True and False Self. In D. Winnicott, ed., *The Maturational Process and the Facilitating Environment.* London: Hogarth Press and the Institute of Psychoanalysis.

Zahn-Waxler, C., E. M. Cummings, D. H. McKnew, and M. Radke-Yarrow. 1984. Altruism, Aggression, and Social Interactions in Young Children with a Manic-Depressive Parent. *Child Development* 55, 112–22.

Zahn-Waxler, C., and M. Radke-Yarrow. 1982. The Development of Altruism: Alternative Research Strategies. In N. Eisenberg, ed., *The Development of Prosocial Behavior.* New York: Academic Press.

Zahn-Waxler, C., M. Radke-Yarrow, and R. A. King. 1979. Child Rearing and Children's Prosocial Initiations toward Victims of Distress. *Child Development* 50:319–30.

# SIX

# The Origins of Morality in Early Childhood Relationships

*Carol Gilligan and Grant Wiggins*

This paper was prompted by an observation we made while listening to the discussion at the conference on "The Origins of Morality in Early Childhood" (Harvard University, 1984). When in the past psychologists traced morality to the child's discovery of the idea of justice, girls and women were seen to have less sense of justice than boys and men. This deficit in moral reasoning was explained in part by women's preoccupation with relationships and with feelings (Freud 1925; Piaget 1932; Kohlberg and Kramer 1969). Now as the focus of psychologists' attention shifts away from moral reasoning and toward moral emotions or sentiments, sex differences seem to have disappeared. Empathy and concern about feelings, once seen as the source of limitation in women's moral reasoning now are considered the essence of morality but no longer associated particularly with women. The question is: What has changed?

The research discussed in this paper was supported by the generosity of Mrs. Marilyn Brachman Hoffman, the National Institute of Education, the Mailman Foundation, and the Picker Foundation. Bernard Kaplan's written commentary on an earlier draft of this paper was immensely helpful to its revision, and many of his insights and clarifications are reflected in this final version. We are also grateful to Diana Baumrind, Sissela Bok, Annette Baier, Lawrence Blum, and to members of the audience at the Chapel Hill Philosophy Colloquim where this paper was read in 1986.

Recent reports of research showing no evidence of sex differences in empathy or moral reasoning (Eisenberg and Lennon 1983; Kohlberg 1984; Walker 1984) are presented as a sign of progress in research methods and in social justice, and they may appear to dissolve the difficult conceptual problems that findings of sex differences pose. But the inference that there are no sex differences in moral development is problematic on both empirical and theoretical grounds. Empirically, sociologists point to striking sex differences in the incidence and forms of antisocial behavior, manifest at the extreme in the statistics on violent crime (Wolfgang 1966; Ishkrant and Joliet 1968; Kutash et al. 1978). Naturalistic observers like parents and teachers as well as psychological researchers are struck by sex differences in aggression among children as well as in the patterns of their social interaction and play (Maccoby and Jacklin 1974; Lever 1976, 1978; Maccoby 1985). On a theoretical level, cognitive developmental psychologists such as Piaget and Kohlberg explain moral development in childhood as a function of peer group interaction; yet differences similar to those which Piaget described continue to mark the games that boys and girls play as well as the forms of conflict resolution that govern the same-sex peer groups of middle childhood. Theorists in the psychoanalytic tradition explain moral development in terms of family attachments and identifications; yet the gender asymmetry which Freud (1914, 1931) encountered as an obstacle to any neat parallelism between male and female development still characterizes family relationships. Women for the most part continue to assume primary responsibility for the care and nurture of young children, and as a result the pattern of childhood attachments and identifications and the pattern of adult moral or "prosocial" behavior typically differ for males and females.

Psychologists have shied away from these observations for a variety of reasons, including the dangers of stereotyping, the intimations of biological determinism, and the fact that in discussions of sex differences there is no disinterested position. Recent claims that there are no sex differences in moral development may reflect the change in the way psychologists are studying morality, the shift in attention away from the problems of relationship that preoccupied Freud in his analysis of family conflicts or Piaget in his study of children's games and toward problems in moral logic or moral feelings per se. Since both males and females demonstrate the human capacity to think rationally and to feel compassion, it is no surprise that researchers measuring morality in these terms find no sex differences in their data. Yet stereotypes of males as aggressive and females as nurturant, however distorting and however limited, have some empirical claim. The overwhelmingly male composition of the prison population and the extent to which women take care of young children cannot readily be dismissed as irrelevant to theories of morality or excluded from accounts of moral development. If there are no sex differences in empathy or moral reasoning, why are there sex differences in moral and immoral behavior? Either there is a problem in the way that empathy and moral reasoning are being measured or the role of empathy and cognition in moral development has been overstated. The question is how to incorporate sociological facts and general observations of what would appear to be morally relevant differences between the sexes into a coherent conception of morality and a plausible account of moral development. To do so, we claim, it is necessary to revise the theoretical frame.

We begin with the issue of perspective because it affects both what observations are made in studying morality and how they are assessed. A major constraint on previous discussions of sex differences in morality has been the assumption of a single moral standpoint, defined as *the* moral perspective, which renders it impossible to talk about sex differences except in the terms of invidious comparison. Cast in these terms, discussions of sex differences are marked by signs of unease, suggesting a discomfort in speaking and yet also a discomfort in not speaking about differences that seem obvious or clear. Freud, introducing his statement that women have less sense of justice than men, begins with a rhetorical gesture ("I cannot evade the notion though I hesitate to give it expression") and then proceeds to align himself with "critics of every epoch" (1925, 257). Piaget disavows any privileged position in describing female moral deficiency, claiming that "the most superficial observation is sufficient to show that in the main the legal sense is far less developed in little girls than in boys" ([1932] 1965, 77). Kohlberg, writing with Kramer (1968), describes the third stage of moral development as "functional" for housewives and mothers, but explains that if women, like men, were to obtain higher status jobs and more education, they too would advance to higher stages of moral development.

Immediately one senses the predicament of the observer who has no place to stand, no neutral position from which to comment on sex differences and no way, for that matter, to avoid the alternatives of moral arrogance and moral self-abnegation which Nietzsche described as quintessentially masculine and feminine stances. The virtue of the sex difference question in discussions of moral development lies precisely in the fact that it renders the issue of perspective inescapable. To ask from what perspective sex differences are being considered leads readily into the question, from what perspective is morality being defined? It is this question that we wish to consider in tracing the origins of morality to relationships in early childhood.

## Two Moral Perspectives/Two Dimensions of Relationship

Apart from our relationships with other people, as Piaget ([1932] 1965) observed, there would be no moral necessity, and this observation becomes central to our position that a perspective on relationships underlies any conception of morality. Recent research on infancy provides compelling demonstrations that the foundations of morality are present early in child development—in the infant's responsiveness to the feelings of others and the young child's appreciation of standards (Kagan 1984; Stern 1985). But to explain the nature of moral feelings and standards, it is necessary to consider how these capacities become organized psychologically, and thus to consider the infant's experience of relationships with other people. Thus, we locate the origins of morality in the young child's awareness of self in relation to others and identify two dimensions of early childhood relationships that shape that awareness in different ways. One is the dimension of inequality, reflected in the child's awareness of being smaller and less capable than adults and older children, of being a baby in relation to a standard of human. This dimension of relationship has been stressed by theorists of moral development in both the cognitive and the psychoanalytic traditions and is reflected by the emphasis placed on the child's feelings of helplessness and powerlessness in relation to others, feelings tied to the fact of being dependent on others who are more powerful. Focusing on the constraint of the young child's situation, psychologists have defined morality as justice and aligned development with the child's progress toward a position of equality and independence.

But the young child also experiences attachment, and the dynamics of attachment relationships create a very different awareness of self—as capable of having an effect on others, as able to move others and to be moved by them. Characteristically young children come to love the people who care for them, desiring to be near them, wanting to know them, being able to recognize them, and being sad when they leave. In the context of attachment, the child discovers the patterns of human interaction and observes the ways in which people care for and hurt one another. Like the experience of inequality, although in different ways, the experience of attachment profoundly affects the child's understanding of how one should act toward other people and the child's knowledge of human feelings. The moral implications of attachment relationships have generally been overlooked in theories of moral development, in part because the passivity of early childhood love has been stressed, rather than the child's activity in creating and sustaining connections with others, and in part because the emergence of self-awareness has been tied to separation and detachment. Yet the experience of attachment generates a perspective on relationships that underlies the conception of morality as love.

To summarize the implications of this discussion, the different dynamics of early childhood inequality and attachment lay the groundwork for two moral visions—one of justice and one of care. The child's experience of inequality and of attachment, sometimes but not always convergent, grounds a distinction between the dimensions of inequality/equality and attachment/detachment which characterize all forms of human relationships. Although the nature of the attachment between child and parent varies across individual and cultural settings and although inequality can be heightened or muted by familial and societal arrangements, all people are born into a situation of inequality and no child survives in the absence of adult connection. Since everyone is vulnerable both to oppression and to abandonment, two stories about morality recur in human experience.

Children know both stories and test them in a variety of ways. American children appeal to justice in the face of unequal power by claiming "It is not fair" or "You have no right"; they assess the strength of care by stating "You do not care" or "I do not love you anymore." In this, children discover the efficacy of moral standards, the extent to which justice offers protection to the unequal in the face of oppression, and the extent to which care protects attachment against threats of abandonment or detachment. The lessons learned about justice and care in early childhood relationships generate expectations which are confirmed or modified in later childhood and adolescence. Two moral injunctions—not to treat others unfairly and not to turn away from someone in need—define two lines of moral development, providing different standards for assessing moral judgments and moral behavior and pointing to changes in the understanding of what fairness means and what constitutes care. By tracing moral development across two intersecting dimensions of relationship, it is possible to differentiate transformations that pertain to equality from transformations that pertain to attachment and to consider the interplay between problems of inequality and problems of detachment. Observations of sex differences in moral understanding and moral behavior reflect a tendency for these problems to be differentially salient or differently organized in male and female development.

The sex difference question, when framed in this way, does not carry the implication that one sex is morally superior, nor does it imply that moral behavior is biologically determined. Instead, it draws attention to two perspectives on morality. To the extent that biological sex, the psychology of gender, and the cultural norms and values that define masculine and feminine behavior affect experience of equality and of attachment, these factors presumably will influence moral development.

For example, the experience of attachment in early childhood may attenuate the experience of inequality by empowering the child in relation to the parent, who otherwise seems unmovable and all-powerful. If girls identify with their mothers, to whom they are attached, and remain in closer physical proximity to them, the experience of inequality may be less overwhelming and the sense of efficacy gained by creating connections with others more central to the organization of their self-concept and to their self-esteem. In adolescence, girls may be less attentive to the consequences of unequal relationships and more apt to focus their attention on the nature or the strength of connection, especially when norms of feminine behavior impede strivings toward equality. If boys are more strongly attached to their mothers but identify with their fathers and do not see beyond their father's authority and physical power, then the experience of inequality and the desire to overcome that status may become more salient and separation or independence more crucial for self-esteem. If recurrent childhood experiences of inequality are less mitigated by experiences of attachment in boys' development and then are compounded by social inequality in adolescence and a high cultural valuation of male dominance, feelings of powerlessness may become heightened and the potential for violence may correspondingly increase.

These schematic observations are intended to suggest the ways in which experiences of inequality and experiences of attachment can interact with one another, leading one dimension of relationship to overshadow the other or to color its meaning. We have indicated how girls may tend to lose sight of the problems that arise from inequality and how boys may tend to lose sight of the problems that arise from detachment. Yet the tension between these two moral perspectives may best illuminate the psychology or moral development by drawing attention to conflicts in relationships that give rise to genuine moral dilemmas.

Seen in terms of either justice or care, the following problems appear to have right, if difficult, answers. Seen from both perspectives, their ethical ambiguity appears. With this shift, one comes to a different understanding of the child who is uncertain over whether to adhere to standards of fairness or to help another child on a test, or the adolescent who is torn between loyalty to particular relationships and loyalty to ideals of equality and freedom, or the adult who wonders in allocating resources whether it is better to respond to the perception of need or to follow principles of justice. Like the dilemma posed by Sartre (1948) about whether a young man should join the resistance or stay with his mother, or the dilemma of mothers who wonder whether to join the resistance or stay with their children, these conflicts can be seen as paradigmatic human moral problems—problems that arise when the demands of equality and the demands of attachment clash.

The metaphor that illuminates our discussion of moral development is therefore the ambiguous figure, illustrating how the same scene can be organized in at least two different ways and also how one way of seeing can cause another to disappear. We will begin with a summary of research on moral orientation to present evidence that the two perspectives we have described are manifest in the ways that people define and resolve moral problems. We then will turn to the question of moral feelings and indicate how the different perspectives on relationship color the meaning of compassion and organize the moral emotions of shame and guilt, love and sorrow. Finally, we will offer an overview of moral development, and the relational life of the child. Drawing on insights we have gained from rereading Piaget and from Bowlby's work on loss and detachment, we arrive at the position that moral emotions, like moral judgments, are not primary data but are effects of relationships. The egocentric fallacy is to assume that strong feelings or clear principles are self-generated or *sui generis*. Our argument is that strong feelings and clear principles are dependent on authentic relationships. Because relationships vary in nature, the conditions that affect relationships and the moral psychologies generated by different forms of relationship become central empirical questions and theoretical concerns. In this paper, we will focus our attention on two dimensions of relationships and suggest their implications for the development of moral reasoning and moral feelings.

## Evidence of Two Perspectives in Moral Reasoning

Evidence that the two moral orientations we have described structure people's thinking about the nature and resolution of moral conflicts comes from studies of the ways people describe moral conflicts they have faced. Analysis of such descriptions indicates that people tend to raise considerations of justice and of care in recounting an experience of moral conflict and choice (see Lyons 1983; Gilligan and Attanucci 1985). In a sample of eighty educationally advantaged adolescents and adults, fifty-five or 69 percent introduced both justice and care considerations (Gilligan and Attanucci 1985). Two-thirds of the people studied, however, (fifty-three out of eighty or 66 percent) focused their attention on either justice or care concerns, so that of the considerations they raised, 75 percent or more were framed in the terms of one or the other orientation. This focus phenomenon was manifested equally by males and females among the high school, college, and medical students and the adult professionals who were studied. But the direction of focus revealed a difference between the sexes. Care focus in moral reasoning, although by no means characteristic of all women, was almost exclusively a female phenomenon in this educationally advantaged North American sample. Of the thirty-one men who demonstrated focus, thirty focused on justice. Of the twenty-two women, ten focused on justice and twelve on care. These findings are presented in the following table, together with the finding of no sex differences in the tendency to represent considerations of justice and care with roughly equal frequency.

|         | Care Focus | Care-Justice | Justice Focus |
|---------|-----------|--------------|---------------|
| Females | 12        | 12           | 10            |
| Males   | 1         | 15           | 30            |

(Average number of considerations per dilemma = 7; range = 4–17)

Source: Gilligan and Attanucci 1985.

The clearest demonstration of moral orientation appears in a study designed and conducted by Johnston (1985) who developed a standard method for assessing spontaneous moral orientation and orientation preference. Johnston asked sixty children, ages eleven and fifteen, from a typical American suburban community, to state and to solve the problem posed by two of Aesop's fables. Most children (fifty-four or fifty-six out of sixty, depending on the fable) cast the problem in the terms of either the justice or the care orientation; either they identified conflicting rights and duties and ordered them by referring to a rule or fair procedure for adjudicating conflicting claims, or they identified the various needs involved and created a solution that was responsive to all of the needs. After the children defined and solved the fable problem, Johnston asked, "Is there another way to think about this problem?" With each fable, about half of the children (more fifteen- than eleven-year-olds) spontaneously switched orientation in response to this question; most were able to explain the logic of both orientations, and only one child did not answer Johnston's subsequent question as to which solution was the best solution. Fifty-nine of the sixty children indicated which of the solutions they discussed provided a better way to solve the problem and explained why it was preferable.

Johnston found both gender differences and fable differences in moral orientation. Boys more often spontaneously cast the fable problems as problems of justice and preferred justice solutions (honoring contracts, respecting rights, acting in accordance with principles of fairness). Girls more often spontaneously cast the problems in terms of care and preferred care solutions (creating ways of responding to everyone's need). Sex differences reached statistical significance in three of the four comparisons presented in the following table:

| | Spontaneous Orientation | | Orientation Preference | |
| --- | --- | --- | --- | --- |
| | Fable 1 | Fable 2 | Fable 1 | Fable 2 |
| Boys | | | | |
| rights | 22 | 21 | 13 | 17 |
| response | 5 | 7 | 13 | 5 |
| Girls | | | | |
| rights | 12 | 15 | 3 | 6 |
| response | 15 | 10 | 24 | 18 |

*Source:* Johnston 1985.
*Note:* The only comparison that did not reach significance at the .01 level or beyond was spontaneous orientation in fable 2.

The girls' preference for innovative solutions to the fable problems corroborates Piaget's observation that girls in their games apply "their ingenuity in inventing new figures" and are "more easily reconciled to innovations" in resolving disputes ([1932] 1965, 77). Johnston speculated that when inequality is heightened in the fable, justice solutions may be more likely, and that when attachment seems more probable, care solutions may be more frequent. One of the most interesting sex differences, however, was the tendency for girls to see attachment where boys saw inequality and for girls to present care solutions as feasible where boys described them as naive and unworkable.

In essence, this research suggests that people understand two logics of moral problem solving and that the analytically distinguishable orientations of justice and care prompt different ways of perceiving and resolving conflicts. The research findings are consistent with our analysis of human relationships and moral development, indicat-

ing that eleven-year-old children as well as adolescents and adults ori-
ent toward the moral values of both justice and care and are capable
of shifting orientations in considering conflicts in relationships.
Langdale (1983) studied moral orientation in judgments of hypothetical dilemmas and reported an interaction between spontaneous
moral orientation (as reflected by self-generated "real-life" moral
conflicts) and the orientation characteristic of hypothetical moral
problems. The validity of the justice-care distinction in the coding
procedure developed by Lyons (1982, 1983) is indicated by Langdale's
finding that Kohlberg's justice-reasoning dilemmas elicited the highest frequency of justice considerations from both males and females
in a life-cycle sample of 144 people. Langdale found sex differences in
moral orientation across four different dilemmas, with women consistently raising more care considerations than men, even in resolving the justice-focused Heinz problem.

It should be emphasized, however, that at this point we suspend
any claim as to the generality of these findings. It clearly will be necessary to examine the vicissitudes of these two orientations among both
men and women embedded in different socioeconomic, educational, and
cultural contexts as well as across a wider range of moral problems.

## The Implications of Moral Orientation for the Study of Moral Emotions

The two perspectives we have designated as a "justice orientation"
and a "care orientation" imply a shift in the conception of what is
relevant to the moral domain. According to this thesis, the two
orientations would not only entail different notions of "morality"
manifest in different forms of moral reasoning, but also different conceptions of the emotions and the relations of the emotions with morality. Certain activities that are treated dismissively from one perspective may be elevated from a different perspective. For example,
forms of human relationship that, from the perspective of a justice
orientation, may be relegated to the status of residues of an outgrown
stage may, from a care orientation, be viewed as significant and even
central. This shift in world view is key to our representation of the
moral significance of attachment relationships, seen not as residues
of early childhood need but as key to the development of what in the
past was called "moral sensibility." Detachment which is highly valued as the mark of mature moral judgment in the justice framework
becomes in the care framework a sign of moral danger, a loss of connection with others. The sharp subject-object distinction that is considered essential to development in most psychological theories thus

is called into question and a more fluid conception of self in relation to others is tied to the growth of affective imagination, namely, the ability to enter into and understand through taking on and experiencing the feelings of others.

In the traditional literature, governed by a predominant justice orientation, shame and guilt have been seen as the pardigmatic moral feelings. Hoffman (1976) has taken the lead in criticizing this view and emphasized the need not only to consider empathy, sympathy, and altruistic motives in conceptualizing morality and moral development but also to pay attention to evidence of empathy, sympathy, and altruism in early childhood. Blum (1980), in his philosophical study of *Friendship, Altruism and Morality*, argues for the moral significance of human connection and personal care and contrasts two modes of responding to others that resemble our contrast between justice and care.

Our conception of the care orientation as grounded in attachments lead us to consider love and sorrow as well as other feelings closely linked to attachment and fears of alienation and isolation as moral emotions. Moral outrage can be provoked not only by oppression and injustice but also by abandonment or loss of attachment or the failure of others to respond. In a study of high school girls, moral passion marked their descriptions of situations in which someone did not listen, recalling Simone Weil's and Iris Murdoch's definition of attention as a moral act. It is important to emphasize that in our conception, love does not imply fusion or transcendence. Instead love is tied to the activities of relationship and premised, like attachment, on the responsiveness of human connection, the ability of people to engage with one another in such a way that the needs and feelings of the other come to be experienced and taken on as *part of* the self. As experiences of inequality and attachment organize moral reasoning, generating a preoccupation with justice and with care, so too these experiences structure feelings of shame, guilt, love, and sorrow.

Shame and guilt and love and sorrow can be traced analytically to experiences of inequality and of attachment in that shame and guilt imply falling below a standard while love and sorrow imply connection. In the individual person, however, these feelings, like these experiences, intermingle. Guilt may be engendered by the inability to reciprocate love; shame as well as sorrow may be provoked by a loss of attachment or by inattention; and sorrow as well as shame and guilt can accompany the experience of oppression or injustice. These feelings define moral experience and clarify moral violation; yet the power of moral feelings coexists with the recognition that such feelings can be interpreted differently in different contexts.

These problems of interpretation are illustrated clearly by the discussion of the word "compassion" in Milan Kundera's novel, *The Unbearable Lightness of Being* (1984). The discussion of compassion begins with the observation that "all languages that derive from Latin form the word 'compassion' by combining the prefix meaning 'with' *(com)* and the root meaning 'suffering' (Late Latin, *passio*)." In other languages, such as Czech, Swedish, and German, the word is translated by a similar prefix combined with a root meaning 'feeling' (19–20). The significance of this etymological distinction is that the meaning of compassion changes from sympathy to love as the relationship implied changes from one of inequality to one of attachment. This shift in meaning, which Kundera draws out in the following passage, is key to our thinking about the nature of moral feelings and the role of emotion or sentiment in moral development:

> In languages that derive from Latin, "compassion" means: we cannot look on coolly as others suffer; or, we sympathize with those who suffer. Another word with approximately the same meaning, "pity" (French, *pitié;* Italian, pietà; etc.), connotes a certain condescension towards the sufferer. "To take pity on a woman" means that we are better off than she, that we stoop to her level, lower ourselves.
>
> That is why the word "compassion" generally inspires suspicion; it designates what is considered an inferior, second-rate sentiment that has little to do with love. To love someone out of compassion means not really to love.
>
> In languages that form the word "compassion" not from the root "suffering" but from the root "feeling," the word is used in approximately the same way, but . . . the secret strength of its etymology floods the word with another light and gives it a broader meaning: to have compassion (co-feeling) means not only to be able to live with the other's misfortune but also to feel with him any emotion—joy, anxiety, happiness, pain. This kind of compassion . . . therefore signifies the maximal capacity of affective imagination, the art of emotional telepathy. In the hierarchy of sentiments, then, it is supreme. (Kundera 1984, 20)

In its English usage, compassion means sympathy, and the tinge of suspicion Kundera's narrator describes extends across the entire discussion of altruism and prosocial awareness, conveying an uncertainty over whether altruistic emotions are really self-interested and whether they are welcomed by the recipient. It is only when compassion means co-feeling that its moral qualities are clear. No longer does one remain distant in the presence of another's feelings, and the opposition between egoism and altruism disappears. Yet the idea of co-feeling goes against prevailing assumptions about the nature of the self and its relation to others, since co-feeling implies neither clear self-other boundaries nor a merging or fusion between self and other, so that one or the other disappears. Considered on a theoretical level, co-feeling, however morally desirable, would seem to be psychologically impossible. Yet the contrast between sympathy and co-feeling occasionally appears in empirical studies, often in conjunction with observations of sex differences in empathy or prosocial awareness. To consider the meaning of co-feeling and its possible significance in moral development, it is necessary first to distinguish more closely between different forms of moral emotions and different ways of knowing others.

Hoffman (1976) suggests that one can feel another's feelings only to the extent that the other's feelings are similar to one's own. Kagan's view of morality as grounded in emotions assumes "a family of feelings, each of which has a prototypic core" (1984, 169). Although feelings are felt by the individual, the suggestion of a family of feelings mediated by standards of feeling to which everyone is assumed to have access leaves open the question of how this access is gained. Our interest in co-feeling lies in the implication that such feeling develops through the experience of relationships which render others' feelings accessible. The distinction between co-feeling and empathy is that empathy implies an identity of feelings—that self and other feel the same, while co-feeling implies that one can experience feelings that are different from one's own. Co-feeling then depends on the ability to *participate* in another's feelings, signifying an attitude of engagement rather than an attitude of judgment or observation. To feel with another any emotion means in essence to be *with* that person, rather than to stand apart and look *at* the other, feeling sympathy *for* her or him. For example, when a child suffers, one may feel the child's suffering as part of one's own or one may observe that the child is suffering and feel concern for the child.

The moral emotions of shame and guilt convey a distance between self and other; to feel ashamed in the eyes of others or guilty for one's wishes or actions toward others is to feel lower than them or perhaps more powerful in the sense of being capable of doing them harm. When one feels ashamed or guilty in one's own eyes, the implication of inequality remains but is structured in terms of self-regard. One has fallen beneath one's standard or failed to live up to one's aspirations, as the terms super-ego and ego-ideal imply.

To see love and sorrow as moral emotions—as feelings that affect the ability to care for oneself and for others and inform the understanding of how one should act or what actions constitute care or cause harm—is to see experiences of attachment and detachment as relevant to moral development. With this shift, the assumptions usually made about relationships in discussions of morality change. For example, the reason love does not connote condescension is not because it implies equality but because it signifies connection. Through co-feeling, self and other, whether equal or unequal, become connected or interdependent. Difference in this context may stimulate interest or signify the potential for an expansion of experience or for detachment and misunderstanding, but it does not imply that one is higher or lower than the other. Conversely, co-feeling does not imply an absence of difference or an identity of feelings or a failure to distinguish between self and other. Instead, co-feeling implies an awareness of oneself as capable of knowing and living with the feelings of others, as able to affect others and to be affected by them. With this shift in the conception of self in relation to others, moral questions change.

No longer does moral inquiry turn on the question of how to live with inequality—that is, how to act *as if* self and other were in fact equal or how to impose a rule of equality based on a principle of equal respect. Instead, moral inquiry deals with questions of relationship pertaining to problems of inclusion and exclusion—how to live in connection with oneself and with others, how to avoid detachment or resist the temptation to turn away from need. The games children play and their friendship patterns reveal their engagement with these questions and enable them to observe the costs of exclusion and to discover what inclusion entails. Children's experiments in inclusion and exclusion, seen most darkly in ostracism and clique formation, lead to some of the more painful experiences of childhood and adult life. But they also prepare for the difficult questions about inclusion and exclusion that people face. The implication of this discussion is that the costs of detachment and the conditions for attachment or connection are lessons that are learned through experience.

The role of feelings in knowledge about attachment and detachment raises the question of how knowledge of feelings is gained and expanded. The infant, responding empathically to the feelings of others, demonstrates co-feeling in its most inchoate form. As the child develops, different experiences of human connection—with parents, siblings, friends, teachers, and so on—may deepen and widen the experience of feelings, expanding the child's vocabulary of feelings and increasing the child's interest in knowing how people feel. The aesthetic sensibilities of children which are evident in their drawings and stories demonstrate their ability to enter into the feelings of others or to imagine affectively how others feel. Thus the child's capacity for co-feeling, on the one hand inconceivable, on the other is clear.

For example, it is the child's and parent's responsiveness to each other that gives life to the relationship between them, imbuing it with the pleasure that comes from responsive engagement with others and creating an interplay of feelings that leads the child to wonder at the adult and the adult to delight in the child. Through the attachment or connection they create between them, child and parent come to know one another's feelings and in this way discover how to comfort and to hurt one another. When the responsiveness between parent and child decreases and their inequality comes to the fore, the child may feel ashamed or guilty in the eyes of the parent, and the parent, at best, looks on the child with sympathy and feels compassion for his or her distress.

This distance between self and other has been celebrated as the mark of the subject-object distinction, the birth of subject-object relations. But it also carries with it the dangers of objectification, the ability to treat others as objects and to feel no connection with them. The sense that safety and insight are gained through detachment is countered by the recognition that in the absence of co-feeling one cannot know what others are feeling, and therefore one may live in egocentric ignorance, dangerously prone to rationalization.

Two descriptions of knowledge thus underlie two ways of thinking about morality. One is the conception of knowledge as arising through the correspondence between mind and pure form, so that moral knowledge becomes the reflective equilibrium between the self and moral principles. Then one can take the role of the others or assume Rawls' original position or play Kohlberg's game of moral musical chairs—all without knowing anything about the other but simply by following the laws of perspective and putting oneself in his or her position. The other conception is of knowledge as gained through human connection, a conception conveyed in the Biblical passage "And Adam knew Eve." The young child's feelings of shame and guilt, love and sorrow, signify the presence of both forms of knowledge and point to their origin in the relationships of early childhood.

In studies of empathy, sympathy, and prosocial behavior such as helping, sharing, caring, and so on, the distinction between compassion in the sense of sympathy and compassion in the sense of cofeeling is generally not made, or, if made, associated with the presence or absence of self-other boundaries. These studies often focus on children's response to distress and equate development with the child's ability to see the distress as belonging to the other and to "own" his or her own feelings. Thus Hoffman distinguishes between the infant's empathic responsiveness and the child's sympathetic distress and sees in this contrast a developmental progression that reflects the emergence of self-awareness and the growth of cognitive capacities.

Hoffman (1977) notes, however, in a survey of the literature on sex differences in empathy, that one of the few instances of clear sex difference is the finding that although girls and boys are equally able to identify and understand the feelings of others, girls also tend to experience the feelings. Along the same lines, Wolf, Rygh, and Altshuler (1984) have observed in analyzing children's narratives that although girls and boys of similar ages have the same repertoire of feelings, they tend to "string" feelings together differently in composing narrative sequences. But the most compelling example of sex differences which suggests the distinction between co-feeling and sympathy arose as a serendipitous observation in a study of reflective thinking and prosocial awareness in early adolescence. The findings of this study, conducted by Bardige, suggest a tension between co-feeling and formal operational thinking in a context where this tension raises a central question about moral development.

Perhaps the seeming implausibility of co-feeling reflects a moment in development when the capacity for co-feeling is lost. Theoretically, we would expect such moments to occur when connection with others is constrained by biological or social or psychological factors and therefore when detachment is more likely. Adolescence is one such time. In this light, we might also expect some adolescents to resist detachment and to demonstrate by their resistance a sense of moral problem.

Bardige (1983, 1985) analyzed the journals kept by forty-three eighth graders who were taking the course, "Facing History and Ourselves: Holocaust and Human Behavior." The children were students in two social studies classes in suburban schools. Bardige set out to trace the growth of logical thinking in early adolescence by analyzing the students' ability to understand complex historical events. In conducting her analysis, however, she noticed that four girls whose journals showed signs of concrete operational thinking repeatedly responded to films and stories portraying violence with language that coupled sadness, horror, or distress with shock and a call for action to stop the violence. Reexamining the journals, Bardige found that this pattern appeared in the journals of eight of the twenty-four girls in the study and one of the nineteen boys. She called the pattern "face-value thinking" to denote the tendency of these students to take evidence of violence at face value.

The limitations of "face-value thinking" were clear and the naiveté of its good intentions apparent; yet the immediacy of perception, the passionate clarity of judgment, the intensity of involvement, and the eagerness to "do something" were striking—particularly in light of the observation that those students whose reasoning was more sophisticated, in that they saw two sides of the story or were capable of seeing through multiple lenses, did not respond to the evidence of violence with the same moral intensity. In one sense, the face-value responses called attention to "the central moral truth of the situation—the fact that violence was being inflicted and the need to stop it." Thus face-value thinking "captures the impulse to respond both emotionally and actively. It allows no excuses for torture and murder" (Bardige 1985, 17).

The fact that this kind of thinking was associated with evidence of what are generally taken to be lower levels of cognitive and moral and ego development led Bardige to reconsider her analysis of the journals and to question whether moral sensibilities are at risk in adolescence. All the students showed personal distress, profound concern, incredulity, and a desire to "do something" in response to the violence they witnessed, but the language they used and the linkages they made were different. Contrasting the "passionate clarity of a 'face-value judgment' [with] the generosity of a 'composite-picture judgment' that looks for the good side, and the integrity of a 'multiple lens judgment' that recognizes that actions that satisfy one's conscience may not be truly helpful," Bardige saw a pattern of gains and losses.

Kant had argued similarly. The moral insights implicit in the ideas and behavior of the common man may well be muted or lost, he noted, in the moral philosopher's ability to "confuse his judgment with a mass of alien considerations and cause it to swerve from the straight path" ([1785] 1948, 22–23). Piaget saw the onset of formal operations in adolescence as carrying with it a danger of the most pervasive egocentrism and thus characterized adolescence as "the metaphysical age par excellence" (Piaget [1940] 1967, 64). Bardige too considered the ways in which a more powerful cognitive framework can also be more dangerous:

> The ability to see both sides can bring a new understanding of others and therefore an enhanced ability to take their needs into consideration. It can also allow a concern for the rights and welfare of the victimizer to obscure the experience of the victim and the reality that the two sides are not equal. The use of multiple lenses can bring a new assumption of responsibility. This ability can also, as several multiple-

lens users pointed out in their journals, be used to rationalize inaction, evade decisions, or shrewdly manipulate others into complacency in the face of evil. (Bardige 1985, 36)

Most striking in the responses of the students who took evidence of violence at face value was the direct expression of feeling in response to the perception of hurt. The expressions of sadness or disgust, coupled with statements of uncomprehending shock, became the ground on which the students felt called to take action. In the absence of face-value thinking, the evidence of co-feeling disappeared from the journals. The more sophisticated thinkers were more likely to locate emotion within themselves and to express sympathy for the victims. Some were suspicious of emotional responses, recognizing how feelings can be manipulated; others spoke of their efforts to overcome their tendency to distance themselves.

Kagan has speculated that "Perhaps each of us is persuaded of the moral rightness of an idea by two different, incommensurate processes. One is based on feelings; the other, on logical consistency with a few deep premises." He goes on to observe that "When a standard derives its strength from either foundation, we find it difficult to be disloyal to its directives. When it enjoys the support of both, as it does for torture and unprovoked murder, its binding force is maximal" (1984, 124). Our analysis of justice and care as two moral perspectives and of sympathy and love as two meanings of compassion corroborates Kagan's suggestion of two moral processes but indicates further how feelings and premises are characteristic of both a justice and a care approach. The focus phenomenon in our studies, where subjects tend to view moral problems largely in terms of justice or care, suggests a tension between the two perspectives, in that the adoption of one tends to obscure the other.

The fact that care focus in moral reasoning appears in our data primarily in the moral judgments of girls and women and the fact that with one exception Bardige found face-value responses to violence only in girls' journals (a third of the girls showed this pattern) keep alive the question of sex differences in moral reasoning and moral feelings and indicate the problems that arise when moral development is assessed from a single perspective. What appears as dispassion within a justice framework appears as detachment or indifference from a care perspective: the ability to stand back and look at others as if one's feelings were disconnected from their feelings and one was not affected by what happens to them. This ability to see relationships in two ways or to tell a story from two different angles underlies what may well be the most searing experiences of moral dilemma, creating an irreducible sense of ethical ambiguity and also perhaps the temptation to shut out one version or one perspective and thus eliminate the problem—the wish to make the conflict disappear.

## Implications for Theories of Moral Development

In the final section of this paper, we wish to consider the implications of our data for describing the moral development of the child. Our metaphor of the ambiguous figure calls attention to the persistent danger that lies in the loss of perspective. It follows from our analysis of justice and care as two moral perspectives that either perspective can represent the concerns of the other within its own terms. Within a justice framework, care becomes a matter of special obligations or supererogatory duties. Within a care framework, justice becomes a matter of including the self as well as others within the compass of care. Yet this effort to construct one orientation in the terms of the other, like attempts to cast the two orientations as opposites or mirror images so that caring is unjust and justice uncaring, misses the reorganization of relationship that occurs with the shift in perspective. To argue whether morality is *really* a matter of justice or of care is like arguing whether the rabbit-duck figure is really a rabbit or a duck.

The care ethic cannot be reduced to a "personal" aspect of morality conceived as justice, as Kohlberg and others have argued.[1] To do so is not only to fail to see that care can be "principled"—governed by standards of authentic relationship—but also to overlook those dilemmas that arise from conflicts between perspectives or from blind spots within one point of view. For example, moral psychology, looking at development from the perspective of the thinking or feeling self, construed as a detached ego attaining its freedom, cannot account for the classic errors of moral blindness or rationalization. Similarly, a moral psychology that represents development only as progress toward equality and mutual respect runs the risk of confusing detachment with objectivity, so that relationships end up serving heteronomous and reified moral norms.

---

1. Kohlberg (1984) criticizes Gilligan's account of metaethics to argue that the ethic of care is "not well adapted to resolve justice problems, problems which require principles to resolve conflicting claims among persons, all of whom in some sense should be cared for." There is, thus, in his view, no "moral point of view" from which to judge in tackling problems of care and responsibility separate from issues and norms of "justice" (p. 231–32). But the "morality of care" represents not merely the sphere of "personal decision-making," as he puts it, but an alternative point of view from which to map the moral domain and reveal "the laws of perspective" (in Piaget's phrase) which describe a relationally grounded view of morality.

Our relationship-focused perspective on morality leads us to see experiences of equality and of attachment as critical to the growth of moral understanding. Looking at the dynamics of development, we pay particular attention to the interweaving of these two dimensions of relationship and thus to conflicts between concerns about justice and concerns about care. When the child's search for equality—the effort to become stronger and more competent, like the adult—comes into tension with the child's search for attachment—the effort to create and sustain authentic relationships, the experience of moral dilemma may be most intense and the potential for moral development may as a result be heightened. Early childhood and adolescence would appear to be such times, since biological growth, new psychological capacities, and new worlds of social experience combine to change the terms of both equality and attachment. Consequently relationships must be renegotiated along both dimensions at these times. To see early childhood and adolescence as periods when the relational dimensions of equality and of attachment both undergo rapid transformation is to see the moral conflicts that young children and adolescents are likely to encounter. The implication that detachment constitutes a solution to such problems in either period is, in our view, the major blindspot in current theories of self and moral development.

In this light, we come back to Piaget's insights about the moral wisdom and generosity of the eleven-year-old child and consider, in addition, Bowlby's work on the ways children rationalize disordered attachments. Piaget's question—"How is it that democratic practice is so developed in the game of marbles played by boys of 11 and 13 whereas it is so unfamiliar to the adult in many spheres of life?"—has never been answered, beyond Piaget's reflection that the eleven-year-old is the "sovereign" in the childhood world ([1932] 1965, 76). This question continues to challenge the assumption of incremental progress contained in stage theories of moral and ego development.[2] Piaget's observation of the eleven-year-old boy's "insights into the ideal or spirit of the game which cannot be formulated in terms of rules" ([1932] 1965, 386) corresponds to our observation of similar insights among girls of eleven into "the spirit of the relationship" which also

2. In fact, we should remember that Piaget argued that moral development could not be understood in stage-theory terms precisely because autonomy was continually at risk in every new relationship of constraint ([1932] 1965, 86)—thus dependent on the social circumstances facing the growing child, the adolescent, and the adult. Furthermore, Piaget also noted the problems in confounding moral development with intellectual development, observing that "an intelligent scamp would perhaps give better answers [to questions about moral conduct] than a slow-witted but really good-hearted little boy" (116). See also Kagan (1984), chap. 4.

cannot be fully articulated at this age. In light of the sex differences we have noted in moral reasoning and moral emotions, the question as to whether insights about games and relationships, equality and attachment, are held in common by children of both sexes may better be phrased as a question of whether boys and girls tend to organize such insights differently in relation to one another. Adolescence becomes a critical time in moral development because the childhood organization of equality and attachment no longer fits the experience of the teenager. Thus the wisdom of the eleven-year-old, about the rules of the game and about the nature of relationships, rather than being solidified and progressively expanded in adolescence, is in danger.

Puberty returns the sovereign eleven-year-old, whose insights into the spirit of justice and care, although inexpressible, constitute the core of moral wisdom, to an insecure position between the relationships of childhood and of adulthood, where the child's assumptions about care and about justice are often radically upset. Formal thinking opens up the world of powerful moral ideals and hypothetical arguments, but puberty also opens up the world of reproductive sexuality and mystifying attachments. The potential for alienated rationalizing and for detached feelings is therefore heightened in the difficult social world of the teenager, especially in the presence of systematic injustice or rationalized indifference on the part of adults. Inhelder and Piaget offer vivid descriptions of the seductions of metaphysics in adolescence and see the adolescent's egocentrism as "messianic," liable to produce private fantasies that even the thinker herself or himself later might find to be "pathological megalomania" (1958, 344). The critical variable for moral development in adolescence may be the development of genuine intellectual and emotional attachments which would counter the potential for such egocentrism. But the question arises: Is Piaget's picture a necessary one? Or are alienation and rationalization a response to inadequately formed or thought-through attachments? In this light, we look at Piaget's own example of the eleven-year-old he identifies as Camp.

Camp, contrary to Piaget's intentions, illustrates how care can override justice, but the example is inadequately explained—in part to sustain Piaget's contention that "equality and solidarity go hand in hand":

*Int:* What do you think about cheating?
*Camp:* For those who can't learn, they ought to be allowed to have
  a little look, but for those who can learn, it isn't fair.
*Int:* A child copied his friend's sum. Was it fair?
*Camp:* He ought not to have copied. But if he was not clever, it was
  more or less alright for him to do it. (Piaget, [1932] 1965, 289)

Surprisingly, Piaget observes, "this last attitude seems to be rather the exception among the children we examined. But no doubt many others thought the same without having the courage to say so." Piaget solves the problem posed by his example by claiming that it illustrates the conflict between solidarity among children and obedience to adult authority and then discusses the Kantian question of whether one should lie to avoid betrayal. But the egalitarian justice that Piaget sees as developing with age among children in correlation with the growth of solidarity between them does not address the issues of attachment and detachment which the example contains. Nor are these issues articulated by Camp.

Camp illustrates compassion in the sense of sympathy rather than co-feeling, distancing himself from the less clever child whom he thinks it "alright" unfairly to help. Thus he implies that one only modifies justice for those in a lower position. But the attachment implications of such dilemmas are often articulated explicitly by girls of this age, who speak of the costs to themselves of turning away from the perception of need in others—the haunting memory of the unheeded cry for help as well as the dangers of "losing all your friends."

Adolescent girls' resistance to detachment has generally been interpreted as a failure of separation and as occurring at the expense of their intellectual and moral growth. Viewed in light of the costs of detachment, it seems instead to contain a different moral insight whose application is not limited to the private sphere. A high school philosophy student, discussing the dilemma posed by Sartre about whether a young man should join the resistance or stay with his mother, illustrates both the coherence of an attachment-based care logic and the contrast between care and justice reasoning:

> If I were the boy, I think that I would have chosen to stay with the mother. I do not know if that would be best, but it is a more immediate and good solution. Are there no other men to be loyal to the state, when he is the only one whom his mother's existence depends on? I feel strongly toward directing actions toward the good of individuals. If everyone did so, logically, these actions would be for the good of everyone.

The response to the mother is grounded not only in the immediacy and reality of her need, but also in the logic which argues that were the norms guiding care in particular relationships lived up to in a general way (i.e., universalizing the norm of attention to each idiosyncratic relationship), social conflict might be unnecessary. Seeing differences between people as offering the potential for creative solutions that are responsive to everyone's need, the student illustrates how the logic of the ethic of care, with its preference for inclusive solutions, is designed to avoid turning moral dilemmas into binary choice, win-lose situations. Yet the inclusive or creative solution does not fit the standard of equality from the justice perspective. If she were to adopt a role-taking stance and put herself in the other person's position, she would assume that the other would have similar needs or duties (vis-à-vis mothers) when in fact that might not be the case. Thus detachment, impartiality, and "ideal role taking" may obscure the possibility of the win-win solution that she imagines.

But there is another point to be made. Co-feeling characterizes the student's approach to solving the dilemma in that she "lives with," rather than reconstructing in her own terms, the mother's need. In this sense, co-feeling underlies respect for the feelings of others and removes the presumption of deciding for others whether or not their needs are "real." It is in this way that the shift from inequality to attachment changes the organization of thinking about the relationship between self and others and makes possible compassion in the sense of love. Of note is that this student reveals this capacity in her own life; while she wishes desperately to be able to decide her future religious orientation and argues for her right to do so, she writes with feeling about her parents' different point of view. Her wish is insightful; she asks not that they agree with her but that they understand her view.

Another high school student, discussing Kohlberg's Heinz dilemma, also sees a problem in detachment, not only in the dilemma itself—the unresponsiveness of the druggist to Heinz and his wife—but also in the implications of what is generally taken to be its right answer, the statement that life takes priority over law and property. Although she is able logically to justify the rightness of Heinz's stealing on these grounds, she finds a problem in saying that one should steal a drug to save the life of a stranger when she knows that in her own city people are dying because they cannot afford medication and yet she also knows that she has no intention of stealing. Thus she sees the "right answer" as logically right but as morally problematic, leaving unaddressed the question of what it means to divorce moral judgment from action and also the question of whether stealing constitutes a good solution to problems of perceived need or unfair distribution.

The current debates about the child's capacity for altruistic feelings and motives have not addressed a crucial point: if such feelings are natural and present in early childhood (and Piaget as well as Kant and Rawls regard them as so—necessary, if insufficient), their loss or harmful transformation must be the *result* of certain kinds of experience. Thus we ask: What experiences might be present in the lives of those who lose these sensibilities? Do some children never lose them, and if so, what form has their experience taken?

Piaget suggested that knowledge of the good is acquired after knowledge of pure duty, but he never indicates how that knowledge is attained ([1932] 1965, 73, 106, 350). Kohlberg claims that his sixth stage integrates caring and justice, but he never describes how caring develops or how one knows what constitutes care (1984, 349–58). What if knowledge of the good is not acquired after knowledge of pure duty but is possessed in embryo form by the girls whom Piaget fails to understand—the girls who do not sanction hitting back as an appropriate response to blows received and more quickly shed egocentrism in the experience of cooperation—as well as by the eleven-year-old marble shooters and exam takers? What if the upbringing and moral experience of girls and the insights of eleven-year-old boys, as reflected in Piaget's own data, point to a different kind of complex, idiosyncratic moral development, dependent on the fate of attachments?

Perhaps the relational experience of girls, not only their connection with their mothers but also their friendships throughout childhood, mitigate against detachment and its attendant egocentrism, keeping both their relational nature and their moral knowledge intact, if unsystematic. The extent to which school-age girls acquire a factual knowledge of human feelings and can explain and predict complex patterns of interaction within a family or school classroom has never been addressed in its significance for moral understanding. Perhaps the quiet uncertainty of so many adolescent women reflects an accurate understanding of their conflicting feelings, the multiplicity of perspectives and possible judgments based on a nonegocentric knowledge of how others feel.

Piaget's work contains the seeds of this argument, lost in the language and the focus on justice considerations and in an overly cognitive reading of his work by Piagetians. Piaget's notion that autonomy develops in peer interaction, often in spite of the parents, merely highlights the essential role of relationships in moral development ([1932] 1965, 190–93, 319). The morality based on a self-evident good, a morality of intention and co-feeling, depends not only on the experience of genuine cooperation but also on the experience of genuine attachment. The loss of the natural moral emotions thus seems less a loss than a repressive transformation where ego developmental needs in detachments adapt moral feelings to personal aims. Thus norms and rules become reified as "self-chosen principles," removed from the relational contexts which give them life and meaning.

If the persistent error in care reasoning is vacillation and lack of clear judgment resulting from a tendency to include all possible ways of seeing, the persistent danger in the justice reasoner is moral arrogance, the irrational faith in the infallibility of judgments from principles rigidly applied to a situation. It follows then that development need not entail moral progress; if attachment is a primary datum, moral wisdom may exist early in the life of the child and be lost in the evolution of relationships. Moral immaturity will consist not in an absence of general moral knowledge but in an absence of the attachments necessary for making moral notions moral insights. The experienced and negotiated relations of the child, particularly in early childhood and adolescence, may provide critical data about both the promise of moral wisdom and the danger of lost moral insight. The question then becomes not how do moral "selves" develop, but what might be the developmental moments in relationships which both promote and threaten moral progress.

Our perspective on moral development as occurring through the transformation of attachment, as well as through the child's progress toward equality, highlights the value of Bowlby's work on loss and detachment in illuminating moral development and suggests further avenues of study. The vulnerable child, due to the physical or psychological loss of the parents' intimacy, experiences a "disordered mourning" resulting in either "compulsive care-giving" or "independence of affective ties." Many of the victims of loss of intimacy are subject to *intermittent* discontinuities in parental affection and profound mixed messages from parents about their love for the child.

How will the child respond to such mixed messages? Bowlby suggests several possible outcomes to this dilemma:

> One is that the child adheres to his own viewpoint even at the risk of breaking with his parent(s). That is far from easy . . . A second and opposite outcome is complete compliance with the parent's version at the cost of disowning his own . . . A third, and perhaps common outcome is an uneasy compromise whereby the child oscillates uneasily between them. (Bowlby 1973, 2:318)

In this most common case, the child oscillates between "two incompatible pairs of models, each pair consisting of a model of his parents and a complementary one of himself." Bowlby observes that while misattribution of the source of anxieties by the child characterizes many rationalizations, the theories which document the child's misattributions offer little evidence that the child's fears are not in fact justified. Bowlby argues that fear of loss of attachment underlies, quite understandably and realistically, many children's rationalizations: they either fear the loss of love or fail to grasp how their "loving parents" can seem so unloving in reality.

The unsuccessfully developed adult might then be highly intelligent but detached and egocentric—prone to unwitting rationalization. The rationalizer would then have called forth a "rational" solution to an irrational problem: the confusing feelings and images generated by inauthentic relationships are resolved through detachment, often viewed, mistakenly, we argue, as the necessary origins of healthy autonomy. Egocentric detachment is, therefore, an avoidable effect of a certain kind of alienating moral experience, not a paradigm case of development. Thus we reverse Piaget's argument, adopted by most Piagetians and consonant with most psychoanalytic accounts of the child's situation. Piaget claims:

> The individual, *left to himself, remains* egocentric . . . The individual begins by understanding and feeling everything through the medium of himself . . . It is only through contact with the judgments of others that this anomie will gradually yield. (Piaget [1932] 1965, 400, our emphasis)

Left to him- or herself, we claim, the individual *becomes* egocentric; able only to feel and understand through the medium of him- or herself, he or she loses contact with the feelings of others and thus must rely on egocentric judgments. In this way, anomie grows.

Acknowledging the universal ground of moral problems in the often divergent aims of equality and attachment requires moral psychology to make major changes in its concepts and methodology. Once we acknowledge that there are (at least two) different moral orientations, not only the locus of our data but our conception of "development," "stage," "self-in-relationship," and "moral maturity" must change to encompass different moral languages and the attendant problems of translation. If moral development begins in and proceeds through relationships, the child's cognitive and affective development must be seen not as final causes but also as dynamic effects of the child's relational life. If egoism is not a given, if co-feeling is not an impossibility, if the aims of equality and attachment diverge as well as converge, moral psychology must make room for a range of moral experience dependent on particular kinds of relationships as well as on cognitive and emotional maturation and on the particularities of societal and cultural context. Thus the domain of morality becomes more appropriately complex. Moral development does not entail the disappearance of moral dilemmas, and the attempt to chart development from one moral perspective only ensures the continuation of a fruitless debate about rabbits and ducks.

We began with a question about the disappearance of the discussion of sex differences. In the course of this paper we have suggested how that discussion might be transformed into a more general dialogue between two moral voices whose deep resonance in human experience suggests their origins in early childhood. In one of Virginia Woolf's novels, the narrator comments, "Either we are men, or we are women. Either we are cold, or we are sentimental. Either we are young, or growing old . . . Such is the manner of our seeing. Such the conditions of our love" (1922, 71–72). In this paper we have suggested that men and women may have a tendency to see from different standpoints or, put differently, to lose sight of different perspectives. Our view of morality as originating in early childhood relationships makes it possible to explain how as men and women we can become both cold and sentimental when genuine attachments fail. It also calls attention to the fact that we are all destined to be unequal when young and to strive toward moral equality as we grow older. While it is true that either we are men or we are women and certain experiences may accrue more readily to one or the other sex, it is also true that the capacity for love and the appreciation of justice is not limited to either sex.

For a variety of reasons, girls and women presently speak more readily about the costs of detachment, although men in various ways have highlighted these costs across time. Perhaps at this moment in history, as psychologists turn their attention to the human capacity for empathy and compassion, we will think more deeply about the ability to respond to feelings in someone who is otherwise a stranger and through that response experience the co-feeling that renders her or him less strange. Valuing that capacity, we may look more closely at the women who have been most closely involved with the much-studied infants and young children, as well as at the increasing involvement of men. In this way, we may alter our manner of seeing and observe how the infant's empathy contains the seeds of co-feeling and how the ability to live with the feelings of others can be nourished and sustained. Then, attending to problems of inequality, especially those encountered by adolescents, we may also attend to the transformations of attachment when we consider the fate of early childhood relationships and chart the course of moral development.

# References

Bardige, E. 1983. Reflective Thinking and Prosocial Awareness: Adolescents Face the Holocaust and Themselves. Ed. D. diss., Harvard Graduate School of Education.

———. 1985. Things So Finely Human: Moral Sensibilities at Risk in Adolescence. Unpublished manuscript, Harvard Graduate School of Education.

Baumrind, D. 1986. Sex Differences in Moral Reasoning: Response to Walker's (1984) Conclusion That There Are None. *Child Development* 57:511–521.

Blum, L. 1980. *Friendship, Altruism and Morality.* Boston: Routledge and Kegan Paul.

Bowlby, J. 1969–80. *Attachment and Loss.* 3 vols. New York: Basic/Harper Colophon.

Eisenberg, N., and R. Lennon. 1983. Sex Differences in Empathy and Related Capacities. *Psychological Bulletin* 94, no. 1, 100–131.

Freud, S. [1914] 1957. On Narcissism. In J. Strachey, ed. and trans., *The Standard Edition of the Complete Psychological Works of Sigmund Freud.* Vol. 14. London: The Hogarth Press.

———. [1925] 1961. Some Psychological Consequences of the Anatomical Distinction Between the Sexes. In J. Strachey, ed. and trans., *The Complete Psychological Works.* Vol 19.

———. 1931. Female Sexuality. In J. Strachey, ed. and trans., *The Complete Psychological Works.* Vol. 21.

Gibbs, J. C., and S. V. Schnell. 1985. Moral Development "versus" Socialization. *American Psychologist* 40, no. 10, 1071–80.

Gilligan, C. 1982. *In a Different Voice: Psychological Theory and Women's Development.* Cambridge, Mass.: Harvard University Press.

Gilligan, C., and J. Attanucci. 1985. "Two Moral Orientations." Unpublished manuscript. Harvard University.

Hoffman, M. 1976. Empathy, Role-taking, Guilt, and Development of Altruistic Motives. In T. Likona, ed., *Moral Development and Behavior.* New York: Holt, Rinehart, and Winston.

———. 1977. Sex Differences in Empathy and Related Behaviors. *Psychological Bulletin* 84, no. 4, 712–22.

Inhelder, B., and J. Piaget. 1958. *The Growth of Logical Thinking from Childhood to Adolescence.* New York: Basic Books.

Iskrant, A., and P. V. Joliet. 1968. *Accidents and Homicide.* Cambridge, Mass.: University Press.

Johnston, K. 1985. Two Moral Orientations, Two Problem-solving Strategies: Adolescents' Solutions to Dilemmas in Fables. Ed. D. diss., Harvard Graduate School of Education.

Kagan, J. 1984. *The Nature of the Child.* New York: Basic Books.

Kant, I. [1785] 1948. *Groundwork of the Metaphysic of Morals.* In H. J. Paton, trans., *The Moral Law.* London: Hutchinson.

Kohlberg, L. 1984. *The Psychology of Moral Development: Essays on Moral Development.* Vol. 2. San Francisco: Harper and Row.

Kohlberg, L., and R. Kramer. 1969. Continuities and Discontinuities in Childhood and Adult Moral Development. *Human Development* 12:93–120.

Kundera, M. 1984. *The Unbearable Lightness of Being.* New York: Harper and Row.

Kutash, I., S. Kutash, L. Schlesinger, and Associates 1978. *Violence: Perspectives on Murder and Aggression.* San Francisco: Jossey-Bass.

Langdale, C. 1983. Moral Orientation and Moral Development: The Analysis of Care and Justice Reasoning Across Different Dilemmas. Ed. D. diss., Harvard Graduate School of Education.

Lever, J. 1976. Sex Differences in the Games Children Play. *Social Problems* 23:478–87.

———. 1978. Sex Differences in the Complexity of Children's Play and Games. *American Sociological Review* 43:471–83.

Lyons, N. 1983. Two Perspectives: On Self, Morality and Relationships. *Harvard Educational Review* 53, no. 2, 125–46.

———. 1982. Conceptions of Self and Morality and Modes of Moral Choice: Identifying Justice and Care in Judgments of Actual Moral Dilemmas. Ed. D. diss., Harvard Graduate School of Education.

Maccoby, E. 1985. Social Groupings in Childhood: Their Relationship to Prosocial and Antisocial Behavior in Boys and Girls. In D. Olwens, J. Block, and M. Radke-Yarrow, eds., *Development of Antisocial and Prosocial Behavior: Theories, Research and Issues.* San Diego, Calif.: Academic Press.

Maccoby, E., and C. Jacklin. 1974. *The Psychology of Sex Differences.* Stanford, Calif.: Stanford University Press.

Piaget, J. [1932] 1965. *Moral Judgment of the Child.* New York: Free Press.

———. [1940] 1967. The Mental Development of the Child. In *Six Psychological Studies.* New York: Vintage Books.

———. 1973. *To Understand Is To Invent: The Future of Education.* New York: Grossman/Penguin.

Sartre, J. 1948. *Existentialism and Humanism.* London: Methuen.

Stern, D. 1985. *The Interpersonal World of the Infant.* New York: Basic Books.

Walker, L. 1984. Sex Differences in the Development of Moral Reasoning: A Critical Review. *Child Development* 55, no. 3, 183–201.

Wolf, D., J. Rygh, and J. Altshuler. 1984. Agency and Experience: Action and States in Play Narratives. In I. Bretherton, ed., *Symbolic Play: The Development of Social Understanding.* New York: Academic Press.

Wolfgang, M. 1966. *Patterns in Criminal Homicide.* New York: John Wiley.

Woolf, V. 1922. *Jacob's Room.* New York: Harcourt, Brace.

# SEVEN

# Particularity and Responsiveness

*Lawrence Blum*

I was asked to reflect, as a philosopher, on the relevance of the data of the social sciences to moral philosophy. But in order to discuss moral development it is first necessary to presuppose some conception of morality. This conception of morality will dictate which aspects of behavior, emotion, and thought will count as components of moral development.

My particular interest is in different conceptions of morality and their relation to an important range of moral virtues—compassion, kindness, generosity, helpfulness, considerateness, sympathy. I will contrast two conceptions of morality. The one I will call "impartialist" fails to provide adequate conceptual space for these moral virtues. The second, which I will call "particularist," is able to express the moral significance of these traits. I will also discuss a quality I call "responsiveness," which I regard as common to the moral virtues mentioned above, and which can be seen in children. I will suggest that responsiveness in children be treated as a developmental precursor to these adult moral qualities. I will not, however, argue for this position directly, but will try to clear away certain philosophical blinders that prevent acknowledging responsiveness as a morally significant phenomenon in both children and adults.

Before proceeding to the argument, I begin with a brief typology of philosophical views of morality and discuss the room which they do or do not leave for the phenomena of moral development.

Many philosophical views of morality show little or no concern for any psychological substratum that explains how a human being does, or can come to, live in accordance with morality. Such perspectives are often justified in terms of some conception of 'reason' or 'rationality.' That is, if rational argument can demonstrate a certain view of morality to be compelling, that is all the philosophical grounding it needs. Some conceptions, for example Kant's, make the further assumption that such rational acceptance is sufficient to motivate conformity to the morality. But it must be admitted that many philosophical views take no stance either way on this point, assuming tacitly that philosophical acceptability has no connection to psychological reality.[1]

This perspective on morality is often grounded in a certain metaethical view, currently discarded by many ethical theorists, that the foundation of the 'ought'—of what is morally right—can have nothing to do with the 'is' of human nature—with how humans behave and feel. In this view the validity of a moral position has absolutely nothing to do with our having prior assurance that our natures allow us to live up to it. Rather, as is true for Kant, it is only because we already accept morality that we know we are able to adhere to it. Or, to put it in its more familiar terms, "ought implies can."

Utilitarianism, despite its status as the chief current rival to Kantianism, is susceptible to this same characterization. The classical utilitarianism of Bentham and Mill took the view that a single principle ought to guide all our actions—to promote the maximum of happiness among all human beings. Mill (1861) claimed that the motives to conform to the utilitarian principle were nothing more than pleasure and pain, and thus were within the scope of ordinary human motives. The trouble with this view, as has frequently been noted, is that the pleasure/pain motivation on which Mill drew works only for the individual and cannot alone generate a broader application of the

1. Augusto Blasi, in his remarks at the conference at which this paper was presented, implied that the perspective sketched here—that philosophical acceptability has no connection to psychological reality—is the paradigm "philosophers' " conception of morality. I hope to be indicating here that this is only one among many philosophical orientations, though it is undoubtedly a very influential one and is really more influential in contemporary ethical theory than it has been in the earlier history of ethical thought. The lack of psychological reality in contemporary ethics has come under recent criticism, most influentially by Williams (1981), but also by Stocker (1976) and others.

utilitarian principle. The latter requires the agent to *abstract from* her own interests or happiness, and to consider *everyone's* pleasure or pain equally and impartially. From the point of view of human motivation, this is really no less problematic than Kant's position, which requires the individual moral agent to take up something like what Sidgwick called "the point of view of the universe."[2]

A second set of philosophical views exhibits a concern with the psychological substratum of morality, but is is not particularly concerned with its *development*. Such views try to indicate some adult psychological capacity in which to ground morality but do not inquire into how this adult capacity could have been developed from various childhood capacities. Such views generally, but not inevitably, base morality on *feeling* or *emotion*, and within this rubric one can distinguish two types. The first, of whom the British empiricists Adam Smith and David Hume are the most famous exponents, sees sentiments, such as sympathy and benevolence, as forming the basis of moral judgment. For Hume, sympathy (corrected for various kinds of parochialism) provides the standpoint from which human beings judge other human beings as possessing virtue and vice. The second view, best represented by Arthur Schopenhauer (1841), sees our emotional nature (in particular, compassion) as underlying our capacity for moral *motivation* rather than moral *judgment*. For Schopenhauer an emotionally based motivation, rather than the capacity for moral judgment, is central to morality. (For this reason Hume is rightly seen as a forerunner of Kagan's [1984] views [see below, p. 320] whereas Schopenhauer is closer to the view that I am advocating.) Nevertheless, although both views ground morality in emotion rather than reason, neither one is particularly concerned with the ontogenesis of moral emotions.[3]

A third category of theories is concerned with both the adult capacities in which morality can be grounded and their development.

2. The convergences between Kantianism and utilitarianism, which otherwise differ in many ways, have been especially emphasized by Williams in his various writings.

3. Aristotle, a philosopher who has come into increasing prominence in contemporary ethical theory, provides a more complicated case. He talks about the formation of virtue and how it depends on having the correct kind of upbringing. However, he is not particularly interested in the specific nature of the child's capacities and does not attempt to identify particular capacities of children as being the developmental foundation of adult moral morality. It should also be noted that to the extent that Aristotle does have a developmental view, his account of morality does not particularly leave room for the sorts of qualities—such as compassion, kindness, responsiveness to the needs of others, care and concern about the welfare of others—on which I will be focusing here.

Some of the most prominent of these theories are of a neo-Kantian nature, such as those of Rawls (1971) and Kohlberg (1981, 1984). Both attempt to specify the way in which a mature morality grows out of specific childhood capacities, sentiments, or ways of thinking, though Kohlberg, as a developmental psychologist, does this more extensively than Rawls. Both views retain the Kantian emphasis on rationality as the foundation of morality but attempt to discard Kant's nonemprical or "transcendental" perspective. Kohlberg and Rawls describe rationality as a specific empirical human capacity with a developmental history. Thus their view abandons the sharp 'is/ought' distinction.

I will argue that this neo-Kantian view of morality gives an insufficient role to the virtues of altruistic responsiveness, and that it fails to give full moral significance to the phenomenon of childhood responsiveness. My own view is closer to a developmental position such as that of Gilligan (1982) than to the neo-Kantians.

I begin the discussion of responsiveness with a few examples, and then move to a definition:[4]

*(Example 1)*
Sarah, twelve months, is sitting with Clara, fifteen months, on
    Clara's mother's lap. The girls have grown up together and are
    very close. Clara is holding a plastic cup which she drops on
    the floor, cries, and points to. Sarah climbs out of Clara's
    mother's lap, gets the cup, and gives it to Clara.

*(Example 2)*
Michael, fifteen months, is struggling with his friend Paul over a toy.
    Paul starts to cry. Michael appears concerned and lets go of the
    toy so Paul has it. But Paul continues to cry. Michael pauses,
    then gives his own teddy bear to Paul; Paul continues crying.
    Michael pauses again, runs to the next room, gets Paul's
    security blanket, and gives it to him. Paul stops crying.

*(Example 3)*
Sarah, two years three months, is riding in the car with her cousin
    Ali, who is four. Ali is upset because she does not have her
    teddy bear, and there is a fairly extended discussion about how
    the bear is probably in the trunk and can be retrieved when
    they arrive at the house. About ten minutes pass and, as the
    car approaches the house, Sarah says to Ali, "Now you can get
    your bear."

4. Example 2 is taken from Hoffman (1976); example 4 is from Ned Mueller's presentation at the conference. The others are from my own and my wife's observations of our own children, their friend, and their cousin.

*(Example 4)*

Two children, twenty-two months and twenty-four months, are close
friends. While playing, one accidentally harms the other who
cries. While the one who harms will not respond to an adult's
admonition to apologize, he seems concerned about his action;
he offers the other child a toy and attempts to reconnect or
apologize to the other child.

*(Example 5)*

Ben, three-and-a-half, is playing on the floor with his sister Sarah, six
months. Ben sees a safety pin and takes it to his mother in
another room, saying that it would hurt Sarah if she got it.

*(Example 6)*

Sarah, three, gives Clara, three, her own Donald Duck hat (to keep
"forever"), saying that she has done so because Clara has
(recently, but not in the moment) lost her (Boston) Celtics cap.

These examples differ in important ways. Some involve greater moral
or cognitive "depth" than others. In example 5, Ben is responding not
to an actual state of harm or distress but to a potential one (Sarah being hurt by the safety pin). In example 2 Michael seems to be "assessing" what will stop Paul's crying; he makes attempts and cognitively processes Paul's reactions to them. Examples 2 and 4 both involve persistence in action. In examples 3 and 6 Sarah responds not to
an immediate state of distress of the other child but draws on her
memory and knowledge of the other child's condition. In example 6
Sarah's responsiveness is not to a specific state of *distress* but rather
simply to what she believes Clara wants or would like. Examples 2
and 4 involve the child's responding to a distress which he himself
has to some extent brought about; this feature is absent in the others.

The six examples share what I believe to be a nonegoistic sentiment or motivation of one child toward another child. By "responsiveness" I refer to an action expressive of an altruistic motive toward
others.[5] Responsiveness is not simply an intention to aid another,
since such an intention can be entirely unaltruistic in its underlying
motivation—for example, merely to gain power over another, to gain
approval of others (e.g., parents), to secure future benefit. Responsiveness is not limited to concern directed toward a specific negative con-

---

5. Thus "responsiveness" is not to be taken as meaning merely "reacting to
another person," e.g., by smiling when a parent enters the room; it must also involve some altruistic concern. But there is, no doubt, a connection between responsiveness in the former, broader sense and in the latter, more restricted sense used in
this paper.

dition of another. It is not limited to actual felt distress, because the other person can be (as in example 5) at risk or in danger without knowing (hence feeling) this, or can even be in a kind of pain without being aware of her pain.[6] Responsiveness is toward another's *condition*, rather than specifically toward some particular *emotion* the other is feeling. Yet the condition need not be a particularly unpleasant one; it can simply be a condition of wanting or being able to be made happier by something, as in example 6 when Sarah gives Clara a Donald Duck cap. It should be noted too that, as defined, "responsiveness" involves the taking of *action* to address another's condition. It thus involves a kind of initiative and is not merely a passive response to another person.[7]

Responsiveness involves both cognitive and affective dimensions. It involves a cognitive grasp of another's condition. Even the twelve-month-old in example 1 seems to understand that the other child is distressed and that this is because she has lost her cup. At the same time the altruistic aspect of responsiveness involves our emotional natures, in that responsiveness is not a purely rational willing of another person's good.[8] The altruistic motivations involved in responsiveness can be understood only by reference to human emotions, though I will argue below that this does not mean that each instance of responsiveness involves a specific feeling-state. The cognitive and affective dimensions of responsiveness are not rightly understood as merely two separate 'components'—a cognition and a

6. As Martin Hoffman has reminded me, Adam Smith ([1759] 1948) notes the possibility and even appropriateness of sympathy for a "wretched" but nevertheless joyous person in the process of losing his reason (77). As Hoffman (1982) himself points out, the ability to respond beyond another's immediate situation to a general condition of the person depends on an advanced level of cognitive development, appreciating the other as a continuous person with a separate identity and history (94), though we can see the rudiments of such a development in some of our examples (3 and 6).

7. The terminology of "responsiveness" is drawn partly from the work of Gilligan (1982). Whitbeck (1983) points out that Gilligan's terminology "may be misunderstood to suggest response to the exclusion of initiation" (83), though this is not Gilligan's intention. Addressing Whitbeck's point, I wish to forestall such an interpretation by building into the notion of responsiveness the taking of action to address another's condition.

8. Whether the purely rational willing of another's good is possible is a question I will not explore here, though its existence in small children can certainly be doubted. The Kantian tradition in ethics, which will be discussed below, claims that such rational willing is not only possible but is the highest, if not the only, expression of morality. A sophisticated contemporary defense of that position can be found in Nagel (1970), though Nagel has modified his position in subsequent writings. I am defining "responsiveness" so as to exclude this purely rational willing.

feeling-state—added together; rather they inform one another. I will try to show how this is so, as well as generally to clarify the nature of responsiveness, by discussing some other psychological phenomena that might be confused with responsiveness or that might be involved in responsiveness but are not coextensive with it.

First of all *merely* understanding another's condition is insufficient for responsiveness, since this understanding can be used for example to manipulate or ridicule.[9] The purely cognitive is not sufficient because it does not ensure the altruistic concern for the other. At the same time I suggest that there is a natural link between knowing another's distress and being concerned or inclined to do something about it, though this inclination can be blocked by contrary inclinations or sentiments. In order for the connection between knowing about and responding to the other *not* to be made, some process must intervene to distance the one person from the other.[10] This view is elaborated by Murdoch (1970), who suggests that to truly know or "see" another person involves having some altruistic sentiment toward that person. Her view depends on construing 'knowing' to include allowing the perception of another person's distress to affect oneself, vividly imagining the other's distress, and the like.[11]

Second, experiencing the same *feeling* as the other person is neither necessary nor sufficient for responsiveness. It is not sufficient, for X could feel a distress caused by Y's distress, and yet X might not have any concern for Y's distress but simply have an impetus to rid himself of his own distress. Hoffman points out that a nonaltruistic identity of feeling may occur in children younger than twelve months whose identities are insufficiently differentiated from others and who thus experience another's distress as occurring within themselves (1976; 131). But as Scheler (1965) notes, this phenomenon—which he calls "emotional infection"—is found in adults as well. Mere identity or similarity of feeling can occur in the absence of the cognitive grasp of the other as well as of the altruistic concern.

In addition, having the same feeling as the other is not necessary for responsiveness. This is partly because in order to be an appropriate target of responsiveness, the other person need not himself have any particular feeling (see above, p. 311). Even when the other is in a particular feeling-state, it is also perfectly intelligible, as Scheler often

9. A good example of a twenty-month-old child showing a sophisticated understanding of another for the purposes of manipulating her is given in Hoffman 1976, 129.

10. An interesting argument for a quasi-necessary link between seeing distress and being responsive to it is made by Ross (1983).

11. A similar argument is given by McDowell (1979).

emphasizes, that a person be truly concerned about another's pain without having feelings of pain or distress herself.

More generally, while responsiveness is grounded in our emotional natures, its occurrence on a particular occasion does not always involve any particular feeling state on that occasion. To say, for example, that I care about Joan, or am concerned about her, is not to say that at every moment I am experiencing some particular feeling-state. One can intelligibly say that one is concerned about someone but is not feeling that concern at that particular moment. And yet one cannot have concern for Joan without having *some* feelings regarding Joan in at least some situations. For example suppose I am concerned about Joan because she is in danger, and then the danger recedes. In order for it to have been true of me that I was concerned about Joan, I must have some feeling of joy, relief, or the like, when I learn that she is out of danger (though the feeling need not occur at some particular moment since some people react to emotionally charged information more immediately than others).[12]

It might be thought that although adults can be responsive without having a state of mind corresponding to that of another person, this would be impossible or rare in children. Although greater development of cognitive abilities allows for adult responsiveness to be less dependent than children's on the limits of an individual's own experience, it does not seem necessary that children with concern for another must share a feeling-state with that other. In example 3, in order for Sarah to be responsive to Ali's distress about her teddy bear, Sarah need not have been in a state of distress herself. It seems more plausible to say that the feeling-state will sometimes be present (perhaps, e.g., in examples 1, 2, 4, 5) and sometimes not; but in any case it is not a requirement for the attribution of responsiveness.

Just as I want to avoid an overly cognitive understanding of responsiveness, so, too, I argue against an overly affective view. But I do not suggest that having the same feeling as the other has nothing to do with responsiveness. In responding to another's distress one can have a comparable feeling within oneself. Being "moved" or "touched" by another person's plight are metaphors employed in describing responsiveness that express the sense of a distinct emotional reaction to another's situation. My argument here is addressed to what I see as an oversimplified and overly affective emphasis, especially on experiencing the identical feeling of the other person.

---

12. The complexities of the cognitive, affective, and motivational aspects of sympathy, concern, care, and the like, are further discussed in Blum (1980, chap. 2).

It might be argued that in the absence of a specific feeling-state, one cannot be sure why the child is acting in an altruistic manner; hence responsiveness cannot be inferred. It is true that the altruistic motivation is a matter of an inference. But what are the alternative explanations? It is not enough to say that the child notes the other child's need and therefore fills that need (by saying where to get the teddy bear, or taking the safety pin away). For it is precisely the intentional helping behavior whose explanation we seek. Could it be 'conditioning'? Complex issues surround this notion, but it seems that the situations in which children are responsive to one another are too diverse to be encompassed by any purely behavioral conditioning. If a child had been repeatedly rewarded for giving another child a cookie, it might be plausible to explain his continuing to do so without invoking any altruistic sentiment or motive toward the other child. But such an account would not seem plausible in some of our examples, in which the children may well not have encountered very similar circumstances before.

For similar reasons a *purely* biological or instinctual explanation would seem insufficient to explain particular instances of responsiveness that are dependent on cognitive understandings in relatively new situations. My account of responsiveness, however, is not meant to exclude a biological or physiological substrate for the capacity for responsiveness; it implies only that an explanation of the exercise of that capacity on any particular occasion requires more than physiology.

Let us focus for a moment on the nature of the cognitive dimension essential for responsiveness—the knowledge of the other person's condition. This knowledge has sometimes been depicted as the subject *inferring* the other's state of mind from a feeling the subject herself has, or has had, in similar circumstances. While such inference may play some role in the assessment of another's state of mind, it cannot be the sole cognitive process involved in understanding another. This is partly because concern for another does not always involve the assessment of a particular state of mind at all—hence it is not an inference *from* the responsive person's own state of mind to the other person's (see above, p. 311). Second, such inference would not account for understanding states of mind *different* from those which one is experiencing (or has experienced) oneself. Third, grasping another's condition, in the context of responsiveness, does not require being in any particular feeling-state oneself (see above, p. 313).

More fundamentally, I suggest a theoretical bias in the premise that our knowledge of others inevitably proceeds from an inference about our own state of mind. This bias, rooted in the empiricist epistemological tradition, presumes a division of self from others, so that one has only indirect means of forging a subsequent cognitive link between self and other. This theoretical assumption has been criticized most powerfully by Wittgenstein (1953), whose view I can only mention, not defend. Wittgenstein sees the commonality between persons sharing a "form of life" as a condition of the possibility of knowledge of others, and indeed a presupposition of any processes of inferences made by one person with regard to another.[13] The notion of the individual subject, generating knowledge of others purely out of his own experience—the paradigm for empiricist epistemology—is, Wittgenstein argues, an incoherent one.

While the issues raised by Wittgenstein's critique of empiricism go far beyond the scope of this paper, I suggest that our ability to grasp another's condition is a more fundamental cognitive process that more specialized uses of inference can only build upon but not replace. Thus, in example 2, while Michael seems to be engaging in inference regarding how to stop Paul from crying, his understanding that Paul is in distress in the first place does not seem a product of such inference, but rather a more immediate grasping of Paul's condition. Once one gives up the epistemological commitment to the idea of the individual knower severed from any fundamental connection with others, the phenomena of responsiveness can be seen more clearly as involving an immediate and noninferential grasp of another's condition.[14]

A similar point can be made about the cognitive process of "projection," in which the subject projects himself into the other's situation, imagining what he would feel, and then attributing that feeling to the other person. Although such a process can be involved in some instances of coming to understand another's condition, it could hardly be all of what is involved in such cases. The model is too egocentered and presupposes a too-sharp separation between self and other. It sees others only on the model of one's own self. It thus fails to acknowledge, as Scheler emphasizes, how understanding others

---

13. The interpretation of Wittgenstein on the matter of knowledge of others is not entirely uncontroversial. For example Wittgenstein is sometimes regarded as a "conventialist," for whom the "forms of life" in question are simply particular social constructions. I follow Cavell (1979) and others in rejecting this reading of Wittgenstein in favor of one in which the sense of connection between human beings which allows knowledge of one another is, at least partly, more fundamental than any socially relative conventional practices.

14. For a comparable critique of assumptions of a too-sharp self-other split within epistemological traditions in philosophy, see Scheman (1983).

means understanding them precisely *as other* than oneself—as having feelings and thoughts which might be different from what one would feel in the same situation.

The use of self as the model for knowing the other is overdrawn here in the 'projection' model of understanding. As Noddings (1984) points out, the understanding involved in caring for another person is generally more appropriately seen on a model of *receptivity* than projection.[15] One "takes in" the other person, opening oneself to the other's feelings, allowing oneself to, so to speak, receive the other person in all his or her difference from oneself. This description of the process of knowing the other seems more genuinely oriented fully to the other person than does that of projecting oneself outward into the other's situation and noting what one would oneself feel.

Perhaps more so than the previously discussed 'inference' model, the 'projection' model fails to apply to many of the cases of childhood responsiveness discussed above. Projection requires a level of cognitive development beyond the children's capabilities.[16] It is not that these children fail to understand the other child's condition; rather, their understanding need not take the form of projection.

An excessively sharp distinction between self and other can be seen in some views of the altruistic, as well as cognitive, dimension of responsiveness. Hoffman's views are interesting in this regard, for the overall thrust of his work is to portray empathy and sympathy as fundamental sentiments in the child that form the foundation of later moral behavior. He explicitly rejects an egoistic construal of the child's basic nature. Hoffman (1976; 135) asks *why* children come to have active sympathy toward each other once they are able to distinguish their own identity from that of others. He answers by saying that they discover that the similarities between themselves and others outweigh the differences. This belief in similarity becomes the foundation of the child's being able to have sympathy for another person.

Hoffman's framing of the issue presumes that prior to the observation of similarities and differences, the child has a sense of her own identity as fundamentally separate from others. The sympathy would occur only *after* the perception of similarity with other children. If this were correct the sense of separateness would always lie at a more fundamental level than any sense of likeness to other children. Likeness would be forged only through explicit assessment of

15. Something like Noddings's point is also made by Scheler (1954, part 1, chap. 3).

16. See Hoffman 1982, 93ff.

similarity, while separateness would need no inference but would be assumed. My suggestion is that, on the contrary, the sense of likeness (which I would prefer to call a sense of connection), on which sympathy is founded, is as fundamental to a child's sense of who she is as is the sense of separateness.

I do not deny that children perceive similarities and differences with other children. Nevertheless, I suggest that empathy or sympathy does not rest on such perceptions but is prior to it. Surely children note some differences between themselves and another child, without that fact carrying weight for them in whether or not they are able to empathize with the other child. For example, they might note that another child has a different color of hair or wears different kinds of clothes. Even differences in skin color do not by themselves lead to a distancing between children, except in contexts where skin color has been communicated to the child (by parents, peers, etc.) as signifying differential value or as requiring distancing. Children's delight in commonalities between themselves and others (having Luke Skywalker dolls, wearing a red shirt, etc.) can involve a greater (though perhaps only momentary) sense of likeness; but I would suggest that the sense of likeness which allows for empathy must lie at a deeper level. The issue here partly involves whether the achievement of identity on the child's part involves a fundamental separateness prior to any sense of relatedness. Perhaps what is needed is a notion of identity formation that builds into it a sense of relatedness to others.[17]

As several recent philosophers have pointed out, the counterposition between "egoism" and "altruism," especially in philosophical discussion, suggests a kind of radical separation between self and others.[18] The notion of altruism, for instance, conveys the notion that one's giving to others is entirely cut off from any concern for oneself,

17. The general critique given here of Hoffman was suggested by some remarks of Gilligan's in a lecture on Hoffman, and is supported by her general perspective on identity and relatedness. (See especially Gilligan 1984.) I have also been influenced in my remarks on identity formation by Chodorow (1979).

Scheler (1954) also sees "fellow-feeling" ("Mitgefuhl") as fundamental to morality. Yet he too, at least by implication, sometimes portrays an excessively 'separated' moral subject. He is rightly critical of all 'egoistic' conceptions of fellow feeling, emphasizing that the other must be seen separately from oneself, and emphasizing both the individual's capability of understanding persons who are quite different from self, as well as the necessity of seeing the other in her own terms rather than one's own; nevertheless, Scheler leaves the achievement of this sort of fellow feeling somewhat of a mystery. He articulates no level of connectedness or likeness between persons which could serve as the foundation for such fellow-feeling.

18. On the egoism/altruism counterposition and its limitations, see Norman 1979, MacIntyre 1967, Blum 1980, chap. 4. See also Gilligan 1984.

or even that it is at the expense of the self. In contrast to altruism, the notions, for example, of 'community' and 'friendship' are relationships in which concern for others, while not reduced to self-interest, is not separable from concern for self. To be concerned for a friend, or for a community with which one closely identifies and of which one is a member, is not to reach out to someone or something which is 'wholly other' than oneself, but to that which shares a part of one's own self and is implicated in one's sense of one's own identity.[19]

I have described responsiveness without speaking much of "empathy," a concept psychologists often employ in this context. Perhaps some explanation is appropriate. First, the definition of "empathy" is variable. Sometimes, as in Hoffman (1976; 126), it refers to the involuntary experiencing of another's emotional state, or "feeling what the other feels" (1982; 86). Kagan (1984; 126), though citing Hoffman, seems to construe empathy as inferring another's experience or state of mind. These two definitions of empathy are not the same, as I have argued above (p. 311). Hoffman's does not necessarily involve cognition, but only a feeling, whereas Kagan's involves cognition but not necessarily any feeling on the part of the empathizer. Furthermore, I have argued that *neither* of these phenomena is necessary or sufficient for responsiveness. Neither one builds in the requirement of altruistic concern for the other.

It should be said that both Kagan and Hoffman occasionally use the term "empathy" in a way that implies the existence of altruistic concern, even though this is not explicit in some of their definitions. In Hoffman's 1982 article, empathy is defined "not as an exact match with another's feeling, but [as] an affective response more appropriate to another's situation than to one's own" (95). If "appropriate" is construed as involving both altruistic concern and a cognitive grasp of the other's situation, this definition comes closer to what I have meant by "responsiveness"; and Hoffman does seem to see this latter

---

19. The general critique given here of the individualist view of the self has been greatly influenced by Sandel (1982). Sandel argues that the Kantian tradition in political philosophy, as seen especially in the work of Rawls (1971), is doomed to failure because it operates with a notion of the autonomous individual abstracted from his or her connections to others. It abstracts from the ways in which our connections to others and our capacities for responsiveness are a central part of our own identifies, rather than being mere sentiments or voluntary commitments. My own remarks are meant in the spirit of Sandel's argument, and, while I recognize their tentativeness, I want to suggest that moral and political theory, as well as moral development theory, require a notion of fundamental connection between persons which can be encompassed within whatever notion of individual identity is central to the theory.

definition of empathy as more accurate than the one mentioned above.

This lack of clarity regarding the definition of "empathy" does not preclude the possiblity of some clearer definition—delineating its cognitive, affective, and/or altruistic components—that will make empathy a phenomenon related to responsiveness. Nevertheless, responsiveness and empathy may still remain distinct phenomena. For the term 'empathy' seems to carry a stronger implication of a distinct affect than does 'responsiveness' as I have understood it, although responsiveness too is necessarily grounded in our affective natures (see above, p. 313).

I have described responsiveness without bringing out its relation to morality. Responsiveness should be seen as a moral phenomenon, and I suggest that responsiveness in children is one developmental forerunner of the adult moral virtues of compassion, kindness, helpfulness, sympathy, and the like, in that these altruistic virtues as well as responsiveness involve altruistic motivation and sentiment toward others. The claim of developmental connection can only be established empirically, but it does involve supplementing one influential view of moral development, namely that moral development consists primarily in the child's moving from a stage of egoism to one of social morality or conformity to social rules. Such a view is shared, for example, by both Shweder and Kohlberg, though Kohlberg has a developmental stage beyond social morality. My own view does not reject the notion that there are some elements of childhood egoism that will have to be transcended; but it suggests that there are elements of mature morality only weakly connected to social rule-following, and that children must be seen as having altruistic capacities as well as egoistic tendencies.

The moral significance of responsiveness does not lie in the child's appreciation of moral *standards*. There is no necessary implication that a child who is responsive to another necessarily thinks of helping the other as conformity to a standard of right and wrong, or good or bad, nor that she sees herself as behaving in conformity with a standard of behavior which defines what it is to be a good person. All that is necessary is that the child understand the other child's state, believe that the other child will be made better off by her action, and have some altruistic sentiment or motivaton toward the other child. Thus the responsive child must believe herself to be responding to an undesirable state of the other child (or at least a state capable of improvement), and must regard her own action as trying to make that state better. But this is not the same as judging that her action is good because of its conformity to a moral standard.

Kagan (1984) has emphasized the emergence of the appreciation of standards in children between the ages of one and two and sees this appreciation as a foundation of the child's morality. He also sees the capacity for empathy as one of the sources of this appreciation of moral standards. Nothing I have said is meant to contradict these views. I suggest only that the moral significance of childhood responsiveness not be seen *solely* in terms of the generation of moral standards. Responsiveness involves ways of feeling, acting, and understanding that have moral significance and value, even if they do not necessarily presuppose use of moral standards.

Thus in example 1 Sarah's getting the cup for Clara manifests a kind of reaction to another child which has some moral significance, even though it would not seem necessary and may not even be plausible to see this one-year-old child's action as deriving from an appreciation of a moral standard. This could be true as well of Sarah (at two years, three months) in example 3 saying to Ali that she can now get the teddy bear which she (Ali) had been wanting. By contrast, in example 5, Ben's removing the safety pin can be seen as partly responding to a general norm saying that it is right or good to look out for his sister, to prevent her getting hurt; but at the same time it seems equally plausible, and certainly in any case possible, that his action stems also from a simple and direct concern for his sister, independent of the expression or codification of this concern in a principle to which he adheres. My suggestion is that the concern as well as the possession of the standard has moral significance.

Kagan sees the development of standards as a phenomenon distinct from what I am calling responsiveness. This is apparent in his emphasis on the power of moral standards to inhibit impulses and actions incompatible with those standards (1984; 131, 143, 152), though for Kagan not all moral standards are related to the inhibition of aggression. But the moral significance of responsiveness does not lie primarily in its power to control the child's impulses. In our examples, the altruistic sentiment is not necessarily being opposed by a hostile, aggressive, or selfish impulse in the responsive children. The moral significance of responsiveness (in both adults and children), I would suggest, lies in the mere self-transcending care and understanding of the other, not in the countering of egoistic impulse.[20]

20. The conception of morality as involving self-transcending but not self-denying care is spelled out more fully in Blum (1980) and Murdoch (1970).

I do not mean to imply that the development of standards is entirely separate from that of responsiveness. It is certainly plausible to link them, as Kagan does, and to see them developing together. The child not only acts out of concern, but comes to see this as good or even right, to feel shame and guilt when failing to do so, and to judge others for such failure. Nevertheless I suggest that even in adult morality the two processes retain some degree of independence. Our caring for others does not *simply* flow from our adherence to a principle of caring for others. Our caring is often generated spontaneously and does not necessarily bring with it the thought that it is a morally good thing to care for others. And similarly, one can act from a moral principle that enjoins caring, but without actually caring or being concerned for the person in question.

Although Kagan is correct in positing some emotionally based concern for others (taking this to be essentially what he means by "empathy") as fundamental to moral development, I suggest that he unnecessarily limits what should be seen as counting for morality when he sees empathy's moral significance almost solely in terms of the generation of moral standards of behavior. This is so even though Kagan distinguishes moral standards for positive prosocial behavior, such as helping and cooperation, from standards for inhibition of aggression. For not all helpfulness and cooperative behavior is generated by, or is explained in terms of, moral standards. Some of it, like caring, is a spontaneous and direct response to a particular person or situation.

I now want to contrast the two major conceptions of morality mentioned earlier, the "impartialist,"[21] and the "particularist." I will argue that particularism, but not impartialism, can express the moral significance of responsiveness and its related virtues (compassion, kindness, care, and so on) in both adults and children.

According to impartialism, which now characterizes Kohlberg's "justice morality" (1984), but which characterized *all* of morality in the earlier versions of his theory (1981), there is one, unitary, distinct "moral point of view," which is impartial, universal, impersonal, objective, and rational. Morality takes the form of universal principles—principles applicable to all human beings—guiding the moral agent to right or obligatory action. To be moral the agent must abstract himself from his individual interests and particular relationships; he must adopt an impartial standpoint favoring no person over

21. The terminology of "impartialism" is that of Darwall, in *Impartial Reason*, an important recent statement and defense of a neo-Kantian position.

any other. Moral principles thus generated cannot be confined merely to the customs or mores of any particular society. They must at bottom rest on a rational and universal foundation that transcends the agent's own society (or *any* particular society, for that matter), though particular principles of his own society which can be validated from that perspective may be included in the set of morally acceptable action-specifying principles. Although most familiarly associated with Kantianism (see above, p. 307), this characterization applies to utilitarianism as well, although in that tradition there is less explicit emphasis on rationality.

The particularist conception includes concern for and caring responses to particular other persons. This concern can take place toward persons standing in a particular, richly textured moral relationship to oneself—for example, friend, family member, student, colleague, comrade, patient, doctor. Or it can be directed at a stranger, standing in no such relationship. (There are also categories between these extremes, such as vague acquaintance, or one's insurance agent.) This concern and care for particular persons is not derived from an impartial point of view nor (necessarily) grounded in universal principles of action. On the particularist view, this concern and care has prima facie moral value, a moral value which can not be fully understood from the impartialist perspective.

The impartialist conception of morality aspires to define a single comprehensive moral point of view. The particularist conception does not aim at a total view of morality; it acknowledges that some of what we regard as "moral" can be understood only from the impartialist perspective but claims that some domains of our moral lives can be understood only by means of particularistic notions. The particularist perspective regards many actions as governed by an interplay between particularist and impartialist motivations.

Both impartialism and particularism are concerned with forms of moral awareness rather than with moral conceptions external to the agent's conscious motivations. Suppose for example that an agent performs an act which is in fact just (e.g., a politician supports a just social policy), but does so for purely opportunistic reasons, having no concern for whether the action is just and can be justified (as it in fact can) from an impartial perspective. In some sense this action "conforms to" an impartial perspective, for from the outside it can be seen to be a "just" action. However, this is not the sense relevant to our discussion, which requires that the agent be *aware* of the action as just and be motivated to perform it *because* it is just (or, in the particularist case, that she be aware that the action will benefit the other person, and that she perform the action because it will benefit this person). An action will thus be spoken of as "impartialist" or "particularist" only if such conceptions inform the agent's consciousness in the performance of the action.

My claims for the particularist view are twofold:

1. Particularity represents a coherent and intelligible form of moral consciousness and motivation distinct from impartiality and one which can figure in an explanation of action. Some actions are in fact performed, at least in part, for particularist reasons (which is not to deny that part of their motivation may also be impartialist). This claim cannot be refuted by showing that the same action *could* be performed from a purely impartialist set of considerations; for this will not by itself call into question the intelligibility of the particularist explanation.

2. There are some morally valuable actions which cannot be accounted for in wholly impartialist terms. Without invoking a particularist perspective one cannot understand them as the morally valuable actions they are.

Faced with the particularist challenge, the impartialist may attempt either of two strategies. The first is to claim that all particularist notions are, at bottom, themselves a form of complex universality and impartiality, so that particularity reduces to impartiality and universality. Such a position denies not only the second claim—that some actions *cannot* be accounted for in wholly impartialist terms—but also the weaker view that particularity constitutes a distinct dimension of a moral consciousness. The second strategy is to acknowledge a distinction of type between impartiality and particularity, but to deny moral value to particularity. I will consider each of these strategies in turn, beginning with the first.

I begin with an example of an action involving a particularistic dimension. Jane is at a committee meeting of colleagues at her work, one of whom is a friend. Jane becomes aware of some distress on the friend's part; the turn which the conversation is taking is unnerving him in a way the others seem not to notice. Jane intervenes in the conversation so as to divert it from the subject causing her friend anxiety, while not embarrassing her friend by calling attention to him. At the same time Jane makes this intervention in a way which does not undermine the progress of the meeting and which thus takes seriously the purpose of the meeting and her responsibility to the group. She continues to participate responsibly in the ongoing task of the group, and awaits the opportunity to find out later from her friend what was going on at the meeting.

The particularistic elements in Jane's action are the concern and sensitivity she shows toward the particular friend, extricating him from an unpleasant and perhaps painful situation; and the responsibility shown toward the particular group of colleagues. To encompass this seeming particularity within a universalist view, the defender of impartialism must show that there is some principle which is universal in form, conforms to the requirement of impartiality, applies to the situation at hand, and, in doing so, specifies the particular action which Jane performs. Such a principle would, however, refute only the second claim by showing the *existence* of an impartialist principle as a possible alternative to Jane's nonimpartialist form of motivation. It would not show that Jane had not acted from a nonimpartialist concern for her particular friend and responsibility toward her particular colleagues. It is important to consider this possibility, however, since the mere existence of an impartialist alternative might be thought to cast doubt on the existence of particularity as a genuinely distinct, motivating, and morally significant aspect of consciousness.

I will consider two ways in which the defender of impartialism might attempt to see Jane's action as essentially universalist and impartialist. The first appeals to 'role' (or 'status') morality. One might say that Jane occupies two roles—friend and colleague. Each of these generates a set of obligations or responsibilities. These obligations, though not universal in the sense of applying equally to all human beings, nevertheless retain a formal universality in applying to anyone occupying that role; yet they are context-dependent and 'particular' in applying *only* to persons occupying the role. Could not Jane's action, then, stem from her dual role-obligations, and in that way conform to universality and impartiality?

In reply let us note first that a role morality in this sense would not necessarily be impartialist in the full sense I have described. For example, the Brahmans in Bhubaneswar, India, on whom Shweder reports in this volume, possess a role morality which (as Shweder describes it) is formally universalist. That is, obligations or prohibitions involved in that role are thought to apply to anyone occupying that role.[22] But a role morality is *impartialist* (in addition to being formally universalist) only if the roles and their attendant obligations are, or are at least presented as being, justified by reference to a stand-

---

22. Shweder notes that his respondents sometimes qualify the application of the role morality so that it is meant to apply only to Indians and not, say, to Americans; for example, it is forbidden, by this code, for an Indian widow to wear bright clothing, but it is not thought to be wrong for an American widow to do so. But this qualification does not count against the role-universalism of the prohibition, since the respondents give an account of the relevant differences between American and Indian widows which makes the prohibition applicable to the latter but not to the former. The relevant role would then be "Indian widows."

point which accords no inherent favor to one individual over any other.[23] As Shweder presents the Brahman morality, the ground of obligation lies not in such an impartial perspective but in a view about a "natural order" of the world, divinely created, and involving functional interdependency between inherently unequal statuses and roles; such a perspective itself provides a rationale (within Brahman morality) for why the impartial perspective is *not* an appropriate one.

Thus a role morality may not be (and, I suggest, typically is not) impartialist, though it may be formally universalist. Role morality also fails to conform to another important feature of impartialism—action-specifying principles. Responsibilities attaching to statuses like 'friend' or 'colleague' cannot be understood solely in terms of principles specifying actions to be performed. While concepts referring to family position such as 'father,' 'mother,' 'parent' signify a social role, and while they involve moral responsibilities, these responsibilities cannot be seen as involving very specific tasks and actions such as those involved in more explicitly delineated social role positions such as police officer, doctor, or accountant in a specific firm. A father has a general responsibility to care for and nurture his children; this is how we understand (the moral dimension of) fatherhood. But this is not to say that there are specific actions that the role morality of 'father' specifies. It does not for example tell me to spend the afternoon playing ball with my daughter rather than (what I would prefer doing) taking her to a ball game, though the former action can be seen as part of my fatherly responsibility to nurture my child and help her develop. Hence any specific fatherly action which is performed will be underdetermined by the role morality and will draw on some particularistic aspect of the agent's response to the situation.[24] But in order to conform to the impartialist picture, the principle itself must (even if only implicitly) specify the action; otherwise something outside of the impartialist moral capacities will (also) be operating to bring about the action.

23. One finds something like such an impartialist account of role-morality in writers defending a "rule-utilitarian" point of view. For an impartialist attempt to ground friendship as a source of special role-like obligations, see Telfer 1971.

24. My argument here is drawn from Melden (1977). However, we can apply Melden's point, as he himself does not, to some elements of the more defined social roles as well, e.g., police officer. There are some dimensions of a police officer's job which, like the parent's responsibility to nurture the child, can not readily be pinned down to the performance of specific actions—responsibilities connected for example with the overarching responsibility to protect the community from harm. Such elements will necessarily involve an irreducible particularity in their application to specific situations.

The same point applies to the morality of friendship. It is certainly part of a serious friendship that one recognizes responsibilities.[25] But it is not clear that such responsibilty consists in principles which dictate that certain actions be performed. The responsibility is better seen as a kind of attitude toward one's friend, which orients one toward noticing certain things (e.g., that the friend is in distress), giving thought to the friend's interests, being willing to go out of one's way to help the friend, and the like. This sense of responsibility functions as a background attitude which conditions but does not determine the particular actions one performs regarding one's particular friends. But unless the role directly generates the action in a given situation, the criteria of impartialist morality are not met. For, in order to know how to implement in the particular situation what the role bids him in general to do (e.g., to nurture his child, to stand up for his friend), the agent will have to draw on moral capacities beyond the mere ability to consult the principle.

A second way in which role morality fails to conform to the demands of impartialism concerns the centrality of *obligation* or *duty* to many versions of that view. As I have portrayed the situation, Jane's action is undertaken not out of any sense of obligation but rather out of a direct response to (Jane's perception of) her friend's anxiety. Even if the action is seen as reflecting some sense of responsibility toward the friend (and in that sense to stem from Jane's 'role' as friend), this does not mean that Jane need think of it as a morally compulsory action. (This suggests that responsibilities are not the same as obligations.) Direct responsiveness to a friend, or to any other person, need not carry with it a quality of "must" or "have to." In addition, not every admirable act of friendship need be seen as part of the responsibilities of friendship. One may out of love or concern for the friend go out of one's way to help him, beyond what one has a responsibility to do.

Finally, in addition to the failure of role morality to satisfy the demands of the impartialist perspective, not all role-related action can be fully accounted for by role morality. A significant dimension of Jane's action is lost if one looks at it simply as the working out of a conflict between two sets of general role responsibilities (friend and colleague). For one's sense of responsibility to one's *particular* friend is not simply (though it is partly) an application of a universal responsibility of friendship. Each friendship has its own particular character and history, generating particular responsibilities and expectations

25. I am not certain whether the language of "obligation" is in place in the context of friendship.

which cannot be fully captured in any listing of general responsibilities. Even if the particular responsibilities of friendship fall under some very general rubric such as 'concern' or 'loyalty,' bringing these to bear on the particular friendship will involve the same particularistic consciousness. For what concern or loyalty comes to, or ought to come to, with regard to a particular friend is grounded in the particularity of that friendship.

To summarize, role morality cannot justify a reduction of particularity to impartiality or universality. For role morality is not necessarily impartialist, and is not expressed solely in terms of obligations. Some roles, and perhaps all, do not generate principles specifying particular actions; so particular actions reflective of roles necessarily involve a particularistic dimension. Finally, the generality of a role morality does not account for the full range of moral responsibilities attaching to specific instances of those roles. The generality or universality attaching to roles does play some part in moral action; but some dimension of particularity remains as an intelligible motivational factor, distinct from universality and impartiality.

The defender of impartialism need not rely specifically on the notion of role morality in attempting to encompass apparent particularity within its own framework. It could be claimed that a principle of sufficient complexity and specificity could capture the particularities of Jane's situation within a universal principle. For example, the specific history of Jane's relationship with her friend would be cashed out as a consideration applicable to *all* friendships involving that particular sort of history. A principle taking this and all other morally pertinent factors into account would be quite restricted in its application, but could still theoretically be utilized by an agent to determine right action, in the few situations to which the principle applied.

If the principle is meant to be stable and directly action-yielding, it is not clear that its theoretical possibility translates readily into a practical reality. In Jane's situation it would have to include a myriad of factors—the particular history of Jane's relationship with the friend, an assessment of the relevant expectations of the friend and the other colleagues, a general characterization of Jane's complex relationship and responsibilities to the colleagues (particularly with respect to the task at hand), an assessment of the outcomes of various acts Jane might perform in the circumstances, and so on. In addition it would have to assign these factors some weight or priority so that the principle would be able to tote up the various considerations and determine a particular action. It is not clear that there could *be* such a statable principle; or that a realistic attempt at one would not somewhere along the line implicitly rely on the agent drawing on some particularistic moral considerations in order to apply it, rather than relying purely on the principle itself. And the principle might well be so cumbersome that few would be likely even to try to make explicit use of it.

Even if such a principle could be constructed, its mere existence would not be sufficient to refute the first claim—that particularistic considerations are fully distinct from impartiality and universality and can figure intelligibly in an account of why someone performed an action. It would refute only the stronger second claim that particularistic notions *must* be invoked to explain some actions. To substantiate the former position requires the further step of showing that the apparently particularistic agent (such as Jane) is "really" or implicitly making use of the (universal) principle in question.

What would substantiate this supposition? Showing that the agent consciously and in the moment at hand actually *consulted* the principle would not be required. For people can be acting according to a principle without consulting it on each occasion. People often initially adopt principles and then come to act on them so systematically and faithfully that the action becomes almost automatic. Yet the principle continues to inform their consciousness of their situation; if stated, they would generally agree to the principle; and the principle would continue to be part of an explanation of why they act as they do.

However, the mere statability of a principle which purports to show what is right to do in a given situation is not sufficient to show that an agent who performs the action in question is acting *from* the principle. As Kant said, he may only be acting "in accordance with" the principle ([1787] 1959, 13). He may hit on the action quite by accident, as someone might come up with the correct answer to a mathematical problem without understanding the problem; or, as discussed earlier (p. 310), he may perform the act for a self-interested reason.

An analogy with grammatical rules can be invoked to show that people operate from or according to principles which they do not consciously consult and of whose existence they may or may not be aware. We say that people follow grammatical rules (and not only speak in accordance with them) because the rules seem to us the best explanation of the speech behavior which we observe. But in the case of morality, this analogy does not necessarily point to universal or impartialist principles underlying the actions of the morally good agent. For, I am contending, a particularist consciousness is precisely an essential component in the 'best explanation' of the moral behavior exhibited by the morally good agent. The grammar analogy suggests that underlying moral behavior there can be a structure which not only externally describes but actually *accounts for* that behavior. My contention is that this structure can consist of concern for particular persons, a sense of responsibility to particular friends, a disposition to compassion, and the like, which are not simply universal principles of action.[26]

A more sophisticated defense of the impartialist position, which avoids the appeal to explicit complex and cumbersome principles, is given by Kohlberg (1982, 520–21). Kohlberg distinguishes between a "moral rule" and a "moral principle." A moral rule is "a general proscription or prescription of a class of actions: for example: 'Do not kill,' 'Do not steal,' 'Love your neighbor'." By contrast a moral principle is a method, such as Rawls's original position, or what Kohlberg sometimes calls "ideal role taking" (1981), for making moral decisions. Kohlberg uses this distinction to suggest that while moral rules are not situation-sensitive, moral principles can be. In ideal role taking, for example, the agent arrives at the correct action in a decision situation by imagining himself in the situation of all the persons who would be affected by his action.

Kohlberg's point can be put by saying that a universally valid, impartial decision-procedure can generate a decision that takes into account the specificity of a given situation, so that actions such as Jane's can be seen as generated by such a "moral principle."

In discussing this claim, I will leave aside the problems in interpreting the procedure itself—for example, problems in the coordination and agglomeration of the different opinions and feelings generated from the ideal role taking process; problems with a particular agent's subjective distortion in attempting to see the situation from the point of view of the other person; and problems about whether the procedure really yields a determinate outcome in many particular situations.

Outside of these issues, Kohlberg's approach avoids some of the problems of the complex universal principle approach, but invites some of the same objections. For one thing it would not show that any given agent who merely performed the action recommended by the ideal role taking procedure was operating *according to* that procedure, even implicitly. The possibility of the agent's having acted in a purely or partially particularistic mode cannot be excluded. More

---

26. An argument against the view that the grammar analogy supports the impatialist conception of morality, as suggested by Quine in his remarks on my presentation at the conference, is made by Williams (1985, 97).

generally, what is the evidence that someone is making use of this ideal role-taking procedure at all? If the problems of interpretation could be solved, then perhaps the procedure can claim to be a rational reconstruction of (some part of) moral rightness. But at best this will tell us only how to determine which acts are right. It will not tell us whether an agent has *acted well* in the sense that engaging in ideal role taking was an essential part of his motivation in performing the action.

A procedure which merely determines which act is right would not be acceptable to Kant, for example. For Kant, what counted for morality was not an externally "right" act, but whether the agent performed the right act from a sense of its rightness. Nor is external rightness, independent of the agent's consciousness, a goal of Kohlberg's enterprise; for he attempts to show that the development of people's actual moral consciousness heads in the direction of (even if, as in the latest formulation [1984], it almost never achieves) the stage of pure universal and impartial decision making. Moreover, in Kohlberg's latest formulation, this impartialist decision procedure is claimed to articulate only one part of morality, namely "justice." Care and beneficence—considerations characteristic of what I call particularity—are seen as aspects of morality lying outside (though not contradicting) this procedure (1984, 227ff). This claim is minimal compared to the claim that particularistic considerations can be reduced to universal ones. My major quarrel with this newer Kohlbergian view is the *primacy* Kohlberg claims for justice over care and beneficence; but I cannot discuss this here.

In arguing that moral agents do not, need not, and should not always act from universal principles or decision-procedures, I am not implying that each situation is so unique that the moral agent facing a problematic situation has nothing to draw on from previous situations to help her make her decision. A compassionate or sympathetic attitude, a habit of paying attention to others, a sensitivity to others' needs—these are components of a person's morality which she brings to a situation and yet which cannot be cashed out as universal principles of action. A person can learn to be more compassionate; this does not mean that she comes to hold new action-specifying principles. What is learned in previous situations is not only which principles to consult in action but, as Murdoch (1970) emphasizes, what to notice, how to care, what to be sensitive to, how to get beyond one's own biases and narrowness of vision.

Someone may reply, "But surely to be compassionate *is* to adhere to a kind of principle." Up to this point I have been construing the word "principle" as involving the prescription of the performance of a certain action in a situation of moral choice; and this is normallly how it is used in impartialist moral theories. However "principle" is not always used in this way. Take for example the injunction "Be kind and sensitive in dealing with colleagues." This might be taken to be a kind of principle which informs Jane's action. It may for example help her to keep from being inappropriately and counterproductively angry at her colleagues' insensitivity to her friend. But such a 'principle' is nothing like a decision procedure. It is not a method by which Jane determines a specific action to perform. Rather it expresses, and perhaps helps Jane to call up in herself, certain sensitivities and attitudes toward others which issue in the particular actions—sensitivities which she must already possess or else adverting to this injunction would have little effect. Principles in this sense, in contrast to their use in the impartialist conception, require other moral sensibilities and capacities for their application, beyond the mere ability to understand the principle and to see that a certain situation falls within its scope. In this sense almost any element in our moral natures could be spoken of as a "principle"; but this would not lend support to an impartialist conception of morality.

I have argued that particularity constitutes a distinct dimension of morality, unreducible to universality and impartiality. Two more differences between the two perspectives are important to note. It is characteristic of the particularistic dimension of ethics, in contrast to the impartialist one, that the agent need not regard herself as doing what is morally right or good. A person can be compassionate and responsive without thinking of herself *as being* compassionate and responsive. Compassion is attributed to someone on the basis, roughly, that she has apprehended, and is concerned about, some negative state of another person.[27] This does not mean that the particularistic moral agent does not know what she is doing, while the impartialist one does. The compassionate person knows that the other needs help and sees her own action as providing it. The same lack of the requirement of moral self-consciousness characterizes other qualities related to sensitivity to particular other persons—generosity, care, concern, thoughtfulness, kindness—as well as of other virtues of a different sort, for instance, courage. (In fact it would be conceivable for someone to exemplify at least some of these virtues—to be, for example, generous, compassionate, or courageous—without even having the concept of that virtue at all, much less applying it to themselves.) By

---

27. For more on the precise definition of compassion, distinguishing it from other other-directed sentiments and virtues, see Blum 1980.

contrast one can only be just, dutiful or principled by knowing that one is doing so, and striving to do so.

This difference between the compassionate person and the just person has nothing to do with whether their actions are to be explained 'subjectively' or 'objectively,' in Kagan's terminology (1984, 19–25). The attribution of both compassion and justice refers to something within the agent's consciousness—concern for the particular other person in the case of particularity, and adherence to a principle in the case of universality. In neither case is the attribution meant to be a purely hypothetical construct, making sense of the agents' behavior from a purely external point of view. Yet in another respect, both are 'objective' in that they both claim to give an accurate account or explanation of an agent's action, not *merely* to report what the agent thinks his motivation to be; they are real, rather than merely apparent, motives. The difference between the two ways of being moral is this—the compassionate agent need not be thinking of herself as acting compassionately in order to be doing so, while the just agent must see himself as acting justly in order to be doing so.

In this regard it is significant that Jane's situation is not one of a "moral dilemma" as traditionally conceived—that is, a situation in which an agent is faced with two or more alternatives of action and must decide which is the "right" action to take. While Jane sees herself as facing a dilemma, this is understood not in terms of "What is the right thing to do?," but rather, "How can I deal with the acute discomfort my friend seems to be in (given the overall situation)?" This means that Jane's goal in the situation is not to figure out which is 'the right' action, but rather simply to figure out how to help her friend, in light of the taken-for-granted commitment to the colleagues' task. Thus while Jane's action is a morally good one, its moral goodness does not involve Jane's consciously striving to perform a morally right act. So, in contrast to impartialist concepts such as justice, obligation, and universal principle, the moral value of particularity does not require the agent to regard her act as having moral value.[28]

28. The possession of virtues in the absence of their self-attribution is discussed by Williams (1981). Shweder, in his paper in this volume, notes that the Kohlbergian conception of morality unrealistically requires respondents to be able to articulate concepts with which they operate in order for the possession of those concepts to be attributable to them. Shweder rightly says that possession of the concepts is prior to their articulation.

My point here takes this observation one step further and is directed against Shweder's view of morality also. Shweder abandons impartialism (as well as the Kohlbergian conception of morality as a product of the autonomous individual) but

This point relates directly to my earlier remarks regarding childhood responsiveness (see pp. 320–21) because childhood responsiveness is a phenomenon that is not essentially dependent on the child's use of terms like "right," "wrong," and "should." In this sense it does not necessarily involve the use of explicitly 'moral' terminology, and perhaps is even developmentally prior to the understanding of such concepts (though for my view it is only necessary that it be at least to some extent developmentally independent of it). Of course the two can also come together, and naturally though not inevitably do so, in explicit norms relating to caring for others, not hurting, and so on.[29]

Acceptance of an important element of adult morality not involving the moral agent's explicit use of moral concepts can help us to accept that there can be an important element in children's moral development that has this character also.[30]

A second important difference between the particularist and the impartialist perspective concerns emotion and sentiment. The impartialist point of view is concerned only with moral *action*; but morality is broader than this. It includes the conveying of attitudes, sentiments, emotions to the other person, which inform and are expressed in the actions taken.[31] For example, it is not sufficient that Jane simply perform a certain action—say the action of changing the subject of discussion. She must do this *in a certain way*, which involves a sensitivity to the other parties involved. Changing the direction of the meeting could have been done in an inappropriate way which called attention to Jane's friend's anxiety, and this would have been contrary to Jane's aim. Or it could have been done in a way which disrupted the process of the work group, and this too would be counterproductive, though not necessarily uncaring. Any appropriate action

---

retains the notion that morality takes the form of formally universal precepts and prohibitions. In his view the individual acting in accordance with morality always knows that he is doing so; that is, he is aware of the precept or prohibition *as* a moral principle or precept. It is this latter feature which I am arguing is not always necessary. In regard to this point, Shweder's own view of morality is still unduly tied to universal principle and right action.

29. The reciprocal effect of direct responsiveness and norms of care is discussed in Kagan 1984.

30. It might be well to point out, however, that one must be cautious in attributing full-blown adult moral sentiments and virtues to children. For instance, in our examples of children's response to the distress of other children, it would not seem accurate to refer to this responsiveness as "compassion," for this concept seems to require a richer cognitive and emotional structure than one would seem to be warranted in attributing to children. Nevertheless it seems to me plausible to see the former as a natural precursor of the latter.

31. An extended argument for this point is given in Blum 1980, chap. 7.

Jane takes in this situation will exhibit an emotionally grounded sensitivity, a compassion, an attentiveness to others. This is not to say that emotional sensitivity is a requirement of all moral action, or even of all moral action of a particularistic sort. Emotional sensitivity is simply one instance of the more general category of attitudes, emotions, sentiments which have at most an entirely subordinate role for impartialism's emphasis on action and principle, but which on the particularist view are allowed sometimes to be essential to an appropriate response to a situation.[32]

In summary, I have argued that the particularistic dimension of morality is genuinely distinct from universality and impartiality, whose significance for morality has dominated moral philosophy and moral development theory. No conception of morality can be complete without taking account of particularity. "Responsiveness" and its attendant virtues of compassion, care, kindness, thoughtfulness can only be understood as grounded in this particularistic morality. Finally, I have suggested that responsiveness in children has moral significance, a significance which can only be understood in light of particularistic morality.

I mentioned earlier that, in face of seeming particularity, either the impartialist could challenge this particularity's distinctness from universality or impartiality; or he could acknowledge the distinctness, but challenge particularity's alleged moral significance. I close with some brief remarks on the latter issue.

The particularist's claim is that compassion, care, kindness, thoughtfulness, concern for others are all virtues and sentiments which have moral significance, just as do the qualities of justice, du-

---

32. It may be that particular moralities of different groups differ in the extent to which the attitudinal/emotional dimension is regarded as significant. Certainly some particular moralities emphasize outward action more than (expressed) inner feeling or attitude. It may be, for example, that the Indian morality which Shweder studied is much more interested in compliance with the rules and precepts than with having the "right attitude." However, it is difficult to imagine a morality which has absolutely no concern whatsoever with the attitudinal dimension. Suppose for instance that a society places great emphasis on deference toward authority and has very specific behavioral forms in which this deference is to be shown; it would still be hard to imagine that there would not be some ways of engaging in this deferential activity which, while formally meeting the correct standard, were out of keeping with its spirit. That is, they would be taken as "conforming in letter but not in spirit," and in that way would not be as appropriate and 'right' as if the actions were done with the proper attitude. If this line of thought is correct, then even in the most 'externally'-conceived conception of moral action, the attitude behind conformity to the rule is seen as relevant to proper conduct.

tifulness, adherence to universal principle, and the like. The particularist will point out that both the former and the latter qualities are part of most people's ideals of character, of what it is to be a good person. Both sets of qualities seem important for moral education; we want our children to be compassionate as well as just, caring as well as principled. We admire people who are kind and compassionate, as we do those who are principled and impartial.

The impartialist challenges this by denying moral significance to the particularistic virtues. But on what basis is this challenge made? It cannot be on the basis that only that which makes reference to a universal, impartial point of view is rightly called 'moral.' For this is precisely the point which the particularist denies, and this denial cannot be met merely by a reassertion of the challenged view.

I suggest that there can be no final resolution of a dispute over the meaning and criteria of the term "moral." To a large extent the dispute is a merely semantic one. But one perspective on that term makes it difficult to allow for the particularist view, and that is the notion that "the moral" points to a unitary phenomenon. Several philosophers (MacIntyre 1966, 1984; Feinberg 1968) have recently proposed that our conception of the domain of the moral is a product of diverse sources, not unified as a single, internally consistent "moral point of view." In his recent work, Kohlberg, responding to Gilligan's criticisms, has proposed that there are two meanings of the term "moral," one relating to justice and one to care and beneficence.

Acknowledgement of a plurality within the domain of 'morality' accords with the particularist perspective. For on that view the moral significance of the impartialist qualities are not denied; but it is simply asserted that the particularist qualities too have a claim on that term, and therefore on the attention of moral philosophers and moral development theorists.[33]

33. I would like to thank Owen Flanagan and Jerome Kagan for very helpful comments on a late draft of this paper.

# References

Blum, L. 1980. *Friendship, Altruism, and Morality.* London: Routledge and Kegan Paul.

Cavell, S. 1979. *The Claim of Reason.* Oxford: Clarendon Press.

Chodorow, N. 1979. *The Reproduction of Mothering.* Berkeley, Calif.: University of California Press.

Darwall, S. 1983. *Impartial Reason.* Ithaca, N.Y.: Cornell University Press.

Feinberg, J. 1968. Supererogation and Rules. In G. Dworkin and J. Thomson, eds., *Ethics.* New York: Harper and Row.

Gilligan, Carol 1982. *In a Different Voice.* Cambridge, Mass.: Harvard University Press.

———. 1984. The Conquistador and the Dark Continent: Reflections on the Psychology of Love. *Daedalus* 113:75–95.

Hoffman, M. 1976. Empathy, Role-taking, Guilt and Development of Altruistic Motives. In T. Lickona, ed., *Moral Development and Behavior.* New York: Holt, Rinehart, and Winston.

———. 1982. Affect and Moral Development. In D. Cicchetti and P. Hesse, eds., *New Directions for Child Development: Emotional Development,* no. 16. San Francisco: Jossey-Bass.

Kagan, J. 1984. *The Nature of the Child.* New York: Basic Books.

Kant, I. 1959. *Foundations of the Metaphysics of Morals.* Trans. L. W. Beck. New York: Bobbs-Merrill.

Kohlberg, L. 1981. *Essays in Moral Development.* Vol. 1, *The Philosophy of Moral Development.* San Francisco: Harper and Row.

———. 1982. A Reply to Owen Flanagan and Some Comments on the Puka-Goodpaster Exchange. *Ethics* 92:513–28.

———. 1984. *Essays in Moral Development.* Vol. 2, *The Psychology of Moral Development.* San Francisco: Harper and Row.

MacDowell, J. 1979. Virtue and Reason. *The Monist* 62, (no. 3):

MacIntyre, A. 1966. *A Short History of Ethics.* New York: Macmillan.

———. 1967. Egoism and Altruism. In P. Edwards, ed., *Encyclopedia of Philosophy.* Vol. 2. New York: Macmillan.

———. 1984. *After Virtue.* 2d. ed. Notre Dame, Ind.: University of Notre Dame Press.

Melden, A. I. 1977. *Rights and Persons.* Berkeley: University of California Press.

Mill, J. S. [1861] 1979. *Utilitarianism.* Indianapolis, Ind.: Hackett.

Murdoch, I. 1970. *The Sovereignty of Good.* New York: Schocken.

Nagel, T. 1970. *The Possibility of Altruism.* Oxford: Clarendon Press.

Noddings, N. 1984. *Caring: A Feminine Approach to Ethics and Moral Education.* Berkeley: University of California Press.

Norman, R. 1979. Self and Others: The Inadequacy of Utilitarianism. In W. Cooper, K. Nielsen, and S. Patten, eds., *New Essays on John Stuart Mill and Utilitarianism. Canadian Journal of Philosophy,* supplementary volume 5.

Rawls, J. 1971. *A Theory of Justice.* Cambridge, Mass.: Harvard University Press.

Ross, A. 1983. The Status of Altruism. *Mind* 42:204–18.

Sandel, M. 1982. *Liberalism and the Limits of Justice.* Cambridge: Cambridge University Press.

Scheler, M. 1965. *The Nature of Sympathy.* Trans. Werner Stark. London: Routledge and Kegan Paul.

Scheman, N. 1983. Individualism and the Objects of Psychology. In S. Harding and M. Hintikka, eds., *Discovering Reality*. Dordrecht: D. Reidel.

Schopenhauer, Arthur [1841] 1965. *On the Basis of Morality* Trans. E. F. J. Payne. New York: Bobbs-Merrill.

Sidgwick, H. [1907] 1966. *The Methods of Ethics*. New York: Dover.

Smith, A. [1759] 1970. *The Theory of Moral Sentiments*. In H. Schneider, ed., *Adam Smith's Moral and Political Philosophy*. New York: Harper and Row.

Stocker, M. 1976. The Schizophrenia of Modern Ethical Theories. *Journal of Philosophy* 73, no. 14, 453–66.

Telfer, E. 1971. Friendship. *Proceedings of the Aristotelian Society*, supplement.

Whitbeck, C. 1983. A Different Reality: Feminist Ontology. In C. Gould, ed., *Beyond Domination: New Perspectives on Women and Philosophy*. Totowa, N.J.: Rowman and Allanheld.

Williams, B. 1981. *Moral Luck*. Cambridge: Cambridge University Press.

_____. 1985. *Ethics and the Limits of Philosophy*. Cambridge, Mass.: Harvard University Press.

Wittgenstein, L. 1953. *Philosophical Investigations*. New York: Macmillan.

# Contributors

Augusto Blasi
Professor of Psychology
University of Massachusetts, Harbor Campus
Boston, MA 02125

Lawrence Blum
Associate Professor of Philosophy
University of Massachusetts, Harbor Campus
Boston, MA 02125

Judy Dunn
Professor of Human Development
Department of Individual and Family Studies
The Pennsylvania State University
University Park, PA 16802

M. Ann Easterbrooks
Assistant Professor of Psychology
Department of Child Study
Tufts University
Medford, MA 02155

Carolyn Pope Edwards
Associate Professor of Education
School of Education
University of Massachusetts, Amherst
Amherst, MA 01003

Robert Emde
Professor of Psychiatry
University of Colorado School of Medicine
Denver, CO 80262

Carol Gilligan
Professor of Education
Harvard Graduate School of Education
Cambridge, MA 02138

Charles C. Helwig
Department of Psychology
University of California, Berkeley
Berkeley, CA 94720

William F. Johnson
Psychiatrist
Child-Adolescent Unit
York Hospital
York, PA 17405

Jerome Kagan
Professor of Psychology
Harvard University
Cambridge, MA 02138

Melanie Killen
Assistant Professor of Psychology
Wesleyan University
Middletown, CT 06457

Sharon Lamb
Harvard Graduate School of Education
Cambridge, MA 02138

Manamohan Mahapatra
Punama Gate Area
Bhubaneswar 751002
Orissa, India

Joan G. Miller
Assistant Professor of Psychology
Department of Psychology
Yale University
New Haven, CT 06520

Edward Mueller
Professor of Psychology
Department of Psychology
Boston University
Boston, MA 02215

Richard A. Shweder
Professor of Anthropology
Committee on Human Development
University of Chicago
Chicago, IL 60637

Catherine Snow
Professor of Education
Harvard Graduate School of Education
Cambridge, MA 02138

Elliot Turiel
Professor of Education
Department of Education
University of California, Berkeley
Berkeley, CA 94720

Grant Wiggins
Adjunct Lecturer
Department of Education
Brown University
Providence, RI 02912

# Index